HISTORY

OF THE

SCANDINAVIANS

AND

SUCCESSFUL SCANDINAVIANS

IN THE

UNITED STATES

VOLUME I

HISTORY

OF THE

SCANDINAVIANS

AND

SUCCESSFUL SCANDINAVIANS

IN THE

UNITED STATES.

COMPILED AND EDITED

BY

O. N. NELSON.

VOLUME I

SECOND, REVISED EDITION

HASKELL HOUSE PUBLISHERS LTD.
Publishers of Scarce Scholarly Books
NEW YORK. N. Y. 10012
1969

First Published 1904

HASKELL HOUSE PUBLISHERS LTD.
Publishers of Scarce Scholarly Books
280 LAFAYETTE STREET
NEW YORK, N. Y. 10012

Library of Congress Catalog Card Number: 68-31266

Standard Book Number 8383-0198-3

Printed in the United States of America

LIST OF COLLABORATORS

Vols. I. and II. of History of the Scandinavians in the United States

III

CONTENTS

Vol. I. of History of the Scandinavians in the United States

CONTENTS

Vol. II. of History of the Scandinavians in the United States

LIST OF BIOGRAPHIES

LIST OF BIOGRAPHIES

LIST OF ILLUSTRATIONS

PREFACE TO THE SECOND EDITION

For nearly ten years I have devoted all my time to the investigation of Scandinavian-American history; and the first edition of my first volume, which appeared in 1893, was far more favorably received than I ever anticipated or dared to hope. Yet it was by no means faultless; and as the pages from 1 to 276 were electrotyped, it was no easy task to correct every mistake. But at great expense of time, labor, and money, all errors of facts and most of the grammatical mistakes have been corrected. Several pages, and even whole articles, have been rewritten. The article on *The First Norwegian Immigration, or The Sloop Party of 1825*, is a new production. Nearly twenty pages of *Bibliography* and some valuable statistical tables have been added. Pages 291-364, dealing with Scandinavian settlements, churches, and schools, in Minnesota, are new matter, prepared for this edition; and the balance of Vol. I. consists of biographies of Scandinavians in Minnesota, most of which appeared in the first edition; but all of them have been rewritten, rearranged, and brought up to date. In fact, the revision and reconstruction of the whole first volume have been so thorough and complete that in many respects it is an entirely new history of the Scandinavians in America, brought up to the beginning of the twentieth century.

The first edition of the second volume was issued so recently (in 1897) and prepared with such great care that hardly any changes were made up to page 236, except in regard to the arrangement of the biographies. The rest of

IX

the work was reset altogether. But owing to the lack of space, several biographies which appeared in the first edition had to be omitted, and some were very much abridged.

It must be admitted that, excepting the church organizations, there are hardly any Scandinavian institutions in this country. Whatever is accomplished in the political, social, or financial spheres by any Scandinavian-American, is accomplished by the individual. Hence, the record of such individuals necessarily has to be an important feature of Scandinavian-American history. Partly to sell my work, and partly to secure the most reliable information on historical and biographical topics, I have personally visited all the counties and cities in Minnesota, Iowa, and Wisconsin where any considerable number of Scandinavians reside.

In selecting and editing the biographies—as well as in preparing everything else for this work—I have endeavored to be impartial. It has been my aim not to be influenced by any religious belief, national prejudice, political conviction, or personal friendship or dislike. In cases where I felt that I might be liable to lean toward one side or another, some of the editors or revisers, whose opinions differed from mine, were consulted. To state the unadorned facts, without literary display or expression of judgment, has been the constant endeavor in regard to the biographical sketches. Yet sometimes it was almost necessary to pass judgment on a man's standing within a certain sphere, and I have not shrunk from doing so, or from permitting it to be done, whenever it seemed advisable or desirable, and when the opinions expressed were by general consent considered to be true.

No one has been allowed to write his own biography, even the editors of, and contributors to, this work having been subjected to this rule. The parties themselves, however, when living, have been permitted to examine their biographies in regard to the facts; but the language used, the views expressed, and the method of treatment, are strictly our own. The proper equilibrium of modesty and self-esteem is a difficult virtue to attain, and some of our Scandinavian-Americans are sadly deficient in this respect. One man, whose chief merit apparently consisted in having been in the lower branch of the legislature a couple of terms, was indignant because his biography did not begin thus: "Hon. ——— is one of the most popular and active Republicans in the state of———." A much larger percentage, however, go too far in the other direction. For an historian to avoid the sins of commission and omission under such circumstances, and at the same time not to offend people, is a Herculean task. Consequently, the biographies of living men are more or less unsatisfactory. At the same time the great pains which have been taken with the biographies, some of which have been revised by half a dozen different parties, ought to make them exceptionally reliable.

In regard to the spelling of the geographical names in the Scandinavian countries, the postoffice directories of Denmark, Norway, and Sweden have been carefully consulted, and in most cases the latest mode of spelling has been followed. The radical changes in spelling which have been adopted by the government of Norway in recent years has a comical side in connection with this work, namely, that several educated Norwegian-Americans do not know how to spell correctly the name of their own birthplace. Whenever possible, not only the *församling* or *prestegjeld* where a person was born has been mentioned, but also the stift or province, and of course the country; this was necessary because several places in the North have the same name; for example, there are in Sweden over 50 places called Säby, and 75 Berg. Whenever it is stated that a person has received a college education in one of the Scandinavian countries, it is meant that he has completed a course at one of the *elementarlärovärken* in Sweden or the Latin schools of Denmark or Norway—the names of these institutions cannot be properly translated, but the best equivalent for them is college. Nearly all the names of newspapers and books, as well as foreign words, have been printed in *Italics*.

For fifty years past numerous attempts have been made by different parties, both in the English and the Scandinavian languages, to elucidate certain features of the life of the Scandinavian-Americans. Many of these productions were meritorious, and a few of them are standard works as far as they go. Among the men making these attempts were several who by intellectual endowment and thoroughness of education were well prepared to undertake and successfully complete their task. Yet, apparently, none of these productions have received sufficient recognition and support to enable any one of the many Scandinavian-American writers to devote time and talent to extensive historical research concerning their countrymen on this side of the Atlantic. That I have been enabled to devote several years to historical investigations, to meet the various and often heavy expenses connected with the preparation and publication of such a large work, and to make a living out of the sale of the book, seems to indicate that my labors are appreciated. This appreciation has not only been manifested by a courteous reception of the author wherever he has traveled, and by a flattering endorsement of his work, but by a generous financial patronage, sometimes involving considerable sacrifice on the part of the admirer of the enterprise. The keen interest which the educated Scandinavian-Americans, especially the clergy, have taken in the history, has incited the author to greater exertion in the prosecution of his labor.

I am indebted to so many people for the successful completion of this edition that it is beyond my power to give full credit to all those who have assisted me in the undertaking. Special mention, however, should be made of Consul G. N. Swan, Rev. Adolph Bredesen, Ernst Skarstedt, Rev. C. M. Esbjörn, and J. J. Skordalsvold, who have carefully and critically revised several important articles and rendered valuable assistance in the completion of the *Bibliography*. The last mentioned has also revised and read proof of the whole work, and without his able aid it might not have appeared in its present form. Elias Anderson and F. L. Trönsdal have taken more than ordinary interest in the enterprise. My wife has looked after the purely artistic part of the work. I am also under obligation to the Lumberman Publishing Company, the typesetter; the Tribune Job Printing Company, who have done the press work; Bramblett & Beygeh, the engravers; and A. J. Dahl & Company, the binders.

Owing to the magnitude of the labor and expense involved in completing this edition, a few years may pass before I shall be able to prepare and publish the third volume, which no doubt will deal with Illinois and some neighboring states.

Partly on account of having different writers to prepare the various articles, no absolutely uniform system of capitalization and punctuation has been maintained throughout this work. Yet the exceptions to the rigid "Rules of Nelson and Skordalsvold" are few and unimportant. Sometimes in quoting from another author, it was inconvenient to use his exact language. In such cases the single quotation mark (') has been employed to indicate that the expression is not my own. As has been said before, no literary brilliancy has been attempted. Hamlin Garland remarked recently: "I believe the well-educated descendants of the Scandinavian settlers of the Northwestern states are closer to Webster's dictionary to-day than are the languid Southerners, or the erudite Easterners." If his assertion be true, I may entertain the hope that the language used in this work is tolerably correct, because the classes of people he refers to have written or revised a large portion of it. The greatest master of history, Edward Gibbon, says, "Diligence and accuracy are the only merits which an historical writer may ascribe to himself." Another celebrated writer, James Clark Ridpath, asserts, "The historian must either lay down his pen or cease to be a partisan;" and on the altar of Diligence, Accuracy, and Impartiality I have laid down the best fruits of my labor.

O. N. NELSON.

MINNEAPOLIS, MINN., January, 1900.

Characteristics of the Scandinavians

AND

REVIEW OF THEIR HISTORY.

—BY—

O. N. NELSON.

This is an age of classification, and mankind has been divided into different races, or types, of men. But history, with a few exceptions, deals only with one race—the Caucasian—because hardly any others have succeeded in becoming civilized. The Hindoos, Persians, Greeks, Latins, Slavonians, Kelts, and Teutons, all belong to the Indo-European branch of the great Caucasian race. The English, the Germans, the Dutch, the Scandinavians, and their descendants in other countries, are all members of the Teutonic family. It may seem strange that the theoretical Greek and the practical Englishman, the fanatical Hindoo and the philosophical German, the rude Russian and the polite Frenchman, should all have, if we go far enough back, a common ancestry. Yet the resemblance of their languages and their mythologies proves that they were once one people, who lived together somewhere. But when or under what circumstances they separated, and migrated to different countries cannot be determined. But if the different nations of the Indo-European branch differ greatly in physical appearance, mental culture, social conditions, religious beliefs, and political attainments, the closest relation exists between the different nations of the Teutonic family. Physically, the Teutons resemble each other; mentally, they are equally endowed. The development of the political history of Sweden is similar to the development of the political history of England. Blackstone, the father of English law, and Stjernhöök, the father of Swedish law, agree on many of the finest points in jurisprudence. Danes, Norwegians, Swedes, Germans, Dutchmen, and Englishmen have a common mythology and common superstitions; but it is only the Scandinavians—Danes, Norwegians, and Swedes—who have, almost, a common language. The Danes and the Norwegians write virtually alike, but differ a little in their pronunciation; nor is it, at all, difficult for a Swede to understand a Norwegian, or for a Dane to understand a Swede. All the Scandinavian people, with the exception of the Icelanders, understand each other's languages

When and under what circumstances the Scandinavians first came to their northern homes has always been a matter of dispute among scholars. Different theories have been advocated. Learned men have maintained that the human race first saw daylight in the *Land of the Midnight Sun*, and that the Paradise of the Bible was located near Upsala, Sweden. The Icelandic sagas claim that Odin, the god and king of the Teutons, taught his people the art of writing and the science of war, and led them out of Asia, through Russia, and colonized the Scandinavian countries. It is only one hundred and fifty years since a noted scientist endeavored to prove that the greatest part of the North could not have been inhabited at the time of the birth of Christ, because most of the land there was then covered with water. Others again assert that Scandinavia has been the cradle of the Indo-European branch of the human race. A well-known Norwegian-American educator and author says: "There is a strong probability that their (the Scandinavian tribes) invasion of the countries which they now inhabit must have taken place during the second century preceding the Christian era." But the latest and most celebrated Scandinavian anti quarians and historians have—by comparing the old skulls, as found in the graves, with the skulls of the present people—come to the conclusion that the same race of people which now inhabit the Scandinavian countries, have been there for thousands of years, at least, before the Christian era commenced.

The Scandinavians entered late upon the historical arena. The Grecian history had begun eight hundred years before even their existence was known. Grecian literature, philosophy, and art had flourished centuries before they could write their own names. The Romans had conquered the fairest part of the earth, legislated for the world, made good roads through the whole empire, and civilized a large portion of mankind, before the Scandinavians occupied houses or fixed habitations, but wandered through the dense forests as semi-savages. The French, English, and Germans had been Christianized four or five hundred years before the Northern people accepted Catholicism as their national religion, and as late as in the sixteenth century some of them still worshiped Odin. This late development, which is no doubt due to the

severity of the climate, and the great separation from the
higher civilization of the South, must be taken into consideration when we compare the Scandinavians with other
nations, and endeavor to determine the quantity and quality
of influence which each nation has had upon the general history of mankind.

That the Northmen, in spite of their lateness, have had a
great influence, and taken an active part in the world's business, no one can successfully contradict. They have not
merely been savage plunderers and rude conquerors, but also
discoverers, civilizers, and organizers. They assisted in over-
throwing the magnificent Roman power, conquered France,
enslaved England, discovered America five hundred years
before the voyage of Columbus, organized the Russian Empire, and liberated Germany from religious and political
thraldom. Of course the greater part of their contact with
other nations and their influence upon other people have
been accomplished through war; but war, until recently, has
been the mainspring of nearly all undertakings. The very
fact that the Scandinavians have, by the might of their
swords, crowned and dethroned foreign rulers; dictated terms
to popes and emperors; fought, both for and against, the
liberties of men; and in many other ways taken an active
part in the affairs of the world, must have had a great influence upon civilizaticn.

The Scandivanian countries were first referred to in
Grecian literature as early as three hundred years before the
birth of Christ. "But," says Geijer, "if the Greek ever knew
anything about them, the Roman again forgot them." But
if the Roman had forgotten them, he was soon to be re-

minded of their existence in a forcible and positive manner, for, under the name of Goths, the Scandinavians became the principal participants in undermining and destroying the Roman power in the third, fourth, and fifth centuries of the Christian era.

By a chain of successful conquests; by good management through very ˙ capable and honest men; by establishing public order, law, and justice; by encouraging literature, science, art, and the accumulation of wealth, the Roman Empire had, in the second century of this era, reached a state of greatness, power, and civilization, which has hardly been equalled, never surpassed by any nation, either of the ancient or the modern world.

The Romans, who had at first assailed the domains of the barbaric Teutons beyond the river Rhine, were in the third and fourth centuries of this era called upon to defend their own territories against the invasion of the very same barbarians whom they had been unable to conquor or subdue. For this purpose a line of military posts had been established along the river to protect the Roman citizens against the invading hordes, being similar to those which the United States keeps on the western borders to protect the whites from Indian outrages.

Of the many different tribes, all belonging to the Teutonic family, who pressed upon the Roman frontier, none were so powerful or intelligent as the Goths.   These Goths dwelt on both sides of the Baltic Sea, and it is said that those who joined their kinsmen to participate in the plunder of the Mistress of the World, crossed the sea from the Scandinavian countries in three ships. But, as later was the case with the Vikings, they were not formidable in numbers, but in courage, endurance, and ferocity. These wild men are described as being very tall, strong, and robust; having white bodies, yellow hair, broad shoulders, wiry muscles, florid complexion, and fierce blue eyes that during excitement gleamed with fire and passion. Physically, they, in general, resembled the people of the whole Teutonic family of today; but, more specifically, they came nearest to the people who now live in the southern part of Sweden and on the Danish islands. Little or nothing is known in regard to the semi-civilization which they had attained to at the time they first came in contact with the imperial power; but they probably had reached a fairly high standard of moral development, and enjoyed some luxuries.

It was with these men, "Who astonished the nations of the South by their reckless courage and gigantic stature," that the imperial army of Rome had to measure swords. It was ancient renown against barbaric ferocity, disciplined order against natural courage, law against anarchy, Christianity against Odin, Latin against Teuton. The Roman fought by prescription, his movements were as regular as clockwork. The Teuton obeyed the commander, but the commander was chosen for his fitness. If the Teutons could not stand their ground, their wives and sisters assisted them. The women fought and screamed with a fierceness never witnessed before or after, save during the French Revolution. The Romans feared the wild yells of the women almost as much as they feared the swords of their husbands and brothers. Rome was doomed. It was to no avail that the barbaric warriors were engaged to defend the Roman territories against barbaric invasion; they, of course, turned traitors. It delayed, but did not change the result.

In the latter part of the fifth century of this era a Teutonic savage sat on the throne of Rome. At about the same time Spain, France, and in fact all western Europe fell into the hands of the Northern hordes.

Now an exhibition was made on the grand stage of the historical theatre that has never, in all the various dramas of human actions, had its likeness. Side by side, on apparent social equality, walked the refined Roman—dressed in his toga—by the rude man from the North—dressed in a goat-skin suit—his long, yellow hair combed towards the four winds. The citizen carried centuries of learning in his head, the luxuries from many countries on his back. He was the poet, the artist, the statesman, and the philosopher.

The Goth possessed nothing; he only knew how to eat, drink, and fight. But he carried the sword of state, before which the proud Roman bowed in humble subjection.

By the fall of Rome, civilization had been thrust backward many centuries. Anarchy reigned supreme. Time rolled on; for centuries the Roman world—yea the world itself—was hidden in darkness. For this wholesale barbarization the Romans themselves were partly responsible. They lacked the frankness, manliness, honesty, and virtue requisite to preserve sufficient moral power to govern decently a great state. The old civilization which Rome represented had lost its force. The Roman believed in nothing. Right and wrong were only relative terms. To him anything which succeeded was right, everything which failed was wrong. The Romans had become greatly degenerated, debauchery and licentiousness were the common practice.

The new race was ignorant, but had strong convictions and high moral principles. To the Goth falsehood was a great vice, secret stealing was a cowardly act, for which no torment was too severe. He robbed openly, he faced his victims boldly. He was honest and frank, living up to his rude ideas of life. The Persians, the Egyptians, the Greeks, and the Romans had their liberties on account of belonging to a powerful, free state. The Teuton was a free man because he was a man; *individuality* was his strongest characteristic.

The native population out-numbered, by far, the invaders, who, nevertheless, swayed the scepter of power. In time the Goths adopted the Christian religion and became somewhat civilized. The slaves became their master's instructors. Out of the Roman confusion rose the modern states. In the eighth and ninth centuries western Europe had been somewhat organized and Christianized, only, however, to be thrown into confusion again by the kinsmen and partly countrymen of the Goths—namely, the Vikings.

Before the fall of Rome little is known of the history, customs, or characteristics of the Scandinavian people; but it is certain that they were tribes of the great Teutonic family, and had, probably, not advanced much above the condition of the semi-civilized races at that time. The Teutons, however, unlike some people, had the talent to adopt new ideas, to assimilate with other people, and to advance. History proves sufficiently that they have been very progressive. The Goths had been the principal participants in the destruction of Rome, but the Goths were not exclusively Scandinavians, because part of the tribe, in all probability, lived in Germany. The Teutons constituted many tribes, no nationalities existed, which, however, commenced to develop shortly after the fall of Rome.

In the seventh, eighth, ninth, tenth, and eleventh centuries—at the time when the foundation of the European kingdoms were in process of construction—the inhabitants of the Scandinavian countries became famous as Vikings. But the Viking practice had been in operation ever since the Teutons and Romans came in conflict with each other. The Scandinavian Viking age is only a continuation of the barbaric flood that deluged the classical civilization. The two may differ in the particulars, but not in the essentials; it is impossible to understand one, without having a clear conception of the other. "All wars hang together," Gustavus Adolphus used to say.

According to Sars, the Scandinavian Viking age is divided into three periods; but it might be more correct to say that there were three kinds of Vikings, as no sharp divisions, in regard to time, can be made. No one can tell when the age commenced. Northern Vikings had, no doubt, practiced their trade ever since the Christian era began, and, perhaps, before. *The First Period:* A small number of chieftains, or one alone, would, at irregular times, gather together crews for a few ships and sail over to England, Ireland, France, or Flanders, where they would plunder a city or a monastery, and quickly return home with their booty. *The Second Period:* An advance was made, not only in the art of war and military management, but even in the systematic plan of robbing defenceless people. Several Vikings club together, take possession of some exposed point—for example, a small island near the coast—erect fortifications, and thus control a large extent of territory. They may remain at one place for years, and forage the surrounding country according to a regular plan, then proceed to their native lands. *The Third Period:* Plundering, robbing, and piracy have been abandoned. The Vikings came as conquerors. Their fleets counted from one to five hundred vessels. Cities were stormed and sacked. They conquered territories, settled them, and governed them. They treated with kings and rulers. Of course the third period, during the ninth, tenth, and eleventh centuries, is without comparison the most important and fascinating. It has had a very great influence both upon the Scandinavian countries and abroad.

The Vikings, who had at first occasionally plundered the western European countries for the sake of pleasure and small profits, commenecd "Piracy as a trade" on a wholesale scale in the first part of the ninth century. "These bold sailors and admirable foot-soldiers" had made a general and perpetual declaration of war on all mankind, but especially on those who possessed any kind of tangible property that was worth having. The seas swarmed with their sails. The miserable people along the coasts of the North Sea, who had lately been Christianized, fled in terror. Priests prayed in vain: "Deliver us, O Lord, from the rage of the Northmen." The world, it was thought, would soon come to an end. Germany, Holland, Belgium, England, Scotland, Ireland, France, Spain, and Italy were all punished with fire and sword, sacked and robbed, drenched in blood and tears.

That time has been called the *heroic* age, the age of *individualism*. Princes had to buy their freedom in gold and cede their territories to the conquerors. Paris was beseiged, Dublin was taken by storm, and in the very heart of London, not far from the celebrated St.Paul's Cathedral, have been found skeletons of old Northern warriors.

Many scattering Scandinavian settlements were made in foreign countries during these terrible times. The Northern people intermarried and mixed with the native population. In a comparatively short time the fierce pirates became Christianized and civilized, giving new vigor and energy to the degenerated people of western Europe. Besides the many smaller settlements, scattered through nearly every European country, the Norwegians colonized Iceland in the latter part of the ninth century; the famous Rolf—also a Norwegian, though several of his followers were Danes and Swedes—wrested Normandy from the weak French king in the first part of the tenth century, and the Danes conquered the whole of England a hundred years later. The colonization of Iceland, and the conquest of Normandy and England were the last and greatest acts of the bloody drama of the Viking age; these were beneficial to civilization, and may be said to have palliated the former atrocities of the Northmen. The Icelanders created a classical literature from which is received the best information we have in regard to the mythology of the Teutons in general, and of the Scandinavians in particular; established a humanitarian, free republic, on the basis of the Northmen's conception of a civil government, which lasted for nearly four hundred years; discovered America five hundred years before Columbus sailed from Spain, and perhaps his knowledge of what they had accomplished partly induced him to undertake the voyage. The followers of Rolf found Normandy in poverty and distress. In a short time they made it the richest, most populous, and most civilized province in France, where the best French language was used. The Normans, being virtually independent of the French monarch, conquered England in 1066, and founded the kingdoms of Naples and Sicily. Danish kings reigned over England, as well as in their native country, of course, for several years, and to-day many English words, laws, and customs are purely Scandinavian. The names of many cities, lakes, rivers, etc., in France, England, Scotland, Ireland, and other countries, have a Scandinavian origin. Several of the greatest noblemen in the western European countries—notably Lord Nelson of England—are descendants of the Northmen.

During the Viking age the boundary lines between the Scandinavian countries were not sharply drawn. In fact the people were at first tribes; then a great number of petty kingdoms were formed. It was not until the latter part of the ninth century that the present divisions of the Northern nationalities were established, and the Scandinavians continued to speak one and the same language for two or three hundred years later. Even after the stronger kings had succeeded in defeating the weaker and adding their territories to their own dominions, which resulted in laying the foundation of the present Northern powers, it was yet a long time before the present boundary lines were established. A large part of southern Sweden, which is now the richest and most populous portion of the country, belonged to Denmark, and some of its western land belonged to Norway. It is, therefore, incorrect to speak about a Danish conquest or a Norwegian colonization, for things were rather mixed up in those days. Yet it is certain that the Swedes participated less in the destruction, and later in the upbuilding of the western European countries than the Danes and Norwegians. The Danes confined themselves principally to England and France. The Norwegians attended to Scotland, Ireland, and other northern islands. The Swedes, being closed out from the North Sea, went east, where they founded the Russian Empire in the middle of the ninth century, and served in large numbers in the imperial army at Constantinople.

The descendants of the Swedish founders of Russia ruled that country until the sixteenth century. In certain parts of Switzerland the people claim, at least they did half a century ago, that they are descendants of the Swedes.

What were the causes which produced the Viking age? The answer is:

First—Although there is every reason to believe that the Scandinavian countries were a great deal less populous than at present; yet, being poorly tilled, and one man often having children by several women, there were more people than could be supported. Some had to seek their fortune in foreign countries. Frequently a father was compelled to drive all his sons away from home to make their own living, save one who inherited his estate.

Second—The religion, the desire for adventure, and the spirit of the times, induced many to leave their native countries to court dangers and turn the wheel of fortune in foreign lands. It was believed that only those who died a violent death were entitled in the next life to associate with the

gods in Valhalla. It was considered a high honor to have
fought successfully in foreign countries. Young princes
received their first education on board of a war vessel. In a
short time the Viking business became a fashion.

Third—The love for freedom and the passion for independence, or the strong individuality, induced many to
leave the North rather than submit to a superior, which
they were especially called upon to do during the latter part
of the period when the stronger kings at home subdued the
weaker. But at the bottom it was essentially a question of
economy. Men's religion often coincides with their business
interests, and that was sometimes the case with the Vikings,
for several of them believed a great deal more in their own
strength than in the powers of the gods.

We must not look at the Vikings through the glasses of
the twentieth century, or judge them according to the standard of modern civilization, but examine them in accordance
with the spirit of the times, and measure them by the influence their deeds have had upon general history. They
honestly believed that "War was the natural condition of
man," and that a legitimate reason for declaring hostility
was, that those who were attacked had valuable property.
After all, this robbery did not differ much from the English
opium war, the plundering of Denmark and France of their
provinces by the Germans, and the treatment of the Indians,
Mexicans, and Spaniards by the United States. The Northmen
were in a kind of continual state of hostility. The modern
wars are so terribly destructive to life and property that
their continuation for a longer period would annihilate the
whole human race. It is true that modern warfare is con-

ducted on a more systematic plan, but the struggles of the Vikings were not altogether irregular. For if anyone besides the great noblemen and kings indulged in the plundering business on a small scale, they were at once driven off the sea as a set of lawless robbers, whom the Vikings themselves considered it to be a moral duty to exterminate. Therefore, according to the spirit of the times, the operation of the Vikings was a perfectly legitimate, honorable, perpetual state of war, limited to certain persons, who made it their profession for the sake of pleasure and profit.

It must also be remembered that the description of these fierce outrages has always been recorded by their enemies. Very often crimes were charged to the Vikings which in reality were committed by, what may be termed, their *camp-followers*, or the worst element of the respective countries in which the Northmen might happen to be.

In regard to the ultimate results, and the benefits to the human race which was the consequence of these bloody times, reference has already been made to the state of affairs at and after the fall of Rome. The same was the case shortly after in the western European countries. For as Prof. Worsaae says, who, perhaps, is the best authority on the history of the Vikings: 'In the first ages Christianity produced among the people, as was the case in other countries besides England, a sort of degeneracy and weakness. Instead of the dire battle of the heathens there were now heard songs and prayers, which, joined with the constantly increasing refinement, made the people dull and effeminate, so that they willingly bent under the yoke of their masters, both spiritual and temporal. In the ninth, tenth, and eleventh centuries the Anglo-Saxons had greatly degenerated from their forefathers. Relatives sold one another into thraldom; lewdness and ungodliness had become habitual; and cowardice had increased to such a degree that, according to the old chroniclers, one Dane would often put ten Anglo-Saxons to flight. Before such a people could be conducted to true freedom and greatness it was necessary that an entirely new vigor should be infused into the decayed stock. This vigor was derived from the Scandinavian North, where neither Romans nor any other conquerors had domineered over the people, but where heathenism with all its roughness, and all its love of freedom and bravery, still held absolute sway.

This admirable description of the condition in England applies, perhaps, with greater truth and force to other western European peoples; for they are in no small degree indebted to the old Northmen for whatever freedom, honesty, virtue, and heroism they now possess. The foundation of the present European states was laid by our ancestors. Out of the confusion, disorder, and anarchy arose a new civilization. From the union of the degenerated western European peoples and the courageous Scandinavians sprung a new, a better, a nobler, a manlier race.

During the Viking periods great changes had taken place at home in the Scandinavian countries. The smaller kingdoms were conquered and united with the larger, thus laying the foundation of the modern Northern states. The many wars degraded the Northmen's honesty and simplicity; foreign corruption, deceit, and luxury were introduced. The old religion had lost its force. Many Vikings asserted that they believed in nothing, save their own strength. The more prudent men did not believe in the old gods. Harold the Fairhaired, of Norway, acknowledged only one supreme being in heaven, the creator of the universe and of mankind. The attention of the Roman church had been directed towards the North by the atrocities of the Vikings, and she sent missionaries thither. The men who had been a terror to Christendom, and the savage plunderers of Europe, became sons of Mother Rome. It is true that they never were very obedient children, and they took the first opportunity offered to be their own masters, yet something had been accomplished. The Viking age ceased, partly because many of the boldest, the bravest, the most independent, and the most turbulent had settled in foreign lands; leaving the weak, the cowards, and the contented at home, who either did not care or did not dare to attack foreign countries, which were now to a great extent defended by their former compatriots; partly because the people in the Scandinavian countries had, at least in name, become Christianized and bowed to the dictates of a pope, who now opened a new field for their barbarity, and gave them a new employment for their swords —namely, the crusades; partly because at home the internal disputes, conflicts of principles, and the struggles connected with the formation of new states, kept the Northmen busy with their own affairs.

From the eleventh to the sixteenth century Catholicism swayed the religious faith of the North. There was, considering the times, a great deal of advance and contact with the more highly civilized nations of the South; yet rude, savage manners were in general practice, and Odin, in many places, was still worshiped. During the greater part of the fourteenth and fifteenth centuries Denmark, Norway, and Sweden were united under one government. But their history is merely a record of internal strife, war, and bloodshed. Denmark, which by means of its superior civilization was the acknowledged leader, became the seat of the government, but the unwise and cruel Danish kings created, by their bloody acts, a hatred between the Scandinavian people, which even the time between then and now has been unable to eradicate. Guided by popular leaders the Swedish peasants rebelled successfully twice, and Sweden separated forever from Denmark in 1521, while Norway for about four hundred years remained virtually a province of Denmark.

Ever since the first part of the sixteenth century Lutherism has been the national religion of the Scandinavian countries, and a hundred years later the famous Gustavus Adolphus became the prime defender of Protestantism, intellectual freedom, and German liberty. The rebellions of the common people of Sweden in the fifteenth and sixteenth centuries, during the Kalmar Union, gained for them a great influence and a confidence in their own strength which they have never since ceased to exercise upon the national affairs. In Denmark, on the contrary, the peasants became almost slaves of the great landowners. But since 1849 the Danes have virtually enjoyed full universal male suffrage, which none of the other two Northern countries possess.* Yet the king of Denmark has a greater veto-power than the king of Sweden-Norway; consequently the people of the former country have, in reality, less political rights than those of the two latter. In Norway nature has divided the country into great valleys; each valley managed its own local affairs;

*In Norway the suffrage was greatly extended in 1898.

the common people knew and cared nothing about the Danish rulers or the doings of the world, and retained their personal independence. In Denmark and Sweden feudalism, aristocracy, and patriotism became more general than in Norway. It is only in this century that the Norwegians have in any sense indicated a desire for nationalization; since 1814, however,—when a very liberal constitution was adopted, and Norway was separated from Denmark and joined with Sweden—they have, perhaps, had a stronger national spirit, and certainly possessed more political freedom than either of the other two Northern people.

The most prominent of the characteristics of the Viking was his strong *individuality*. His love for freedom, his desire for personal independence, amounted to a passion. He would endure the rigid climate of the north, the burning sun of the south. He would sleep beneath no other roof than the arch of heaven, use bark for bread, drink rain-water as a beverage, make the forest his habitation, and have the wild beasts for his companions. But he would never give up one inch of his rights as a free man. The people of the classical countries were free men, because they belonged to a powerful and free state; they boasted of their citizenship. The Northman was a free man because he was a man, he boasted of *himself* and the deeds he performed. The same passion for freedom has run through the whole Scandinavian race from the earliest time to the present day. A great portion of the Vikings left their native lands because they refused to submit to a superior chief. No king or ruler has been able, for any length of time, to be the absolute master of the Scandinavian people. No foreign nation has been powerful enough to subjugate them. Sweden and Denmark have dethroned their obstinate monarchs, Norway dared to draw the sword against Europe and demand national independence. The Scandinavians were the last people who submitted to the Catholic yoke; they were the first to cast it off. Today the Swedish-Norwegian and Danish kings have as little authority and power as any rulers in Christendom. To be free and independent has always been the greatest ambition of every true Northman.

The second characteristic feature of our savage ancestors is *courage*. Bravery, however, sometimes turned into a fierceness that could hardly be distinguished from insanity. War was their profession. They hunted men as well as wild beasts, but prefered men who possessed some kind of valuable property. "For they deemed it a disgrace to acquire by sweat what they might obtain by blood." And whether we wander with the Goths when they plunder and destroy Rome, or sail with the Danes and Norwegians when they dethrone English kings and humble proud French monarchs, or live in the camps of the Swedes when Gustavus Adolphus and Charles the Twelfth dictate terms to popes and emperors, or accompany the Northern immigrants when they clear the dense forests of Wisconsin and subdue the wild prairies of Dakota, we find that they all excelled in endurance, heroism, and courage. In fact the Scandinavian warriors have been so noted for their fearlessness that they have conquered by the very terror of their names. Honor on earth and salvation in heaven, joy in this life and happiness in the next, could only, according to their religion, be gained by physical, brutal prowess. Their doctrine was that only the brave warriors who died a violent death were in the next life entitled to associate with the gods, fight in the celestial abode, enjoy the companionship of young maids, drink wine, and eat pork.

Stubbornness, firmness, and determination are qualities which the follower of Odin has been largely blessed with. To him no defeat was final. Failure meant only delay. He overcame all opposition, conquered every obstacle, defied every difficulty. Mountains, oceans, deserts, rivers, must not hinder his purpose. Charles the Twelfth during his childhood examined two plans. Under one plan, which showed how the Turks had taken a town in Hungary from the emperor, were written these words: "The Lord hath given it to me, and the Lord hath taken it from me; blessed be the name of the Lord." After the young prince had read this, he wrote under the other plan, which showed how the Swedes had taken Riga about a century before: "The Lord hath given it to me, and the devil shall not take it from me." Charles the Twelfth was a good representative of Scandinavian stubbornness.

Besides being independent, stubborn, and courageous the old Viking was, on the whole, *honest* and *truthful*, but terribly *revengeful*. Mercy seldom entered his harsh breast. He never forgave an offense. "He had a sense of honor which led him to sacrifice his life rather than his word." A promise once given, either to a friend or an enemy, had to be carried out unconditionally. Yet deception and cunning might be practiced in war, but the highest honor was bestowed upon those who were open and frank towards their enemies, kind and merciful towards the weak and those who sought protection. Deception and cunning they never tolerated among each other. One of the noblest characteristics of the Northman was the brotherly union which he entered into with a friend or antagonist whom he could not conquer or subdue. This union, which was the most sacred that could be entered into, was effected by opening each other's veins, mixing their blood, and taking an oath that they would share each other's joy and sorrow in this life, and revenge each other's death.

Hospitality was an essential part of the Northmen's religion. There was a kind of unwritten social law which compelled every person to entertain, to the best of his ability, the time not being limited, and free of charge, anyone, either his best friend or his worst enemy, who should ask or be in need thereof. And no guest needed to fear to be molested or imposed upon. This custom of hospitality is yet to a great extent practiced in the rural districts of the Scandinavian countries.

The Northmen had a *higher respect for women* than most heathen nations. It is true that they bought their wives of their fathers-in-law. The Romans sometimes stole their wives. But after the bargain had been once made the women were generally treated with respect and dignity, and their place in the house was that of free beings, not slaves. The men were attached to home and family, and, of course, enjoyed the wine and the feast.

It is true that civilization has changed their manners, customs, mode of thinking, ideas of right and wrong, and to some extent even their appearance. Yet at bottom the Scandinavians of today are the same as their ancestors were a thousand years ago. "Civilization," says Carlyle, "is only a wrappage through which the savage nature bursts infernal as ever."

The diverse influences of Denmark, Norway, and Sweden have developed different characteristics of the people in the respective countries. But the people of the northern part of Sweden differ more from the inhabitants of southern Sweden than the latter do from those who live on the Danish islands—the last two having a very fair complexion, being the purest descendants of the Goths; the former are often as dark as Frenchmen, which is also the case with many Norwegians, and those residing in Danish Jutland.

The Danish islanders and the southern Swedes in particular, and all the Danes in general, are open and frank, easy to become acquainted with, polite to strangers, not specially witty, but refined and polished in their intercourse with other people. They are industrious, frugal, peaceable, and possess a great amount of push, energy, and business shrewdness. They are not so much of agitators and extremists as the Norwegians, nor as aristocratic and conservative as the northern Swedes, but a combination of both. In business they are democratic, in social affairs they prefer the class distinction. Both in politics and commerce they are conservative. Risky speculations, and radical reforms are repugnant to their very nature. They will answer you by *yea* and *nay*, but prefer the *ifs* and *buts*. Their motto is: "In the sight of our Lord all men are 'Smålänningar.'" This part of the North is by far the most populous and wealthy; the people are more business-like and cosmopolitan in their ideas than any other Scandinavians. In their social intercourse they pay less attention to the form than the substance; they are less earnest, but more courteous than the Norwegians. They have been called the *Germans* of the North.

A northern Swede, and especially a Stockholmer, is reserved, hard to get acquainted with, conservative, but above all, an aristocrat. He is proud of his country, its history, and himself. Business is not in his line. He is the poet, wit, historian, statesman, philosopher, and patriot. He must dress well, comply rigorously with the latest rules of etiquette, and drink the most expensive wine. He has a large assortment of bows, bobs, courtesies, and hat-liftings, varying according to the age, sex, condition, and class distinction. The class distinction is greater and more varied in Sweden than in any of the other Scandinavian countries. The northern Swedes have been called the *Frenchmen* of the North.

The Norwegians are less ceremonious than the Danes or Swedes, as no class distinction exists among them; they treat strangers with a certain kind of cold courtesy, and do not appear to be anxious to make anybody's acquaintance. They are independent, somewhat haughty, radical, progressive, extreme, and above all, Norwegians. Religious, political, and social changes must not be hindered, but promoted. They are more earnest and turbulent than any of the other Scandinavian people, but lack that smoothness and courtesy which the Danes especially master with great perfection. They are bold sailors and daring adventurers, resembling more than anyone else the old Vikings. The Norwegians have been called the *Englishmen* of the North.

These different characteristics of the Northmen are, of course, as has always been the case, largely due to "The climate, the soil, and the general character of the countries."

The southern part of Sweden, and Denmark are largely productive prairies, where the climate is rather even the whole year round; no great changes occur in the seasons to compel the people to make any extraordinary exertions. The country is rich, productive, and thickly settled; consequently, social and financial intercourse is so frequent that the people out of necessity become courteous, refined, enterprising, and broad-mined. This part of the North was first civilized and Christianized. Later, the introduction of feudalism and the enslavement of the peasants could easily be accomplished here, where, unlike Norway and northern Sweden, no great mountain walls and deep fjords defended the weak against the encroachment of the strong. But the same European influence which in the middle ages compelled these people to submit to the spirit of the times, has at present made them the broadest and most cosmopolitan of all the Northmen.

In the northern part of Sweden nature is stern, the winters are severe, existence must be obtained by hard toil, and activity becomes a necessity. It was the brave people from Dalarne who in olden times often insisted upon their rights of free men, and twice enforced their demands by the sword. It is due to the population of northern Sweden that she has one of the most brilliant histories in Christendom, and that the peasants have never, as was the case in Denmark, been chained to the soil, but have always exercised a great influence upon the political affairs. But the grand careers of Gustavus Adolphus and the Charleses have had a tendency to make the Swedish people proud, which is but natural, for few countries, and certainly neither Denmark nor Norway has such a renowned history. The nearness of Russia, French influence, and a brilliant history have been the chief agencies in making the Swedes a conservative, a polite, and an aristocratic nation. "Sweden," a Dane says, "is the one of the three kingdoms which, according to its whole history and present position, is called upon to take the leadership in all foreign Scandinavian politics. The nation has still a vivid memory of its participation in the great European strifes in the days of the Gustaves and the Charleses, and takes continually the greatest interest in all great political questions. That country has, furthermore, what the other two kingdoms have not, a class especially adopted to be the bearers of such a policy. It cannot be denied that the great foreign questions are the most difficult to grapple with for the democracies. Sweden, more than Norway and Denmark, has something of an able national aristocracy. Norway has no noblemen at all, and the few in Denmark are too fresh from absolute government, and it seems also—although some of them are very wealthy—that they are hardly to the same extent as in Sweden, interested in the economic life of the country. While in Denmark we only find few names like those of Moltke, Bille, and Frijs, prominent in its foreign politics; in Sweden we still find a number of names from the great European wars—skjölds, svärds, hjelms, stjernas, kronas (or all the names ending in words as shield, sword, helmet, star, crown, etc.)—as leaders in agriculture, mining, banking, or other important interests of the country. Nor can it be denied that such a class, as a rule, has a better understanding of the great questions than a pure democracy of peasants or of workingmen in the cities."

.In Norway "The ocean roars along its rock-bound coast, and during the long, dark winter the storms howl and rage, and hurl the waves in white showers of spray against the sky. The Aurora Borealis flashes like a huge shining fan over the northern heavens, and the stars glitter with keen frosty splendor." The many deep cut valleys, protected by mountains and fjords, are by nature independent principalities. Even when the country was a province of Denmark each valley governed its own local affairs. The Norwegians are, like the elements that surround them, daring, independent, radical, and turbulent.

An educated Danish-American speaks about the Scandinavians at home in the following manner: "If we look for the differences in character between the Scandinavians and the Anglo-Saxons, we find that our countrymen, with all their solid qualities, are lacking in that energy which probably, more than anything else, characterizes the English and American nations. The average Scandinavian has at bottom a good deal of the same nature as the Anglo-Saxon. He is rather cold and taciturn. Southern people even find a certain kind of brutality in his nature, but they admire his strength of character. Outward, as well as inward, the Scandinavian and the Anglo-Saxon are probably more alike than men of other nationalities. It is only when it comes to activity that the Scandinavians fall back compared with the pushing and enterprising Anglo-Saxons. This difference has not always existed. Energy, individuality, and love of freedom were just as characteristic of the old inhabitants of the Scandinavian north as they are at present of the English speaking race, especially in the greatest period of their history, that of the Vikings, when the Normans, Danes, and Swedes conquered half of Europe, and the Danish blood on French soil, the Normans of Normandy, instituted the greatest development of the mediaeval epoch.

"But the old Scandinavians did not keep up this great evolution of force at home, whether this was due to the mollifying influence of Christianity, or to the destruction of the small independent communities by the larger kingdoms, or to both together which ended the old life of continuous fighting. The northern empire of Canute the Great, as well as the later of the Valdemars, were even more short lived formations than the Frankish empire; and at no later period of their history have the Scandinavians been able to make any great extension of their power. They have developed a respectable civilization, but no great enterprise, and they are not counted among the leading nations of the world. Only the poet can now sing, 'Again shall the glorious race of the North lead to victory the freedom of nations.' In actual life they are at present a more modest people.

"There is certainly in this respect a great difference between the three Scandinavian nations. The Swedes have formerly been more apt to go to extremes. Although they are not lacking in any of the more solid qualities of the Danes and Norwegians, they have in their composition more of the French *elan* than their brethren; and they have at least a certain kind of pushing energy. We shall not attempt to decide whether this is due to the difference in climate—there being in Sweden more of the stirring, continental difference between the seasons, more frequent changes from heat to cold than in Denmark or Norway; or to the accidental historic development which connected Sweden, more than Denmark-Norway, with general European politics; or, finally, to the old difference in race between the remarkably gifted people of the Svear north of the great Swedish lakes, and the Goths and other Scandinavian tribes farther south. The Danes are certainly a people of extreme moderation. They are unbearably conservative in business, where they work respectably, but seldom exert themselves very much. In their religion they rarely show much zeal, although, as a rule, on the other hand, they are far from being professed free-thinkers. In art, their national school copies with truthfulness the characteristics of the country and of the people, but lacks all brilliancy in colors and in ideas. Molesworth, an English ambassador of two hundred years ago, in describing the country and the people, speaks of their extraordinary moderation in virtues as in vices; and thus it certainly cannot be their absolute government which has produced all this respectable mediocrity in the nation. The temperate climate makes one day like another, and their isolated location allows the people to live their own life free from the great European movements. The Norwegians have more earnestness, as their soil and climate are harder and more severe than the fertile Danish country and the moderate Danish climate. But their location has kept them still more apart from general European matters, and their greatness as a seafaring nation can hardly keep up with the changes of the times. It was in the former Danish-Norwegian state largely due to the Norwegians that the sea was called the 'Path of Danes to praise and might.' Lately came the epoch of steam, which made even navigation a question of machinery and money rather than of personal prowess and ability. Already when navigation and commerce went over distant parts of the world and through greater seas, the very location of England and Holland gave them an advantage over the natives of the North. Nature contributed its part, and together with free government made the Anglo-Saxons the real successors of the Scandinavian Vikings in enterprise and energy. Today this natural advantage in the location of Great Britain is again neutralized by the marvelous development of the railway systems of the world; and not only the political preponderance, but also the new changes of communication by land, that is making Germany—and especially the Prussians, these able German colonists on Slav territory —the successful competitor of England. This, too, is one of the main causes of the greatness of the United States; and it is especially—as everybody knows—the railways which at this moment make the great American West the main field of development of the whole Teutonic race. This is now, more than any other part of the world, what in olden times the northern and western seas were in Europe. Here there is room for the individuality and energy of our race; for the free development of co-operation of all human forces.

"This feature of moderation, so prominent in the characters of the present Scandinavians, also shows itself in their internal policy. Honest administration and justice are characteristics of their national life."

In a letter to Prof. Hjärne, of Upsala, Sweden—pub- in The North in 1893—Björnstjerne Björnson characterizes the Norwegians in this manner: "The Norwegians are, in my opinion, not that people in the North which is least gifted or has the weakest character. But its fate has brought it to such a pass that it has not had enough cohesive power, not enough sense of national honor; therefore its aims are not far reaching. It is not so grand as the Swedish people (not so flippant either, perhaps). It is not so industrious and faithful as the Danish people (not so zealous either, perhaps). It takes hold and lets go, it lets go and takes hold of persons and aims. It will exert itself to the utmost; but it demands speedy and signal success; its ambition is not so great as its vanity. Hot-headed, impetuous in small things, it is patient in great ones, so that with all its faults it has talents for a noble deed, provided the conditions are present. But the condition of conditions is the right of self-determination in order that it may concentrate its bias for adventure and its talents in forming new things and, if possible, in making these an example for others. The Norwegian people must needs take the lead in certain things. If its craving for honor and its character can be marshaled in a spontaneous exertion for the accomplishment of a certain purpose, you may see that it is capable of something, and the North shall be benefited by us."

It is, however, not fair to blame the Scandinavians at home for their lack of energy and enterprise. Nature is against them. The countries, on the whole, are barren and unproductive, the opportunities for safe investments are scarce, and a speculator after having once failed will find it extremely difficult to re-establish himself in business. Consequently the people become conservative in business, as well as in politics and in religion. Diligence and frugality has to be adopted, not as a matter of choice, perhaps, but as a matter of necessity. In the United States the country is new, undeveloped, and rich; a failure, or even several, can be amended, which induces us to become bold speculators, and daring advocates of new social, religious, and political theories; changes and excitement become a passion; everything is conducive to activity; the air we breathe is commercial. In the North all this is reversed. Yet it would be wrong to accuse the people of sluggishness. For whoever has seen Stockholm, hewed out of the rocks, or Kristiania—both located nearly a thousand miles farther north than the northern boundary line of the United States, and having about the same latitude as the central part of Alaska and the extreme southern portion of Greenland—must admit that they possess all the energy and enterprise which nature permits them to exercise. Taking into consideration the harshness of the climate and the barrenness of the soil in the greater part of the Scandinavian countries, no one can deny that the people have shown more push and perseverence in supporting themselves by cultivating these districts than any of the other nations—all of which, as a general thing, have been more favored by nature. It is not difficult to live in splendor when one has plenty, but it takes skill and prudence to manage to make a comfortable livelihood out of a small income. The Scandinavians at home have not only supplied their physical wants, but are among the most civilized nations on earth. Their lower schools—the bulwark of a nation—are excellent, and certainly better than the much-boasted of American common schools. Denmark, Norway, and Sweden are among the five European states, which virtually have no illiterate classes of people.   In Russia only 21 persons out of a hundred can read and write, in Italy 58, in Hungary 61, in Austria 75, in Ireland 76, in the United States 78, in Great Britain 91, in Holland 92, in Germany 99, and in the Scandinavian countries 99½.

It is true that the people of the North are somewhat inclined towards drunkenness, and crimes and vices are, of course, as is the case in every country, committed.   Yet in the Northern countries, where large cities can hardly be said to exist, where the poorer classes of the community are scattered through the farming districts and not congregated in dirty quarters of great cities, morality naturally stands high.   And whoever has, by actual observation, compared the facial expressions of the lower strata of humanity in the country districts of the North with those of the same grade in the large European and American cities, must certainly come to the conclusion that the former are morally so far superior to the latter that no comparison can properly be made between them.

History of the Scandinavian Immigration.

—BY—

O. N. NELSON.

The Icelanders discovered America, as is well known, about the year 1000, and the Scandinavians have, in all probability, emigrated to the United States ever since the country began to be colonized. For example, Hans Hansen Bergen, of Bergen, Norway, came with the Dutch emigrants to New York as early as 1633, and became the ancestor of a large American family by that name. In the Dutch colonial and church records he was variously called *Hans Hansen von Bergen*, *Hans Hansen de Noorman*, etc. He married a Dutch lady, was quite a noted character in those early days, and his name has, perhaps, been mixed up with the supposed Danish-Norwegian colony at Bergen, N. J., which should, according to some questionable authorities, have been founded there in 1624. Although there is every reason, and some historical evidence for assuming that there were Danes and Norwegians in America at that time, they were not numerous enough to establish a distinct settlement.

The well-known Swedish colony was founded at Delaware River in 1638, and a Swedish clergyman preached in his native tongue in Philadelphia as late as 1823. United States minister to Sweden-Norway, W. W. Thomas, writes: "New Sweden as a distinct political organization under the Swedish flag, existed but for seventeen years. Yet, brief as was its life, this little colony occupies a memorable place in American history, and has left a lasting impress upon this continent. Most of the Swedish colonists continued to live on the banks of the Delaware, and their descendants have ever been, and are today, among the most influential and honored citizens of the three states of Pennsylvania, Delaware, and New Jersey. The man who, as a member of the Continental Congress, gave the casting vote of Pennsylvania in favor of the Declaration of Independence, was a Swede of the old Delaware stock—John Morton. And when the civil war burst upon the land, it was a descendant of New Sweden, the gallant Robert Anderson, who, with but a handful of men, calmly and bravely met the first shock of the rebellion at Fort Sumter. Surely, love of freedom, and patriotism, and state-craft, and valor came over to America, not only in the *Mayflower*, but also in that Swedish ship, the *Kalmar Nyckel*."

The brave Captain Bering, a Dane, entered the service of Peter the Great, and discovered the strait which bears his name, in the first part of the eighteenth century. It was on his discovery that Russia based its claim to Alaska, which afterwards was bought by the United States. The early Swedish immigrants in this century found countrymen of theirs in Charleston, S. C., who had come to this country during the previous century.

In the first year, 1820, when the United States commenced to record the number of immigrants who arrived, 20 are registered from Denmark and only three from Sweden-Norway.   It is a remarkable fact that the total sum of the Danish emigrants from 1820 to 1840 equals in number the total sum of both the Norwegians and Swedes during the same time; yet the Danish immigration has never been very heavy, reaching its maximum of nearly 12,000 in 1882, when, on the other hand, 30,000 Norwegians and 65,000 Swedes arrived. Since, the immigration of all the Scandinavian countries has declined. The Norwegians never exceeded a thousand a year until 1843, the Swedes not until 1852, and the Danes not until 1857.

It seems that the early Danish immigrants in this country and the Swedish colonists at Delaware River should have been the means of spreading reliable information in regard to America in their respective countries, and thus become factors in making the emigration from Denmark and Sweden much earlier than from Norway. But it is just the reverse. The Danes, however, have been too busy in re-constructing their affairs at home, and on that account have, probably, been prevented from participating in the movement towards the West. The common people in Sweden knew nothing about the colony at Delaware River, the relation between these settlers and their father-land had virtually ceased before the present century commenced. Such adventurers as Kleng Person came in direct contact with the laboring classes of Norway, and thus hastened the American fever in that country. The Kleng Persons of Denmark and ` Sweden appeared on the scene much later. Nor must we forget that before the middle of this century a citizen of Sweden

was required to have a special permit from the king and
pay three hundred kronor* before he could leave the
country, while the constitution of Norway granted that
freedom to every man. It must also be remembered that
the conservatism of the Danes and Swedes has somewhat
hindered their westward march, while the passion for radical
changes among the Norwegians has been the means of promoting their emigration.

The emigrants of today have a great deal of trouble with
their baggage, steamship agents, hotel runners, and impos-
ers of all kinds. Yet their annoyance and inconveniences are
small in comparison with the misery which the early pioneers passed through. Before the middle of this century no
regular steamers plowed between the North and this country, no Western railroads existed. The Scandinavian emigrants rode after a horse team to a seaport at home, where
they often had to wait for weeks before a chance could be secured to embark for England, France, or Germany, where
they again had to rest in patience for a while until a sailing-
vessel brought them across the stormy Atlantic. Sometimes several emigrants clubbed together and hired or
bought a small, old ship; others again took passage on a
merchant-vessel. Generally the journey lasted from two to
six months. Provisions often failed, sickness and suffering
always occurred, and more than once starvation and hun-
ger stared them in the face. From New York they generally
proceeded to the Northwest by slow boats up the Erie
Canal and continued the tedious journey on the Great Lakes.

"In early times migrations consisted of movements of
whole tribes in a career of conquests, and differed radically

*In "Sjelfbiografi", p. 10, by Rev. S. B. Newman, it is asserted that emigrants had to
give bonds for the amount mentioned.

from emigration, which is a movement of individuals." The wandering of the Goths and other barbarians at the time of the fall of Rome, and to a certain extent the conquests of the Vikings, were migrations. The early colonies of America, for example, the Swedish settlement at the Delaware River in the first part of the seventeenth century, were not private affairs, but national, under the direction of the respective governments; they also differed from emigration. The great stream of human beings who have sought and seek homes on the American continent and in Australia in the nineteenth century are emigrants. But if migration, colonization, and emigration have differed in their nature, the causes which have lead the Scandinavians, and to a great extent other people, to participate in these movements have always been the same.

What have been the chief motives and main causes which have induced the one-and-a-half million Scandinavians to exchange their northern homes and settle on the wild prairies and in the thick forests of the Western continent in the nineteenth century? *First:* The Northern countries, on the whole, are barren and unproductive. The wealth, and especially the best part of the land, has been, to a great extent, concentrated in a few hands. And although the Scandinavian countries in many places are not thickly populated, yet the land being poor, unequally divided, and not always cultivated to its fullest capacity, a large portion of the intelligent, industrious, and prudent classes have been compelled to drag out their lives in poverty. The idea of dependence was repugnant to their very nature. But revolution against the powers that be and the property of other people was almost equally objectionable, for civilization has made the fierce and turbulent Northmen law-abiding people. Yet revolutionary movements, on a small scale, of the laboring classes were attempted during the first part of this century, both in Denmark and Sweden. In Denmark these movements of the people resulted in important changes. Property was revolutionized. The greater part of the land before 1849 belonged to the large estates; the laboring people and tenants, being bound to the soil, were virtually slaver of the great land owners; but since most of the land has passed into the hands of small and middle-sized farms; and the people now exercise a great influence upon all affairs pertaining to the government. This reconstruction of Denmark has, no doubt, hindered the Danish emigration, which before 1880 did not reach 5,000 in number a year, and has never exceeded 12,000 annually. In southern Sweden, however, an attempted revolution failed totally; some of the leaders got drunk when action was necessary. But on the whole little has been attempted or accomplished by revolutionary movements to better the economical conditions of the Scandinavians at home. Nor can it be denied that feudalism, a strong central government, a mistaken idea of patriotism, the great distinction between the classes, the religious belief that the superiors must be obeyed in all things, and the continuous preaching of contentment by the clergy to the masses, had induced the descendants of the independent Vikings to submit slavishly to the condition of things. But the spirit of freedom was not dead, it only slept. Kindle the spark and the old Viking blood will again boil with fire of passion and seek for adventure, conquests, and liberty. And when the report reached the North that beyond the Atlantic Ocean, freedom of conscience, liberty of thought, and, above all, independence in life, could be attained by honest toil, struggle, and self-sacrifice, they were at once ready to embrace the opportunity. But as a people they move slowly, they are more conservative than radical; consequently their emigration began late, which, however, was largely due to the fact that no reliable information in regard to the Western World could reach the poorer and middle classes, scattered, as they are, over a large tract of territory thinly populated.

Secondly—A few Scandinavian sailors and adventurers had settled in the United States in the early part of this century. Some of them were educated men. In letters to relatives, contributions to newspapers, and, above all, by personal visits to their old homes, they pictured in fine colors the economic, social, religious, and political advantages to be gained in the New World. They created a sensation among the laboring and middle class, which has resulted in changes at home that may be said to be revolutionary in their nature. When Scandinavian-Americans visited the North, the people would travel on foot, during the cold winters, long distances to hear their wonderful tales—some are said to have been a professional expert in the art of tale-telling. Ole Rynning's book, *A True Account of America*, which was published in Kristiania in 1839, was read by everybody. Gustaf Unonius, who with his wife and a few others arrived in America in 1841, and may be said to have given the first impulse to the Swedish emigration, was looked upon in America as a curiosity, and his letters to the press in Sweden created a great excitement. Col. Hans Mattson, who came to this country in 1851, says: "At this time the Swedes were so little known, and Jennie Lind, on the other hand, so renowned in America, that the Swedes were frequently called Jennie Lind men." When he visited his native country in 1868, the people flocked to see him, the servant girls drew lots who should wait upon him, and the one who succeeded in having the honor, expressed her disappointment that "He looked just like any other man." In the early times the opinions in the North regarding America differed. Class opposed class. The clergy, the school, the press, and the upper classes leagued together in opposing the whole emigration movement. The clergy maintained that to emigrate to a foreign country was a sin against the fourth commandment: "Honor thy father and thy mother, as the Lord thy God commandeth thee; that thy days may be long, and that it may go well with thee upon the land which the Lord thy God giveth thee." But these pious men omitted to mention that their God had brought his chosen people out of the bondage of Egypt. In the public schools, children were taught that to emigrate was a crime against patriotism. The press ridiculed the whole movement and published the contributions from Scandinavian-Americans only as a matter of curiosity, and as a specimen of American mendacity. Scandinavian travelers, tourists, and those who had ruined their financial and social conditions in the old country, often went to the United States and described in the newspapers at home the sufferings and horrors which awaited the emigrants, and the barbarity of the American nation. Frequently these accusations were true. In the early part of this century the emigrants were swindled, defrauded. ill-treated, robbed, murdered, and even sold as slaves into the Southern states. According to the Constitution of Norway, which is one of the most liberal in Europe, those who were convicted of a penitentiary offense, and those who had emigrated to a foreign land, were put on an equal footing. To emigrate in those days was considered a crime by all the Northern powers. Henrik Wergeland wrote:

> "Did ind hvor Fyrren suser ind
> Tör ingen Nidding vandre,
> Som har forglemt i trolöst Sind
> Sit Faedreland for andre."

Thirdly—Religious persecution and military service have not compelled many Northmen to leave their native lands. For, excepting Eric Janson's party from Sweden, few have emigrated on account of direct religious oppression. On the whole, and especially in later years when the Northern emigration has been heaviest, the religious laws of the Scandinavian countries have been very liberal. But it cannot be denied that indirectly the religious narrowness, the unfavorable and unjust religious laws, have had a great influence in promoting the movement, especially in starting it; yet sometimes the emigrants have mistaken law and order for oppression, and left their native lands on account of their wrong notion of liberty. Quite frequently the very opposition of the clergy and the educated classes lead the working people and farmers to cast the dice in favor of the Western World.

Fourthly—After the pioneer immigrants had succeeded, by

sending letters, newspapers, and special information for emigrants published by steamship and railway companies, to
their relations and friends in the North, but, above all, by personal visits to their old homes, in giving a true, but sometimes
an exaggerated, account of the condition of things in
the United States, then the emigration   assumed   enormous
proportions.   It became a fashion.

Smith, in his book *Emigration and Immigration*, says:
"Emigration is sometimes spoken of as if it were simply the
operation of an individual coolly and rationally measuring
the advantages to be gained, and thus advancing his own
ecconomic condition and that of the country to which he
comes.   Nothing could be farther from the truth.   Emigration proceeds now under the numerous influences, the efforts
of steamship companies, the urging of friends and relations,
the assistance of poor law authorities and charitable societies, and the subtle but powerful influence of popular delusion
in regard to the New World."   Another authority, speaking
especially in regard to the Scandinavian emigration, which
Smith does not, although his assertions apply to it as well
as to others, writes: "With a few minor exceptions the whole
movement has been unorganized, though agents of steamship and railway companies, and even some of the states,
have systematically worked up immigration sentiment in the
Northlands."

There are certainly very few Scandinavian paupers and
criminals who have, as has been the practice in other
European countries, and especially in England, been sent to
foreign countries by the government, local communities, or
charitable associations.   Yet, in by-gone days, philanthro-

pic societies in Sweden have paid the passage to America of liberated criminals.

To sum up the causes which have induced one-and-a-half million Northmen to emigrate to the United States in the nineteenth century, the main reason has at bottom been the same as that which produced the Viking age, namely, *material betterment*. Yet, as was the case with the Northmen, the *love for freedom and adventure*, especially as the unjust religious, social, and political conditions have been rather oppressive to the middle and laboring classes, has, during the whole history of the Scandinavian emigration, been a powerful factor in promoting the movement. It was adventurers, and those who were hostile to all class distinction, that gave the first impulse to the movement, and may be said to have directed the Northern immigrants towards the Northwest.   While, as was the custom in the heroic age of the ninth and tenth centuries, *the spirit of the time and the fashion of the age* have in latter years induced many young people in the Scandinavian countries to court dangers and turn the wheel of fortune in foreign lands. The man who dared to leave his native country has always been admired for his courage and bravery, although his motives have often been questioned. To emigrate has of late been looked upon as the proper thing to do for those who were ambitious and possessed sufficient energy to become successful in foreign lands. It has always been considered a great shame to return to the North, even for a short visit, before a person has been successful abroad, and few have done it. In recent years, letters, newspapers, and printed informations for immigrants, which have been sent to relatives at home, visits of prosperous im-

migrants to their native lands, and inumerable prepaid passage tickets "Have been the most powerful preachers of the
New World's advantages."

Age, sex, and occupation prove that the Scandinavian
immigrants are the cream of the working classes. According
to the United States statistics, 62 per cent are males, 65 per
cent arrive between fifteen and forty years of age, 11 per cent
are over forty years of age, and 24 per cent are children
under fifteen. During the years between 1881 and 1890,
1 person out of 5,914 was a clergyman, 1 out of 5,089 a
musician, 1 out of 7,236 a physician and surgeon, and 1 out
of 3,074 a teacher—in other words only 1 out of 1,017 had
a profession, while 1 out of 12 was a skilled laborer, and
one-half of the Scandinavian immigrants were either farmers, merchants, or servants.

Nor is there any reason to assume that they change their
occupations a great deal when they arrive in this country, for,
according to the United States census of 1870, 1880, 1890,
25 per cent of the Scandinavian population were engaged
in agriculture, and 50 per cent labored at what was called
"All classes of work." It is a notable fact that 1 out of 4 of
every Scandinavian engages in agriculture, while only 1 out
of 6 of the native Americans, 1 out of 7 of the Germans, and
1 out of 12 of the Irish, follow the same profession.

It is partly on account of their great love and fitness for
farming that the Scandinavians have been considered by
nearly every American political economist to be the best immigrants which the country receives. "It is," says an authority, "to the Scandinavian immigrants from Norway,
Sweden, and Denmark, that the Northwest is largely indebt-

ed for its marvelous development." "The Scandinavians,"
adds another, "especially, take to farming. They have succeeded where the Americans with better start have failed.
They have acquired farms and now live in a state of great
comfort. In a certain sense it is the survival of the fittest."

A fair proportion, however, of the younger element of
the Scandinavian immigrants pursue studies in this country,
either at some of the Scandinavian institutions or in American colleges, and later attend to the professional need of
their countrymen. And although not very many, propor-
tionally, of the highly educated classes emigrate; yet unquestionably, taken all in all, the people who exchange the
North for the United States are, on the 'aggregate, mentally
better endowed, and morally superior to those who remain
at home. In the first place, as a general thing, criminals,
paupers, and idiots are cared for by the Northern governments, and are not permitted to leave. The poor and the
vicious classes cannot pay for their own passage, nor receive
a ticket on credit. Cowards dare not, and fools have not
sense enough to emigrate. It is the old story of the Vikings.
Gathering together hap-hazzard a thousand Scandinavian
emigrants on any vessel which is destined for the United
States and an equal number of those who remain in the
North, and the former will, in regard to age, sex, physique,
mental endowment, and moral purity and courage, be
superior to the latter. Smith, the latest and one of the best
authorities on the emigration question, says: "It is often
the poor and degraded who have not the courage nor the
means to emigrate. When emigration is brought about by
the free action of a man's own mind, without extraneous

aids or influences, it is naturally the men who have intelligence, some financial resources, energy, and ambition that emigrate. It requires all these to break loose from the ties of kindred, of neighborhood, and country, and to start out on a long and difficult journey. On account of that the best people emigrate, therefore the government objects." Secondly, a well school-trained man is not always the best naturally endowed. Besides, even educated emigrants must possess courage, energy, and perseverance in order to succeed in foreign lands. It is only the liberal and broad-minded people of the higher classes who in any sense can exchange their native customs and manners, and adopt the habits of other nations. It is harder, perhaps, for a cultured man, who has acquired a permanent character and fixed ideas, to forget his native soil than it is for an illiterate person—the former's patriotism is founded on reason, the latter's on sentiment. The fact that the majority of the educated Scandinavians at home have been hostile towards and not participated much in the emigration movement has been an important factor in hastening the Americanization of the Northern people.

Those having had a home training, and especially the clergy, whose duties it is to guide the intellectual improvement and moral conduct of the people have generally been men of broad culture and liberal views, who have founded, or promoted, great Scandinavian-American educational institutions, where the younger elements of the people have been educated, and the latter became the leaders of the Northern race in the New World. It is true that these institutions have been managed somewhat according to a different method than most American colleges, yet they have been, and are, the stepping stones towards Americanization. And it certainly is, from an American standpoint, far better that the clergy and other men of learning have been educated in Scandinavian-American schools than that they should have been imported—which otherwise would have been absolutely necessary—from the Northern countries.

The different location of each country and the diverse historical connections with foreign countries have made a little variation in the character of the Northmen at home. But these differences are slight, being on the whole merely artificial, and can hardly be said to apply, to any great extent at least, to the Scandinavians in this country. For the immigrants upon their arrival in the United States generally discard their artificial acquirements and begin to practice their natural endowments, namely: courage, determination, industry, frugality, and perseverance. It is remarkable how quickly, for example, a northern Swede will dispense with his elaborate system of bows, bobs, courtesies, hat-liftings, and adopt the practice of simpler manners; this he often does in spite of himself, for quite frequently he is not a believer in the American simplicity of intercourse; especially is the cold and unceremonious business relation, which is in such contrast to what he has been used to, repugnant to him. Yet even on the streets or in the stores in Stockholm you can easily detect a person who has been in America, perhaps, only for six months; the man has been simplified. But in spite of the fact that the Scandinavians become quickly Americanized, only retaining their original boldness, frankness, and firmness, yet their different training shows itself in many ways. For

example, the great political agitation which has been in
operation in Norway ever since the beginning of this century,
has created among the Norwegians a taste and ability
for politics in which neither the Swedes nor the Danes
can, or will not perhaps, compete with them, not even
in this country. Between the years of 1880 and 1900
there were, according to the United States census, from
ten to one hundred and fifty thousand more Swedes in
America than Norwegians, yet during that period only one
Swede was elected to the United States congress, while at
the same time seven Norwegians had a seat in the national
House of Representatives. It may be argued, which of
course is true, that the Norwegian immigration is older than
the Swedish, consequently the younger elements of the Norwegians have had a longer time and a better chance to
become acquainted with the political machinery of the nation than their brethren; but even granting this, it yet
remains a fact that in Minnesota, where the immigration of
one nationality is just as old as the other, about 170 Norwegians and only 80 Swedes have represented their districts
in the two legislative bodies of the state from 1857 to 1900;
and although the population of the former has, until lately,
outnumbered that of the latter, it is not in proportion to
their political preponderance. Yet it must also be remembered that only 21 per cent of the Norwegians live in cities
of over 25,000 inhabitants, where 32 per cent of the Swedes
are to be found. The Norwegians thus scattered throughout
the farming districts and smaller towns have a better chance
to be elected to local offices and to the state legislature than
those residing in large cities. The greater political activity

of the Norwegians in comparison with the Swedes is also
apparent by the former's greater variation in the choice of
political parties. Some of the best educated Scandinavian-
Americans are Democrats, Prohibitionists, or Populists; yet
the great majority of the Swedes have always been, and are,
Republicans, which is also, but to a less extent, the case with
the Norwegians. Two of the seven Norwegian-American con-
gressmen were elected by the Populists.

The difference in the characters of the two people shows
itself also, to look at it from an historical standpoint, in
their religion. For, while the Swedish-American Lutheran
Church has progressed smoothly, uninterruptedly, and undivided, the Norwegian-Americans have wrangled about theological dogmas, and divided Lutherism into six different
and distinct organizations; some of which, however, have
again been united into one body.

The Danish immigration is more recent, consequently
they do not stand out so prominently in political and religious matters as the other two nationalities, but on the
whole they resemble the Swedes in being conservative.

Thirty-two per cent of the Swedish-American population,
twenty-three of the Danish, and twenty-one of the Norwegian, reside in cities of over 25,000 inhabitants each; this
does not, however, sustain the general opinion, that
the Swedes and Danes are better business men than the
Norwegians; but as the Danes and southern Swedes at home
seem to have a natural instinct for financial undertakings,
it is probably correct.

But on the whole the difference in the character between
the three Scandinavian-American nationalities is small and

short-lived. After a few years residence in this country, and very often not even among the emigrants on board of the ship that brings them, can any distinction of the separate Northern nationalities be detected. In the second generation only the old Northmen's fearlessness, energy, and strong will-power, clothed in American manners, are visible. Of course, the physical features often change considerably in a few generations.

The Scandinavians are justly proud of their Viking age. The kings of Sweden have always styled themselves "King of the Swedes, Goths, and Wends." The Danes and Norwegians point with pride to their conquests in France, Great Britain, and Ireland. Prof. Worsaae says: "The greatest, and for general history the most important, memorials of the Scandinavian people are connected, as is well known, with the expeditions of the Normans, and the Thirty Years' War." It is true that Rolf, Knute the Great, and Gustavus Adolphus, have had, either directly or indirectly, a great influence upon civilization. But, excepting the Thirty Years' War, the greatest, and for the human race the most important, memorials of the Scandinavian people are connected with their discovery of, colonization in, and emigration to the United States. John Ericsson, the greatest Scandinavian-American, was more of a benefactor to humanity than either Rolf, or Knute the Great, or both together. (We refrain from mentioning other influential Scandinavian-Americans because many of them are living at present). 'The emigrants coming from the narrow valleys of Norway, the mines and forests of Sweden, the smiling plains of Denmark, the rocky shores of Iceland, with hearts of oak and arms of steel, are building empires in this Western continent.' They have torn themselves away from home, country, relatives, friends, brothers, sisters, and parents. They have cleared prairies and forests, built railways, and mined the earth in a foreign land. They have by hard and honest toil, struggle, prudence, frugality, industry, and perseverance succeeded against adverse circumstances in creating comfortable homes for themselves on American soil. They have in war and peace, in commerce and literature, in the pulpits and legislative halls, distinguished themselves, done their duties towards their adopted country, and been an honor to their native lands. But these peaceable and industrious emigrants from the North have not received the same recognition, either at home or abroad, as the savage and plundering Vikings. How long will it take before the victories of peace shall be more renowned than those of war?

The well-known Col. Hans Mattson uses the following language in the conclusion of his *Minnen*: "Yes, it is verily true that the Scandinavian immigrants, from the early colonists of 1638 to the present time, have furnished strong hands, clear heads, and loyal hearts to the republic. They have caused the wilderness to blossom like the rose; they have planted schools and churches on the hills and in the valleys; they have honestly and ably administered the affairs of town, county, and state; they have helped to make wise laws for their respective commonwealths and in the halls of congress; they have with honor and ability represented their adopted country abroad; they have sanctified the American soil by their blood, shed in freedom's cause on the battlefields of the revolutionary and civil wars; and though proud of their Scandinavian ancestry, they love America and American institutions as deeply and as truly as do the descendents of the Pilgrims, the starry emblem of liberty meaning as much to them as to any other citizen.

"Therefore, the Scandinavian-American feels a certain sense of ownership in the glorious heritage of American soil, with its rivers, lakes, mountains, valleys, woods, and prairies, and in all its noble institutions; and he feels that the blessings which he enjoys are not his by favor or sufferance, but by right; by moral as well as civil right. For he took possession of the wilderness, endured the hardships of the pioneer, contributed his full share toward the grand results accomplished, and is in mind and heart a true and loyal American citizen."

But not only have the Northern immigrants created permanent monuments in the New World, but they have also exercised a great reflex influence upon the affairs of the Old World. For, while Gustavus Adolphus defended Protestantism and German liberty, which resulted in the intellectual and religious freedom of the world, it was Swedish-Americans who introduced in Sweden the faith of the Baptists in about 1850, and Methodism fifteen years later,* and were largely instrumental in securing that religious toleration in their native land which their ancestors had fought for in foreign countries. A Norwegian-American introduced Methodism in his native country in 1849, and Danish-Americans commenced to preach that doctrine in Denmark shortly after. It certainly shows a great amount of bigotry, narrowness, and ignorance, not to say villainy, of the governments at home, that Baptists should, on account

*The work of the English Methodists in Sweden in the early part of the nineteenth century was interrupted, but was resumed by Swedish-Americans in 1865.

of proselyting,   be sent out of the kingdom by the civil
authorities of Sweden as late as in 1851; that Norwegian
Lutheran clergymen should endeavor, by force, to prevent
the Methodists from worshiping God according to their
own conscience, and bury their dead according to their own
rituals, as late as in 1860; or that Swedish ministers should
refuse to grant the permission of burying a Methodist pas- ·
tor, who was a citizen of this country, in the state cemetery
because, they said, he had been a *false prophet*, and the widow
was compelled to appeal to higher authorities in the name
of the American nation, as late as in 1867. Nor were these
atrocities simply the result, or relic, of barbarian laws, for
until forty, or even twenty years ago, religious intolerance
was the accepted theory and common practice of the majority of both the educated classes and the masses in the Scandinavian countries. It must, however, be remembered that
the clergy of the state church thought it was their religious
duty to prevent what they deemed to be false religions to
be imposed upon the people under their charge. Often the
missionaries who represented the new sects were uneducated
men whose procedure was unwise. For example, the Jansonites in Sweden publicly burned all religious books, except
the Bible. This, of course, was unlawful and they had to
suffer the consequences. But the numerous letters and newspapers which the immigrants have sent to their relatives at
home, and the frequent visits of Scandinavian-Americans to
their native lands, have had an immense influence **in**
moulding the public sentiment in favor of more political,
social, and religious freedom. And public sentiment **not**
only governs republics, but even shakes monarchs on their

thrones, and bends the will of bishops. Today the Northmen at home enjoy, virtually, full religious freedom and possess a great amount of political liberty—blessings which they ought, at least to a great extent, to be thankful for to their countrymen across the Atlantic Ocean.

The Scandinavian-Americans, however, have not con-·fined themselves to the political, social, and religious conversion of the old folks at home, their influence has also been of a more material nature. About fifty per cent of the Scandinavian emigrants arrive by prepaid passage tickets secured by relatives here. During each year of 1891 and 1892—according to the estimate of A. E. Johnson of the great emigration firm, A. E. Johnson and Company—six-and-a-half million dollars in actual cash was sent from this country to the North by well-to-do immigrants to their relatives. It is impossible, however, to arrive at anything like a correct conclusion in regard to what amount of wealth in the shape of presents, prepaid passage tickets, and actual cash which Scandinavian-Americans have transferred from the United States to the North. Smith, in his excellent book *Emigration and Immigration*, estimates that each immigrant sends to his native country $35, and from 1820-99, according to United States statistics, not far from 1,500,000 Northmen have settled in this country. If each of them returned $35, the total sum transfered from here to the Scandinavian countries, would, during that period, amount to $52,500,000.

Each immigrant, however, brings with him a certain amount of capital, which Smith estimates to average from $68 to $100, but in 1898 the Scandinavian immigrants

did not average that, according to the estimate of the commissioner of immigration.   "It costs," to quote Smith,
"about $652.50 to bring up a child in Europe till 15 years
of age, and twice that amount in the United States.
But this estimate does not mean the real value of men; they
are not valued in dollars and cents.   But every immigrant
must represent labor capacity worth at least the value of a
slave, which was $800 or $1,000 before the war, but being a
free man he may not choose to work.   But it is figured that
each immigrant is worth $875."   Assuming that each Scan-
dinavian immigrant has brought $75, which added to $875,
the value of his labor capacity, amounts to $950, and multi-
plying that amount by 1,500,000, the number of immigrants
we find that the Scandinavian countries have sent—or rather
permitted to be transferred—to the United States one billion
four hundred and fifty million dollars ($1,450,000,000) worth
of property in the form of human beings and what valuables
these have brought with them. Even subtracting the $52,500,-
000 which have been returned in the shape of prepaid tickets,
presents, and cash, it yet leaves the United States in a debt
of $1,397,500,000 to the Scandinavian countries.

The Chinamen are, perhaps, intellectually equal to any
people, yet China can never reach a higher civilization than it
has attained to until the population is, in some way, reduced.
Civilization and luxury go hand in hand.   A highly cultured
people must have elbow room for their activity.   Simply
a bare physical existence cannot elevate a nation, no matter
how well intellectually the individuals may be endowed.
That the Scandinavian countries have had a heavier population than could be decently supported will, perhaps, not be

seriously disputed; consequently the emigration has fur-
thered their development. Facts prove the assertion. The
social and political aspects, the relation between the employer and employe, have been revolutionized in Norway
since emigration began. It is true that other causes have
assisted in extinguishing class distinction, yet emigration
has been the main factor. But then the emigration has also
been so heavy that, taking into consideration only the immigrants themselves and their children, there is now (1900)
half as many Norwegians living in this country as there are
in the whole of Norway. In Denmark and Sweden, where
the emigration in proportion to the population has not been
so heavy as in Norway, the effect has been less marked. Yet
it has had great influence upon the social and political conditions. Wages have certainly been raised in both countries
as the direct result of the emigration. Besides Scandinavian-Americans often import, and introduce to the trade in
this country, goods manufactured in the North; some of
them have returned home and established new industries;
thus the manufacturing interests of the Scandinavian countries have been extended, furnishing new employment to
their people, and increasing their national wealth.

Yet in spite of this widened commercial activity, and beneficial political, social, and religious influences, the governments of the Northern powers have always looked upon
emigration as a loss to their countries. A Danish-American
wrote in 1885: "At present the official world, the press,
and, on the whole, the higher classes, are rather hostile to
the whole movement. At the best, they ignore it. They
have not yet arrived at the same conclusions in regard to it

as have the leading statesmen in England. They regard emigration as a loss to the old countries. They have the Greek-German view of the state as having interests apart from and above those of the individual. The existing state is, in their eyes, sacred, and not — as it is understood in England and America — identical with the interests of the individual members of the body politic. Secondly, they do not recognize the wholesome influence of the emigration on the people at home. It takes away from the rising population in a good many districts from one-eighth to one-fourth of its laborers. Such a decrease has considerable influence in raising wages; and employers in the first instance only look on what they lose; they do not recognize that the better-paid workingmen, as a rule, give more valuable, and, therefore, not at all dearer, work. It is true that the great political influence of the emigrants on their old home at present contributes largely to strengthen the elements of opposition to the powers that be; but a self-conscious, independent people makes actually a stronger community."

It is impossible to determine, either by statistics or by any historical records, the exact causes which have induced the majority of the Scandinavians to settle in the Northwest. It is, no doubt, partly due to chance, climate, the direction which the early Scandinavian pioneers, especially Rev. O. G. Hedstrom, gave to the movement; but, perhaps, more on account of the Northwest being just opened for settlement at the time when their emigration began. When some Norwegian emigrants arrived at Milwaukee, Wis., in 1839, in search of suitable land, an old settler warned them against the climate of Illinois. He placed two men before them, one strong and healthy, the other weak and lean. Pointing towards the former, he said: " There you see a man from Wisconsin; the other is from Illinois." The Norwegians remained in Wisconsin. Slavery might, in the early days, have prejudiced them from going south. It is certain that movements of Scandinavians in that direction have at different times been attempted, but always failed.

Prof. Babcock, of the University of Minnesota, who has made a special study of the Scandinavians in this country, and being a native American his opinions have a specific value, writes in *The Forum* for September, 1892, as follows: "The passion for the possession of land and for independence that goes with it have characterized the Scandinavians from the earliest times, and it is that which has made them so valuable as citizens of the Northwest. Had they preferred to huddle together in villages or, still worse, to crowd into large cities, the progress of this section would have been materially slower. Until within the last eight years the towns have claimed only a small percentage, and now probably not more than ten per cent come to settle in towns. Scanty means', a spirit of economy, and a fearlessness for hard work and temporary privation, have made them frequently pioneers in settling new territory. With the extension of new railroads into northwestern Minnesota and the Dakotas, and the opening up of Government and railroad land, great numbers of Scandinavian immigrants, and Scandinavian settlers from older portions of the West, have settled here. All of the eighty counties of Minnesota, save possibly two, have representatives of all three Scandinavian peoples; whole townships and almost whole counties are tilled by them.

In the newer counties of Minnesota and the Dakotas thirty
and even forty per cent are of Scandinavian parentage. In
the older portions it is said to be possible to travel 300 miles
across Wisconsin, Iowa, and Minnesota without once leaving Scandinavian-owned land. Though in every large city
and town in the Northwest there are Scandinavians engaged in commercial enterprise and the professions with
marked success, it yet remains true that the great majority
are farmers.

"One of the most important indirect results of the love
for land-ownership is the hastening of naturalization. To
take up homestead claims one of the first conditions for a
foreigner is a declaration of intention to become a citizen;
so the prospective farmer at once takes out his first papers;
and the first step in naturalization is made. This done,
natural inclination leads him to perfect his title of full
citizenship. But the Scandinavian immigrant hardly
needs any great incentive to citizenship. In politics he
is as much in his element as an Irishman in New York
City. His aptitude for politics and his interest in public
affairs are natural. Be he Norwegian, Swede, or Dane, he
hastened and moved in an atmosphere electric with independence and individualism. The Norwegian celebrates the
Fourth of July all the more loyally, because on the seventeenth of May he commemorated in the same way the establishment, in defiance of all Europe, of the Norwegian constitution of 1814. The Dane is fresh from the constitutional
struggle begun in 1849; the Swede has had popular representation since 1866: consequently the Scandinavian immigrants have had some considerable political education when

they arrive. The ballot and independence are not meaningless terms to them; the exercise of them is their right, not merely their privilege. Certainly no class makes greater effort than the Scandinavian to become naturalized; none enters upon the rights and duties of American citizenship with more enthusiasm or honest, intelligent appreciation of its high privileges. Statistics from Minnesota show some interesting facts bearing upon this question, comparison being made with the Germans, who rank among our best immigrants. By the census of 1885 the Scandinavian population was 43.2 per cent and the German 30.1 per cent of the total foreign-born population. Of the increase of foreign-born population for five years ending with 1885, the Scandinavian was 48.2 per cent, the German 30.9 per cent. For the same period, of the total naturalizations (first papers) the Scandinavians took out 56.3 per cent and the Germans 23.2 per cent. Or, looking at the matter in another way, for the same half-decade the Scandinavians who were naturalized were 35.4 per cent of the increase of Scandinavian population for the same time, the Germans 22.9 per cent. Similar statistics for other half-decades give approximately the same results.

" The political affiliations of the Scandinavian voters till about 1886 were almost invariably with the Republican party. The opposition to slavery rallied every son of the Northland, and no soldiers were braver or more patriotic than the Scandinavian Fifteenth Wisconsin regiment and Scandinavian companies in other Wisconsin and Iowa regiments. The suppression of the Rebellion, the abolition of slavery, the passage of the homestead law to which they owed so much—all appealed powerfully to their political senses. New-comers found their predecessors in the Republican party; they found it the party in power in the State and generally in the Nation; its principles were acceptable, and so they too became Republicans. Since 1886, however, less reliance can be placed upon a solid Scandinavian vote, though this element has never been the ready tool of "bosses." It has ever been a ruling rather than a ruled element. The immigration of the last eight years has had a larger percentage from the cities, and a larger percentage has settled in the cities, so that "labor questions" have affected them; local political issues have, to their credit, sometimes shaken their old allegiance more or less, as, for example, prohibition in Iowa and North Dakota, high license in Minnesota; the Bennett law in Wisconsin temporarily drove them out of the Republican party; the Farmers' Alliance, People's party, etc., have drawn Scandinavian recruits from both of the old parties; the tariff and other national questions have divided them as well as other thinking men in both great political parties. However, the majority of them are still and will continue to be Republicans, though no party can mortgage their vote for any election.

"Coupled with the love for politics among them is the love for religion and the Church. The vast majority are Lutherans of one branch or another. At any rate, they are Protestant enough to satisfy the most fastidious Catholic-hater, for a Catholic in Norway or Sweden is a rare, suspicious object. The dissenting movement among the Scandinavian Lutherans in America is comparatively strong. At one time there were six divisions of the Norwegians alone, though recently three of them united. The rigid adherence to the forms and practices of the mother-state Church is weakened, while, on the other hand, the liberal and atheistic movements have made slow progress, even among the dissenters. The churches, with a few exceptions, have not maintained regular elementary schools. Poverty, isolation of the families of the great farming class, and the desire to conform to American customs have all lead to a very general patronage of the common schools. The church school is usually open during public-school vacations, if at all, and instruction confined to religious teaching and the use of the mother-tongue. All this has contributed to the rapid Americanization of the second generation. For higher education, the church maintains numerous and well-patronized seminaries and colleges, while the high-schools and the State universities throughout the Northwest have a large Scandinavian attendance, auguring well for the future. In the University of Minnesota, for example, located in the same city with two Scandinavian colleges, during the past year one hundred and seventy-five students, out of thirteen hundred and seventy-four were of Scandinavian parentage.

"The Scandinavians, with all their virtues, are not without faults. They are often narrow-minded, in the city sometimes clannish and given to making demands, political and social, as Scandinavian-Americans. The Swede is frequently jealous of the Norwegian, and *vice versa*. But as a class they are sober, earnest, industrious, and frugal. They are not driven here; they come of their own accord and come to stay, not to get a few hundred dollars and return to a life of idleness. They come not to destroy our institutions, but to build them up by adopting them. They come from countries not potent or glorious in European affairs, and therefore the more readily denationalize themselves, that they may become entirely American. The most of them are plain, common people, strong, sturdy, and independent, required to unlearn little, ready and able to learn much and learn it well. They still have the same powers of adaptability and assimilation that made Rollo and his Northmen such good Frenchmen, and Guthrun and his Danes such excellent Englishmen; and using these powers among us today, they are, or are rapidly becoming, irreproachably and unimpeachably American."

The well-know Prof. H. H. Boyesen writes in the *North American Review* for November, 1892: "The Chicago papers, at the time of the trial of the Anarchists, complimented the Scandinavians of the West on their law-abiding spirit, and the counsel for the accused emphasized the compliment by requesting that no Scandinavian should be accepted on the jury. He declared his intention of challenging any talesman of Norse blood on the ground of his nativity. Although this man probably had but slight acquaintance with Norsemen, the instinct which bade him beware of them was a correct one.

"There is no nation in Europe that is more averse to violence, and has less sympathy with Utopian aspirations than the people of Norway and Sweden. They have been trained to industry, frugality and manly self-reliance by the free institutions and the scant resources of their native lands; and the moderation and self-restraint inherent in the cold blood of the North make them constitutionally inclined to trust in slow and orderly methods rather than swift and violent

ones. They come here with no millenial expectations,
doomed to bitter disappointment; but with the hope of
gaining, by hard and unremitting toil, a modest competency.
They demand less of life than continental immigrants of the
corresponding class, and they usually, for this very reason,
attain more.   The instinct to save is strong in the majority
of them, and save they do, when their neighbors, of less frugal habits, are running behind. The poor soil of the old
land and the hardships incident upon a rough climate, have
accustomed them to a struggle for existence scarcely less
severe than that of the Western pioneer; and unilluminated
by any hope of improved conditions in the future. The qualities of perseverance, thrift, and a sturdy sense of independence which this struggle from genergtion to generation has
developed, are the very ones which must form the corner
stone of an enduring republic.

"It is therefore a fact which all students of the social
problem arising from immigration have remarked that the
Scandinavians adapt themselves with great ease to American institutions.   There is no other class of immigrants
which so readily assimilated, and assumes so naturally
American customs and modes of thought.   And this is not
because their own nationality is devoid of strong characteristics, but because, on account of the ancient kinship and
subsequent development, they have certain fundamental
traits in common with us, and are therefore less in need of
adaption.   The institutions of Norway are the most democratic in Europe, and those of Sweden, though less liberal,
are developing in the same direction.   Both Norsemen and
Swedes are accustomed to participate in the management of

their communal affairs, and to vote for their representative in the national parliament; and although the power given them here is nominally greater than that they enjoyed at home, it is virtually less.   The sense of public responsibility, the habit of interest in public affairs, and a critical attitude towards the acts of government are nowhere so general among rich and poor alike as in Norway and Sweden, notwithstanding the fact that the suffrage is not universal.   No great effort is therefore required, on the part of Norwegian and Swedish immigrants, to transfer their natural interest in public affairs to the affairs of their adopted country, which now must concern them closely.   With increasing prosperity comes a sense of loyalty to the flag, and a disposition, perhaps, to brag in the presence of later arrivals.   To be an old settler is a source of pride and is recognized as a title to consideration.   A large majority of the old settlers participated in the war, and naturally shared in the sentiment of militant loyalty and devotion to the Union which animated the Federal army.   This is, perhaps, the chief reason why the Scandinavian element in the United States is so overwhelmingly Republican; for the newly-arrived immigrant, having no comprehension of the questions dividing American parties, is apt to accept his politics from the respected "old settler" and veteran, and feels safe, at the end of five years, in voting as he votes.   Thus it happens that the war feeling with its attendant hostility to the South, is transmitted to those to whom the war is but a dim tradition, and the militant politics of the veteran survives amid a peaceful generation that never smelled powder.

"It is notable that, though in many of the earliest Norse

settlements the descendents of the first settlers are still living, there is very little but their names (often Anglicized) and a certain Norwegian cast of features to indicate their Scandinavian origin. They speak English, and, if they have ever learned Norwegian, have usually forgotten it. They have intermarried with American families, and live, think, and feel as Americans. I have had letters from many of these people, asking me to suggest Norwegian names for their children, or inquiring about certain localities in Norway from which their parents or grandparents came. It would seem, judging by the rapipity with which they have adopted American speech and modes of life, that the problem of the assimilation of the immigrant may be safely left to time, without the interference of artificial agencies. But it must be remembered that fifty or sixty years ago, the Scandinavian nationalities were completely lost in the ocean of American life, which beat upon them on all sides, and they had no choice but to drift with the current. I am far from believing now that they, or any other nationality, are strong enough to remain permanently alien in our midst; but they are surely able to resist, for a whole generation, the influence of our national life, and make the process of national assimilation extremely diffcult for their children.

"The Scandinavians have been accused of clannishness, and not without cause. It should, however, be considered that the immigrant, of whatever nationality, has no choice but to be clannish, unless he chooses to associate with those who look down upon him, or dispense with social intercourse altogether. Native Americans are not in the habit of welcoming the immigrant with cordiality; and they have often good reason for regarding him with eyes not altogether friendly. Social intercourse can only be agreeable among people who recognize each other as equals, and no man can be blamed for shunning the society of those who refuse to grant him this recognition. It is, therefore, inevitable that alien communities should grow up in our midst as long as we permit the stream of immigration to pour unimpeded down upon our shores. Each new arrival is attracted to the locallity where he has friends or kinsmen; and when he has laid aside a little money his first desire is to draw more friends and kinsmen after him. Around this nucleus a constant aggregation of homogeneous alien elements will gather.

"There is continual complaint in the Scandinavian papers of the West that the nationalities which they represent are not recognized in the distribution of offices; and it is alleged that in the cities and counties, where the Scandinavians twice out number the Irish, the later have a larger representation in municipal and county offices. The reason of this is not a lack of aptitude for public affairs on the part of Norwegians and Swedes; for, on the contrary, they take as naturally to politics as goslings do to water. But it is rather because they have not learned to suspend personal spites and resentments for the sake of a larger end to be gained. They have not learned party discipline nor the faculty to assert themselves as a unit. From the American point of view this is perhaps not a matter of regret, but rather of congratulation. For we have already a pestiferous abundance of alien nationalities which have the insolence to claim recognition, not as bodies of American citizens, but as Irish, Germans, Bohemians, and Poles; as if in that capacity they have any right to participation in the government of the American republic."

Smith in his book, *Emigration and Immigration*, says that the American traits are: *First*, " The f.ee political constitution and the ability to govern ourselves in the ordinary affairs of life;" *second*, " The absence of privileged classes;" *third*, "The economic well-being of the masses;" *fourth*, "Love of law and order, ready acquiescence in the will of the majority." In a political sense these peculiarities are virtually common to both the Americans and Scandinavians; for even if the latter have had privileged classes in their native lands, they certainly are not in favor of such an arrangement. It is no wonder then that the Scandinavians become — according to all authorities on the subject — quickly Amercanized in regard to all political affairs.

What then is the reason that the majority of the American people and many of the educated Scandinavian-Americans accuse the Northmen of clannishness? In the first place those people differ from each other socially. The American has a broad knowledge of men and things. He can and does approach a stranger with the same ease with which he meets a friend of several years' standing. He questions everybody. He recognizes no class distinction, but associates with everyone who is worthy of his confidence. He is energetic, ambitious, excitable, and extreme. He is remarkably liberal and tolerant on all religious, political, and social questions; but equally narrow-minded and bigoted in regard to his patriotism. America, in his estimation, is the only country under the sun fit for civilized man to live in. He points with just pride to the rapid development of the nation. He boasts of, and sometimes exaggerates, the natural, undeveloped resources, and of the great future of his country. He jokes with everything, even the most sacred. A city council will grant a license to a saloon or house of ill-fame one day, the next Sunday all the individuals who compose the council will attend a revival meeting and pray for the conversion of mankind. If a foreigner, who knew nothing about the life in America, should attend a political mass-meeting, or a large religious revival gathering, he would certainly come to the conclusion that the whole nation was either drunk or insane, or perhaps both.

The Scandinavian, on the other hand, is less excitable, enterprising, and ambitious, but more solid, reserved, and conservative. He does not live by jerks, but progresses slowly and surely. He is more moderate in his virtues as well as in his vices. He will attend church once or twice Sunday, and perhaps devote part of the day in visiting a friend or taking a walk. The latter practice is considered to be a great sin among the Puritans. The Scandinavian-American seldom meets the Yankee except in business relations, or at a political convention, although he may occasionally attend a woman's suffrage meeting or an American church sociable, and make a short, formal call at the Yankee's house to be introduced to the family.

The superior social aptness, the great religious and social activity of the American woman leads the Northman to conclude —as a Norwegian wit expressed it—that all she does is to dress herself, attend church, and take care of her nerves. The United States statistics show that the Scandinavians are less apt to marry American ladies than any other foreigners, although they more frequently inter-marry with other nationalities than any other immigrants.

The Scandinavians seldom see the admirable home life for which the Americans are justly noted. They judge the latter as he appears in business life, and conclude that the Yankee is simply a financial and political boomer who is too shrewd and unscrupulous to be depended upon. Their conclusion in regard to business is, on the whole, correct, but in regard to society it is utterly wrong. For no nation is more sympathetic, humanitarian, devoted to kindness, and liberal towards charitable objects than the Americans. Secondly, the conservatism and slowness of the Northmen is often mistaken for clannishness. They settle in large bodies, not with the intention of being exclusive, but because it is convenient, and often their only choice; here they attend to their own affairs without thinking anything about Americanization. Struggle for existence, in many cases, requires all their strength.

But the American nation has nothing to fear in regard to the foreignism of Scandinavians. They very rapidly adopt the virtues as well as the vices of their adopted country. It is, perhaps, better that a people is a little slow in becoming Americanized, than to hasten too much. A person who takes out his naturalization papers on the day he arrives at Castle Garden, either does not know his obligations to the new country, or doesn't care to perform any duties to any land; in either case he is not likly to be a desirable citizen. All the Scandinavian immigrants use American furniture and machinery, their style of dress and mode of living are essentially American—all of which has a powerful influence in

Americanizing them. It is true that there are Northmen who have lived in this country thirty years, yet are unable to speak fifteen English words correctly; but this class of people are an exception, not the rule.

Of course their manners, customs, and language are often a strange combination of Scandinavian-Americanism and would make an excellent theme for a novelist. They sometimes talk about, "spika English," "travla på stimbåten," "maka monni," "mova avej," "go to mitingen," "been chitad," "got a yobb," and, "sinjä Yankee Doodle." But most of them agree with H. Stockenstrom:

> "Men jag mest prisar den nya Svenska,
> Som är så olik den fosterlänska."

The bad habit of having a feast of eating and drinking at funerals, which is customary in the Scandinavian countries, is sometimes practiced here also. For example, we read about the early Norwegian settlers in Wisconsin how they astonished the minister at a funeral by presenting to him a glass of whisky between the singing of the first and second stanza, saying: "It is customary in our country to take a glass between the singing of each stanza." And with the hymn book in one hand, a glass of whisky in the other, and the corpse before them, the mourners shed tears over their departed friend. Half-way between the house and the cemetery they repeated the act. This, however, is an extreme case. It is seldom carried to such excess in the North, and far less—if practiced at all,—among the Scandinavian-Americans. For, on the whole, the Northmen in this country adopt American manners and customs. The more progressive element of the first generation speak English from choice, the second from necessity, and the third knows little about the language of their grandparents. Yet it is to be hoped that the Scandinavian-Americans of today will never become so completely transformed that they lose their character, courage, earnestness, frankness, strong convictions, self-possession, and indomitable will-power.

According to the United States census of 1870, 1880, and 1890 the Scandinavians have the best records of any nationalities in the country, either foreign or native, in regard to crime, vagrancy, pauperism, deaf and dumb, and blind. In addition they take most readily to farming, become quickly Americanized, and possess a better education and have more money at their arrival than any other immigrants. It is no wonder then that nearly every political economist admits that they are the best immigrants which the country receives.

W. W. Thomas, United States minister to Sweden-Norway, wrote in 1891 as follows: "Probably not less than 2,000,000 Swedes and their descendants are now living in our country and call themselves Americans. In fact the day will soon come when the United States will contain more citizens of Swedish descent than Sweden herself; and we will be not only the newer, but the greater Sweden, as we have already become the greater England." Col. Hans Mattson, in his *Minnen*, published in 1890, says: "When we take into consideration the numerous Swedish colonists that settled in Delaware, Pennsylvania, and New Jersey in the seventeenth century, and their descendants, together with the descendants of Scandinavian emigrants of the last seventy years, I think it is safe to estimate the total population of Scandinavian descent at over four millions, or fully one-sixteenth of the entire population of the United States." These estimations, however, appear to be simply assertions and not based upon any kind of statistical figures or computations, and are, perhaps, too high. Yet in 1900 there were in this country about one-fifth as many Danes as in Denmark, one-third as many Swedes as in Sweden, and one-half as many Norwegians as in Norway. In 1890 one person out of every twenty-five in the United States, was a Scandinavian, either by birth or by descent in the second generation. By the most careful computation of statistical figures, it is a conservative estimate to assume that, in 1900, there are in this country three million Scandinavian-born or having Scandinavian parents.

The Icelandic Discoveries of America.

—BY—

S. SIGVALDSON.

The origin and cause of the movement that led to these discoveries seems to have had their birth in Norway in or about the year 872, when King Harold Fairhair, in a naval battle, overcame the jarls, or independent princes, of that country, and subdued them to his vassalage. Such a subjugation could not be tolerated by the haughty and heroic Northmen, and they were forced to seek relief in other countries more congenial to their free and independent natures. In support of this the histories tell us that a general movement took place; the jarls and Vikings took to their ships, invoked their God of Storms and set sails for distant shores. Some steered to the South and founded homes for themselves in the sunny climate of sourthern Europe. But we are especially concerned with the northern branch of this army, which discovered and settled on the islands in the North Atlantic, especially Iceland.

This noble and historic island is said to have been first discovered in 874 by the heroic Viking Ingolf. It was on this island, especially, that a strong and free republic soon grew up, and to its sturdy sons, we claim, belongs the immortal honor of the discovery of America.

This republic, entirely independent, and consisting of the bravest and boldest of the Northmen, soon developed into a community of wealth and culture; now renowned the world over for its rich literature in old sagas, poetry, and chronicles. It is thus evident that all these combined afford the most reliable authority for the early settlements, achievements, and discoveries of the Northmen. Hence it is mainly from these, as authorities, that we relate the following historical facts, undisputed by the best modern historians.

In 876, about two years after the discovery of the island, we are told by the chronicles, that a certain settler, by the name of Gunnbjorn, was driven on to the coast of Greenland in a storm, that his ship was fettered in ice all through the winter, but as soon as spring came they were able to return to Iceland. A great many years after, about 983, another settler, by the name of Erik the Red, got into a quarrel with his foe, and a homicide was the result. For this Erik was condemned by the court, according to the laws of the land, and to escape punishment, as well as to satisfy his nature for exploration and discovery, he fitted out a vessel, and with a few companions set sail for the land of Gunnbjorn. After a few days sailing he discovered Greenland and explored it along the coast each side of Cape Farewell during the next three years. He finally settled down on a grassy plain near the coast, which he was pleased to call Greenland, and from thence the whole country has derived its name.

After three years, however, he returned to Iceland, but only to induce a greater number of emigrants to embark for Greenland. We are thus told that in re-crossing he had a

fleet of twenty-five ships, but, unfortunately, eleven of them
perished in the high seas of the North, and but fourteen
reached Greenland.   However, the remainder built up a prosperous colony in the country, which lasted for 400 years.

One of the men who came over to Greenland with Erik,
Hjerulf by name, had the distinguished honor of being the
father of the first white man, who saw the main land of
North America.   This man's name was Bjarni.   The event
came about thus: during the summer that Hjerulf went
over to Greenland with Erik, his son Bjarni had been absent
in Norway; and being unconscious of his father's journey,
Bjarni sailed home to Iceland the following autumn to pass
the Christmas with his father.   But on arriving in Iceland he
found that his father had emigrated to Greenland; he therefore immediately set sail to follow his father to that country.

On the way over, a cloudy sky and foggy weather attended his voyage, the crew lost their way, and were for
many days borne before the wind without knowledge of their
course.   At length the weather brightened up somewhat, and
Bjarni sighted land in the distance, but to his disappointment,
he soon discovered that it was a coast without mountains,
covered with woods, instead of the great mountains of ice
that he had been told he would see on the coast of Greenland.   They therefore put the ship about and sailed for two
more days, when they again sighted land, but neither this
answered the description of Greenland.   Again they went to
sea, and having sailed for four days more with the same
wind, the coast of Greenland was seen to loom up in the distance.   Fortunately enough, Bjarni landed on the very
promontory where his father lived.   He then assumed control

of his father's estate, and dwelt with him the remainder of his life.

This accidental finding of land by Bjarni excited little curiosity until it came to the ears of the famous Leif, the son of Erik the Red, who at this time, about 999, came over to Greenland from Norway.   This Leif Erikson, the real discoverer of America, bought the vessel of Bjarni and manned it with a crew of thirty-five men, leaving Greenland in the autumn of the year 1000, and sailing to the South, for the express purpose of discovering the lands previously seen by Bjarni. Good fortune attended. Some distance to the southward, Leif discovered a barren coast, now known to be the northern coast of Newfoundland. Having rested here for some time, the discoverer again put to sea, sailing farther southward, and in the space of a few days came upon another coast, covered with thick woods. Here he landed and inspected the country around, now known by the name of Nova Scotia. But soon he once more set to sea, and, having now sailed for two more days, with a northeast wind, he for the third time sighted land, and pulled ashore "At the estuary of a certain river." Here they found the country pleasant, the river full of fish, and the land abounding in grapes. With this Leif was so pleased that he called the land he had discovered, Vinland. The location of *the third discovery* corresponds the closest to that about Massachusetts Bay.

Pleased as they were with the country, Leif determined to pass the winter here, his men accordingly built up some huts at this place, and in them they dwelt through the winter. In the spring Leif and his men started home for

Greenland with a cargo of timber, and reached the abode of his father, Erik, in safety. This discovery of Leif created much talk in Greenland, and Thorvald, his brother, thinking the land had been "too little explored," begged leave of Leif, and obtained his ships for another voyage, made in 1002. Thorvald succeeded in finding the lands, and the huts that Leif had built. Here it is said they made their winter quarters, supporting themselves on fish through the winter of 1002-3.

In the spring they went on exploring along the coast. But having sailed some distance they fell in with "savages," and in a fight that followed Thorvald was killed. Shortly after that the remainder returned to Greenland.

Again it is said in the sagas, that in the summer of 1006, there came from Iceland a noble and a wealthy man, Thorfinn Karlsefni by name. This man, we are told, fell at once in love with the beautiful woman, Gudrid, the widow of Thorstein Erikson, brother to Leif, and as a natural consequence they were united in marriage, and the event was celebrated by a merry wedding.

This woman Gudrid is said to have persuaded her husband, Karlsefni, to sail for Vinland, and that she succeeded to such a degree that Karlsefni left for Vinland in the spring of 1007, with a sufficient force to found a colony, having three or four ships, with 160 men, some women, and a cargo of cattle on board. America was safely reached. In this very year Gudrid gave birth to a child, and they named him Snorro. He was thus the first white child born in America. By way of remark, it may be noted here that such men as the learned antiquarian, Finn Magnusson, and the renouned sculptor, Thorvaldsen, have taken pride in tracing their ancestry to this first white American boy, Snorro. But to continue: this company of Karlsefni is said to have dwelt in the country for the three following years, but then to have returned again to Greenland. Karlsefni had to give up his enterprise on account of the hostility of the natives. Many of their crew had lost their lives, when the remainder returned home, 1010, with a cargo of timber, skins, and furs. The latter two of which they had obtained from the natives.

Yet another party sailed for Vinland, 1011, but with even less success. A quarrel arose among their number, which ended in cruelty and bloodshed within their own flock. After their return to Greenland, 1012, ends the account of all the important attempts to explore and colonize Vinland, or America, as far as the Northmen are concerned.

As previously stated, this gives the outline of discoveries and voyages made by the Northmen in the tenth and eleventh centuries, as related by the sagas and annals of Iceland. And in saying this, as much is said, as if these great historical events were backed by the strongest authority.

Any one that is thoroughly acquainted with the spirit of the old sagas, their simple and unambitious style, together with their minute detail and accuracy of statement, cannot for a moment hesitate to accept their narrative as undisputable history. This in fact, is the conclusion that the learned world has arrived at.

Besides this verifying power of the spirit and accuracy of the sagas themselves, innumerable coincidental facts, and important finds in Greenland and even in America, absolutely prove that the Northmen were the first and last true discoverers of America. This seems a very strong statement to make without giving sufficient arguments to prove the assertion. But it is here taken for granted that a detailed account of all the coincidental proofs now revealed by the best authorities on this subject, is unnecessary, and could not come within the scope of this little essay. Let it rather be sufficient to say that these discoveries of the Northmen were known to some of the learned Europeans up to 1350, at least. A passage here quoted from the *Antiquitates Americanae*, clearly proves that the native Indians, also, possessed some traditions about the Northmen in America. This is the passage: "There was a tradition current with the oldest Indians (in these parts) that there came a wooden house and men of another country in it, swimming up the river Assoonet, as this (Tonton river) was then called, who fought the Indians with mighty success, etc."

Besides all this, an appeal to common sense ought to tell us that the Vikings, the boldest navigators of ancient times, men who visited or plundered every nook and corner of Europe, so to speak, could not help but to discover America, after once having discovered Greenland.

To support that the history of these discoveries was known through Europe, we have the account of the French author, Gabriel Gravier, (together with many others,) in his work, *Découverte de l'Amérique par les Normands*, that Gudrid, wife of Karlsefni, made a journey to Rome, where she was well received, and that she here certainly told about her voyage in America, and it is also here said that the facts thus

revealed by Gudrid, although kept as a profound secret by
the papal authorities, had without a doubt a great influence
on subsequent discoveries.

We have thus shown that the discoveries in America by
Leif Erikson are proven by accurate records in Iceland, that
the history of these discoveries was known through Europe,
and especially in Rome, that this history of the Northmen is
verified by subsequent coincidental discoveries, and the remains of ruins and relics, and finally, that the old traditions
of the Indians in America must necessarily remove every
shadow of a doubt.

What then can be the value of the so-called discovery of
Columbus? Columbus himself professes to have gone to,
and beyond Iceland, whether he got any information there
in regard to America is not certain, but a great sailor and
a rover that he was, together with his genius for geography
and ambition for discovery, make it very probable, and
indeed almost certain, that he did obtain the necessary information for his great subsequent voyage. If not, what did
he go to Iceland for? Two facts are certain, and that is, that
he would naturally endeavor to obtain any information connected with his conceived enterprise, and since there was
nothing to hinder him from getting this information, either
from the people in Iceland or their sagas, what are we to in-
fer but that he did? Secondly, if he did obtain some knowledge there about America, it is equally certain that a man of
his ability and sagacity, would have sense enough to remain
tacit about it, if for his silence he would be rewarded with
the immortal glory of discovering the better half of the
world. Or how could the man help but to get the necessary

information from his advisors in Rome, who knew all about it? This indeed is so strongly hinted at in one of the accounts of Columbus that nothing but the blindest prejudice can dismiss its significance. The fact of it all is that Leif Erikson is the true discoverer of America, while Columbus was merely the first emigrant to America from Spain.

The First Swedish Settlement in America.

—BY—

EMMA SHERWOOD CHESTER.

[*Published in the Scandinavia in 1884.*]

To the human trait of avarice may be attributed the world's most rapid advance in every department of commerce and its subsequent arts. The alluring sparkle of gold has led men to dare all latitudes and seas, however strange, however obstinately closed, however strewn with dead men's bones; and from the new world of North and South America there has streamed for centuries the light of a beacon such as this. The Northmen, the Spanish, the French, the English, the Dutch—an army of adventurers—have come, have seen, have generally conquered. To their magnificent courage or insatiable greed, the doors of knowledge and of wealth have opened, and the majority of these early colonists have gained their ends,—the acquisition of territory at any risk, the extortion of gold at any cost. But higher motives and more enduring principles were brought to us across the seas when religious intolerance drove the spirit of martyrdom to our shores. The Puritans, the Huguenots, the Swedish fugitives from the Protestant-Catholic wars colonized those states in

(87)

which slavery with its attendant evils found its most inse-
cure footing; and on the banks of the Delaware, the only
humane policy ever devised for dealing with the Indian race,
was instituted by the pious Swedes. "Slaves," said Gustaf
Adolf, "cost a great deal, labor with reluctance, and soon
perish from hard usage; but the Swedish nation is industrious and intelligent, and hereby we shall gain more by a
free people with wives and children." This would appear to
be a stroke of economy rather than a principle of morality,
but in the instructions of the Swedish government to Governor Printz, with regard to the Indians, the genuine piety of
the Swedish administration is exhibited. Article IX reads as
follows: "The wild nations bordering on all sides, the governor shall treat with all humanity and respect, and so that
no violence or wrong be done to them by Her Royal Majesty, or her subjects aforesaid; but he shall rather   *   *   *
exert himself that the same wild people may be gradually
instructed in the truths and worship of the Christian religion, and in other ways brought to civilization and good government, and in this manner properly guided. Especially
shall he seek to gain their confidence, and impress upon their
minds that neither he, the governor, nor his people and sub-
ordinates are come into these parts to do them any wrong or
injury, but much more for the purpose of furnishing them
with such things as they may need for the ordinary wants of
life."

Religious dissensions, the most bitter and cruel of all an-
imosities, had scattered broadcast over Europe, in the seventeenth century, the seeds of fermentation and unrest. So
that when William Usselinx, a native of Antwerp, Brabant,

proposed to Gustaf Adolf in 1624, the despatch of a Swedish
colony to America, it was as if he had provided an outlet for
the bursting national heart. Gustaf seized upon the plan
with enthusiasm. He concentrated upon it all of his talents
as a statesman, and the result was a scheme which for brilliancy and liberality of design has had no parallel in the annals of colonization projects. Usselinx was the founder of
the Dutch West India Company, of which he was also for
several years a director. Becoming dissatisfied for some reason with the management of the company, he severed his
connection with it, and proceeded to Stockholm. He appears
to have been a man of more than ordinary ability, which
was exhibited in the projection more than in the execution of
great enterprises. He was the agitator of more conservative men, and to him is accredited the first conception of a
Swedish colony in America, at a time when Europe was
absorbed in the seriousness of home affairs. The Thirty
Years' War was at its height, and Protestant Danes and
Germans were exposed to the fury of the storm. Gustaf
Adolf was as yet but a looker-on, conscious of the inevitable
part which he must soon assume, and burdened with anxiety
for his unhappy subjects. Usselinx appeared at an oppor-
tune moment. He proposed the founding of a trading company in Sweden, whose operations should extend to Asia,
Africa, and America, the territory included in the project
being, indeed, almost unlimited, He expatiated to the king
upon the advantages certain to accrue from the enterprise,
that carried objections before it. He appealed to his philan-
thropy by depicting the opportunities for spreading the
Christian religion among heathen nations. He asserted in

positive terms the pecuniary gain which would eventually be added to the Swedish crown; and, as a clinching argument in favor of the immediate undertaking of the scheme, he pointed to the suffering condition of the Protestants in the kingdom, and the horrors to which they were exposed. The king foresaw in it a benefit not to be defined by Usselinx's terms. While he recognized in it the direct solution of a problem which had long vexed his mind, he also perceived moral and political blessings as likely to arise from it, which the eye of a great statesman only can descry through centuries. In the warrant for the establishment of such a company, we find these words: "Know ye, that by a petition, the honest and prudent William Usselinx has humbly shown and proved to Us how a general trading company here from our kingdom of Sweden, to Asia, Africa, America, and Magellan could be established," etc.   *   *   *   "Such being the proposition which he made, we have taken it into consideration, and that we cannot disapprove of it, nor do we see, but what it is sure, that if God will give success, it shall tend to the honor of His holy name, to our and the state's welfare, and the advancement and advantage of our subjects. We have, therefore, graciously received, and with pleasure approved of it, and consented that the said company be organized and established," etc. * * * "Given and signed in our royal palace at Stockholm, the 21st of December, 1624.   GUSTAVUS ADOLPHUS."

A commercial company endowed with the privilege of founding foreign colonies, was therefore incorported at Stockholm, May 21, 1627. The charter provided the existence of the company for twelve years from May, 1625 to May, 1637, during which time no capital was to be withdrawn, nor new stockholders admitted. Usselinx was to have for his services, past, present, and future, "one per mille of all goods and merchandise which were bought and sold in the company." It was decided that the contributions of capital should not proceed from any single country, but that all Europe should be invited to share in the enterprise, both with the subscription of means and the despatch of colonists. Prof. Odhner regards this as a move of expediency rather than disinterestedness, as the finances of Sweden were then in a state of depletion. But the character of Gustaf Adolf would surely admit a more generous construction, namely, that he wished *all* suffering people to share in its possible advantages.

The persons who took part in this remarkable company were his majesty's mother, the Queen Dowager Christina, the Prince John Cassimir, the Royal Council, and the most distinguished of the nobility, the higest officers of the army, the bishops and other clergymen, together with the burgomasters and aldermen of the cities, as well as a large number of the people generally. For the direction and execution of the plan, there were appointed an admiral, vice-admiral, chapman, under-chapman, assistants, and commissaries, and a body of soldiers fully officered. Such was the plan proposed by the greatest man of his time. But God disposed otherwise. Upon the eve of the fruition of his designs, Gustaf was summoned to his supreme mission as defender of the Protestant faith in Europe. Brilliant triumphs distinguished him in other spheres, but through them all he preserved an undiminished interest in the plan which had been thus temporarily, as he believed, frustrated. At the battle of Lützen he lost his life, bequeathing to his chancellor, Oxenstierna, who was also his beloved friend and coöperator, "the jewel of his crown," *i. e.*, the project which had lain so near his heart.

Oxenstierna exerted himself to the utmost to carry out the intentions of the king, but his efforts were unsuccessful, chiefly on account of an impoverished treasury. The final outgrowth of his exertions was a conception far inferior to that of Gustaf. "I think it to be regretted," said Provost Stillé, upon the occasion of the presentation of a portrait of Queen Christina to the Historical Society of Pennsylvania, "I think it to be regretted that while we possess the portrait of Queen Christina, we have not those of her great father, Gustaf Adolf, and of Oxenstierna. I firmly believe that those two men, in their scheme for colonizing the shores of the Delaware, are entitled to the credit of the first attempt in modern times to govern colonies for a higher purpose than that of enriching the commercial and manufacturing classes of the mother country. No doubt the expectation of extending Swedish commerce was one of the motives which led to the founding of the colony, but it seems always to have been a subordinate one." Some Swedish historians claim that an emigration took place as early as 1627, under Gustaf Adolf; but this is no where substantiated. The Cabots had sighted Delaware as early as 1496, but they had in all probability passed it by. That Hudson saw the Delaware Bay, on August 28, 1609, is confirmed by the log-book of his mate, Juet. And in 1623 the Dutch took possession of the shores of the Delaware. But there is no authority for stating that the Swedes ever visited this locality before 1638. At the age of six Christina succeeded her father, and from that time until she was eighteen, the kingdom was under regency, thus giving to Oxenstierna an opportunity for deliberating upon the best methods for advancing the plans of Gustaf. In May, 1635, he visited Holland on political business, and there saw Samuel Blommaert, Swedish commissary at Amsterdam, and a partner in the Dutch West India Company. Prof. Odner, of the University of Lund, had the good fortune a few years ago to discover, in the Royal Archives of Sweden, a package containing letters from Blommaert to Oxenstierna, concerning the first expedition to Delaware. In these letters Blommaert broaches the subject of a Swedish expedition to the coast of Guinea. About one year later a Dutchman named Spiring visited Oxenstierna in Sweden. He had recommended himself to the chancellor by a certain shrewd business capacity, and was employed in the Swedish service. Upon his return to Holland, after this visit, he wrote to Oxenstierna regarding commercial matters, and the letter is now in the Oxenstierna Collection of the Royal Archives at Stockholm. He had talked with Blommaert of the Guinea scheme, and had heard through him of a man who could give reliable information on the subject. This man was Peter Menewe, destined to become the second governor of the State of Delaware. Menewe was a native of Wesel, in the county of Cleves, Holland. He was a member of the Dutch West India Company, and had served as governor of New Netherlands, in America, from 1626 to 1632. This territory of which the Dutch held stout possession, extended from the Delaware to the Hudson, and in the capacity of governor, Menewe resided at New Amsterdam (now New York City).

As the result of some disagreement, he was dismissed from
his office in 1632, and returned to Holland, where he was
brought to the notice of Blommaert by Peter Spiring. His
prolonged residence in America had no doubt given him a
thorough knowledge of the locality, and he was, of all available persons, the one best qualified to lead the enterprise now
proposed. These three Blommaert, Spiring, and Menewe,
met at the Hague, early in 1637, and held a consultation,
which it was deemed best, should be private, on account of
the possible interference of the Dutch West India Company.
It was found that the Guinea plan would involve too heavy
an expenditure of means, and they therefore turned their
thoughts to North America. Prof. G. B. Keen has translated in full a letter from Menewe to Spiring, then in Sweden,
in which he offers his services to the Swedish government, as
the founder of a colony in "New Sweden," on the banks
of the Delaware.   The letter is extremely interesting, and
Prof. Keen's translation may be found in the *Pennsylvania
Magazine*, No. 4, Vol. VI.   It is dated "Amsterdam, June 15,
1636," and contains an estimate of the expense of such an
expedition as was proposed; "half of which," he says, "I
myself, will guarantee, Mr. Spiring assuming the other half,
either on his own account, or for the crown, the same to be
paid at once in cash."

To this plan the Swedish government gave its cheerful
consent. Half of the money was subscribed by Menewe,
Blommaert, and their friends; half by the three Oxenstiernas,
Clas Fleming (virtual chief of the admiralty), and Spiring.
"The consequences, of this design," said the chancellor, "will
be favorable to all Christendom, to Europe, to the whole

world." He, too, like Gustaf Adolf, possessed the eye of a
seer. On August 9, 1637, the admiralty issued a passport
for two ships, the *Kalmars Nyckel*, and the *Vogel Grip*. The
former was a man-of-war, the latter a sloop. Both were
well supplied with provisions, and merchandise for traffic
with the Indians. Besides Menewe, the only person expressly named as taking part in the expedition are Henrik
Huyghen, probably Menewe's brother-in-law, a Swedish surveyor named Måns Kling, and a religious instructor named
Reorus Torkillus. The remainder of the emigrants, in the
neighborhood of fifty, were largely composed of criminals—
Swedes and Finns. That New Sweden was used as a place of
banishment for miscreants, we have evidence in "A Proceeding of the Fiscal against and sentence of Gysbert Cornelissen
Beyerlandt," in these words:

"Thursday being the 3d February, 1639, Ulrich Leo-
poldt, fiscal plaintiff, against Gysbert Cornelissen Beyerlandt. Plaintiff demands that defendant be sent to
Fatherland and condemned, as quarrelsome persons usually
are, who wound soldiers in the fort, as defendant has lately
done in Fort Amsterdam.

"The fiscal's demand on and against Gysbert Cornelissen Beyerlandt having been seen, and everything being
maturely considered, he is condemned to work with the
company's blacks until the first sloop shall sail for the South
River, where he is to serve the company and pay the wounded
soldier fl. 15, the surgeon fl. 10 for his fee, and the fiscal a fine
of fl. 10."

Various causes conspired to hinder the embarkation of
the little company until late in the autumn, when bad weather

at sea still further opposed them, so that the voyage was not continued until near the close of 1637. Little is known of the details of this voyage. That it was very circuitous is implied from the course taken by Governor Printz several years later. Printz sailed south past the Portugese and Barbary coast, until he found the "Eastern passage" when he veered directly across toward America, landing at Antigua, where he spent Christmas. He then proceeded on his voyage past Virginia and Maryland, to Cape Henlopen, and landed at Fort Christina about six months from the time of leaving Stockholm. As Printz stopped at Antigua, it is probable that Menewe, who is supposed to have come directly here, was not so long in making the voyage.

In 1630 the Dutch had taken possession of the banks of the Delaware, and early in the spring of 1631 planted a colony of more than thirty persons, just within Cape Henlopen, on Lewes creek. Here they built a little fort, and erected the arms of Holland. They named the country Swaanendale, and the water Godny's Bay. The care of the little settlement was entrusted to Gillis Hosset, first governor of Delaware. But Hosset soon fell into altercations with the Indians, who revenged the murder of one of their chiefs in the established Indian fashion, destroying the fort and all its occupants. From which period the Dutch abandoned this particular locality of Delaware. Menewe landed at Cape Henlopen, and purchased of the Indians the same land which the Dutch, almost the same day, eight years before, had bought. He named the cape Paradise Point. The grant of land included all of that territory on the west side of the river from Cape Henlopen to the Falls of Santickan, and extending several days journey inland,—according to some authorities, "to the great falls of the river Susquehanna, near the mouth of Conewaga creek." The land was surveyed by Måns Kling, and stakes were driven into the ground as landmarks. The deed was written in Dutch, as the Swedes were not yet familiar with the Indian language. It was subscribed to by five Indian chiefs, and sent to Sweden for preservation. Unfortunately the deed was destroyed by the fire of the royal palace in 1697. The Dutch at Fort Nassau protested against the invasion of the Swedes, and Governor Kieft, of New Amsterdam, formally objected, saying: "The whole South River of New Netherlands has been many years in our possession, and secured above and below by forts, and sealed with our blood. *Which even happened during your administration of New Netherlands and is well known to you*, etc. Thus done (Thursday being the 6th of May, Anno 1638." The South River trade was very important. Two vessels, leaving there in 1644, are said to have had a cargo of twenty-one hundred and twenty packages of beavers, and thirty-six thousand four hundred and sixty-seven packages of tobacco. There was, therefore, considering the circumstances, reasonable ground for dispute in the matter. Menewe, however, seems to have disregarded the protest of Kieft, and to have made no allusion to it in his letters home, for he says in a letter to Blommaert that he "traveled some miles into the country to discover whether there were any Christian people there, and made signals by firing cannon, but received no response to indicate their presence." He continued his course up the river to a place called by the Indians Hopockahacking, but named by the Swedes

Christina, after their queen, who was then eleven years old.
At this point, on Minquas (Christina) Kil, Menewe appears
to have determined to remain, from the first; although Vander Donk states that he (Menewe) represented to Vander
Nederhorst, the agent of the Dutch West India Company in
the South River country, that he was on his way to the West
Indies, and had stopped to take in wood and water, after
which he should continue his voyage. But upon the return of
the Dutch, somewhat later, they found the Swedes cultivating a little garden, the seeds of which had already sprung up.
Upon their third visit they perceived Menewe's intentions to
be unmistakable, for he had commenced the erection of a
fort. In vain Governor Kieft protested, and at last suc-
cumbed. Various reasons are given for this submission, which
on the face of it is unaccountable, considering the superior
numbers of the Dutch. One writer states that the charter of
the Dutch West India Company forbade declaring war with
a foreign state or the native Indians, without the consent of
the states general of the United Netherlands. Another reason given for Kieft's uncharacteristic mildness on this occasion is the Protestant amity which existed between the
Dutch and Swedes, and which found a bond of union in that
period of disintegration.

The *Kalmars Nyckel* cast anchor at a natural wharf of
rocks (foot of Sixth street, Wilmington), and upon these
rocks a fort was built, whose southern rampart extended
within a few feet of the creek. Directly under its walls, on
one side of the creek, was a basin called the harbor, where
vessels might lie out of the current, the creek at this point being navigable for large craft. Owing to alluvial deposits,

this basin is now filled up, although the original outline as drawn by Lindström, surveyor to the Printz's expedition, is still perceptible, and accords with Lindström's plan. The fort was built on an elevation, accessible, as has been said, to large vessels on one side, but otherwise surrounded by bogs and sand-banks. The site is now occupied by the extensive workshops of Wilmington. The fort served for the residence of the garrison, and there was also a structure for the storing of provisions and merchandise. Both were of logs. Subsequent investigations have brought to light an iron bridle from which a portion of the head-stall is broken, and an irregular fragment of a common tin plate. Both of these articles are now in the possession of the Historical Society of Delaware.

Here the Swedes seem to have prospered, for there exists a letter from Governor Kieft, dated July 31, 1638, in which he accuses Menewe of monopolizing the fur trade of the Delaware by underselling the Dutch and conciliating the Indians; and, indeed, the Swedes are said to have exported thirty thousand skins during the first year of their residence in New Sweden. Upon the completion of the fort, and about three months after entering the Delaware, Menewe prepared to return to Sweden. Kieft's letter mentioned above, also speaks of Menewe's leaving, which would imply that he went sometime in that month (July, 1638). He had taken all precautions for the welfare of the colony in his absence, and left twenty-three men under command of Måns Kling, and Henrik Huyghan. To Kling was consigned the duties of a military commander, and to Huyghen the care of civil matters. They were directed to defend the fort, and continue the traffic

with the Indians. The *Vogel Grip* was sent to the West
Indies in advance to exchange a cargo brought from Gothenburg, and Menewe followed in the *Kalmars Nyckel*. He arrived at the island of St. Christopher in safety, where he
exchanged his cargo, and, possibly, met his death. Concerning his fate there is much conflicting evidence. Nearly all
writers agree in declaring that he returned to Fort Christina,
where, after serving the colony for three years, he died, and
was buried. But Prof. Odner has recently announced that
this is incorrect, for which statement he presents what he
believes to be indisputable evidence. In a letter to Blommaert, dated June 8, 1639, Clas Fleming speaks of the
necessity of providing a successor to Menewe at Fort
Christina; and for his theory that Menewe was lost at sea,
Prof. Odner refers to Blommaert's letters to the chancellor,
dated November, 13, 1638, and January 28, 1640. The
inferences are as follows: While exchanging his cargo at St.
Christopher, Menewe was invited to board a Dutch vessel
called *The Flying Deer*, and while thus entertained one of the
terrific hurricanes known to that country arose, dismantling
and foundering many ships. As neither *The Flying Deer* nor
any of her crew was ever seen again, it would seem that
Menewe perished in this manner. The *Kalmars Nyckel*
escaped, and took every means for the recovery of her commander, but he was seen no more, and the vessel pursued her
way to Sweden. Encountering rough winds which disabled
her, she retired to a Dutch port, to await repairs and further
orders. The sloop *Vogel Grip* returned to Fort Christina,
took in a cargo of furs, and procceeded to Sweden, where
she arrived at the close of May, 1639, making the voyage

from Christina to Stockholm in five weeks. The little colony, then left to itself, became discouraged, and was about to abandon the settlement, when Peter Hollendare was appointed the successor of Menewe, and Clas Fleming assumed the direction of the work in Sweden.

In 1639, the ship *Kalmars Nyckel*, which had suffered damages at sea, was repaired and equipped in Holland, with the view of despatching a second Swedish colony to America. Cornelis Van Vliet, a Dutch captain, who had been for some time in the Swedish service, was selected as a man well qualified to take command of the vessel; but upon his appointment, there arose an unexpected difficulty in obtaining emigrants. This was supposed to be due to the fact that the long and, at that time, dangerous voyage, antecedent to settlement in a country inhabited by savages, presented inadequate attractions. But there seems to have existed, from the first, a personal prejudice against Van Vliet, which, as was eventually proved, was not without grounds. No one volunteered to accompany him, and it was at last found necessary to make a draught upon such married soldiers as had evaded service, and others, guilty of evil offences, together with their wives and children. Thus provided with emigrants, the perplexity of raising funds presented itself, the country having been drained of its resources by wars. But at this juncture, Blommaert and Spiring, with their customary zeal, came forward, and advanced the requisite means. The *Kalmars Nyckel* was accordingly equipped, and provided with another crew, concerning whom little is known. The governor appointed to accompany the expedition, as successor to Menewe, was Peter Hollendare, who signs himself

Ridder (knight). Having thus far vanquished her obstacles, the *Kalmars Nyckel* left Gothenburg in the autumn of 1639, destined, however, to meet with still further discouragements. Upon entering the North Sea, she sprang a leak, and was obliged to put into Medemblik for repairs; again she started, only to encounter fresh disasters, until the growing dissatisfaction with both crew and vessel was vehemently oppressed. Van Vliet was accused of dishonesty in victualling the ship, and was convicted of the charge, upon the examination which was immediately ordered by Blummaert. Mr. Spiring thereupon commanded Van Vliet's discharge, and appointed Pouwel Jansen (probably Dutch) in his place, a new crew also having been hired. But continued misfortunes beset them at sea, and it was not until February 7, 1640, that the *Kalmars Nyckel* made the successful effort to sail from Texel. At this point, the name of Blommaert, so distinguished in the records of the earliest exposition, disappears from the current chronicles; and it is supposed that he either died, or retired from the Swedish service, the former supposition being the more credible.

Hollendare's colony landed at Christina, April 17, 1640, a little more than two months after leaving the Texel. They found the settlement left by Menewe in good condition (Kieft's letters being the only authority to the contrary),but, for want of an executive head, and having heard nothing from home, they appear to have entertained doubts, at this period, as to the expediency of trying to maintain their national independence. It is probably that they would have allied themselves to the interests of the Dutch, had it not been for the Hollendare's arrival. Professor Odhner who has prosecuted the search with much zest, declares that he has been unable to discover any record as to the way in which Menewe's colony occupied their time after his departure, with the exception of a partially destroyed *Schuldt Boeck*, kept by Henrik Huyghen, from the year 1838, the contents of which are meagre and afford little information. Concerning the people whom Hollendare found upon his arrival, and he himself took with him, he says in a letter to the chancellor: "No more stupid or indifferent people are to be found in all Sweden than those which are now here." He appears to have encountered the opposition of Måns Kling, whose rough experience had taught him the impracticability of certain theories advanced by Hollendare for dealing with the Dutch, and who may have found subordination to a novice in these matters hard to brook. Hollendare purchased land of the Indians for a distance of eight or nine Swedish miles above Fort Christina, erecting three pillars for a boundary. (These continually renewed purchases of land from the Indians remind one of an American child-expression, "Indian-giver," meaning one who presents a gift and then takes it back). Incipient protests were made, from time to time, by the Dutch, but none of serious consequence. About this time the Swedes also purchased of the Indians a considerable tract of land on the east side of the river, having already bought, as has been stated, the territory on the west side. According to Hazard's Annals, a general sickliness prevailed among both Swedes and Dutch, during Hollendare's administration, and it was deemed expedient to take measures at once for the strengthening of the colony.

In May, 1640, therefore, Måns Kling was sent to Swe

den in the *Kalmars Nyckel*, for the purpose of laying before
the government the necessities of the settlement; and in May,
1641, Kling left Stockholm in the *Charitas*, a vessel which
had been prepared at the above place, at a cost of about
thirty-five thousand florins. He took with him a company
of mining-people and "roaming Finns," the later being a race
inhabiting the Swedish forests. They numbered thirty-two
persons, four of whom were criminals, the remainder going
either as servants to the company, or to better their condition. Måns Kling was accompanied by his wife, a maid, and
a little child. He was appointed to serve as lieutenant on the
pay of forty *rix-daler* a month, beginning May 1, 1641, and
was also granted by Clas Fleming, as a present, fifty *rix-
daler* expectancy money. Sailing from Stockholm, Kling repaired to Gothenburg, where he was joined by the *Kalmars
Nyckel*, and (probably) other emigrants. The two vessels
left Sweden, in 1641, constituting the third expedition to the
Delaware. Soon after their arrival at Christina, a new company, under the name of the West India or America company, was formed, and it was decided that the crown should
pay the salaries of a governor and such other officers as might
be needed for the advancement of the colony. Hollendare's
last letter to the chancellor was dated December 3, 1640, and
little more than the writer has stated is known of his administration.

The fourth expedition, under Governor Printz, proved to
be the largest, and in point of numbers, the most important
of the expeditions sent to Delaware. The chief personages
who took part in it were the governor, his wife, and daughter
Armgott, the Rev. Johan Campanius (Holm), and Måns Kling,

who had returned to Sweden, in 1641. Johan Printz, lieutenant-colonel in the Swedish army, was appointed Governor
of Delaware, August 15, 1642. He was granted four hundred *rix-Daler* for traveling expenses, and two hundred dollars silver for his annual salary, to commence January 1,
1643. His "Instructions" were dated at Stockholm, August
15, 1642; and on the 30th of the same month, "a budget
for the government of New Sweden" was adopted. Herein
are mentioned a lieutenant, a surgeon, a corporal, a gunner, a
trumpeter, besides twenty-four private soldiers; also, in the
civil list, a preacher (Campanius), a clerk (Knut Persson), a
provost (Johan Olafsson), and a hangman, the whole estimate
of salaries amounting to three thousand and twenty *rix-daler*.
The Company's "servants," and those who went to improve
their condition, were called freemen; while the malefactors
were retained in slavery, and occupied ground appropriated
for them, there being no intercourse between the two classes.
According to Campanius, it had proved greatly to the detri-
ment of the colony for criminals to be permitted to share in
its advantages, and the embarkation, for this purpose of any
person of bad repute was forbidden in Sweden. Such as had
already come out were required to return, many of whom
died at sea. The official "Instructions" instructed Printz to
go to Gothenburg by land, as being more expeditious.
Whether he did so, or whether he went in the ship *Fama*,
which sailed from Stockholm and was joined at Gothenburg
by *Svanen* and (acording to Acrelius) the *Charitas*, is un-
certain. He was instructed to be governed by the skippers
and officers of the ships, as to the course he should take;
whether "to the north of Scotland, or through the channel

between France and England." According to Acrelius, and other authorities, he sailed south. The expedition left Gothenburg, November 1, 1642, and arrived at Christina, February 15, 1643. The first official report sent by Printz from New Sweden is lost, but in a private letter to the chancellor, dated April 14, 1643, he says: "It is a remarkably fine land, with all excellent qualities a man can possibly desire on earth." Yet, during this first year, there was great mortality among the Swedes, which Printz, in his report for 1647, attributes to hard work and insufficient food; for upon receiving board and wages they did well enough. In this year, on the 7th of September, Reorus Torkillus, the clergyman who accompanied Menewe, died at Christina. In this year also, came Johan Papegäja, with a letter to the governor, recommending his "employment, protection, and advancement." He afterwards married the governor's daughter Armgott, a haughty lady, who exercised a tyrannous disposition over the Swedes. On the 6th of November, 1643, Queen Christina granted Tinicum Island to Printz, and here he established his residence. His mansion, which he named "Printz Hall," is said to have been "very handsome." Adjacent to it were an orchard and pleasure house; and here also, Fort Gothenburg was erected, the whole island being frequently spoken of as New Gothenburg.

While the governor's arbitrary temper rendered him, in time, odius to the people, his executive ability must command the highest praise. Neither Menewe nor Hollendare had done more than to break the roughest ground of the enterprise, and it remained for their successor systematically to establish means for the permanent protection of the new set-

tlement, Fort Christina having been repaired, and Fort
Gothenburg completed. Of the forts projected and finished
by Printz, the following are the chief:

(1) Elfsborg. This was on the eastern side of the river,
about two miles below Christina. It was usually garrisoned
by twelve men commanded by a lieutenant, and had eight
iron and brass guns. At this point of vantage, Printz is said
to have exercised great authority over the Dutch, whose
movements were thus worried and frustrated by him. The
statement of most historians that he weighed at this time,
upwards of four hundred pounds, is regarded by Hazard as
a mistake, and probably refers to a relative of the govern-
or's. Certainly, were it Printz himself, the active duties of a
soldier must have soon reduced the formidable bulk. Although Elfsborg was considered a very valuable site, it
became uninhabitable on account of the mosquitoes which
infest New Jersey, and was soon abandoned.

(2) Manajunk. This was a "handsome" little fort on
the Schuylkill. It was made of logs, filled up with sand and
stones, and surrounded by palisades cut very sharp at the
top. It was mounted with great guns.

(3) Korsholm. This fort was at Passajunk, in the neighborhood of Chinsessing, and was commanded by Swen
Schute. On the other side of it was a substantial house
called Wasa, built of hickory, and two stories high. It was
defended by freemen, although not strictly a fort. About a
quarter of a mile further up, on the "Minquas Road," Printz
built a similar strong house, and also the first mill in Delaware, calling the place Möndal. Private residences and plan-
tations rapidly sprang up, centering chiefly upon Tinicum

Island. The place of Olaf Stillé, a Swede who was much
beloved by the Indians, is indicated on Lindström's map, and
was probably on the Schuylkill, southwest of Philadelphia.
From him is descended Provost Stillé, of the University of
Pennsylvania, the name being one of the very few which remain uncorrupted. Thus the colony was strengthened and
enabled to control the Indian trade of the Schuylkill. That
Printz was not always scrupulous in his methods of gaining
an end, is certain, but that he endeavored to serve his country in the best way compatible with his vindictive and
ambitious temperament must be conceded. This much may
at least be said of him. He was the first real pioneer which
the State of Delaware had seen, and upon his retiring from
the service the prosperity of the colony steadily declined.

The Indian policy pursued by the Swedes, in accordance
with the instructions given to Printz, cannot be over-
estimated. The important paragraph contained in Article 9
has already been quoted. Article 5 reads: "The governor,
God willing, have arrived in New Sweden, he must, for his
better information, bear in mind that the boundaries of
which our subjects have taken possession, *in virtue of the
articles of contract entered into with the wild inhabitants of
the country, as the rightful lords*, extend," etc., etc. That
this policy, steadily pursued by the Swedes, and afterwards
imitated by Penn, was ever abandoned by the American
nation, remains a lasting shame. In the financial burden
and moral obloquy attaching to our Indian Bureau, we have
the legitimate fruits of the course we have pursued.

In the year 1644, the ship *Fama* returned to Sweden with
a cargo, which we give in Printz's own words: "One

thousand three hundred whole beavers, 299 half beavers, 537 third parts of beavers; great and small together, 2,139 beavers; again, tobacco, 20.467 pounds (Swedish), in 77 hogsheads; again, my own tobacco—which partly I received from foreigners and partly I planted myself— 7,200 pounds, in 28 hogsheads, sent home to the shareholders in Sweden, that they may either reimburse me at 8 *styfver* per pound, or graciously allow me to sell it elsewhere." On the 25th of November, 1645, a great calamity befell the colony; which may best be described in the governor's words: "Between 10 and 11 o'clock, one Swen Wass, a gunner, set Fort New Gothenburg on fire; in a short time all was lamentably burnt down, and not the least thing saved except the dairy. The people escaped, naked and destitute. The winter immediately set in bitterly cold" (as cold, he says elsewhere, as he had ever experienced in northern Sweden). "The rivers and all the creeks froze up, and nobody was able to get near us (because New Gothenburg is surrounded by water). The sharpness of the winter lasted until the middle of March; so that if some rye and corn had not been unthrashed, I myself, and all the people with me would have starved to death. But God maintained us with that small quantity of provisions until the new harvest. By this sad accident the loss of the company is 4,000 *riks-daler*." His personal loss was estimated at 5,584 *riks-daler*. Whether his own house was destroyed I am unable to discover. According to his own account it would be inferred that it was, while Ferris states that it remained standing for more than one hundred and twenty years, "when it was accidentally destroyed by fire." What might have been the motive of Swen Wass for committing such a deed can only be surmised. He was sent home in irons and remanded to the Swedish government for justice. The buildings were reconstructed as soon as possible.

On the 1st of October, 1646, the Swedish ship *Haij* (sometimes called *The Golden Shark*) arrived, bringing the first news that had been received from home in two years and four months. She was sent back in the following February with a cargo of "24,177 pounds of tobacco, the whole in 101 casks, of which 6,920 pounds were planted in New Sweden, 17,257 pounds were purchased." The governor and other officers of the colony had received instructions to draw their salaries from the duties on tobacco, but as the revenues from this product had not been large, it was found necessary for them to obtain their subsistence from other sources. It was probably with regard to this period that Stuyvesant wrote to the commissary at the Delaware River: "The Swedish governor receives no succor, nor has he to expect any for the present, as I have been informed, trustworthily." During the year 1646, violent altercations with the Dutch occurred, and, according to Acrelius, the arms of Holland, which had been erected at Santickan, were torn down by the Swedes. In this year also, a wooden church decorated in Swedish fashion, and situated on Tinicum Island, was consecrated September 4, by the Rev. Johan Campanius.

Concerning the year 1647, we obtain an inferential account from Printz's Report, dated February 20th of that year, and sent to the chancellor with Johan Papegäja. The entire number of souls in the colony at that time was one hundred and eighty-three. The quarrels between the Dutch and the Swedes had continued, and Printz writes with exasperation: "It is of the utmost necessity for us to drive the Dutch from the river, for they oppose us on every side. (1.) They destroy our trade everywhere. (2.) They strengthen the savages with guns, shot, and powder, publicly trading with these, against the edict of all Christians. (3.) They stir up the savages against us, who, but for our prudence, would already have gone too far. (4.) They begin to buy land from the savages, within our boundaries, which we had purchased eight years ago, and have the impudence in several places to erect the arms of the West India Company, calling them their arms; moreover, they give New Sweden the name of New Netherland, and dare to build their houses there." Hudde declares that when he sought to present the earlier claims of the Dutch, the governor replied that "the devil was the oldest possessor of hell, but that he sometimes admitted a younger one." As to the English, the Report says: "I have at last been able, with the authority of Her Majesty, to drive them from hence." In the same Report he announces that the trade has declined, and that some of the most useful members of the colony have intimated their wish to return home; among others, Henrik Huyghen, whose services were very valuable, and the clergyman, Campanius. He himself begs to be released from his post, and to return to Sweden, in the next ship. The chancellor's reply is to the effect that Printz could not yet be spared, and that it would be advisable to raise the salary of Campanius, as an inducement for him to remain. In this year, the *Svanen* arrived with goods from home, although the chancellor had been unable to fulfill all of the governor's requests thus soon.

The reply of the chancellor was brought back by Lieutenant Johan Papegája.

The year of 1649 recorded the murder of two Swedes by
the Indians, the first occurrence of the kind that had been
chronicled. As a rule the relations of the savages with the
Swedes were of the most friendly nature, although Printz
complained at times that when the latter no longer had
what the Indians wanted, they were liable to trouble with
them, there being, apparently, no other mode of expressing
amity. Campanius gives a quaint account of an Indian
council called to discuss the advisability of destroying the
Swedes, who no longer had "cloth, blue, red, or brown;" nor
"kettles, brass, lead, guns, nor powder." The verdict, however, was, that "We, native Indians, will love the Swedes,
and the Swedes shall be our good friends. * * * We shall
not make war upon them and destroy them. This is fixed
and certain. Take care to observe it." The same writer
accords to Printz "a complete suit of clothes, with coat,
breeches, and belt, made by these barbarians, with their
wampum, curiously wrought with the figures of all kinds of
animals"—the extravagant cost being "some thousand pieces
of gold." For the next two or three years, the struggle between Swedes and Dutch for supremacy, was a pretty even
matter, the declining strength of the Swedes being supplied
by re-enforced aggressiveness, while the Dutch remained superior in numbers.

In 1651 the Dutch built Fort Cassimer (now New Castle, Delaware), against which Printz protested withont
effect. The name of the fort was a singular selection, inas·
much as it is Swedish rather than Dutch. The governor's

desire to return to Sweden had been steadily increasing, and he renewed his appeal to be recalled. The colony was degenerating, less because of the relaxation of Printz's efforts than of the insufficient response from home. Clas Fleming died in 1644, and his successor had not been appointed. Queen Christina, contemplating the abdication of her throne, and inheriting none of her father's love for the enterprise, manifested little interest in the welfare of the colony. In Stuyvesant, Printz had found his match for love of power and unyielding determination. Under his administration, the strength of the Dutch was augmented, and, impatient at the delay of the government in recalling him from a situation which was becoming highly preplexing, Printz sailed for home before the arrival of his order to return, which was dated December 12, 1653. He left his administration in the hands of his son-in-law, Lieutenant Papegája, who, from prolonged residence there, must have been familiar with the requirements of the office. Some of the colonists applied to Stuyvesant for permission to come under the jurisdiction and protection of the West India Company, a request which, for reasons politic, was not granted. Upon his return to Sweden Printz was made a general, and in 1658 he was appointed governor of the district of Jönköping. He died in 1663. Johan Papegája, Vice-Governor of Delaware for a period of eighteen months, was succeeded by Johan Claudius Rising, in 1654.

On the 12th day of December, 1653, the College of Commerce of Sweden nominated Johan Claudius Rising as Commissary and Assistant Councillor to the Governor of New Sweden. Rising was a native of the then Swedish province

8

of Pommerania, and had been court-martialed for some military offense during the Thirty Years' War. He was accompanied on his expedition to New Sweden by Peter Lindström, royal engineer, a clergyman named Peter ——, and various officers, both civil and military. He was allowed 1000 *rix daler* for traveling expenses, and an appropriation of 1,200 dollars silver per annum, together with such emoluments as might be derived from the South Company. He was also to have as much land in New Sweden as could be cultivated by twenty or thirty peasants. Although appointed as assistant-councillor, or lieutenant-governor, Rising at once received precedence from Papegája, who had served as vice-governor since Printz's departure; so that in Rising was vested the office of fifth governor of Delaware. He was directed to strengthen the Swedish possessions on South River, and to subjugate the Dutch by measures of amity, as far as possible. He sailed from Gothenburg early in the year 1654, in the ship *Aren*, Captain Swensko. Acrelius states that so great was the number of emigrants desirous of accompanying this expedition, that hundreds were left behind for want of sufficient passage-room for them.

They arrived in the Delaware, or Southriver, on Trinity Sunday, in the latter part of May, 1654. Sailing up the river as far as the Dutch Fort Cassimir—now New Castle, Delaware—they fired a salute of two guns, in response to which two men came down to learn the character and intentions of their visitors. They returned to their commandant, one Gerrit Bikker, and informed him that it was a Swedish vessel, with a new governor, who demanded the surrender of Fort Cassimir, claiming that the ground upon which it stood was Swedish property. Astonished at this presumption, Bikker took time to digest it, during which Rising informed himself with more certainty as to the condition of the Dutch garrison. Assuring himself that it was feeble he landed with thirty men, who, dispersing themselves over the fort, again demanded its surrender at the point of the sword. Bikker, stupidly bewildered at the unexpectedness of the attack, and commanding but ten or twelve men, yielded his side-arms, and attempted no defence. The gallant Lieutenant Gyllengren took possession of the guns, and, striking down the Dutch flag, raised the Swedish colors in its stead. The fort was named Fort Trinity, in memory of the day of its surrender. Bikker complained bitterly to Stuyvesant of the ruthless and inhuman manner in which he and his men were driven from the fort; while Acrelius, on the other hand, declares that a correct inventory of the property was taken, and that each man was permitted to remove his own at discretion. They were at liberty to leave the place, or to swear allegiance to the Swedish crown. Fearful of the consequences of falling into the hands of the Dutch, after his surrender, Bikker took the oath of allegiance. Concerning this affair, the Dutch records state: "We hardly know which astonished us more, the attempt of the newly arrived Swedish troops to make themselves masters of the Southriver and our fort, or the infamous surrender of the same by our commandant." Of strategic genius Rising made no exhibition on this occasion, but for prompt and audacious *sang froid*, he may be heartily commended. He rebuilt the fort, and a plan of it was drawn by Engineer Lindström, a copy of which was, and may still be, in the possession of Mr. Thomas Westcott,

of Philadelphia, although the original was destroyed in the
fire at Stockholm in 1697. Rising now found it incumbent
to renew the former treaties with the Indians, and a meeting
was therefore appointed for June 17, 1654, at Printz Hall,
on Tinicum Island; when, flattered and pacified with gifts,
the Indians reiterated their promises of friendship and the
council closed with feasting and firing of guns. The energies
of Rising and Lindström were largely directed to investigation and classification of the resources of the country, which
were duly reported to the home government. Rising, who
came to New Sweden without a wife, and subsequently
appealed to the chancellor for such a commodity, took up his
residence in the fort at Christina.

In August, 1654, Oxenstierna, Chancellor of Sweden, died;
and, upon the abdication of Christina, the reins of government fell into the hands of her cousin, Charles Gustaf. In
the meantime, the Dutch, who had never recovered from their
indignation at the seizure of Fort Cassimir, meditated revenge; and it was not long before the instruments of retali-
ation were placed by auspicious circumstances in their hands.
In the latter part of September, 1654, the Swedish ship
Haij, a small and weather-worn vessel of forty to fifty tons
burthen, met with a curious misadventure. She was commanded by Hendrik Van Elswyk, of Lübeck, Factor of the
High Crown of Sweden, and by some error or culpable
intention of the pilot, was guided out of course into the
North River, to a position behind Staten Island. Elswyk
was compelled to send to New Amsterdam for a pilot to re-
lieve them of their difficulty, and thus gave the Dutch information of his presence. The *Haij*, with its cargo, was seized

on suspicion of evil intentions, and while the crew were permitted to remain on the vessel, Elswyk was sent to the Southriver with instructions to Rising to settle the difficulty with the Governor of New Netherland. At a meeting of the Director-General and High Council, at New Amsterdam, on the 20th of October, 1654, a formal offer of the restitution of the ship *Haij*, with its effects, was made to Rising, on the condition that Fort Cassimir should be restored to the Dutch. Assurance was also given that in such an event, friendly and neighborly intercourse would be resumed. A pass was accordingly issued for Rising to visit New Amsterdam, but, tenacious of Fort Cassimir, he refused to make such a settlement. Elswyk addressed the following protest against the seizure of the *Haij*, to the Director-General and Council:

"Noble, Honorable Director-General," etc: "On the 22d of September last I landed, either through the carelessness, or perhaps wanton malice of my pilot, in this river of New Netherland, with the ship *Haij*, intrusted to me by the Royal Swedish General Chamber of Commerce, on behalf of the Honorable South Company. I sent some of my people in a boat here to New Amsterdam, as to good friends and neighbors," [The gloss of amity between the Dutch and Swedes at this time appears to have been very thin, and an illustration of the saying, "A man convinced against his will, is of the same opinion still."], "to engage a pilot, who, for a money consideration, would bring us to the Southriver. Arrived here, my men, both born Swedes, were taken to the guard-house, and I was fetched from the place where I was by the Honorable Vice-Commander with eight musketeers, and placed here in the house of Sergeant Daniel Litschoe, but the ship itself was also brought up from the Raritan Kil, by the Honorable Director-General, our flag hauled down, and the ship continually occupied by soldiers and people. Now, although it is asserted that his noble Honor, Johan Rising, Director of the Government of New Sweden, had taken your Honor's pretended Fort Cassimir, and that, therefore, your Honors have seized this ship with its cargo, such a pretext has no basis or foundation whatever, because the said Fort was erected in 1651 by his noble Honor, your Director-General, rather by overwhelming force than with right and equity, upon the territory of H. R. M. of Sweden, our most gracious Queen; the then Swedish governor protesting against it, so that the aforesaid Honorable Governor, Johan Rising, has not taken it from your noble Honors, but has only repossessed himself of what belongs to Her Royal Majesty of Sweden, herself," etc., etc.

This the Dutch regarded as a mere begging of the question, and they continued to reiterate their grievance in the unlawful and insufferable taking of Fort Cassimir. They relaxed none of their claim to their legitimate possession of it, and openly expressed their suspicion that the ship *Haij* had "lost her way" with no friendly intentions. They now, accordingly, took measures for hostile advances against the Southriver Swedes. The ship *Balance*, armed with thirty-six guns, and commanded by Frederick de Coninck, was instructed to proceed directly from Holland to New Netherland, and there to await further orders. She arrived on the 15th of August. On the 19th a call for volunteers was issued. "If some lovers of the flourishing, well-being, and safety of this newly-opened province of New Netherland are willing and inclined to serve the Director-General and Council, either for love or a reasonable salary and board money, they will please address themselves to his Honor, the noble Director-General himself, or to one of the honorable gentlemen of the Council, and inform them," etc. Signed,

"P. STUYVESANT,

"NICASIUS DE SILLE,

"CORNELIUS VAN TIENHOVEN."

An order to captains of vessels in the harbor was also issued, to furnish men, ammunition, and provisions. Such as refused were impressed. Van Tienhoven and Coninck were ordered to board ships, and request amicably, or, if refused, command from each ship two men, two hundred pounds of codfish, two or three small barrels of groats, one barrel of meat, with one barrel of bacon, and three hundred pounds of bread; also as much powder as they conveniently could spare. The French privateer, *L'Esperance*, was also chartered. Jews were exempted from service, owing to the antipathy of other soldiers to do service in conjunction with them. A tax of sixty-five stivers per month, "until further orders," was, however, imposed upon each Jew over sixteen and under sixty years. "When your Honors shall have carried the expedition to a successful end," says a letter in the Dutch Records, dated May 26, 1665, "the land upon which Fort Christina stands, with a certain amount of garden land for the cultivation of tobacco, shall be left to the people, as they seem to have bought it with the knowledge and consent of the Company, under the condition that the aforesaid Swedes shall consider themselves subjects of this State and Company. This for your information and government."

On the 5th of September the expedition sailed for the Southriver. It consisted of seven vessels and between six and seven hundred men. Upon arriving at Fort Cassimir they at once took measures for seizing the fort. Swen Schute, was the commander in charge, and had been informed of the intentions of the enemy. Rising had instructed him to hold the fort, and above all, not to allow the Dutch to pass without firing upon them. Schute disobeyed the latter injunction, and permitted the Dutch fleet to pass the fort without molestation, the force of his own garrison convincing him that discretion was the better part of valor. Upon being commanded to surrender he begged time to consult with Rising, but this was refused. Meanwhile fifty Dutch sailors had established themselves in the passes between Fort Cassimir and Fort Christina, thus cutting off Swedish communication and hope of relief. At this, Swen Schute claimed the privilege of sending an open letter to Rising, but this also was denied, and accordingly, on Saturday morning, September 16, 1655, Schute boarded the *Balance*, and signed the capitulation. He was severely censured by Rising for allowing the Dutch to pass the fort, without firing, and for subscribing to the capitulation on board a Dutch vessel, instead of in "some indifferent place." The surrender was allowed to be inevitable, owing to the overpowering strength of the Dutch forces. The entire population of Swedes on the Southriver at that time numbered something like four hundred, including women and children, in opposition to whom the Dutch presented six or seven hundred armed men. Swen Schute, together with other Swedes, took the oath of allegiance to the Dutch.

Perceiving that designs were entertained against Fort Christina, Rising sent Elswyk to remonstrate with Stuyvesant, for seeking to obtain possession of the entirely legitimate property of the Swedes. Not to be dissuaded, however, the Dutch besieged Fort Christina, in the rear. The Swedish garrison consisted of but thirty men, with insufficient ammunition and provisions. Hopeless of immediate success, and unable to sustain a prolonged resistance, Rising, therefore, after a gallant defence, surrendered Fort Christina on the following terms :

1. " That all cannon, ammunition, provisions, and supplies, together with other things belonging to the Crown of Sweden, which are in and around Fort Christina, shall belong to and be preserved as the property of the Swedish Crown and the Southern Company, and shall be under the power of said Governor, to take it away or deliver it to Governor Stuyvesant, with the proviso that it shall be given up on order.

2. " Governor John Rising, his superior and inferior officers, his officials and soldiers shall march out of the fort with drums and trumpets playing, flags flying, matches burning, with hand and side-arms, and balls in their mouths. They shall first be conducted to Tinnecuck [Tinicum] Island, to which they shall be taken in safety, and placed in the fort which is there, until the Governor sets sail upon the ship *Waegh*, [*The Balance*] upon which said Governor Rising, his people and property, shall be conducted to Sandy Huck, situated five Holland miles the other side of New York, under safe conduct, within at least fourteen days.   Also the Governor and Factor Elswyk shall in the meantime have allowed

them four or five servants for attending to their business, whilst the others are lodged in the Fortress.

3. "All writings, letters, instructions, and acts belonging to the Crown of Sweden, the Southern Company, or private persons which are found in Fort Christina, shall remain in the Governor's hands to take away at his pleasure, without being searched or examined.

"4. None of the Crown's or Company's officers, soldiers, officials, or private persons shall be retained here against their wishes, but shall be allowed to go without molestation along with the governor, if they so desire.

5. "That all the officers, soldiers, and officials of the Crown and of the Southern Company, and also all private persons shall retain their goods unmolested.

6. "If some officials and Freemen desire to depart, but are not able to go with the Governor and his party, they shall be allowed the time of one year and six weeks in which to sell their land and goods, provided that they do not take the oath of allegiance for the period that they remain.

7. "If any of the Swedes or Finns are not disposed to go away, Governor Rising may take measures to induce them to do so; and if they are so persuaded, they shall not be forcibly detained. Those who choose to remain shall have the liberty of adhering to their own Augsburg confession, as also to support a minister for their instruction.

8. "Governor Rising, Factor Elswyk, and other superior and inferior officers, soldiers, and Freemen, with all their property which they wish to take away, shall be provided by the Governor-General with a sound ship, which shall receive them at Sandy Huck and convey them to Texel,

and thence immediately by a coaster, galliote, or other suitable vessel to Gothenburg, without charge; with the proviso that said coaster, galliote, or other vessel shall not be detained, for which the said Governor Rising shall be answerable.

9. "In case Governor Rising, Factor Elswyk, or any other official belonging to the Swedish Crown, or the South Company, has incurred any debts on account of the Crown or of the Company, they shall not be detained therefor within the jurisdiction of the Governor-General.

10. "Governor Rising has full freedom to make himself acquainted with the conduct of Commander Schute and that of his officers and soldiers in regard to the surrender of Sandhuk Fort [Fort Cassimir].

11. "Governor Rising promises that between the 15th and the 25th of September, he will withdraw his people from Fort Christina, and deliver it up to the Governor-General.

"Done and signed the 15-25th of September, 1655, on the parade between Fort Christina and the Governor-General's camp.   "PETER STUYVESANT,

"JOHN RISING."

SECRET ARTICLE.

"It is further capitulated that the Captain who is to convey Captain John Rising and the Factor Henry Elswyk shall be expressly commanded and ordered to put the aforesaid Governor Rising and the Factor Elswyk on shore, either in England or in France; and that the Director-General shall lend to Governor Rising, either in money or bills of exchange, the sum of three hundred pounds Flemish, which the said Governor Rising engages to repay to the Governor-General, or his order, in Amsterdam, within six months after the receipt. In the meantime he leaves as a pledge and equivalent the property of the Crown and Southern Company now given up. Hereof we give two copies signed by the contracting parties.

"Concluded September 15-25th, on the parade between Fort Christina and Governor-General Stuyvesant's camp.

"PERER STUYVESANT.

"JOHN RISING."

Nineteen Swedes subscribed to the oath of allegiance to the Dutch. Rising did not immediately return to Sweden, and the arms and ammunition of the Crown were not redeemed.

Thus fell, after an independence of seventeen years, the Swedish political power on the Delaware. Had it not been for the rashness of Rising in stirring up the enmity of the Dutch, it might still have survived. Yet the chief cause of its subjugation, doutless, lay in the magnificent maritime resources of Holland, as opposed to the poverty of Sweden in that respect. Help came slowly and insufficiently to the Swedes from home, at this time, while Holland had but to beat the drum in her streets, and the colony of New Netherland was promptly re-enforced.

Not thus ignominiously perished the seeds of moral integrity and thrift planted by the Swedes upon the Delaware river. Scattered broad-cast, they bloom today in countless American homes.

The First Norwegian Immigration,

The Sloop Party of 1825.

—BY—

O. N. NELSON.

Many writers have discussed the origin, cause, and effect of the first Norwegian immigration to the United States in the nineteenth century. It would be difficult, indeed, to find a subject which has been treated so extensively, and at the same time in such an unsatisfactory manner, as that topic. This is not to be wondered at, considering the chaotic condition of the material which had to be relied upon. Hardly any of the very first Norwegian immigrants, say from 1800 to 1840, were educated men; and, of course, they never kept any kind of diaries or written memorandums. "Kleng Peerson looked upon himself as the pathfinder and father of the Norwegian immigration." But the "father" does not seem to have left behind him any productions of his own in regard to his relation with the early Norwegian immigrants; and not a single one of the members of the Sloop family,

125

who sailed from Stavanger in 1825, appears to have published anything with reference to the journey from Norway to America until nearly fifty years later, and then only a brief and unimportant communication in a Norwegian-American newspaper (1).

As far as is known, it was not until 1839, eighteen years after Kleng Peerson's first landing in America, that any account of the Sloop party appeared in print. This was the little book by Ole Rynning, who came to this country a couple of years before its publication. The work was intended to be an emigrant guide rather than a history, and hardly more than two pages are devoted to the Sloop folks. The author asserts, however, that some of the people sent letters to Norway during their first years of residence upon American soil; but none has ever been made public, and, in all probability, not even preserved. From forty-five to seventy years had passed before any serious attempts were made to gather materials with reference to the Sloop party, and all publications dealing with the subject are based upon the assertions of the immigrants themselves or their children (2). The lack of documentary evidence in the case is so obvious that no writer on the topic has been able to reproduce, or even to mention, a single original document in support of his assertions or theories. A few newspaper notices referred to the Norwegians at the time of their arrival in New York

---

(1) R. B. Anderson's "First Chapter of Norwegian Immigration," p. 79.

(2) Prof R. B. Anderson, in his history, "The First Chapter of Norwegian Immigration," claims, on page 93, 'to have talked with eight of the Sloop passengers, and corresponded with two more.' But some of these were infants when they crossed the Atlantic, and consequently their assertions in regard to the journey can only be taken as hearsay evidence. This volume was published in 1895, nearly three-quarters of a century after the people had left their native land.

in 1825, and these notices are contradictory in detail. In 1896 the writer of this article received a letter from Rev. Emil Riis, Lutheran clergyman at Skjold, who had examined *Kirke-bögerne* at that place and at Tysvär, from which places several of the passengers on the sloop hailed. But there is no record in these books of any persons having removed to America during the years of 1820-28. The entire absence of any official account of the movement is remarkable, especially as it was not unlawful to emigrate in those days. Could it be possible that the Quakers objected to comply with the civil law of the land in regard to securing permission to discard their citizenship, which they considered to be a very heavy burden? But, apparently, all the emigrants were not Brethren, or even dissenters from the state church; and their motive for secretly deserting their native land, as they must have done, is even more mysterious than the conduct of the followers of George Fox. A copy of Stavanger's *Toldbog* for 1825 has been secured through the courtesy of N. R. Bull, secretary of the government statistical department in Kristiania, who positively asserts that there is no record in *Toldbögerne* of the sloop Restauration after the year 1825. But the 27th of June of said year the sloop, owned by Johannes Stene and belonging to the Stavanger district, but built in Egersund, was registered to sail for America and elsewhere with a cargo of iron, shipped by three or four different firms. L. O. Helland is reported as being captain, but no mention is made of any passengers. In this connection it should be observed that Helland is not mentioned at all in Prof. Anderson's *First Chapter of Norwegian Immigration*, although all the people who are supposed to have participated in the voyage are enumerated, and it is claimed that Lars Olson was captain, and Lars Larson the principal owner of the sloop.

Under such circumstances it is not strange that the writers on the subject should disagree, at least in detail; for in the absence of authentic records, and during the lapse of a quarter to three-quarters of a century, what a chance for imagination and misrepresentation to supplant the real facts! Perhaps all who have had any experience in gathering historical data on settlements, have found that different individuals, who have all participated in the affairs of the settlement, give conflicting accounts of comparatively recent events. A large number of people are unable to recall incidents of their own lives which happened a few years before. Several of the men consulted by the writer of this article have forgotten when they were married, and some do not know when or where they were born.

In 1807 Denmark and England were at war with each other. During that year some Norwegians, who of course were subjects of the king of Denmark, were captured by the foe. During their confinement on a prison ship near London they received pamphlets containing Barclay's Apology; and at one time, in 1814, Stephen Grellet preached to seven hundred prisoners, most of whom were Danes and Norwegians, and about forty of them appear to have been converted to Quakerism. After peace had been declared in 1814, the prisoners returned to their native land, and the Friends began to advocate the humanitarian doctrines of George Fox among the descendants of the savage Vikings of the North, especially in and around Stavanger and Kristiania.

One of them, Lars Larson, had remained in London one year after his release, employed in the family of the noted Quaker and philanthropist, William Allen. Larson, on his return to his native city, Stavanger, became very active in promulgating the new doctrines ;in the vicinity of his birthplace. During their seven years of harsh imprisonment by a professedly Christian nation, the Norwegian Friends had become attached to the religion of peace, which they tried to hand down to their children, and to spread among their neighbors. But in doing so they came in conflict with the civil and ecclesiastical powers of the land. It must be remembered that religious tolerance was just then becoming a virtue, or a fashion, in Europe, and a necessity in America. Norway had not quite reached that stage. *Skandinaven,* commenting on this subject, said, among other things: "The fact that no state church was established in this country at the time of the adoption of the constitution, was simply due to an historical necessity, and was not the result of greater religious toleration than was found in other countries at that time. Most of the different church denominations were represented in the colonies, and the only religious dogma on which they could agree, was that no state church ought to be established."

The constitution of Norway, adopted in 1814, has been much praised for its liberal and humanitarian principles. But at least certain parts of it seem to have been prepared with too much haste, and approved without due consideration. This especially appears to have been the case in regard to the stipulation about religion. By a large majority the convention at Eidsvold adopted the following, which

9

was intended to be the constitutional creed of the nation: "The Evangelical Lutheran religion shall remain the official religion of the state. All Christian religious sects shall be granted liberty of religious worship; but Jews and Jesuits shall be kept excluded from the kingdom. Monastic orders must not be tolerated. Those inhabitants of the country who profess the public religion of the state shall be obliged to educate their children in the same."

But when the constitution became public property, article II., which contains the legal religious dogma of Norway, reads as follows: "The Evangelical Lutheran religion shall remain the official religion of the state. Those inhabitants who profess it shall be obliged to educate their children in the same. Jesuits and monastic orders must not be tolerated. Jews shall be kept excluded from the kingdom." It may be proper to remark that the prohibition in regard to the Jews was removed in 1851, principally through the efforts of Henrik Wergeland. But what became of the sentence, "All Christian religious sects shall be granted liberty of religious worship?" Who was responsible for the change? Where did the members of the convention have their ears when the constitution as a whole was adopted? These questions have been and are just as much of a conundrum in Norway as what the Silverites call "the crime of 1873" and "Section 22 of the Dingley bill" are in this country. In the absence of any constitutional provision in regard to the free exercise of religion outside of the state church, recourse was had to older laws on the subject, which greatly perplexed the government and became a hardship to the few Friends who resided in Norway. The Quakers, as is well known, not only reject the sacraments and confirmation, oppose religious ceremonies at weddings and funerals, and object to pay taxes to the state church; but they also refuse to take judicial oaths, to perform military duties, and to contribute to the maintenance of military establishments. It is evident that even if the constitution of Norway had granted full religious freedom to every individual upon the face of the earth, yet the Friends would have come in conflict with the fundamental laws of the kingdom, which prescribe that every citizen, without regard to birth or fortune, shall perform military service in defense of his country. But it is natural that the clash should first occur in regard to the mode of worship, rather than with reference to the oath and martial duties. To many people religion is an earnest reality and an every-day concern; while judicial oaths and wars are generally considered to be more of necessary evils than indispensable articles. It cannot be disputed that the Quakers suffered considerably, especially during the years of 1830 to 1845, on account of their refusal to comply with the ecclesiastical and civil laws of the kingdom. They were compelled to have their children baptized and confirmed, as well as to observe all the outward requirements of church and state, including the payment of taxes. They were forbidden to propagate the doctrines of their sect, ordered to abstain from all proselyting, and prohibited from allowing any converts to join their society. On the failure to observe these conditions they were fined, and even the dead who were not buried in consecrated places were exhumed, and interred in accordance with the legal prescriptions. On the other hand, the Friends were often treated with leniency; exempted from paying the fines imposed upon them; and their marriages, entered into contrary to law, permitted to remain in full force. Their life and property received the same protection as that of any other subject, notwithstanding that they objected to pay the same taxes as other people. Perhaps no country has been so little cursed with religious bigotry and persecution as the Scandinavian peninsula. No institution of inquisition was ever planted among them, no blood of heretics ever stained their soil. Nor does it appear that the Norwegian government intended to oppress the few defenseless Friends within its dominion; for already in 1817 a commission was appointed to devise means by which they could be permitted to worship God in their own fashion. It took many years, however, before that result was obtained; but what they suffered in the meantime seems to have been more in consequence of meanness, on the part of certain officials, than of any intended persecution on the part of the government (3). Even if some of the Friends emigrated on account of the lack of religious freedom in their native places, they appear to have been more than willing to return to the ills they knew of after having enjoyed the liberty of America for only a few years. For according to *Sandfärdig Beretning om Amerika,* by Ole Rynning, the emigrants who had settled at Kendall, N. Y., suffered greatly during the first four or five years for the very necessities of life, and desired to return to old Norway, but did not have the means to do so.

By a large number of writers, notably Prof. R. B. Ander-

(3) Most of the facts mentioned in the two paragraphs above have been deducted from "W. A. Wexels's Liv og 'Virken," by Rev. A. Mau, published in Kristiania, 1867, and it is considered to be very reliable by Prof. Georg Sverdrup, who has made a special study of that interesting period of Norwegian history.

son, religious persecution has been given as the main cause of the movement from Stavanger to America in 1825. Consequently it was deemed wise to discuss that part of the emigration problem somewhat extensively. But there is no authentic record to show that a single man, woman, or child of the fifty-two persons who emigrated in 1825, ever came in conflict with the laws of Norway on account of their religion. The only Quaker in the Stavanger district who suffered for his belief, prior to 1826; was Elias Tastad, and he did not emigrate. The main hardships of the Norwegian Friends befell them from 1830 to 1845. At the latter date religious freedom was virtually established in the kingdom.

Stephen Grellet and William Allen were very zealous Quakers, and both became famous as philanthropists. The former was a French nobleman, who had been compelled in early life, during the French revolution, to seek refuge in the United States, where, shortly after his arrival in 1795, he joined the society of Friends. After having resided continuously in this country for a period of twelve years, he for over a quarter of a century wandered from one European country to another, visiting palaces and dungeons, and urging everybody to practice "peace on earth and good will among men." He even preached to the Pope in Rome, who listened with respect to his exhortations. He kept a diary, which afterwards was published in book form. In 1818 he writes: "I had been under great apprehension as to how I could be of the least service in the great work of my dear Lord in Norway and Sweden, for neither dear Allen nor myself understand their language." And again: "Enoch Jacobson, a Norwegian, one of those I saw during my last visit to this nation, on board the prison-ship of war, and who there became convinced of the Friends' principles, having heard that I proposed to return from America to visit Norway, etc., has just arrived in London. He has come under the apprehension that he would find me here, and that it was his duty to come and render me any service in his power." This Enoch Jacobson together with another man had tried, but failed, to organize a society of Friends in Kristiania. Grellet, Allen, and Jacobson sailed directly from London to Stavanger, where they arrived in 1818. In their journals the two former speak highly of the morals of the people, and of the courtesy and intelligence of the officials; but do not by a single word refer to any persecution of their co-religionists in Norway. The Lutheran clergymen received them with open arms, and attended some of their meetings. They both mention, as an illustration of the virtue of the people in the vicinity of Stavanger, that during a quarter of a century only one person had been sentenced to death, although the district contained 40,000 inhabitants; that the prison was kept by an old woman, and she had only one man in it, who was a perfect model of a culprit. Grellet and his companions remained in Stavanger for about one week, visited families, assisted the half a dozen or more Quakers in securing a suitable hall to meet in, and helped them in perfecting the organization. It should be remembered that Lars Larson, the founder of the society of Friends in Stavanger in 1816, had served for some time in the family of William Allen. Considering the familiarity with which Grellet for a whole week associated with the people, it is almost impossible to conceive that they should not know that America was his adopted country, especially when, as before noted, Enoch Jacobson was well aware of the fact that Grellet resided in the United States. According to George Richardson's *Society of Friends in Norway*, Lars Larson also, it seems, met in 1822 a young man from North America, who probably was a Norwegian by birth. It is hard to believe that the Quakers were so absorbed in thinking about heavenly things as to neglect to inquire of visitors from beyond the Atlantic in regard to the location and conditions of the continent to which they departed a few years later. The Scandinavian common people are generally very inquisitive about such matters. In fact B. L. Wick—his article appeared in *The Friends*, Philadelphia, 1894—who investigated the subject a few years ago in London, maintains that it was Grellet who first advised the peasants to emigrate, partly on account of their poverty, and told them that America offered many advantages; for example, a better economical future, free exercise of religion, and relief from military duties. The reason they did not at once act upon his advice is easily explained. The cautious and somewhat slow Norwegian peasants needed time to think about the matter, and to arrange their small affairs. There were persons in the North who really decided to emigrate a quarter of a century before the feat was actually accomplished. Perhaps the Norwegian prisoners during their confinement in London harbor, or some Norwegian sailors during their travels, had heard something about America, and circulated the rumor among their countrymen at home years before Grellet's visit. At any rate it must be admitted that if the Quakers at Stavanger selected, in 1821, Kleng Peerson and another man to go to America and investigate with a view to establishing a colony of Friends in the New World, as some writers seem to believe, then it is absolutely certain that the people must have had some information about the Western continent, as it is purely nonsense to suppose that any rational beings would try to send men in search of a suitable place in which to locate a settlement, to a country never heard of.

But even though it is virtually certain that the Quakers in Norway knew something about America before Kleng Peerson emigrated in 1821, it does not necessarily follow that they sent him and another man thither for the purpose of finding a suitable place to establish a Norwegian settlement. Kleng was not a highly respected character in the vicinity of his home, partly on account of his marriage with a very old but rich woman, whom he expected to support him, being too indolent to earn his own bread and butter. It was the same shiftless individual, who during the greater part of the remainder of his life wandered on foot through a large portion of the Western states, living upon charity, sleeping under the open arch of heaven, or cheating people for his lodging; and who in 1843 was thoroughly whipped in New York because he had defrauded some of his poor countrymen, whom he pretended to assist (4). His companion on the supposed trip of investigation had an exceedingly bad reputation (5). Both of these men probably pretended and were considered to be Quakers, or at least favoring the tenets of that sect. But if they had any religious conviction

(4) J. R. Reiersen's "Veiviser," p. XXVI.

(5) "Billed-Magazin," Vol. I., p. 102.

at all, it did not, perhaps, in any way affect their thoughts
or actions, except "to imbue them with a strong belief in the
devil." Even assuming that most of the Friends around
Stavanger were not of a high intellectual order, yet they
could hardly have been so stupid as to expect to be able to
deduce honesty from the united action of two rascals—to use
one of Carlyle's expressions. But there are also other reasons,
besides probabilities, for believing that Kleng Peerson and
his companion were not sent out by any one to examine the
New World. It is positively asserted in *Billed-Magazin*
(6) that both Kleng Peerson and his companion secretly
deserted their families and went to Gothenburg, Sweden.
It may be proper in this connection to remark that at the ripe
age of sixty-five, Kleng also wedded, and again abandoned, a
Swedish woman at the Bishop Hill colony in Illinois, where
he remained a very short time as member of Eric Janson's
religious communistic organization (7).

In Gothenburg the two men heard about America, which
country they undoubtedly also knew something about before,
and proceeded thither on a merchant vessel. Kleng Peerson
returned to Stavanger in 1824, after having remained in the
state of New York for three years, and gave a glowing
description of the New World, by which he gained a reputation as an excellent story-teller, not to say as a perverter of
the truth. But in spite of his shortcomings, he, no doubt,
exercised some influence in hastening the departure of some
of the peasants. On the other hand, it is claimed that Kleng
Peerson possessed many good traits, and evidently was a

(6) Vol. I., p. 102.

(7) Anderson's "First Chapter of Norwegian Immigration," p. 189.

fairly faithful guide to several parties of Norwegians in search of suitable land where settlements could be established. Prof. Th. Bothne, in his *Lutherske Kirkearbeide blandt Nordmändene i Amerika*, calls him a tramp, and it cannot be denied that he possessed many of the faults and virtues of a genuine tramp. But it should be remembered that this class of people often treat each other with an altruism that even a Tolstoi might admire, and possibly Kleng Peerson gratified the better part of his nature by enduring and enjoying his wanderings in order to serve his compatriots on this side of the Atlantic. He died in Texas in 1865, and it seems that the contradictions of his life followed him to the grave. The inscription on the small stone monument, which his countrymen in that state raised to his memory, reads as follows: "Cleng Peerson, the first Norwegian Emigrant to America. Came to America in 1821." Now it is a fact, as has already been stated in the first volume, page 35, that Hans Hansen Bergen came to this country as early as 1633, and there are many reasons and some evidence for believing that other Norwegians also came at the very dawn of the immigration period. At least one Norwegian, Thomas Johnson, who had served under the famous Paul Jones in his naval victories, was in America during the Revolutionary era, and sat among the gods in the gallery in the congressional hall, Philadelphia, 1781 (8). In 1818 Soren Gustavus Norberg, a native of Kristiansand, came to the United States and settled at Salem, Mass., where he took out his naturalization papers five years later, calling himself Andrew Peterson. He married an

---

(8) Anderson's "First Chapter of Norwegian Immigration," p. 27.

American woman, and one of his sons, an American Methodist clergyman, has produced copies of original documents
in regard to his father. Undoubtedly other Norwegians,
besides those mentioned, came to this country years before
Kleng Peerson arrived, but enough has been said to prove
that he was not "the first Norwegian immigrant to America,"
even in the nineteenth century.

Most authorities agree that on July 4, 1825, Restauration, a small sloop, loaded with emigrants, iron, and brandy,
left the wharf of Stavanger, destined for America. As has
been asserted on pages 107-11 in the second volume, the
first shipload of Norwegian emigrants who came directly
from their native land to the state of Wisconsin, embarked
at Skien the 17th of May, 1839. It seems rather strange
that the departure of these two noted emigration parties
should have occurred on the two great national holidays of
the United States and Norway. This coincidence might,
accidentally or purposely, have happened; but probably the
apparent agreement of dates is to be found in the human
desire to try to harmonize their past actions, no matter
how insignificant, with more important events. The Sloop
party consisted of 52 persons, including women and children.
The majority of them were probably Friends, although
there were in 1821 only six men and five women in the
whole vicinity of Stavanger, Skjold, and Tysvär (9)—
where all the Sloop folks hailed from—who professed to
believe in the doctrines of George Fox. But some of these
did not emigrate in 1825, notably, Elias Tastad, the only
person in that district of the kingdom of whom there is, up

(9) Mau's "W. A. Wexels's Liv og Virken," p. 174.

to 1826, any record of having come in conflict with the law of the land on account of his religion. According to Prof. R. B. Anderson, "Six heads of families converted their scanty worldly possessions into money and purchased a sloop which had been built in the Hardanger fjord, between Stavanger and Bergen, and which they loaded with a cargo of iron. For this sloop and cargo they paid $1,800 (Norwegian money). While six of the party owned some stock in the vessel the largest share was held by Lars Larson, who was in all respects the leader of the enterprise."

The forerunners of civilization, both in the eastern and the western states of this country, have generally been reckless men of questionable moral character. The brute courage and vices of our trappers and hunters have been more conspicuous than their virtue or humanity. This does not imply that they have not been useful and necessary elements; in fact, they have been indispensable to a higher development of mind and matter. They have been necessary vanguards of the miners, loggers, and farmers; these, in turn, have been followed by the merchants and professional men, who have supplied the former with luxuries, and attended to their spiritual and intellectual needs. What has been said about the trappers and hunters is also true, at least in most cases, of the very first immigrants from every European country. The cruelty and bloodthirstiness of the first Spaniards is too well known to need repetition. The English Puritans came to this country in order to be allowed to worship God in their own fashion, and to deprive every one else of the same privilege. The majority of the passengers on the first vessel which carried Swedish colonists to Delaware in 1638 were transgressors of the law. During the whole emigration period it has, in general, been the courageous and discontented classes who have participated in the movement; for the simple reason that the contented always stayed at home, and the timid never dared to go. But before the movement had become somewhat regular, and the knowledge about America certain, the courage of the emigrants bordered upon recklessness, and their discontent was closely allied to anarchy. It was, with few exceptions, the extreme and radical element of all countries, those persons who had little to lose and everything to gain, who first cast the die in favor of the New World. There is no reason for believing, and still less for asserting, that the first Norwegian emigrants, the Sloop party, were either above or below the first emigrants from other countries at that time. One writer on the subject says: "They were men of the poorest classes of the communities whence they came, but not paupers or criminals. They were squeezed out from the bottom of society, escaping, as it were, through cracks and crevices. The average quality, however, steadily improved from the first." Most of them were Quakers, and B. L. Wick claims that there were three classes of persons who had accepted, or pretended to accept, the teachings of the Friends: First, those who honestly believed in the doctrines; secondly, those who did not care for Quakerism, but disagreed with the teachings of the state church; thirdly, those who were poor and hoped to be assisted, and were helped by the society of Friends. He adds: "There are perhaps many to-day in Norway who were not Friends, if it were not for the pecuniary assistance derived." To the second class should be added those who did not care for any religion, but joined any new movement out of curiosity or to gain notoriety; in other words, they were mere religious tramps. It is, of course, impossible to ascertain the proportionate number of these respective classes. But the second class, especially, must have been quite large, considering that in later years a great number of Quakers around Stavanger joined the Baptists and Methodists when the latter denominations began their work in Norway. In this country many of the Friends became Mormons and infidels, and some returned to the Lutheran fold. While there is no method by which it can be absolutely ascertained which of the three classes mentioned predominated on Restauration, yet the actions of those people during the voyage indicated, at least to a certain extent, their character. The Quakers have generally prohibited their members from using liquors or tobacco, and they have in most cases practiced what they preach. Not so, however, with Sloop party Friends. For, they not only unlawfully sold liquor in the English harbor Lisett in passing through the British channel; but after having found a cask of wine floating in the ocean near the island of Madeira, on the coast of Africa, they all became so drunk that the vessel drifted into one of the harbors of the island without any visible sign of life on board, and without hoisted flag (10). The officials at the fort, supposing that some dreadful contagious disease had killed all the people on board, aimed their cannons at the sloop; but the party got a chance to sober up before entering the other world, one of the

(10) "Billed-Magazin," vol. I., p. 71.

passengers staggering up and hoisting the Norwegian flag. It is reasonable to assume that while in this intoxicated state they did not address each other in the usual Quaker language of *thee* and *thou*, nor answered all questions by *yea* or *nay*, but had recourse to some more forcible Norwegian expressions. The stupidity and carelessness manifested on this occasion by the so-called captain and officials deserve the severest condemnation. Their negligence amounted to a crime, and if such a case had been tried before any maritime court in Christendom, the offenders would undoubtedly have been sentenced to several years' imprisonment. The leader and principal owner of the sloop, Lars Larson, was the one who had fished up the cask (11), notwithstanding that he had been converted to Quakerism in England, and had been the first one in Stavanger to open up his house for Friendly meetings; but this time he, with the rest, seems to have drowned, or perhaps intensified, his religious enthusiasm with some excellent wine.

It is generally maintained by all writers on the subject that before the party left the harbor of Funchal, into which they had drifted during their state of intoxication, they were well supplied with provisions by the American consul at that place, who also bestowed other favors upon them. In Prof. R. B. Anderson's history, page 72, it is claimed that J. H. March, who was appointed consul in 1816, was the man who showed the Norwegians such courtesies. But in a recent letter to the writer of this article from the department of state, Washington, D. C., it is asserted that the consul at Funchal was absent from 1824

---

(11) Anderson's "First Chap. of Nor. Immigration," p. 58.

to 1827, during which time the duties of the office were performed by his brother, Francis March. Some authorities, however, assert that the party were not at the island of Madeira at all, but in the harbor of Lisbon, Portugal (12). Fourteen weeks after their departure from Stavanger they reached New York. Here they attracted considerable attention, especially as the so-called captain was arrested for having a larger cargo and more passengers than the law permitted such a small vessel to carry; but he was released. They were also duly referred to by the American newspapers. But they were in such destitute circumstances that the New York Quakers had to assist them financially before they could proceed any farther. Besides the Friends, some other persons, who came to the wharf out of mere curiosity, gave the impoverished Norwegians some money. The sloop and cargo had cost them nearly $2,000; they sold it all in New York for about a quarter of that amount.

Most stories, real or fictitious, have a hero or a heroine; and a large number of writers have represented Kleng Peerson to be the hero of the Sloop party. Although no mention has been made of the means by which he first found out that such a continent existed; yet from the general trend of the presentation it appears as if these authors wanted mankind to believe that Kleng Peerson in some mysterious way, perhaps by his "inner light," discovered some information about the New World, and then imparted part of his wisdom to some Norwegian peasants, who at once dispatched him thither. After three years of thorough study of the new country, he, according to the

(12) Wist's "Norske Indvandring," p. 15.

general version, returned and conquered a portion of the kingdom of Norway with his tongue, and then again hurried across the Atlantic ocean to make final preparation for the arrival of the Sloop party. It is the unpleasant duty of the historian to cut through and destroy the delicate veils which have been woven around events and individuals, and present them to the world in their naked truthfulness, as far as it is possible to do so. The improbability, and even impossibility, of Kleng Peerson having been the evangelist who first preached the new gospel about America to the Norwegians, and the object of his first visit there, have already been discussed. But the meager and questionable evidences in regard to what part he played, after his return to Norway in 1824, in effecting or hastening the organization of the Sloop party, are neither positive nor negative, being about so equally balanced as to prevent any certain conclusion. He came to Norway one year before the party sailed, and probably returned to New York shortly after, without having any knowledge whatsoever of the preparations for departure going on in the vicinity of Stavanger. When the Sloop folks arrived in New York in the fall of 1825, they appear to have met him there by accident, rather than by previous arrangement. If he had been the real instigator of the movement and the chief organizer of the party, it seems he would have accompanied the emigrants across the ocean. They needed him. Prof. R. B. Anderson says: "Instead of risking his life in the sloop he had again gone by the way of Gothenburg, Sweden, and was already in New York ready to receive his friends and to give them such assistance as he was able." But whatever might have been the motive of Kleng in proceeding before the other emigrants, cowardice or prudence could hardly have been the cause. His whole life is a protest against the assumption. The same author cites a New York newspaper notice of 1825, which appears to justify the theory that Kleng was sent in advance. But for historical accuracy newspapers are, in general, not very reliable, and this seems to be the case at the beginning of the nineteenth century as much as at the beginning of the twentieth century, because all the newspaper citations which said writer quotes in regard to the Sloop party are contraditory in detail. On the other hand, some of the ablest Norwegian-American scholars who have studied the subject, question the justice of the honor accorded to Kleng Peerson, refusing to ascribe to the Sloop party any special credit for having promoted the subsequent Norwegian emigration. For example, J. B. Wist not only doubts the particulars, as generally stated, about Restauration, but boldly asserts that the passengers on the same had little or no influence, either directly or indirectly, on the Norwegian immigration, or in any way directed its course. Nicolay Grevstad says: "What gave the first impetus to emigration from Norway may be put under the category of historical accidents. It was also an accident that the first emigrants were dissatisfied with the religious conditions under which they had been living. At that time rumors about America began to spread among the people along the coast of Norway. And if Kleng Peerson had not emigrated, others would have done so, either at that time or a little later on. Popular migrations always have an economical root. The emigration from Norway, as well as from other European countries, is a result of the strained economical conditions prevailing in the Old World, and the hope of doing better in the New World. All other conditions are only tributary circumstances of comparatively subordinate importance."

From New York harbor the majority of the Norwegians proceeded, late in the fall of 1825, to Kendall, then called Murray, in Orleans county, N. Y., where, it is asserted, most of them bought land. Prof. Anderson says: "Kendall is in the northeast corner of Orleans county on the shores of Lake Ontario. Here land was sold to the Norwegians by Joseph Fellows at five dollars an acre; but as they had no money to pay for it, Mr. Fellows agreed to let them redeem it in ten annual installments. The land was heavily wooded, and each head of a family and adult person purchased forty acres." In order to be absolutely certain in regard to this transaction, the writer of this article sent a list of names, which included most of the adult males of the Sloop party, to the district attorney of Orleans county, Thomas A. Kirby, and requested him to make a careful investigation of the county records in relation to the supposed real estate deal between Joseph Fellows and the first Norwegian immigrants. He answered as follows: "From my examination of the records of the Orleans county clerk's office I do not find that Joseph Fellows ever deeded any property about the year 1825, situated in the town of Kendall, or Murray, to any of the individuals named in your communication to me of October 15th, 1898. Later on, in 1835, a Joseph Fellows, of Geneva, deeded property to different individuals, but not any of them corresponded with any of the names that you have given me. The records do not disclose, as far as I can

ascertain, that Kleng Peerson bought any land or had anything to do with the transaction; but our early records, of
course, are not absolutely accurate." It is useless to theo-
rize about the failure of the Norwegian settlers at Kendall to
secure proper titles to their farms, or to discuss their trials
and triumphs at that place, as nearly everything in regard to
them is clouded in obscurity. Joseph Fellows, who was a
Quaker, appears to have been very generous to them, and it
would be unfair to assume that he tried to defraud them out
of their property. Consequently, they themselves must have
been unable to comply with the stipulations about the bargain, and probably he, on that account, sold the land to other
parties in 1835, and at about that time several of the
original settlers sought new homes in some of the Western
states, especially in La Salle county, Ill. With probably one
or two exceptions, not a single descendant of the Sloop folks
now reside at Kendall. There are some Norwegians today,
but they are later arrivals.

In conclusion it must be said that the real historical facts
about the Sloop party are few and contradictory. Taken all
in all, the sum and substance of the whole affair seems to be
this: The Stavanger Quakers had through Grellet, as well
as by other means, learned about America and discussed the
desirability of emigrating some time before Kleng Peerson's
first departure or return; but, being poor and slow to decide,
the execution of their wishes had of necessity to be delayed.
Parts of the story, at least, have apparently been invented
by the participants for the sake of gaining notoriety. Judging from the course which they pursued, it would be more
reasonable to believe that the Cape of Good Hope was their

intended destination, instead of New York. Considering their unlawful trade in England; their idiotic conduct at the island of Madeira; and their extreme poverty, it is useless to argue about, or specify, the cause or causes which led to the departure. The Sloop party desired to get out of Norway in order to improve, in some way, their material condition, and to taste the sweet experience of adventure—exactly the same motives which underlie the whole Viking and emigration periods. Religious persecution may have been the pretext, but in reality was not the cause. The temperament of most of the people on the Restauration was such that they would have tried to emigrate, even if the whole universe had been blessed with the utmost religious freedom. The progeny of the Sloop people seem to have been as completely lost in the ocean of cosmopolitanism as the doings of their forefathers are obscured by uncertainties. Even the commonly strong cohesive power of religion has been unable to hold any number of them together either in regard to faith or habitation. Considered as a unit, the immigrants of 1825 have practically exercised no influence; as individuals they and their offspring have, no doubt, been peaceful citizens and desirable subjects; but, apparently, hardly any of them have possessed those marked characteristics of push and energy so common to the Norwegians in the nineteenth century. Many Norwegian-Americans have made a wide reputation for themselves in a few years. But with the possible exception of Col. Porter C. Olson, a brave Illinois soldier during the Civil war, not a single descendant of the Sloop party appears to have distinguished himself in any line during the seventy-five years that have passed since the Restauration sailed from Stavanger to America with the first party of Norwegian immigrants.

Swedish Colony at Bishopshill, Illinois.

—BY—

MAJOR JOHN SWAINSON.

[Published in Scandinavia in 1885.]

In a spirit of patriotic exultation one of the poets of Sweden proclaims his native land the "Homestead of freedom on earth." In a political sense this boasting expression may be justified. From the earliest dawn of fable-mixed history, when Sigge Fridulfson first founded the embryo Swedish commonwealth, up to the present time, the kingdom of Sweden proper has never been conquered by a foreign foe. Provinces beyond the sea were won and lost, but the sea and mountain-girt eastern part of the Scandinavian peninsula, the ancient Swea and Götha-land was, from time immemorial, inhabited and possessed by a people governed by laws of their own making and by constitutional kings either of their own choosing or inheriting the throne by constitutional succession. The practice of entailing estates— that pernicious inheritance from the feudal middle-age— which at one time prevailed to a rather alarming extent, was checked in its growth by the "reduction" of Charles XI., and was finally abolished by legislation in the beginning of this

(135)

century. As a consequence, the bulk of the land always remained in the hands of a class of independent yeomen, the
owners in fee simple of small freeholds, subject only to taxes
to the crown and to the municipality, and the owners themselves entitled to representation in the national legislature.

But in this so much praised and cherished freedom of the
Swedish people, there was one essential element wanting.
Religious liberty did not exist. According to the law of the
land every native Swede must belong to the established Lutheran church, whether or not his religious convictions
agreed with the doctrines of that denomination. The penalty for apostacy was exile. It may seem surprising, almost
incredible, that such a law—until within the last twenty
years, when it was abolished, or, at least greatly modified—
could prevail among such an enlightened and progressive
people, but such was nevertheless the fact, and to explain
how such a law could remain in force so long is both difficult
and would require a more extended review of the history of
the reformation in Sweden than space here will permit. It
may, however, not be out of place to say a few words on the
subject.

Gustavus Vasa, the father of modern Sweden, also became its religious regenerator. Under his auspices, at the
Diet in Westerås, in the year 1527, the Swedes severed their
connection with the Church of Rome, and adopted the principles of Martin Luther. This was effected quite peaceably,
the only opponent being the primate of Sweden, Gustavus
Trolle, archbishop of Upsala, who made war on the king,
but was speedily put down, captured and sent out of the
country. With this exception the whole clergy, more or less

willingly, it may be supposed, consented to the change. Romanism was done away with, but the church organization was retained.   The bishops and clergy, now suddenly transformed into good Lutherans, were in most instances permitted to remain in charge of their offices; a new archbishop, a disciple of Luther, was appointed, and thus the church of Sweden became the oldest Protestant Episcopal church in the world, with its clerus comitialis, successio apostolica, and every other concomitant for a complete organization.

During the reign of Gustavus Vasa and that of his oldest son and nearest successor, Ericus XIV., the work of strengthening the reformation went on peaceably. Monastaries and nunneries were abolished and their rich estates turned over to the crown; the Bible was translated into the Swedish language, and every measure adopted to put the new-born Protestantism on a firm basis, But King Ericus, being taken prisoner dethroned and finally murdered by a conspiracy headed by his own brother, John, the latter ascended the throne. His spouse, Queen Catherine, a Polish princess, was a devoted Roman Catholic, and by her influence the king became a secret convert. Their son and heir, Sigismund, was educated in the Roman church, and strenuous efforts made to re-establish Romanism in the kingdom. In the meantime Prince Sigismund, on account of his mother's family connections, had been elected king of Poland, and at the death of his father returned to Sweden at the head of a Polish army with the avowed purpose to crush Protestantism and once more put the Swedes under the rule of the papacy. The designs, however, were frustrated. The Protestants gathered under his uncle, Duke Charles, the

youngest and most able son of Gustavus Vasa, and after
several bloody encounters Sigismund had to return to Poland, having been unable to effect his purpose, was debarred
from the Swedish succession and lived and died as king of
Poland.   Duke Charles, a staunch and devoted Lutheran,
was now elected king, and the Lutheran Protestant church
with an episcopal organization, became the established
church of the kingdom.   But against the secret machina-
tions of the court during the long reign of John III. and the
open attempts of Sigismund to re-establish the dominion of
the papal power, the young Protestant church doubtless had
a hard struggle to maintain itself, and since it issued from
the ordeal victorious, it is reasonable to suppose that strin-
gent measures were taken forever to prevent a recurrence,
and to this source, in our opinion, must be traced the laws
against religious freedom in Sweden, which until quite recently, have remained in force and both at home and abroad
have attracted so much criticism; mostly, however, abroad,
for the Swedish people were, and we think, are yet, most devoted Lutherans.   Any apostasy from the established
church finds little favor or sympathy among the Swedish
community at large, and there is not in the whole Roman
calendar a saint, whose memory is held in higher veneration
among the faithful than is among the Swedish Lutherans
that of the Great Reformer.   But while these laws were
still in force, they were in reality a dead letter and almost
unknown, because there was no occasion for their application; and we cannot remember many instances where the
penalty of exile has been inflicted. Public worship among
the Swedes in any other form than according to the estab-

lished church, or conducted by other persons than the regular clergy, was forbidden, and if attempted, would doubtless be prohibited.

While such a state of things existed, there lived, some forty years ago, in one of the Middle Provinces of Sweden, a man by the name of Eric Janson. He was born December 19, 1808, the son of a small farmer. On account of the poverty of his parents he was prevented from attendance in the public schools, and consequently his book learning was of the most limited kind, being principally acquired by the aid of the minister of the parish while preparing for his first communion. The tendency of his mind was religious. He maintained that already at an early age he had experienced a deep repentance of sin and become a convert, feeling at the same time the greatest desire to gain knowledge in matters spiritual. For this purpose he read with avidity all books on such topics within his reach, but he soon threw them all away as unsatisfactory, and thenceforward the Bible became his only study for guidance and consolation.

Eric Janson remained with his father until he was twenty-seven years old, when he married and first rented but afterward purchased a small farm. He was distinguished for honesty, sobriety, and the most untiring industry, and in the whole neighborhood he was recognized as the hardest worker in the field. During this ceaseless toil his interest in religious matters, far from diminishing, was constantly increasing. He felt an unconquerable desire, a glowing enthusiasm, which exhorted him to make known his thoughts outside the immediate circle of his home. With this end in view, in the spring of 1842, he made an excursion to the adjoining province of Helsingland, where he put himself in communication with some piously disposed people and held a number of religious meetings. This visit he repeated and in the course of two years he returned time and again to the field of his missionary work without any molestation. Those who heard him, among whom often were found several of the more progressive of the regular clergy, assert without hesitation that Janson was a most forcible preacher, that his religious tenets in no essential respect were different from the fundamental principles common to all Evangelical churches, and that his style of delivery and mode of teaching and exhortation nearest resembled those of the Methodists. The movement swept over the Province with the strength of a tornado. People by thousands flocked to hear the new preacher; the churches stood empty; families became sundered, some adhering to the old church, others following the new, and finally the Jansonites, as they were called, disdaining any other book but the Bible, publicly burned all other books of religious content, including the Common Prayerbook of the Church of Sweden. This brought matters to a crisis. The authorities, fearing serious disturbances, had Eric Janson arrested in the spring of 1844. After a short imprisonment and a hearing before the governor of his Province, he was discharged with instructions to again appear whenever wanted. During the following two years he made repeated attempts to continue his religious work among the people, but was each time arrested and suffered imprisonment on three or four occasions. Finally, disheartened and despairing of success in his native land, Eric Janson, with a few faithful followers, escaped over the mountains into Nor-

way, in January, 1846, from whence he repaired to Copen-
hagen, where he embarked on a vessel which landed him in
New York in the spring of the same year.   In the month of
July following he finally arrived in the hamlet of Victoria,
Knox county, Illinois.

Prompted by these repeated annoyances and persecutions,
Eric Janson and his followers resolved to forsake their native
ₗand and find new homes in America, for it was not Eric
alone who suffered.   Several of his adherents had been subject to fine and imprisonment for the most trifling offenses
against the old and obsolete "Conventicle-law."   Eric, previous to leaving the country, had made all necessary preparations, and appointed four trusty friends as leaders of the
movement.   But it is safe to say, that in his colonization
plan, did not enter any of those communistic and socialistic
principles, which afterwards found a practical application in
the colony.   These were the fruits of necessity.   In preparing
to leave, those of the Jansonites possessed of any property,
converted this into ready cash, retaining only necessary
clothing and bedding.   But now it was found that one thousand one hundred persons wished to join the intended colony, and of these only a smaller number were able to defray
the necessary expenses.   The aggregate of their means was
now made a common fund and put in the hands of trustees,
with the object of assisting the needy to follow their brethren.   Every one contributed his all, some as much as from
two thousand to six thousand dollars.   Some of the emigrants had debts, and these were paid from the common
treasury.   Some were soldiers, and their release from the
army was purchased with means from the same source.

In our days of perfect communication by rail and steamer, when a trip from Sweden to America can be easily and comfortably made in about two weeks, it is hard to imagine the hardships of such a voyage forty years ago. Emigration was then unknown and no vessels found fitted for that purpose. The only Swedish ships trading on America carried cargoes of iron and were often old hulks of inferior quality. In several such vessels, temporarily fitted up to receive emigrants, the first parties of Jansonites left their native land in the spring and summer of 1846. One of these vessels, with fifty passengers, was never heard of; another was wrecked on Newfoundland, but the people saved; a third was five months on the way, during which time the unhappy emigrants suffered greatly from both sickness and famine.

But one after another these several parties joined their leader in Victoria, Illinois, so that by the end of the year 1846 their number amounted to about four hundred.

In the meantime, Eric Janson, anticipating the arrival of his friends, had purchased several pieces of land in the neighborhood, some of which had improvements; but as townsite for the new settlement was selected the southeast quarter of section 14, in Weller township, Henry county, which was bought of the government for two hundred dollars, and the intended town was named Bishopshill, which is a literal translation of Eric Janson's native place (Biskopskulla) in Sweden.

The first care now was to prepare shelter for all this people. For this purpose were built several large log houses and two tents of large dimensions, besides which a turf house served as a kitchen and dining-room; but these accommodations proving inadequate, resort was had to what in the west is popularly called "dug-outs," which are merely cellars with a roof over, and a door and window in front, the most suitable place for such a resort being a sloping hillside. Of these twelve were built, generally twenty-five to thirty feet in length, eighteen in width, furnished with bunks on the sides, a fire-place in the rear, and rooming twenty-five to thirty persons.

It may easily be understood that among a people with whom religion was paramount, the first thought was to prepare a place of worship, if ever so primitive. With this end in view they first dug a ditch two feet deep, and in this, on a foundation of timber, a middle wall of logs was built, from which a roof of canvas was stretched to both sides. On the north side was the pulpit and entrance; on the south the fire-place; the whole seating eight hundred to one thousand people. In this tabernacle, during the fall and winter, service was held twice a day on week days, and three times on Sundays. Eric Janson himself rose at five o'clock in the morning and roused the people to morning prayer, which often lasted two hours. The second service was in the evening. During the summer these meetings were discontinued and supplemented by an open-air midday meeting in the grove.

Nor was school instruction neglected. At such times, when the weather did not permit outdoor work, instruction by competent teachers, was given to the full-grown people, of whom many were ignorant in reading and writing, the above church-tent being used as a school-room, while for the children school was kept in one of the dug-outs. Besides these there was also another institution of learning of far greater pretentions. The Jansonites, being convinced that the depository of all the saving truths of the Christian religion was found within their little community, considered it their duty to let their light shine before men by missionaries sent out from the colony. For this purpose twelve of their brightest young men were selected to devote themselves to the ministry and put in system the Jansonian theology, but first and foremost to learn the English language, their studies being led by the more advanced members of the society.

One of the earliest difficulties the colonists had to contend with was to provide flour for bread, the nearest gristmill being twenty-eight miles distant, and this, as well as some others, still farther out of the way, often out of order. To obviate this trouble a watermill with a large wheel was built at the creek running through Bishopshill. Unfortunately, however, the water supply in the creek was often so small that it could not furnish the mill with necessary power. This new trouble was overcome in a manner both ingenious, simple, and practical; the health of the young theologians, the elders thought, might suffer by the effects of a too sedentary life, and to obviate this they were, at intervals between their studies, invited to step inside the wheel of the mill, and put this in motion by tramping at such occasions when the water supply was short in the creek. Somewhat later a windmill was put up in the other end of the village, and between the wind power on one side and the tramping theological candidates on the other, the needs of the people for bread were pretty well filled. Some years afterwards, however, a fine steam mill was built which supplied not only the colony, but the whole surrounding country with breadstuff.

Several additional pieces of land were now purchased for the colony, and on two of these were found timber as well as sawmills, so that hereafter the colony had ample supply of lumber. Nor was the farming interest neglected. Three hundred and fifty acres of prairie land was broken the first year, of which part was sowed with flax, and the remainder with wheat. In the native province of a majority of these people the cultivation of flax and the manufacture of linen is one of the leading industries, and soon became of the same importance to the colonists in their new home.

In the summer of 1847 the colony received an addition of four hundred adult emigrants, besides children. To provide shelter for these became of prime necessity, and several more dug-outs were built. But the consequences of living in the unhealthy, ill-ventilated dwellings, showed themselves soon. Sickness set in, mostly chills and fevers, and many fell victims to these diseases. But better buildings were, after some time, provided—first small frame tenements and houses of sun-dried brick, and later, large and substantial brick houses. In the summer of 1849 a party of Norwegians, on their way to join the colony, was attacked by cholera between Chicago and Bishopshill, and brought with them the disease, to which one hundred and forty-three fell victims, among them Eric Janson's wife and children. The following year another party of Jansonites, numbering one hundred and fifty, was assailed by the same fell destroyer, on a steamer between Buffalo and Milwaukee, and hardly one-half of the number reached their destination. But while the number of colonists was thus increased by accessions from the old country, their ranks were constantly diminished by the influence of Jonas Hedstrom, a Swede, and zealous Methodist missionary, who persuaded between two and three hundred of the Jansonites to leave the colony and join his communion.

We have above alluded to the cultivation of flax and the manufacture of linen by the colonists. The weaving was the exclusive work of the women, who devoted themselves to the work with the most untiring energy, as evidenced by the fact that during a period of ten years, from 1847 to 1857, 130,309 yards of linen and 22,569 mats, besides what was used for home consumption, were disposed of at highly remunerative prices, the manufacture finding a ready sale in the surrounding country. After the last named period the manufacture was discontinued, except for their own use, on account of competition from the eastern states.

Another and still more important industry was the cultivation and adaption for sale of broom-corn, which has proved one of the greatest sources of income for the people of Bishopshill.

Even to this peaceful and religious community did the California gold fever penetrate. Their old fundamental principle, "Godliness with a content mind is winning enough," had given way for a desire to make money, and in the spring of 1850 an expedition consisting of nine men, with necessary outfit, was sent to dig gold in California. After many hardships the party reached the gold-land, but all, except one who died and another who remained on the Pacific coast, returned the year following, the trip merely paying expenses.

In the fall of 1848 there arrived at Bishopshill a man who called himself Root, although many suspected that this was an assumed name. He was a man of education and good address, but a base adventurer and desperado withal. Having gained the good will of the community, he applied to be received as a member of the society, which was granted. Later on he married a young woman of the colony, a cousin of Eric Janson, the express ante-nuptial agreement being, that if Root ever wanted to discontinue his connection with the society, he should also part with his wife and the latter be allowed to remain at Bishopshill. Dissatisfaction with the new member soon was apparent. In this industrious hive he was a drone, and spent his time either in hunting or absenting himself from the colony at short intervals. On his return from one of these trips he found that his wife had presented him with a son. He wished now to take her away from Bishopshill, which was resisted. Thwarted in an attempt of forcible abduction, and after twice without success attacking the colony at the head of a mob, he finally sued Eric Janson for the possession of his wife. One day, while the litigation was going on, at the May term, 1850, of the court in Cambridge, while all had left the court-room for dinner except Eric Janson, Root entered, and calling Janson by name, shot him dead. The murderer was arrested, and he was sentenced to three years in the penitentiary. Having served out his term he went to Chicago, where he soon after died in great misery.

The gloom which the death of Eric Janson had thrown over the colony did not slacken its industry. The material progress hastened forward with large strides. The annual earnings were considerable. Large tracts of land were purchased, but the colony not being incorporated, such lands must be bought in the name of some member, which, in case of death of the nominal purchaser, often caused great trouble at the probate court. In the meantime everything remained without any legal organization. The same men who had been nominated as leaders by Eric Janson upon leaving Sweden, still had charge of all the affairs of the colony, and administered the same according to their own sweet will. It had, however, always been considered only a temporary arrangement, which in time must be supplanted by something permanent.

In the year 1853 the colony was incorporated under a charter of the legislature of Illinois. By its provisions the management of all the temporal affairs of the colony was vested in seven trustees, who were to retain their offices for life, or on good behavior. It seems the community, whose interests were at stake, was never consulted or even given an opportunity to express a wish in regard to the choice of these trustees. As a matter of course the same persons who had in their keeping all the resources of the colony ever since they left Sweden, had their names put in the charter to fill these responsible positions. They were: Jonas Olson, Olof Johnson, Jonas Erickson, Jacob Jacobson, Swan Swanson, Peter Johnson, and Jonas Kronberg. Of these five were from the parish of Söderala, and related; and the rest of the parishes from Sweden were represented by the other two trustees. Nobody at the time seemed to understand the danger of this charter. At least nobody protested. The men had hitherto enjoyed unlimited confidence, why not hereafter? Besides, the spiritual interests were paramount in the hearts and minds of the colonists. Temporal matters were of subordinate importance to the religious idea which was the foundation of the colony, and kept its members together.

We had occasion this year to visit the colony, and were received with the greatest kindness and hospitality. Everything, seemingly, was on the top of prosperity. The people lived in large, substantial brick houses. We had never before seen so large a farm, nor one so well cultivated. One of the trustees took us to an adjacent hill, from which we had in view the colony's cultivated fields, stretching away for miles. In one place we noticed fifty young men with the same number of horses and plows cultivating a cornfield, where every furrow was two miles in length. They moved with the regularity of soldiers. In another part was a field of a thousand acres in broom corn, the product of which, when baled, was to be delivered to Boston parties at Peoria, and was supposed to yield an income of fifty thousand dollars. All their live stock was exceptionally fine, and apparently given the best care. There was a stable of more than one hundred horses, the equals of which would be hard to find. One evening I was brought to an inclosure on the prairie, where the cows were milked. There must have been at least two hundred of them, and the milkmaids numbered forty or fifty. There was a large wagon, in which an immense tub was suspended on four posts, and in this each girl, ascending to the top by a stepladder, emptied her pail. The whole process was over in half an hour. On Sunday I attended service. There was singing and prayer, and the sermon, by one of the leaders, contained nothing that a member of any Christian denomination might not hear in his own church. Altogether, I retain the most agreeable remembrance of this visit.

It would be pleasant to stop here, for the rest of this little sketch is a mournful tale, and I shall pass through it as quickly as possible.

The first account of the affairs of the colony was given by the trustees in the year 1855. According to the same the real and personal property amounted to about $500,000, and the debts to $18,000. Now the trustees, having under their absolute control all the resources of the colony, gave themselves up to speculation. They made the new town of Galva, a station on the Chicago, Burlington and Quincy Railroad, near Bishopshill, the principal place of their operations. Here they built a large warehouse and also opened a store of general merchandise. They dealt in grain and lumber, speculated in railroad and bank stock, and carried on a large pork-packing house. On all these different undertakings, it is asserted, they lost heavily; on the pork-packing alone about $60,000. Thus the resources accumulated by the hard labor of the colonists were squandered in a short time.

The next report of the trustees, delivered in 1860, showed assets to the amount of $846,277, from which must be deducted debts of $75,645, leaving a balance of $770,-632 This statement was not satisfactory to the colonists, and the accounts being given in the hands of a special Master in Chancery, he discovered a further liability of $42,-759.33, which the trustees tried to conceal. This discovery, of course, made the colonists lose confidence in their trustees.

Added to this came religious dissensions. A party of Shakers from Pleasant Hill, Kentucky, had gained entrance in the colony and found not a few adherents to their peculiar doctrines. Marital relations were interfered with, the young people were forbidden to enter matrimony, families were sundered, the whole colony was broken up in warring factions, and of the strong religious feeling that kept them together in the days of Eric Janson, hardly a vestige was left. Dissolution was inevitable and was at hand. It took place on February 14, 1860, and was still further perfected in 1861. Property to the value of $592,793 was divided among 415 shareholders. The remainder of the property, according to the statement of 1860, amounting to $248,861, was put in the hands of the old trustees to pay the accrued debt of $118,403.33, and five years time given them to effect the liquidation; but it being soon apparent that the sum thus put aside for paying the debt was not sufficient, on account of a number of worthless items, a further amount of $52,-762 was delivered to the trustees by the colonists. At the expiration of five years the trustees informed the people that $100,000 were still needed to pay the debt, and actually collected in cash $56,163.71. Time rolled on. The trustees never gave any statement about payment of the debt, but instead of this, in the beginning of the year 1868, came notice that a still larger amount was required to settle the obligations of the colony. This brought matters to a crisis. Forbearance ceased to be a virtue. The unfortunate colonists appointed a committee to wait upon the trustees and demand an account, and the latter flatly refused anything of the kind, litigation commenced, which lasted five years,

when a verdict was given by which the colonists were made
to pay $57,782.90, of which amount $46,290 were expenses
for the suit and lawyers' fees. Besides this the colonists dur
ing the litigation assumed responsibility for the whole of the
old colony debt with interest amounting to $158,000 minus
the amounts paid in between the years 1860-1868. Thus, to
pay a debt in 1860 of $118,403.33, these ill-fated people
have actually expended in cash $413,124.61, and in prop-
erty $259,786, or in the aggregate $672,910.61. This seems
absurd and incredible, but the above are all official
figures.

Finally, it may be remarked that the majority of those
now dwelling in this at the outset so ultra-religious colony,
do not belong to any church organization. That they are
utterly indifferent to theological dogmas is hardly to be wondered at when we remember the chaos in this respect prevailing and the number of schools they have passed through
without finding anything tenable. But from this we must
not conclude that the moral standard is low. It may, on
the contrary, truly be said that the general morality is nowhere better, and that the population in and around Bishopshill is distinguished for honesty, strict sobriety, peaceful-
ness, and enduring industry.

This article, published in "Scandinavia" in 1885, was carefully revised, especially
in regard to facts, by Skordalsvold and myself in 1899. We found it was largely based
upon, often being a literal translation of, a chapter of "Svenskarne i Illinois," by Johnson and Peterson. The same is true of M A. Mikkelsen's history, issued in 1892. In the
latter work it is asserted that the majority of the Jansonists became Methodists; that
the shops, mills, and factories in the town are empty; that everything presents the
appearance of a deserted village, with only about 330 inhabitants. The third volume
will contain a biography of Eric Janson, and additional information on the colony.—
EDITOR.

The Fifteenth Wisconsin, or Scandinavian, Regiment.

— BY —

P. G. DIETRICHSON.

[Published in Scandinavia in 1884.]

Already from the very outbreak of our late civil war, a great many Scandinavians in the northwestern states entertained the idea of forming a volunteer regiment, and, as soon as the public appeal had been issued by the Governor of Wisconsin, Honorable Alexander W. Randall, our countryman, responded with hearty promptitude. The formation of this regiment, which became known as the Fifteenth Infantry of Wisconsin, was commenced at Camp Randall, Madison, in December, 1861. Its members were chiefly composed of the Scandinavian population of that state. The Honorable Hans Heg, formerly state-prison commissioner, was appointed colonel of the regiment, and, under his supervision, the organization was effected. He had previously been renominated as commissioner, but a desire to serve his country in the field led him to choose the duties of a soldier. The regiment roster was as follows:

(153)

HANS C. HEG, Colonel.

K. K. Jones, Lieut.-Colonel.   Charles M. Reese, Major.
Hans C. Borchsenius, Adj.   Ole Heg, Quartermaster.
Stephen O. Himoe, Surgeon.   S. I. Hansen, 1st Assist. Surgeon.
G. F. Newell, 2d Assist. Surgeon.   C. L. Clausen, Army Chaplain.

CAPTAINS.   FIRST LIEUTENANTS.

Company A—Andrew Thorkildson.   Company A—Emanuel Engelstad.
    "   B—Ole C. Johnson.   "   B—Joseph Mathiesen.
    "   C—Frederik R. Berg.   "   C—Hans Hansen.
    "   D—Charles Campbell.   "   D—Albert Skofstad.
    "   E—John Ingmundson.   "   E—William Tjentland.
    "   F—Charles Gustavson.   "   F—Thor Simonson.
    "   G—John A. Gordon.   "   G—Henry Hauff.
    "   H—Knud J. Sime.   "   H—Andrew A. Brown.
    "   I—August Gasman.   "   I—Reynard Cook.
    "   K—Mons Grinager.   "   K—Ole Peterson.

SECOND LIEUTENANTS.

Company A—Oliver Thompson.   Company F—Svend Samuelson.
    "   B—George Wilson.   "   G—Will. A. Montgomery.
    "   C—John T. Rice.   "   H—John L. Johnson.
    "   D—Christian E. Tandberg.   "   I—Martin Russell.
    "   E—John M. Johnson.   "   K—Olaus Solberg.

On the 2d of March, 1862, the regiment left Madison
amid the cheers of the people, having been escorted to the
depot by the Sixteenth Regiment, Colonel Allen, who gave
them their good wishes and an earnest farewell with the
voice of a booming cannon.   The Fifteenth had nearly nine
hundred men, a few of them Americans, while some of the
Norwegians had been in America less than a year.

The material of the regiment looked hardy and active,
and some of its number had served in foreign armies.   On
their route to Chicago, they encountered a snow-storm, and,
at one point, were obliged to shovel their way through it,

but, at their arrival in Chicago, they were cordially met by the Scandinavian society, Nora Lodge, and by them presented with a flag, having, on one side, the American colors, and on the reverse, the American and Norwegian arms united, the Norwegian being the picture of a lion with an axe, on a red field.   The committee that made the presentation consisted of Messrs. S. T. Gunderson, G. Roberg, A. Anderson, A. Loberg, and C. Dietrichson.   From Chicago they proceeded to St. Louis, where they were ordered to Bird's Point, Mo., opposite Cairo, and at that place they disembarked for the purpose of going into encampment.   However, the regiment did not engage in any action of importance until they joined an expedition of fifteen hundred men to Union City, Tenn., where a force of rebels were to be captured.   They left Hickman, Kentucky, on the 11th of June, in the afternoon, and went to within four miles of Union City, where they camped for the night.   The march was very rapid.   Everybody was arrested on the road who was likely to advertise their approach.   The next morning, shortly before seven, the first shots of the pickets were heard, and soon after our forces opened on the rebels, who fired their camp and fled, leaving swords, pistols, and much clothing behind them.   Among other trophies taken was a secession flag, captured by Company G, on which was inscribed: "Hill's Cavalry; Victory or Death," from which it would be legitimately inferred that the whole regiment was killed, since that was the only alternative of victory.

Thence the regiment moved to join Davis' division, and entered Florence, Alabama, on the 26th of August.   But, already on the twenty-eighth they joined in the march to

Nashville, to intercept General Bragg in his raid into Kentucky, and his threatened invasion across the Ohio. Beyond Nashville they proceeded with Buell's army through Bowling Green and Murfordsville, reaching Louisville late in September, wearied, worn, ragged, and hungry, on account of their long and trying march, during a part of which they had subsisted on half-rations, and suffered greatly for want of water.

In common with the Union army, they moved next to Chaplin Hills, near Perryville, and of their part in that battle a brief relation will be in order. The Fifteenth Wisconsin, of General Gilbert's corps, formed in line of battle in the woods, at some distance from the severest fighting. One company was sent forward as skirmishers, and was soon engaged with the enemy in force. The brigade, which was commanded by Colonel Carlin, supported Sheridan's division. They had scarcely emerged from the woods before the rebels begin a retreat to the protection of their artillery. The surface of the country being broken, some shelter was afforded to the brigade, and, by passing exposed positions with rapidity, it suffered but little loss. This advanced regiment continued to press the enemy, who were constantly retreating, and planted their batteries where they found it convenient. After the advance had been made in this manner for about a mile, a brief halt was ordered, but, upon ascertaining that the rebels were yet in retreat, the Union soldiers again rallied and pursued them. Another halt was ordered within a quarter of a mile of the village, and the men lay down behind a small elevation of ground. The rebels kept up their fire upon them with canister and shell, while the Union troops replied with their rear artillery, which threw shell over the heads of their advanced troops into the line of the enemy. At length, after a running fire of about two hours, the brigade was ordered to retire. In accomplishing this they captured thirteen wagons loaded with amunition, and succeeded in bringing with them over one hundred prisoners. The battle continued until darkness closed the scene, being extremely fierce in the latter part of the afternoon. But, as daylight passed away, our flag was triumphant, our troops occupying the ground held by the enemy in the morning, with his right wing turned. The destruction of life had been apalling. The woods, cornfields, and open spaces were, in many places, strewn with the slain. The remaining soldiers slept on their arms, with their dead comrades around them, and the next morning only the rear gaurd of the enemy was within reach of our guns.

The Fifteenth Regiment was next employed at Crab Orchard, as a provost guard, for a week, and thence proceeded to Edgefield Junction, where, in November, they joined an expedition, commanded by Lieutenant McKee, fifty miles down the Cumberland river, in search of Morgan's guerrillas. They returned, after five days, with half a hundred prisoners, many horses, mules, and wagons, having destroyed guerrilla premises, a distillery, whiskey, salt, and grain. General McCook complimented them in high terms on their success. The regiment moved then to Nashville, where they were occupied with skirmishing and guarding forage trains until December 25th.

On Christmas eve, 1862, the decision was made to advance the next day. At dawn the troops broke up camp,

and poured along the highways with shouts of joy, the great
mass little thinking how many of them, or who, were soon
to fall in battle.   McCook's three divisions advanced on the
Nolinsville pike, meeting the enemy's artillery and cavalry,
skirmishing all the way, and closing the day with a sharp
fight. The Fifteenth Wisconsin was in this force, and gradually drove the rebels to a strong and nearly impregnable
gorge in a mountain (Knob Gap), which they had fortified
by a force of dismounted cavalry and eight pieces of artillery.
The order was given to Colonel Carlin to capture that battery.   He commissioned Lieutenant-Colonel McKee, of the
Fifteenth regiment, to undertake the desperate task. Accordingly, Colonel McKee led the brigade line of skirmishers.
They approached to the very mouths of the artillery, which
opened upon them with shot and shell.   But these intrepid
men steadily advanced, followed by the brigade, which soon
poured in a tremendous fire, which caused the rebels to yield,
leaving one brass six-pounder behind, marked "Shiloh,"
they having captured it in that battle.   In this charge Colonel Heg was conspicuous in his gallant attempt to reach
the before-mentioned cannon; and he took possession of it
in the name of the Fifteenth Wisconsin.   On the morning of
the 30th, the regiment was formed in line-of-battle, made a
cautious advance, and Company E, under Captain Ingmundson, was sent out to skirmish, and encountered the enemy
about noon.   The regiment was soon ordered to support the
skirmishers, and in the engagement Captain Ingmundson
was slain.   Colonel Heg retreated slowly, and his men, taking refuge behind a fence, held the position until dark, and
rested upon their arms during the night, in the severe cold,

without fire. On the next morning, at four o'clock, the regiment was in line-of-battle. They first supported a battery,
and then took a position from which they at length were
forced to retire, the rebels advancing upon the Fifteenth in
solid columns. At this point, Colonel McKee and some others
were killed, and several wounded. Colonel Heg then withdrew his men to avoid an overwhelming force of the enemy.
Again he posted his troops behind a fence, within four or five
hundred yards of the Murfreesboro' pike, and poured some
destructive volleys into the rebels. Still they were too many
for him to withstand, and he crossed the turnpike, rallied his
men, and remained there the rest of the day. The losses on
the 30th and 31st of December were: Killed, fifteen;
wounded, seventy; missing, thirty-four; total, one hundred
and nineteen men. The report of Brigadier General Carlin
testified to the great bravery, both of privates and officers,
in these engagements. The Scandinavian blood was thoroughly tested, and found to be inferior to none in point of
courage and endurance.

After the Stone River battle the regiment partook of the
suffering of Rosecrans' army for want of clothing, provisions, and tents. January 31, 1863, they went on a scouting
expedition against Wheeler's and Forrest's forces, tarried a
few days at Franklin, and returned. Other expeditions and
outpost and picket duties engaged them until the movement
of Rosecrans' army, June 24th, toward Chattanooga. In
August they crossed the Cumberland mountains, and en-
camped at Stevenson, Alabama. Their brigade laid the pon-
toons across Tennessee river, and they were the first to pass
over. They crossed Sand and Lookout mountains, and

joined the main part of the army, near Chicamauga creek,
on the 18th of September. The next morning, at eight
o'clock, they were in motion, and soon after noon hurried
forward at a double-quick into line-of-battle, to fill a gap
through which the rebles were striving to pass and cut our
army in two. Colonel Heg's brigade was formed in two lines,
the Fifteenth Wisconsin and Eighth Kansas in front, the
former having the right. They were at once pushed forward
through dense underbrush, and had not advanced more than
fifty yards when they met and drove the rebel skirmishers.
Still advancing, they encountered a heavy fire from the
enemy's main line. After a severe fight, the Eighth Kansas
wavered and left the Fifteenth unsupported, which was soon
compelled to fall back also, bearing with them most of their
wounded. Captain Johnson, of Company A, was killed in
this action. An Illinois regiment was now sent forward, with
the Fifteenth for its support. After a short but hard struggle, the Illinois regiment was forced back, and retreated over
the Fifteenth, which was lying down. The regiment now
became hotly engaged. The troops in line of their rear, supposing that the regiment which had fallen back was the last
of the Federals in front, opened fire upon the Fifteenth.
Thus, placed between the fire of friends and foes, there was
no alternative except to break up the regiment and escape as
they best might manage. The enemy now attacked and
routed the rear line, continuing the pursuit across a field,
where the Federals rallied, reformed, and checked the elated
foe. The regiment was, however, not organized again that
day, but the men in detachments joined other commands
near them and remained on the field. At night, Lieutenant-

Colonel Johnson collected his scattered men. Throughout the day Colonel Heg was intensely active in encouraging his brigade, and himself set an example of noble valor. Unfortunately he was wounded by a shot in the bowels, near the close of the day, and died in the field hospital during the night. In his report, General McCook mentions with special honor the name of this fallen hero.

The regiment was called up next morning at three o'clock, and placed in a commanding position on the Chattanooga road, to the right, and in reserve. At ten o'clock in the morning the battle commenced with terrible fury. The brigade, now commanded by Colonel Martin, was ordered to fill the gap made by the withdrawal of General Wood. Hardly had they got into line before they were hotly attacked. The men, protected by rude defenses of logs and rails, twice repulsed the rebels, with great slaughter, after which, both flanks being turned, they still held out, hoping for reinforcements, until nearly surrounded, when they broke and attempted to save themselves. They were the last to leave their position. Many were captured, including Lieutenant-Colonel Johnson. All efforts to rally the men near the Chattanooga road proving fruitless, the retreat was continued a mile, when a tenable position was reached, and the scattered men of the regiments were gathered and consolidated into one force. They held a position here until five o'clock in the afternoon, when they were ordered five miles further to the rear, where they bivouacked for the night, and the fragments of their regiment were brought together. Captain Johnson, of Company A, and Captain Hauff, of Company E, were killed. Major Wilson and Captain Gasman had received some severe wounds.

Captain Hansen, of Company C, and Second Lieutenant C. E. Tandberg, of Company D, were both fatally wounded.

The Fifteenth Regiment subsequently engaged on the fortifications at Chattanooga; a part escorted a supply train to Stevenson, the rest cut and rafted timber for pontoon bridges, and, all united, moved out of Fort Wood, at Chattanooga, under command of Captain Gordon, on the 25th of November, to engage in the assault on Missionary Ridge. On the same morning, Hooker set out for Lookout Mountain toward Rossville, driving the enemy before him down its eastern declivity, and across the valley toward the ascent of Missionary Ridge at our right. He was detained three hours by building a bridge across the Chattanooga creek, but at half-past three in the afternoon was approaching on the Rossville road. That approach was to be the sign for the other forces to move. At twenty minutes to four o'clock, six signal guns are fired, and the long-waiting, ardent troops leap forth first to carry the rifle-pits at the foot of Missionary Ridge. As they arrived at the base of the mountain, the rebel pickets swarm out of their pits in great amazement, and flee before them. As yet no command had been given to go beyond the base, but they stop not for orders. A few moments' delay is caused to re-form the line, and then they start up the ascent. Front and enfilading shots from musketry and fifty cannon are plunging down upon them. Some fall; the rest press dauntlessly on; they clamber up the side, leaping ditches, jumping logs, advancing in zigzag lines, rushing over all obstacles, dodging, if they can, the missiles of heavy stones thrown upon them by the rebels, and thrusting aside their bayonets, until they reach the top, beat back the enemy, and take the ridge.

The Fifteenth Wisconsin then proceeded to reinforce Burnside, at Knoxville, marching one hundred and ten miles with scanty rations.   From that place they made various short marches, and December 25th moved to Strawberry Plains, seventeen miles from Knoxville, and there aided in building a railroad bridge.   January 15th, 1864, at Dandridge, they were joined by a party of convalescents, who, on their route from Chattanooga, had just taken part in a severe engagement with Wheeler's cavalry at Charleston, Tennessee, routing the rebels, whose loss was ten killed and one hundred and sixty-seven wounded and prisoners.   In January they had orders to proceed on a veteran furlough to Wisconsin, but the threatening movements of the enemy forbade their going, and they still kept at duty in the field.   Early in April they moved southward to join the Army of the Cumberland, and, encamping at McDonald Station, Tennessee, made preparations for the spring campaign.   The first design was to reach Atlanta, one hundred and thirty-eight miles southwest of Chattanooga, one of the most important towns of Georgia, a large manufacturing place, where an immense amount of arms, amunition, and clothing for the rebel army was made. The route to Atlanta lay, in part, over a rough, mountainous country, but the charm of spring was then upon it, and the desolation of war had not yet come. On the 8th of May, Howard's corps (Fifteenth and Twenty-fourth Wisconsin Infantry) carried a ridge near Buzzard Roost, but found it too narrow for operation in order to carry the pass near it. The Rebel-General Johnson soon saw that if he remained in the entrenchment around Dalton, his communications would be cut off, and he therefore left his cherished position on May 12th, retreating on a short line to Resaca, which was eighteen miles farther toward Atlanta. On the morning of the 14th, the Federal spies set upon the enemy in their entrenchment at Resaca. During the battle two of the enemy's guns were silenced by the Fifteenth Wisconsin, and a desperate charge made by the rebels was repulsed with heavy loss to them. Five of the regiment were killed and twelve wounded. Yet our troops were making such inroads upon the enemy's works that, during the night of the 15th, they quietly evacuated Resaca, and retreated toward Kingston, thirty-two miles farther south, and thence to Dallas.

The cavalry division, under Sherman and McCook, pursued the enemy on their retreat from Resaca, and the whole army quickly followed, crossing the Ostanula river. The roads were very rough, the marching careful and slow. Johnston, meanwhile, took a shorter route, and, with the larger part of his army, reached Dallas first. The Fifteenth became engaged in the heavy skirmishing and fighting on the 27th, and, as they were crossing a ravine, exposed themselves to a heavy fire from the enemy's artillery. They made a desperate charge, and came so near the rebel breast-works that some were killed within a few feet of them. They found it impossible to dislodge the enemy, but succeeded in establishing our line within fifteen yards of their fortifications. They held this position for more than five hours, although exposed to a severe fire of musketry. The enemy, having been reinforced, charged upon their weakened ranks, until at length they were forced to retire, leaving the dead and wounded on the field. On the next day, May 28th, the Federals, having thrown up defenses four miles from Dallas, were attacked by the enemy in force. Our men saw the attack as it was coming, and, throwing up some slight defenses, reserved their fire until the rebels were within sixty feet of them. The heavy shot of the enemy crushed through the Union ranks, but they firmly held their ground. At given signal, a thousand muskets sped their deadly bullets with unerring aim at the yelling, exulting foe, and volley after volley, in rapid succession, mowed down their deep and thick ranks. The Federal artillery joined their fire, and the ground occupied by the foe was soon strewn with the mangled, the dying and the dead. Once driven back, they rallied and rushed forward again; three times they came, three times they were repulsed, and then fled, leaving a great number of wounded and dead. This was the principal battle of Dallas.

On June 23d the Fifteenth Regiment was actively engaged in the assault upon the rebel position at Kenesaw mountain, where it suffered a loss of six killed and wounded. From this time to the 3d of July, when the enemy evacuated, it participated in advancing, skirmishing, and driving the enemy from line to line of their works on Pine, Lost and Kenesaw mountains. Afterward they pressed forward in pursuit of them toward the Chattahooche river, and captured a number of rebels. Again, and sadly, the rebels took up their retreat, leaving their perfected and expansive defenses on the Chatahooche, removing their heavy guns seven miles to Atlanta, and falling back with their main army toward the fortifications of that city. Then Sherman moved a part of his own forces across the river, took possession of the rebel works, and of certain important strategic points in that direction.

The Fifteenth was in reserve at the battle of Peach Tree Creek on July 20th, and marched then toward Atlanta, and joined in the siege. The regiment was engaged in picket and fatigue duties until August 25th, when they joined in the movement to the south of that city, and participated in the engagement at Jonesboro, returning to Atlanta the 9th of September. During the fall they were ordered to perform provost guard duty and various functions of a similar nature, until their final muster out, February, 1865, at Chattanooga.

The recruits and veterans of the regiment, seventy-two in number, were transferred to the Twenty-fourth, and subsequently to the Thirteenth Wisconsin.

Three hundred Scandinavian soldiers, or just one-third of the entire Fifteenth Regiment were killed on fields of battle or died in our army hospitals. Their names will be a roll of honor in all times to come!

As far as facts are concerned, this article was carefully revised by Skordalsvold and myself in 1899. In regard to other Scandinavian Civil War soldiers from Minnesota, Iowa, and Wisconsin, see pp. 303-4, Vol. I., and pp. 66-8 and 119-21, Vol. II. Soldiers from Illinois and some Eastern states will be referred to in the third volume.—EDITOR.

Historical Review of the Danish Evangelical Lutheran Church in America.

— BY —

REV. ADAM DAN.

The Danish Evangelical Lutheran Church in America is an independent organization, and not connected with any of the Scandinavian, German, or American synods in this country. The church has its own government and constitution; but as many of her ministers have received their education in Denmark, and have been assisted financially, by an annual sum appropriated by the Danish Parliament, as well as by private contributions of some church people at home, the Danish-American Lutheran Church considers herself as a branch of the Church of Denmark, and is so considered by her. And in the interest of our church in this country a committee exists in Denmark called *Udvalget*, consisting mostly of theological professors from the Royal University of Denmark, and clergymen of high rank. But no laws are dictated to us from abroad, the mother church has never made any attempt of ruling in purely local matters; yet it has always been our practice to regard *Udvalget* as the highest au-

thority from which we look for a decision in all matters of
controversy, in fact the authority of *Udvalget* is recognized
by our church constitution. Consequently the church government of the Danish-American Lutheran Church is neither
episcopal nor synodical.

The first beginning of our church in this country was
made in 1871. Many Danish-Americans had previously sent
letters home wherein they had stated their longing after
church services in the mother tongue, which at that time
could not be satisfied, as there existed no Danish Lutheran
church in this country.* Norwegian ministers tried to meet
the religious wants of the Danes, but only a few could be
reached by them, and the Norwegian clergymen joined the
Danes in sending a "Macedonian cry" to the mother church
at home. This gave the impulse to the formation of *Udvalget*
in 1869, with the purpose of helping the Danes in this
country to secure ministers. In 1871 one clergyman and
two laymen were sent to the United States. The clergyman
visited and held meetings in many Danish settlements, and
investigated other matters in regard to the Danes in this
country, then returned to his native land.

One of the laymen, A. S. Nielsen, was ordained shortly
after and became pastor at Cedar Falls, Iowa, then preached
in Chicago for fourteen years. The other layman, R. Andersen, became a student at Augsburg Seminary, was ordained
in 1872, and has for many years been pastor and missionary
among the emigrants and seamen in New York and Brooklyn. In 1871 both Rev. N. Thomsen and the writer of this
article arrived and took charge of Danish Lutheran congregations in Indianapolis, Ind., and Racine, Wis., respectively.

---

*Apparently, two or three purely Danish Lutheran congregations existed before
1871. For example, Rev. M. F. Wiese, a Dane, organized one at Indianapolis, Ind., in
connection with the Norwegian Synod, April 17, 1868.—EDITOR.

Both these men had been missionaries, the former in East India and the latter in Jerusalem, in the Holy Land. The above named four persons were the first clergymen of the Danish Lutheran Church in this country.

In 1872 the Danish ministers, together with some laymen, organized the Church Mission Society, at Neenah, Wis., and at the same time commenced the publication of *Kirkelig Samler*, which has ever since been the official organ of the church. In 1874 the society changed its name to The Danish Evangelical Lutheran Church in America, effected a stronger organization, and adopted a constitution.

At first the work was missionary in its nature, and the ministers often had to make long and troublesome journeys on foot or on horseback, in order to reach the scattered Danish settlements. In latter years the clergymen have had more regular charges.

In 1880 the church became the owner of a school, patterned after the Danish high schools, which had been founded at Elk Horn, Iowa, two years before; but in 1887 the whole plan of the institution was changed, and we lost control of it in 1890. Two or three smaller schools are controlled by members of our church. For some years we had a theological seminary at West Denmark, Wis., but in 1896 we established a theological seminary and college combined in Des Moines, Ia., at a cost of about $20,000. We have also an orphans' asylum in Chicago, where many poor children are cared for and educated.

During the twenty-nine years of church life of our church there have been many controversies of different nature. The first and one of the most important disputes arose about 1872, between the Church Mission Society and the Norwe-

gian-Danish Evangelical Lutheran Conference, together with
other Norwegian Lutheran church organizations, in regard
to some local church property, but more especially in regard
to theological questions. The property question was settled
by the judicial courts in Racine, Wis. But the teaching of
Grundtvigianism, the doctrine held by the renowned Danish
bishop and poet, N. F. S. Grundtvig, permitting, among
other things, a more liberal interpretation of the Bible—as advocated especially by the writer of this article—has never died
out.* For in late years the same question has been agitated
in our church and has called forth many articles in the papers
and hot words at the aunual meetings. Today there are two
factions among us, the followers of Bishop Grundtvig, and
the so-called *Mission People;* both are recognized by the
Church of Denmark as belonging to the Lutheran church,
and they are about equal in strength.‡

Our church as a body is small, having only in 1900 about
50 ministers, 80 congregations, and 8,000 communicant
members, more than half of whom are to be found in the
states of Iowa, Illinois, Wisconsin, and Minnesota. Yet
we have organizations in all the central Northwestern as
well as some of the Eastern and Western states. The value
of the church property amounts to about $250,000. We
have a mission among the Mormons in Utah, where a great
number of Danes have settled and believe that faith. We in
this country do not have any mission of our own among the
heathens, but we contribute annually a fair sum to the dif-

---

* It should be observed that the well-known Rev. C. L. Clausen, also a Dane, who
for many years was one of the most prominent Lutheran clergymen among the
early Danish-Norwegian settlers in this country, leaned also, at least at first, towards *Grundtvigianism*.— EDITOR.

‡The controversy and separation of the two parties are discussed in Vol. II., pp. 52-5.
The statistics on this page are brought up to date by myself, and the last half of page
169 has been rewritten for this edition.—EDITOR.

ferent Danish missions in East India and among the Jews in the Holy Land.

Every congregation has a Sunday school.   Some congregations support permanent teachers who every day give religious and secular instruction, both in Danish and English, to the children.   In other places Danish students teach during the summer vacation, and in some instances the clergymen keep school every Saturday the whole year round.

The church has successfully tried to establish Danish colonies or settlements in Shelby county, Iowa; in Lincoln county, Minn.; in Clark county, Wis.; and in the southern part of Texas.

Historical Review of Hauge's Evangelical Lutheran Synod in America.

—BY—

PROF. G. O. BROHOUGH.

Every effect has its cause. When the church had the most temporal power, the distinctive Christian doctrines were the most neglected. This seeming paradox becomes clear when we remember that Christ's kingdom, though *in* the world, is not *of* the world. Religion is an individual relation and cannot be forced into existence by the mandate of a temporal ruler. During the Dark Ages church life had sunk to its lowest ebb. Bishops robbed, priests swore, the Bible was replaced by the "Picture-book," and prayers were mumbled in a foreign tongue. The lethargic soul could not lift its drowsy gaze beyond the symbol. But the onward sweep of the glad tidings was not to be stopped, only retarded. "Truth crushed to earth shall rise again." The great movements of the crusades had given an opportunity to compare, and comparison educates. The people had become conscious of their own strength and the scarecrows of the tyrants had become exposed. Scholasticism, which for centuries had

(173)

skirted the ocean of free thought, breaking every wave of advancing opinion, was rapidly giving way. There was seeming uniformity and peace, but not the quiet that results from the equipoise of the elements. It was the calm that pre-cedes the storm. The ship of progress simply drifted. The ominous storm-swallow circled about the mast-head. The sky was overcast by portentious clouds, and the dark but quiet sea gave indications of an approaching storm. Tide after tide came rolling shoreward, until finally, at the close of the fifteenth century, the crashing wave of the Reforma-tion burst with a terrifying roar against the timeworn in-stitutions, tumbling them out of the way. This cleared the close and stifling atmosphere. As the dead-weight of igno-rance and superstition was lifted, the human mind expanded. Thought advanced and colossal figures came upon the stage to give direction to that thought.

The Reformation gave to the world an open Bible. The effect was wonderful. When that Bible was again in danger of being closed, Gustavus Adolphus, "the greatest Teuton of them all," on the plains of Lützen, sealed with his own blood the religious liberties of Teutonic Europe.

The pendulum of progress swings from one extreme to another. During the Middle Ages, the "Age of Faith," an appeal lay to authority only. At the close of the eighteenth century, reason and experience were considered supreme arbiters. This tendency is called *rationalism*. The term was first used by Kant. "Rationalism is that tendency in modern thought which claims for the unaided human reason the right of deciding in matters of faith. It asserts the prerogative of the intellect to be supreme arbiter in all departments of revealed truth.   It requires certainty as the condition of its favor, and, with Wolf, promptly rejects what does not come before it with all the exactness and clearness of a mathematical demonstration."   The sources of rationalism were various, embracing different countries as well as different departments of investigation.   The pantheism of Spinoza was a welcome substitute for the heartless doctrine by which God was excluded from his own creation.   The deism of England was industriously propagated in Germany, where the works of Herbert, Hobbes, Tyndal, and Woolston were circulated among the people.   In France the influence of Voltaire and the encyclopedists was unbounded.   It was not till the latter half of the last century that a reaction set in, heralded by such men as Jacobi and Schleiermacher.

Rationalism, like a huge billow, had swept over the whole of Christendom attacking everything that impeded its progress, leaving moral slime and desolation in its wake.   It even dashed up against the rock-ribbed shores of old Norway, lashing its filthy scum far into her peaceful valleys. The clergy of Norway enjoy the reputation of being hospitable and intelligent; but at this juncture they seem to have partaken of the " deep sleep " that had fallen on the Christian church.   Rationalism was rampant at the University and thence spread to the country districts.   On Christmas morning, the worthy pastor took occasion to inform his flock on improved methods of constructing stables and mangers.   In expounding the text about the " sower and seed " new or improved methods for tilling the soil came in for consideration. This was excellent information, no doubt, but it was not the Gospel of Christ, which he was commissioned to preach.

As the last century drew to its close, a peasant lad, Hans Nilsen Hauge (pronounced Howgey) appeared on the scene. Being thoroughly aroused and converted at an early age, he felt impelled to preach the Gospel to his kinsmen and neighbors. For a layman to preach was not only unusual, but *unlawful*. He was warned—he wavered. Being of a modest and retiring disposition, he seriously doubted his own fitness. His conscience, however, would give him no peace, and soon his fearless and persuasive testimony had been heard in every hamlet and valley in the country. Persecutions followed thick and fast. Meetings were broken up, the worshipers were rudely dispersed, and Hauge himself was dragged into prison. Ten times was he incarcerated; he literally rotted in a common jail. All this for no other crime than admonishing his countrymen to lead a Christian life according to the teachings of the established church, and assisting his followers to gain a livelihood by developing the resources of the country. In our age of toleration, we are astonished that such a man should be persecuted. And yet, humanity has always been prone to abuse its benefactors. Every age has starved its Homer, poisoned its Socrates, banished its Aristides, stoned its Stephen, burned its Savanorola, or imprisoned its Galileo. The imprisonment of Hauge did not have the desired effect. The spark soon kindled into flame. Other laymen arose to continue the work and a mighty impulse, that no human power could check, swept over the land. This persecuting attitude of the church toward the revival movement created a wide cleft between the state clergy and the more zealous Christian element of the laity. The difficulty was augmented by the fact that

many of the clergy held the tenets of Grundtvig, a Danish
divine of considerable influence, who differed from the established faith in many points.   This naturally created distrust,
as the laity were sticklers for pure doctrine as well as for
holy living.

It should be stated, however, that in spite of these diffi
culties Hauge and his friends never entertained the idea of
leaving the state church.   They did not desire to form a new
and separate church organization.   All they wished was a
spiritual revival—the introduction of spiritual life into the
dead forms.   Consequently, in Norway, they all worship and
commune in the same church.   The revival movement, on the
other hand, has had a salutary influence on the state church
and the chief professors of theology at the University of
Norway have of late been the friends and allies of the
movement.

In 1839, Elling Eielsen, a lay preacher and a staunch
supporter of Hauge, came to the United States and settled
in the Fox River settlement, Ill.   In Chicago, then but a
traders' post, he preached his first sermon on American soil.
The first Norwegian Lutheran "meeting house" was erected
under his care at Fox River, shortly after his arrival in this
country.   Eielsen was an energetic man and a zealous
preacher.   The burden of his discourse was, "Repent and
believe."   Soon he had visited all the places in the Northwest
where his countrymen had settled.   As an itinerant he suffered untold hardships, but his zeal never flagged.   As an
evangelist, he was emminently successful; and had he possessed the talent for organizing that he had for preaching,
the future church historian might have had a different story

13

to tell. As an organizer he was sorely deficient. The people, however, soon began to feel the need of a formal organization. His friends at Fox River, therefore, requested
Eielsen to "seek holy orders." Accordingly, Eielsen repaired
to Chicago and was ordained, Oct. 3, 1843, by Rev. F. A.
Hoffman, D. D., pastor of a German Lutheran congregation
at Duncan's Grove, 20 miles north of Chicago.*

The ordination of Eielsen satisfied a long felt want of a
clergyman, and, save Eielsen's uncompromising warfare
against sin, peace and order reigned throughout the congregations. This condition of affairs, however, was not long to
continue. Soon after Eielsen's ordination, Rev. J. W. C.
Diedrichsen, ordained in Norway, and C. L. Clausen, a Dane,
and ordained by Rev. L. Krause in this country, appeared on
the field and commenced preaching among the Norwegian
and Danish settlers. Both of these men leaned, more or
less avowedly, toward the teachings of Grundtvig,† Clausen,
however, renouncing these tenets in later years. Diedrichsen,
in a patronizing way, offered to "affirm" Eielsen's ordination. This was rejected as an imposition.‡ Eielsen and his
followers did not seem to trust the late comer who appeared
in the insignia of state church, vaunting its authority. Eielsen soon regarded Diedrichsen as a rationalist and the latter retorted by accusing Eielsen of fanaticism. As to the
truth of these mutual accusations, future historians will
have to judge. It seems plain, however, that the two op-

---

* See copy of credentials of ordination at Chicago, Cook county, Ill., under date
of October 3, 1843.

† See *Wisconsinisme*, by H. A. Preus, p. 5, also *Syv Foredrag* by him : quoted
by O. I. Hattlestad in *Historiske Meddelelser*, p. 32.

‡ See *El. Eielsen's Liv.*, by Brohough and Eistensen, p. 65.

posing factions of Norway had been transplanted to American soil where the contest between true piety and stifling formalism was to be continued.   If this be true, it gives us a reasonable clue to the schism in the early Norwegian Lutheran church in America.

In 1846, on Jefferson Prairie, Wis., Rev. Elling Eielsen and his friends organized a society called The Evangelical Lutheran Church in America, adopting what has been called the "Old Constitution."   In 1875 this constitution was somewhat modified and the name changed to Hauge's Norwegian Evangelical Lutheran Synod in America.   But Eielsen and a few of his friends, being displeased with the new name and the new constitution, withdrew, continuing to labor in accordance with the "Old Constitution" and retained the old name of the organization.

The need of a school was soon felt, and in 1854 some property was bought at Lisbon, Ill., with a view of founding an institution of learning.   On account of disagreement among the leaders, however, the project was abandoned.   In 1865, another effort was made in the same line in Dane county, Wis., and cand. theol. Aaseröd was engaged as principal.   He did not seem to possess the sympathy of the people and the school failed for want of support.   In 1867 the Synod purchased three acres of land in Red Wing, Minn., and commenced breaking ground and procuring materials for a school building.   Meanwhile flattering offers were made by parties at Chicago, and operations were transfered to that place.   A feeble attempt was made at setting the machinery of the school in motion, but the wheels soon clogged and the Synod lost whatever means it had invested.   During all this

time the Synod had grown, and the increasing demand for
ministers and teachers made the want of a school more
keenly felt from year to year. In 1878, by the aid of H. M.
Sande, of Goodhue county, a handsome and convenient
school property was bought at Red Wing, Minn. It had
formerly been a first class boarding school, and owned by a
corporation. In the fall of 1879 Red Wing Seminary opened
its doors to students, and classes were organized both in the
collegiate and theological departments. During the school
year of 1898-9 there were seven instructors and about 150
students. Since the school opened, 180 young men have
graduated from the two departments. This is the only
school controlled, directly or indirectly, by the synod.

During its nearly 55 years of existence the Synod has
given freely to the cause of missions. A modest but steady
stream of contributions from its congregations and missionary societies has poured into the coffers of the Mission Society
of Norway to be distributed over a not insignificant missionary field. Of late a great interest has been aroused in
the missionary work in China. Several persons are already
in the field and are supported wholly, or in part, by contributions from the Synod. The home mission work has also
come in for a modest share of attention.

It is difficult to give accurate statistics as the officers
are remiss in sending in the required reports. The last
United States census has palpable errors. According to the
official report of 1899 there are about 100 ministers and professors in the Synod. It numbers nearly 230 congregations,
scattered over several of the states in the Union, but one-
third of the members reside in Minnesota. The Synod has,

THE OLD SWEDES' CHURCH, PHILADELPHIA.
BUILT 1700.

THE VIKING SHIP
EXHIBITED AT WORLD'S FAIR, CHICAGO, 1893.

PROF. R. B. ANDERSON, MADISON, WIS.

in 1900, in the neighborhood of 30,000 members; probably 18,000 of them are communicant members, the remaining being children not yet confirmed. The total value of the church property amounts to about $600,000.

Budbaereren is the official paper of the Synod; a children's paper is also published.

Sunday schools are maintained in nearly every congregation and three or four months parochial school is usually taught during the summer season.

Of late the aspect of the Synod has somewhat changed. Many peculiarities have been modified. From the seminary at Red Wing have come many able and earnest young men to fill up the serried ranks of the clergy. With these young clergymen have come renewed zeal, more liberal ideas, and broader views. In the *main*, however, the organization has maintained the characteristics of its youth—a vigorous onslaught, both from pulpit and in private, on the common foibles of humanity and the popular forms of vice; such as drunkenness, swearing, Sabbath breaking, etc. Lay preaching, under proper safeguards, week-day prayermeetings, and great simplicity in the forms of worship, are favored. The old questions, however, so hotly contested in earlier days, have lost their spell. It is doubtful if the magical words of *Slavery*, *Predestination*, *Priestly Robes*, etc., can ever again become the rallying cry of any Lutheran body in America. The dream of the younger element in all these bodies is a strong, united, Lutheran church, lifting up the war cry, "Christ is risen!"—advancing in solid phalanx to do battle for Christ and His Kingdom.

Historical Review of the Norwegian Evangelical Lutheran Synod in America.

—BY—

REV. JOHN HALVORSON.

Although a few persons had previously arrived in this country from Norway, the regular Norwegian emigration to the United States did not commence before 1836, when two ships from Stavanger brought about 160 people who settled at Fox River, La Salle county, Ill. From this year onward the emigration continued steadily and most of the immigrants settled in Illinois and southern Wisconsin; later in Iowa and Minnesota. For a number of years, however, they were without religious instruction, and had no ministers of the Gospel who could preach to them in the language they understood, and according to the faith in which they had been baptized and confirmed. The first ordained Norwegian Lutheran clergyman who came to attend to the spiritual wants of his countrymen in the Northwest was Wilhelm Dietrichson. He arrived in 1844. C. L. Clausen, a Dane, who had previously studied theology in Denmark, was ordained by a German Lutheran pastor, Rev.

Krause, of Milwaukee, and commenced to serve Norwegian and Danish congregations in 1843. The next arrivals of ordained ministers were H. A. Stub, and A. C. Preus, from Norway.

In 1851 the first endeavors were made to combine the scattered Danish and Norwegian congregations into one organization; but as the first constitution which had been adopted was found to contain Grundtvigianism, then prevalent in Denmark, the organization was dissolved the following year. A new constitution was adopted in 1853, at Koshkonong, Dane county, Wis. The Synod of the Norwegian Evangelical Lutheran Church in America was thus organized. Seven ministers and 28 congregations united in forming the new body. The constitution was revised in 1865, and ratified two years later.

The Synod adheres to the old biblical faith and Christianity as taught in the Holy Scripture and confessed in the three ancient symbols, the Apostolic, the Nicene, and the Athanasian creeds, in the unaltered Augsburg Confession, and in Luther's smaller catechism. It is strictly orthodox and conservative in matters of faith, and no friend of new forms of doctrine. It holds to the plenary inspiration of the Bible, not only as to contents, but also as to its words, and believes that it is the only perfect rule and guide of faith and conduct. The total depravity of man by the fall in Adam, justification by faith in Christ alone without the works of the Law, and the efficacy of the Word of God and the two sacraments as means of grace, by which the Holy Spirit potently calls, regenerates and sanctifies sinners, are the three distinctive doctrines which it constantly holds forth without fear and without compromise.

Although the first clergymen in the Synod were graduates of the theological department of the University of Norway and were ordained ministers in their native land, the Synod was never financially supported by, nor was it organically connected with, the church in the fatherland. It at once became independent in its management. In matters of church government the Synod is democratic; the congregations alone have the right to call and depose pastors; the pastor is called not for a definite term of years, but to serve for life or during good behavior, unless called away to places of greater need or importance. The Synod in its relation to the congregations is purely advisory. Its object is, according to the constitution, "To keep watch over the purity and unity of doctrine, as well as of the development of Christian life; to superintend and examine into the official conduct of its members, (professors, pastors, and religious instructors) as well as into the religious standing and work of the congregations; to reconcile in matters of dispute in regard to church questions; to erect and manage institutions of learning for the education of ministers and religious instructors; to establish and carry on home and foreign missions; to promote the use and distribution of the Bible, religious text-books, hymn-books, and devotional literature."

Owing to the union of church and state in Norway, many different religious tendencies were held together by external ties in one church. When these tendencies were transplanted to a free soil, they soon caused the formation of distinct church parties, or synods, all claiming to adhere to the Evangelical Lutheran faith and confession. Lay preaching, quite prevalent in Norway in the early part of this century, was first carried on among the Norwegians in this country by Elling Eielsen, who became the founder of Hauge's Synod; but the Norwegian Synod, in accordance with Article XIV of the Augsburg Confession, believes, "That no man should publicly in the church teach or administer the sacraments, except he be rightly, or regularly, called."

During the Civil War, when the slavery question was everywhere agitated, the question arose in the Synod, if slavery, or the relation of life servitude, was an injustice and sin in itself, or if it ever could exist, or had existed in a lawful manner. The Synod took the position, accepted at its annual meeting in 1861: "That, although according to the Word of God, it is not sin in itself to hold slaves, still slavery is in itself an evil and a punishment from God, and we condemn all the abuses and sins connected with it, as we are also willing, when the duty of our calling requires it, and when Christian love and wisdom demand it, to work for its abolition." This biblical question concerning the life servitude, permitted according to the Old and New Testaments, could not be quietly considered in such a time of national agitation; and much excitement with accusations and threats, especially against the ministers of the Synod, was the result. Hauge's Synod and the Swedish-Norwegian Augustana Synod held the view that slavery was sin in itself. On account of the controversy arising out of this discussion, the Norwegian Synod suffered the loss of Rev. L. C. Clausen and several congregations.

In the controversy regarding the Christian Sunday the Synod adhered to Art. XXVIII of the Augsburg Confession, which explains the Lutheran view. In the controversy on absolution the Synod held that absolution is the proclamation of the Gospel, to many or to one individual, potently administering forgiveness of sins to sinners, but requiring faith for its acceptation and proper effect. In connection with this doctrine the question was also raised if forgiveness of sins was prepared for all sinners, in Christ Jesus, and the whole world thus might be said to be justified in him. This expression the Synod defended according to the Bible: Rom. 5, 18, "Even so by the righteousness of one the free gift came upon all men unto justification of life." The other bodies claimed that justification could only be used with regard to those who accepted Christ by faith, which is the generally accepted meaning of justification. The doctrinal controversies on these questions were carried on in conferences and public meetings as well as in the secular and religious press. In 1871, the parties dissatisfied with the strictly conservative policy and confessional rigor of the Synod, together with seceders from the Augustana Synod, organized a new religious denomination, the Danish-Norwegian Evangelical Lutheran Conference.

But even during these years of controversy the Synod was constantly increasing. Numerous congregations were organized all over the Northwestern states, especially in Wisconsin, Iowa, and Minnesota. The number of ministers also increased rapidly, and it was found expedient to divide the Synod into three districts. This was effected in 1876 at the meeting of the church held in Decorah, Ia. The districts comprise within their limits all the states and territories in which Norwegian Lutherans have settled.

At the district meetings each congregation is represented

by one lay delegate and by its minister, as voting members; only such ministers having the right to vote as serve a congregation formally united with the Synod.

Every third year the Synod holds its meetings, presided over by Rev. H. A. Preus, who has held the office of president uninterruptedly for thirty-two years,* being first elected in 1862. Between the synodical meetings the management is exercised by the church council, consisting of the four presiding officers, and of four lay members, elected by the three districts, and one member elected by the Synod at large.

During the first years of its existence the Synod was dependent for its pastors and instructors upon the university and seminaries of Norway; and from 1848 to 1858 received fourteen theological candidates from the university at Kristiania, who accepted charges as pastors in the Northwestern states. Three of them, however, returned to Norway, and during the troubled times of the war but few accessions were made from the mother country. For this reason, and also in order to obtain men better acquainted with the conditions and needs of our church in America, it was found necessary to provide a theological seminary for the education of ministers in our midst. As both the means and men for such an undertaking were scarce, the Norwegian Synod in the year 1855 sent delegates to visit and confer with several English and German Lutheran synods in the United States. In the German Evangelical Lutheran Synod of Missouri, Ohio, and other states, they found a church that adhered strictly to the Lutheran faith and principles, with a college and theological seminary at St. Louis, Mo., under the management of the noted Prof. C. F. W. Walther. Here

---

*At his death in 1894, Rev. V. Koren succeeded him.

the delegates met with a hearty welcome, and the German Synod invited the students of the Norwegian Synod to attend their seminary on the same conditions as their own. With great love and fraternal good feeling the German brethren assisted and encouraged the struggling Norwegian Lutherans in the infancy and poverty of their church; and their aid was gratefully accepted.

In 1859 Rev. Laur. Larsen, then a pastor in Wisconsin, was appointed by the Norwegian Synod as its professor at Concordia College and Seminary, St. Louis, Mo. When the classical department of Concordia College was removed to Fort Wayne, Ind., in 1861, the Norwegian Synod had so far gained in strength that it determined to conduct a college of its own, which began its work the same year in the parsonage at Half Way Creek, near La Crosse, Wis. Prof. Laur. Larsen was appointed president, which position he has filled with great fidelity through all the changes and improvements in the college till the present date. In 1862 the college was removed to Decorah, Ia., where land had previously been secured. In 1864 the cornerstone was laid to a large building, and the next year the present Luther College was dedicated with imposing ceremonies in the presence of 6,000 Norwegian Lutherans from far and near. This was the first higher institution of learning erected by the Norwegians in the United States. That a building of such proportions, at a cost of $75,000, could be completed during a period of such internal and external strife was due mainly to the untiring faith, energy, and self-sacrifice of Prof. Laur. Larsen, and Rev. V. Koren, as well as to the joint efforts of the Lutheran pastors and church members in the Northwest.

The instruction at the college was at first given by two professors, but as the number of students rapidly increased, others were appointed, and in 1874 we find seven professors and over 200 students. In 1874 a new addition was completed at a cost of $23,000. Residences for the professors, and a large brick church were also provided, and the grounds were greatly improved. As the Norwegian people Americanized, the college endeavored to keep up with the transition. English became more and more the medium of instruction, and other branches of study were added, so as to give all the facilities of an American college and still retain the thorough linguistic and historic training of a European gymnasium. In 1881 the course of study was extended to seven years, with a preparatory, a normal, and a classical department, and the number of professors and instructors was increased to nine. In 1889 the college buildings were destroyed by fire, but at the meeting of the three districts the same year it was resolved immediately to rebuild them. The next year they were again completed at a cost of $56,000. The attendance, which, during previous years of doctrinal controversies, had dwindled down to 118, now again increased, so that since 1890 it has averaged about 200 Luther College has received four legacies, amounting to $9,500.

It had originally been the intent to add a theological department to the college at Decorah, but men and means were not at once available, and the Norwegian students still, for a number of years, studied theology at the German Concordia Seminary at St. Louis, although this seminary had, for a number of years, no Norwegian professor, after Prof.

Larson removed. As many as twenty Norwegian students at one time pursued their studies here, and the graduates from this seminary form the main body of the clergy of the Nowegian Synod.

In 1872, to further promote the spirit of Christian fellowship, the Norwegian Synod joined with four German Lutheran synods in organizing the Synodical Conference, which at one time intended to erect and support a theological seminary for all the synods connected with it; but the plan was frustrated. The Norwegian Synod then, in 1876, bought the Soldier's Orphan's Home, Madison, Wis., for a theological seminary. This institution, called Luther Seminary, began with a practical, and afterward added a theoretical department; the first accepts students of Christian knowledge and experience, who, on account of advanced age or other circumstances, are debarred from pursuing a college course, but still possess abilities and a desire to enter the ministry; the latter requiring a classical, or college education for admission. In 1888 the seminary was removed to Robbinsdale, near Minneapolis, Minn., where fine buildings had been erected at the cost of $30,000. The faculty consists of three professors, who also edit the official organ of the Synod, *Evangelisk Luthersk Kirketidende.* In 1893, 47 students attended the seminary.

Thus the Synod took charge of the academic and theological training of its adults, but a still more difficult task was found in how to provide relgious instructors for the children. There was a manifest necessity of having schools where more extensive and systematic religious instruction could be given than that offered in the Sunday schools. As no such schools were provided for by the state or by the American churches, the need and the difficulty of this work was seriously felt.   Instructors for the parochial schools were sometimes taken from Norway, or men were employed who had received an academy training in this country.

A normal department for the educating of instructors in religion was attempted in connection with Luther College, and a special professor was called for this department in 1878; but the connection with the classical department did not work well, and the normal department at Luther College was given up in 1886.   After several unsuccessful attempts a normal school for preparing teachers, both for the English common school and for Lutheran parochial schools was built in Sioux Falls, S. D., at the cost of $16,000.   It commenced work in 1889, with three professors, and in the winter term of 1898-9, had a total attendance of 115 students, of both sexes.

Besides these schools, owned and controlled directly by the Synod, a number of academies and high schools have sprung up within the last ten years, owned and controlled by private corporations within the Synod.   Among such can be mentioned: Willmar Seminary, established 1882, which in 1892 had an attendance of nearly 400 students; Albert Lea Lutheran High School, with an attendance of 200 in 1892; Lutheran Ladies' Seminary, Red Wing, Minn., of which the cornerstone was laid in 1893.   This is the first institution of its kind among the Scandinavians in this country.   It is to be exclusively for lady students who desire instruction in all branches of knowledge especially useful to women; business, art, housekeeping, dressmaking, etc., to-

LUTHER COLLEGE, DECORAH, IOWA.

AUGSBURG SEMINARY, MINNEAPOLIS, MINN.

ST. OLAF COLLEGE, NORTHFIELD, MINN.

gether with instruction in religion. Stoughton Academy, Stoughton, Wis., has an attendance of 140 students; Bruflat Academy, Portland, N. D., 90; Aaberg Academy, Devils Lake, N. D., 80; and Park Region Luther College, Fergus Falls, Minn., 200. The Pacific Lutheran University, Tacoma, Wash., completed in 1894, has buildings amounting to $100,000.

The Synod also owns and supports Bethany Indian Mission, Wittenberg, Wis. This institution obtains Indian children from the Winnebago tribe, and civilizes and Christianizes them. This school is also partly supported by the United States government.

Martin Luther's Orphans' Home at Madison, Wis., contains 36 orphans, who are cared for and instructed by the Synod.

Missions, supported partly by the Synod, in connection with other branches of the Lutheran Church, are: The Jewish Mission, in Montreal, Canada; the Negro Mission, in the Southern states; the Zulu Mission, in South Africa; the mission among the Mormons, in Salt Lake City, Utah; and Sailors' Mission, in New York and Brooklyn. The greatest mission work, however, is the *Home Mission* among the scattered Norwegian immigrants.

While the Norwegian Synod was in its greatest prosperity, a time of great strife and trial came upon it. In 1880 a controversy arose between Dr. F. A. Schmidt, of the theological seminary at Madison, Wis., and Dr. C. F. W. Walther, and others, in the German Missouri Synod, about the doctrine of election and predestination; the former claiming that the Missouri Synod taught a Calvinistic

On pp. 317-35, Vol. I., and pp. 23-37, 129-34, and 145-51, Vol. II., more recent statistics and more detailed accounts may be found in regard to most of the institutions referred to on the last five pages, which practically remain as they were published in 1898.— EDITOR.

theory concerning election; the latter maintaining Schmidt
and his followers held synergistic views. The controversy
which thus began in the German, soon found its way into
the Norwegian Synod. The question was discussed at ministerial conferences and annual synodical meetings, but no
agreement between the contending factions seemed possible.
Excitement ran high, and public discussions were held by
representatives of both parties, all through the Synod. At
the theological seminary and at Luther College the faculties
were divided; the majority, however, adhering to the views
of Walther and the Missouri Synod, while Prof. Schmidt had
the greatest following among the lay people. At a conference in Decorah, Ia., in 1884, each faction drafted a full statement of their faith, with proofs and testimonies attached, for
the consideration of the people. The *Confession* of Schmidt
and his followers was signed by 72 ministers and professors
in the Synod; the *Explanation* of the "Missourians" by
107. The Schmidt faction declared that they could no
longer support or attend the institutions of the Synod, which
were controlled by "Missourians." An opposition college
and theological seminary was established at Northfield,
Minn., where the opponents of the Synod controlled the St.
Olaf School. Hither Prof. Schmidt removed with some of
the theological students, and Luther Seminary at Madison
was almost deserted; but instruction was still continued
with two professors and seven students in 1886. The attendance at Luther College also dwindled down to 118, and
the finances of the church were in a bad condition.

At the next joint synod in Stougton, Wis., it was resolved, "That the establishment of an opposition seminary

at Northfield was in violation of the constitution of the Synod, a breach of agreement, a virtual division, and could not be tolerated; therefore, the members, who had supported this work, were advised to acknowledge their error and desist from it." Fifty-seven members signed a protest, declaring their intention to continue the seminary at Northfield, and seceded from the Synod. This example was soon followed by the congregations, and in the following two years fully one-third of the ministers and congregations seceded and organized The Anti-Missourian Brotherhood. Before the division, the Synod, according to the parochial reports for 1886, numbered 194 clergymen in office, 77,399 communicants, and 143,867 souls.

During the last years of the predestination controversy the proper work of the Synod had been almost at a stand still. The debt had increased, and missionary work had languished. But when the division was effected, and confidence and internal peace restored, new energy was awakened and successful attempts were made to restore finances to a better condition. The contribution of the churches for the different synodical and missionary purposes amounted, in the year ending May 1st, 1892, to $34,830, but has frequently exceeded $50,000.

According to the reports for 1899, the Synod contained nearly 300 clergymen and professors, 800 congregations, 70,000 communicant members, and about 125,000 souls. The total church property is valued at about 3,000,000.

From 1885 to 1891 annual meetings were held with the other denominations of the Norwegian Lutheran Church, discussing the questions which divided them, with a view to further an agreement and union. Although the efforts have not been void of good, they have been temporarily given up, pending the internal strife in the United Church.

Another matter seriously discussed at present is the transition from Norwegian to English. At all the institutions of learning the greater part of the instruction is given through the medium of the English language, excepting at the theological seminary, where a chair in English has been a long-felt want. English Lutheran missions have been established at Chicago, and Minneapolis, and many of the clergy do part of their work in English. The Epiphany English Lutheran Conference, organized in St. Paul, Minn., in 1892, consists of both Norwegian and German pastors. Its aim is to cultivate and promote the use of the English language in the Lutheran churches of foreign extraction, in order to retain the old orthodox faith and establish it on American soil. For, while the Norwegian Synod is noted for its conservatism as to doctrine and church principles, it endeavors to promote the education and influence of its people in all good objects.

Historical Review of the Scandinavian Baptists in the U. S. and in the North.

—REVISED AND APPROVED BY—

REV. FRANK PETERSON.

The Baptist faith was introduced into Denmark as early as 1839. In that year Rev. John Gerhard Oncken, a German, came to Copenhagen, where one of his assistants had succeeded in gathering a few believers. These were baptized by Oncken and organized into a church; the first of its kind among the Scandinavian people. These proceedings, very innocent in their nature, created quite an excitement in Denmark, where the Lutheran state church was looked upon as the only orthodox Christian body. The Baptist missionaries were denounced and persecuted as a dangerous element promulgating heresy and disorder. The members and pastor of the newly organized church were summoned before the magistrates and admonished to desist from their work. A decree was passed by the department of state whereby they were forbidden to hold meetings, to baptize, or to administer the Lord's Supper. But persecution since the day of Christ has always been a means of spreading the teach-

ings which it has been endeavoring to stamp out. It proved
so here. Private meetings were held, and the attitude of the
state and church towards the believers in the faith only
served to make them more zealous and devoted. The Baptist church in Copenhagen soon numbered thirty-two members, and several churches were organized in other places.
Meanwhile the persecutions went on. Oncken, and the minister of the church in Copenhagen, Peter Moenster, were
hunted by the police, and a reward was offered for their apprehension. In 1840 Moenster and his brother were arrested and imprisoned. The latter was banished from the
realm, and, upon his refusal to leave his native land, was
sentenced to a long term of imprisonment. The persecution,
not confined to the leaders, but carried on against their followers as well, soon became unbearable, and Oncken resolved
to go to England to enlist the sympathies of his brethren
in that country in their behalf. He obtained a recognition
for these as being regular and well ordered churches of Christ,
established upon apostolic basis. A deputation of English
Baptists went over to plead with the Danish government for
a milder treatment of their brethren, but to no avail. Another attempt to aleviate the harsh condition of the Danish
Baptists was made by the American and Foreign Publishing
Society, which sent Professors Conant and Hackett over to
petition the King. Through their efforts the King was at
last persuaded to grant what was called the Law of Am-
nesty, by which certain privileges were granted the Baptists, among others that they could assemble privately, and
administer the Lord's Supper. But they were still forbidden
to administer baptism, and were required to have their chil-

dren baptized by the regular ministers within the age required by law. They were still subject to fine and imprisonment, and their children were often taken by the clergy
to be baptized into the state church, for which they were
compelled to pay, or if they refused their goods were
seized. To these persecutions the Danish Baptists were
subject until 1850, when they at last obtained religious liberty. The church, however, during these years of adversity,
had prospered, and in 1900 we find about 25 Baptist
churches and 3,700 members in Denmark, in spite of the fact
that a great number had emigrated to America during the
long period of religious persecution.

The beginning of the Baptist church in Norway is of a
more obscure origin. This faith was first introduced into
that country by German colporteurs, probably about the
years 1845 or '50, but it gained little ground at first, and
was subject of no general attention until 1868. About
1857, F. L. Rymker, a Dane, arrived in the northern
part of Norway and began his fruitful missionary work
there. Rymker, at first a Danish sailor who through some
ill fortune had lost one leg, was led to his view of Baptism by
Mr. Isaac T. Smith, a member of the Baptist Church for Seamen in New York. After his conversion Rymker was sent
as a missionary to Denmark, where he worked for some
years among the wounded and crippled of the navy. He
then went to Norway, and after ten years labor in that
country he had ordained two ministers and organized six
churches, with an aggregate membership of two hundred.
In 1869 a Swedish basket maker, O. Hanson, also entered upon
the missionary work in Norway, and through his preaching

twenty-eight persons were soon converted, and a church was organized. In 1900 there were about 2,200 Baptists in Norway. The various churches scattered throughout the country have of late years been organized into the Norwegian Union of Baptist Churches. In 1892 the American Baptist Missionary Union took charge of the missionary work in Norway, and steady accessions are being made to the church.

In Sweden the Baptist mission began its work a little later than in Denmark, and here, as in the other countries, the field was first entered by independent missionaries. Capt. G. W. Schroeder, who had embraced the Baptist faith in New York, was the first to bring the faith to Sweden. In 1847 F. O. Nilsson, also a sailor, who had been brought to the same views by Schroeder, was baptized, and the first Baptist church was organized in 1848. The following year Nilsson was ordained in Hamburg, Germany, and returned to Sweden to preach the Gospel to his countrymen according to his faith. But being opposed by the authorities, he was put in prison. Upon being released he renewed his preaching and was again imprisoned. Three different times Nilsson was thrown into prison, and twice he appeared before the High Court. At last, in 1851, he was banished from the country, when he went to Denmark, and from thence to America. In Copenhagen he met and baptized Rev. A. Wiberg, who was destined to continue the missionary work in Sweden. Wiberg was an educated man, and a minister in the state church in Sweden. After his conversion and baptism he went to America and engaged in colporteur work. While there he published a book on Baptism, which gained a wide circulation in his native land, and through which quite a number were converted to the faith. In 1855 the Publication Society of Philadelphia established a system of colportage in Sweden, and Wiberg was sent as superintendent. On his return he found about five hundred Baptists in Sweden, despite the fact that they had been, and still were, subject to considerable hardships. In 1856 Wiberg began to edit a paper called *Evangelisten,* which soon gained a wide circulation. Ten years later he built a chapel in Stockholm with money which he had raised in England and in America. The work progressed rapidly, many more workers entered the field, among whom were Rev. G. Palmquist and his brothers, and soon the faith gained entrance into higher circles. After a visit to America, Wiberg returned to Sweden in 1866 and started a theological seminary in Stockholm, called the Swedish Bethel Seminary, which began its work with two professors and seven students, and, under the presidency of K. O. Broady, D. D., still continues. In 1900 there were about 570 Baptist churches and 40,000 members in Sweden.

As far as is known, the first Swedish Baptist in the world was John Asplund, who for some time had served in the British navy; but he deserted and came to North Carolina in the latter part of the eighteenth century. In this country he was immersed, ordained, and drowned in 1807. He traveled on foot through all the original thirteen states and gathered materials for a statistical Baptist year-book, which was published in 1790 and re-issued in new editions for some years afterwards. It is claimed that two copies of this remarkable book are in Colgate University, Hamilton, N. Y.

But it is very doubtful if Asplund ever tried, or had a chance, to propagate his faith among the Swedes either in the old country or in America. Although the before mentioned Capt. G. W. Schroeder had been immersed in East River, N. Y., as early as 1844, thus becoming the second Swedish Baptist in the world, and perhaps some other Swedish-Americans had accepted his views before 1852; yet no organization of Swedish Baptists existed in this country before that year. Consequently, the missionary work among the Swedish people began a little earlier at home than in the United States, but in both cases it was commenced by Swedish-Americans, and the American Baptists have during the last thirty years paid out nearly one million dollars in order to convert the Scandinavians on both sides of the Atlantic. Owing to the hardships to which the Baptists in Sweden were subjected during the fifties and sixties, many of them were compelled to emigrate as soon as they had accepted this faith. This may partly explain why there are about twice as many Swedish Baptists in the United States, in proportion to the population, as there are in Sweden. One person out of every 60 Swedes in this country is a Baptist, but only one person out of every 125 in Sweden confesses that faith.

The first Swedish Baptist church in this country was organized at Rock Island, Ill., the 13th of August, 1852, by Gustaf Palmquist. Shortly after, mainly through the efforts of Palmquist and F. O. Nilsson, organizations sprung into existence in different parts of Iowa, Minnesota, and Illinois, so that in 1860 the various churches had a total membership of about two hundred and fifty communicants. The missionary work among the scattered settlers was often attended with serious difficulty, but the zeal and faithfulness of the missionaries seldom flagged. Most of them were men who were used to hard manual toil, and few had received the advantages of a higher education. But in a new country such men can generally accomplish more than persons of great learning, the former being nearer to the people. The pioneer preachers went on foot long distances and often suffered privations, but the faith was preached to the people even in the remotest settlements. The church grew rapidly and has always continued to do so. Excepting the Lutherans, the Swedish Baptists in the United States are today more numerous and conservative than any other religious organization among the Swedes in this country. Not including those who are members of purely American congregations, there were about 12,000 Swedish Baptists in 1890; ten years later they numbered in the neighborhood of 21,500, being the greatest percentage of increase which any Swedish church in the land has had during this period. The value of the property amounts to nearly $800,000 in 1900, having doubled in a decade. There are about 310 congregations, grouped in a dozen conferences. Of these conferences the one in Minnesota is the largest, next in size comes the Illinois conference.

The Danish-Norwegian Baptists in the United States are not numerous; no attempt has been made to write their history: consequently, facts in regard to them are not easily obtained. It appears that Hans Valder, who lived among the American Baptists at Indian Creek, Ill., accepted the religious views of his associates in 1842. He was licensed to preach, and in a couple of years about twenty Norwegians in La Salle and Kendall counties were immersed, constituting a kind of society without being regularly organized. Valder was ordained in 1844, and for some time received a salary of $50 a year from the American Baptists and $13 from his countrymen. He worked at manual labor part of the time, and was soon compelled to quit preaching altogether in order to support his family. The society was only a temporary affair, as most of its members seem to have moved to Iowa and Minnesota in the early fifties. It is claimed that the first regularly organized Danish-Norwegian Baptist church in this country came into existence at Raymond, Racine county, Wis., the 10th of November, 1356. Rev. L. Jörgensen, a Baptist from Denmark, who was supported by the Americans, organized this church as well as several others. During the latter part of the fifties, some Danish Baptists settled at New Denmark, Brown county, Wis., among whom was Rev. P. H. Dam, who, under the auspices of the American Baptist Home Mission Society, began, in 1863, to organize congregations in eastern Wisconsin. But even where the cradle of the Danish-Norwegian Baptists stood, the progress of the work has been very slow, for in 1900 they had only about 1,000 communicant members in the whole state of Wisconsin. In 1880 the total number of congregations in this country was about 25, with 1,700 communicants and twenty ministers. Today (1900) in the neighborhood of 5,000 persons belong to the 80 Danish-Norwegian Baptist churches, grouped in seven conferences. The value of the property is about $110,000. Hardly more than one person out of 300 of the Danes and Norwegians in the United States is a Baptist.

The Scandinavian Baptists in this country can hardly be

said to exist as independent associations, because they co-
operate in organic connection with the American Baptists,
through whom all missionary work, home and foreign, is
carried on. Yet the dozen Swedish Baptist conferences have
united in forming the Swedish Baptist General Conference,
which holds meetings once a year. The Danish-Norwegian
Baptists have not effected a union of their different conferences. The general conference among the Swedes was organized in 1879. It has no authority over the conferences or
individual congregations composing the same, but is merely
a union of the Swedish Baptists for the purpose of facilitat-
ing the work, such as missions, Sunday school work, and
the distribution of religious literature. Each congregation
sends one or more delegates to the meeting of the general
conference. The same close connection with the American
Baptists is manifest in regard to the education of the young
men who intend to become ministers. The Scandinavian
Baptists in this country have, generally speaking, never
operated a school of their own, but in 1871 Rev. J. A. Edgren,
a brother to the learned linguist, Hjalmar Edgren, began to
teach the Swedish students in the American Baptist theological seminary, Chicago, and in 1881 Rev. N. P. Jensen, a
Dane, became his assistant. In 1884 a regular Danish-
Norwegian department was established in connection with
the seminary. At the same time the Baptists in Denmark
and Norway decided to have their candidates for the ministry educated at this institution, and about thirty-five young
men have during the last fifteen years come directly from
those countries to pursue studies at the school. In 1884
the Swedes had their own school in St. Paul, Minn., and then

for two or three years it was kept at Stromsburg, Neb. But in 1888 they again united with the American institution in Chicago. When the seminary, in 1892, became a part of the University of Chicago, regular Swedish and Danish-Norwegian departments were established in connection with the divinity school of this institution. From 1871 to 1900 about 275 Swedish and 125 Danish-Norwegian students have pursued theological courses, only a part of them, however, having completed their studies. In later years three Swedish professors and an equal number of Danish-Norwegian instructors are employed in the school, and the combined annual attendance averages about fifty in the two departments. Besides the attempt to prepare young men for the position of clergymen, several Scandinavian-American Baptist newspapers and religious tracts are published in the interest of the work.

Owing to the scarcity of historical documents with reference to the Baptist work in the Scandinavian countries, most of the facts were gleaned from the histories of G. W. Hervey and T. Armitage, both American publications. In the second edition I have personally corrected all mistakes of facts that could be detected; but did not change the language of the article, except pages 201-4, which were rewritten by myself, and revised by Rev. Frank Peterson. In making corrections and additions, official church reports have mostly been relied upon, but in a few cases I have consulted newspaper articles and G. W. Schroeder's history of the Swedish Baptists.—EDITOR.

Historical Review of Scandinavian Methodism in the U. S. and in the North.

— BY —

REV. N. M. LILJEGREN.

In 1771 Dr. C. M. Wrangel, who for several years had been a Lutheran Minister among the Swedes at Delaware River, and who had met John Wesley in England, became the leader in organizing a religious society in Stockholm, Sweden, called *Pro Fide et Christianissimo*, which exists today. This may be said to have been the first Methodistic attempt in the North, for although Dr. Wrangel was and always remained a Lutheran, yet he acted upon the advice of Wesley and had been very friendly toward the Methodists during his ministerial duties in this country. When the well-known English manufacturer, Samuel Owen, settled in Sweden in the first part of this century, he brought with him two Methodist ministers, Stephens and Scott, who were of the same faith as himself. Scott was an earnest, active, and bold man, who fearlessly attacked the religious and social evils, built what is now, Bethlehems Church, in Stockholm, and organized the first temperance society in Sweden. The religi-

ous movement at that time became intense and swept
over parts of the kingdom with the strength of a tornado.
In Helsingland the Jansonites, who in their style of delivery
and mode of teaching and exhortation resembled the Methodists, publicly burned all the religious books, except the
Bible. For this great excitement and fanaticism Scott was not
responsible; yet the opposition, in their passion and hatred,
drove him by force, at the risk of his life, from Sweden in
1842.

In 1825 O. G. Hedstrom, a Swede, landed in New York.
He was converted to Methodism, and for some time preached
for American congregations. But when the Scandinavian
emigrants, in the early forties, commenced to arrive in New
York by the hundreds and thousands, annually, he attended
almost exclusively to their spiritual wants. He was the
founder of the Swedish Methodism in America, and to a certain extent, also, of the Norwegian-Danish, for in 1847, O. P.
Peterson, a Norwegian, was converted to that faith by him.
Peterson visited his native country two years later, and for the
first time, introduced Methodism into Norway. He returned
to America in 1850, and the following year began missionary
work among his countrymen in the Northwest. Chr. B. Willerup, a Dane, was the first who introduced Methodism
among the Nowegian-Danish people in this country, in 1850;
for five years he preached for the Norwegian pioneers in Wis_
consin. It is a notable fact that although the emigration
from Norway preceded the Swedish by ten or fifteen years,
yet the Methodistic missionary work among the former immigrants began five years later, at least, than it did among the
latter.

As a general thing the Methodists are noted for their earnestness and strong religious convictions. The early Scandinavian-American Methodists, although most of them were uneducated, were not slow in appealing to their American brethren for aid in carrying on missionary work in their native lands. The Americans, with their usual sympathy and liberality, granted their request.* In 1855 Willerup was sent as superintendent of the work in the Northern countries, which commenced at once in Norway, shortly after in Denmark, but not in Sweden until 1865. Soon a few other Scandinavian-American missionaries followed him; yet it was not until V. Witting was appointed superintendent of Sweden, in 1868, that the work progressed in that kingdom. After the severity of the religious laws had been relaxed—which was done in Sweden in 1873, and in Denmark and Norway a little earlier—Methodism spread rapidly over the Northern countries. In 1876 conferences were organized, both in Sweden and Norway, but the work in Denmark has progressed very slowly, until recent years. According to the report of the Methodist Episcopal Church for the year ending 1899, there were about 16,000 members in Sweden, 5,800 in Norway, and 3,200 in Denmark, or totally 25,000, distributed among a population of about nine and a half million people. Each country has a small theological school. The value of the church property in all the Northern countries amounts to nearly $800,000.

The Methodists from the North have done their full share in developing the material resources of the country and attending to the religious, social, and moral uplifting of their countrymen in the New World. They are, perhaps, the most

---

* According to the annual reports of the Missionary Society of the Methodist Episcopal Church, said organization has paid out over two and a half million dollars during the past forty years for missionary work among the Scandinavians. One million dollars has been devoted to the Scandinavians in this country; the balance of the sum has been spent in the North.—EDITOR.

ardent temperance workers of any of the Scandinavian-American religious organizations. Even their opponents admit that the two Hedstrom brothers in many ways assisted the immigrants and directed the whole Scandinavian movement toward the Northwest.

From the Atlantic to the Pacific, from the Great Lakes to the Gulf of Mexico, where any Scandinavians are to be found, there are also Scandinavian Methodist churches. As a general thing the Swedes, Norwegians, and Danes, in a new settlement, unite and erect a common church, where they all worship God together; the differences in their languages being so small that they easily understand each other. But as the membership increases they usually divide into Swedish, and Norwegian-Danish congregations. A Norwegian-American historian says: "The Scandinavian Methodist Church in America is not a unity, not any undivided whole. It is made up of two separate branches, vis., the Swedish and the Norwegian-Danish." Yet, in nearly all the new and smaller localities, the two branches generally have churches in common.

In 1877 the Northwestern Swedish Methodist Conference was organized, and in 1892 it was agreed to divide said organization into three conferences. The Norwegian-Danish Methodist Conference was organized in 1880. Each conference is divided into districts, each district is presided over by an elder. An American bishop is chairman at the annual conferences. In fact, the Scandinavian Methodists are closely connected with their American brethren. In the Eastern and Western states the Scandinavian congregations belong to American conferences.

Not including those who belong to purely American congregations, there are about 16,000 Swedish Methodists in this country in 1900, and 8,000 Norwegian-Danish. Not one person out of every 300 is a Methodist in Sweden, while over one out of every 100 Swedes in this country belong to this organization. In proportion to the population there are more than twice as many Norwegians in America who are Methodists as there are in Norway. The Swedish Methodists in this country have about 170 churches, valued at $800,000; the Norwegian-Danish have 115 churches, valued at $330,-000. This valuation of the church property does not, however, include the parsonages, which may be estimated to be worth $130,000 and $70,000, respectively.

Several newspapers are published in the interest of the work, *Sändebudet* being the Swedish church organ, and *Den Christelige Talsmand* the Norwegian-Danish. There are two Methodist theological departments connected with the Northwestern University at Evanston, Ill., one Swedish, and one Norwegian-Danish, where young men are prepared for the ministry.

Some of the assertions in the first paragraph of this article are evidently based upon weak and questionable evidence. To affirm that Pro Fide et Christianismo was organized upon the advice of Wesley, thereby indicating that he was the originator of the fundamental principles of said society, does not appear to coincide with the actual facts. The society in Stockholm was modelled after the Society For Promoting Christian Knowledge, the oldest and one of the greatest associations connected with the Church of England, which was founded in 1698, five years before the birth of Wesley. All the Swedish Methodist historians on both sides of the Atlantic, and perhaps some others, seem to have misinterpreted the position of Dr. Wrangel, even going so far as to call him a de facto Methodist. For example, T. M. Erikson, in his history of Methodism in Sweden, styles Wrangel "the pioneer of Methodism in Philadelphia," and asserts that at his death the influence of that sect ceased in Sweden, at least for a time. The same sentiments are expressed by the authors of the semi-official history of Swedish Methodism in this country. These writers assume that because C. M. Wrangel was a pietist, a friend and admirer of Wesley and his work, therefore the former must have accepted the religious views of the latter and become a converted Methodist. But would not the following syllogism be equally correct: John Wesley, being a pious man and friendly towards Wrangel and his work, therefore the former must have accepted the faith of the latter and become a good Lutheran? The relation between these two men, as far as religious co-operation is concerned, appears to be as follows: Wesley endeavored to reform the abuses, real or supposed, of the Episcopal Church of England —with which he never severed his connection. Wrangel, being a progressive man, sympathized with all movements of this nature, and on his return from the United States visited Wesley, Oct. 14, 1768, and requested him to send some piously inclined persons thither to preach the Gospel, which was granted. Considering the need of devout instructors in America and the friendly relation existing between the churches of Sweden and England, such request was very natural, especially as separation from the state organizations had not at that time become a general practice. Afterwards they corresponded with each other. But not a single letter or document has been produced to indicate that the society in Stockholm was the result of Wesley's advice, or that Wrangel had become a Methodist. It may be that Wrangel was influenced by Methodism, but so was also Wesley by the teachings of Luther; for, according to Wesley's own assertion, quoted in "Johnson's Cyclopædia," he became converted through the writings of the German reformer.

The opposition to Rev. George Scott was not so much against his Methodism as against his ingratitude. At first he had been exceptionally well received in Stockholm, some of the Lutheran clergymen even assisting him in his missionary efforts. But during a journey in the United States, in 1841, he had several times severely criticized the morals and religion of the Swedes, who resented this by driving him out of the city.

The following are some of the authorities which have been consulted in regard to the above note, or notes: "International" and "Chambers's" cyclopædias, "Nordisk Familjebok," C. A. Cornelius's "Svenska Kyrkans Historia efter Reformationen," "Wesley's Journal," T. M. Erikson's "Metodismen i Sverige," and "Svenska Metodismen i Amerika."—Editor.

Historical Review of the Swedish Evangelical Mission Covenant of America.

— BY —

REV. E. A. SKOGSBERGH.

In order to fully understand the origin, development, and history of the Swedish Evangelical Mission Covenant of America, it is at first necessary to glance at the religious condition in Sweden in the nineteenth century. In the first part of this century rationalism[1] swayed the religious thought of the majority of the Swedish clergy. Many of the ministers in the Lutheran state church were negligent, and spiritual life had in most cases been supplanted by stale forms. In 1842, a pious but uneducated peasant, Eric Janson, commenced to hold devotional meetings in Helsingland, in the northern part of Sweden. About the same time Rev. George Scott, an English Methodist minister, began to preach in Stockholm, and shortly after the Baptists commenced to introduce their faith around Gothenburg.

All these movements were more or less hostile towards the Lutheran state church of Sweden, and the majority of

---

1 Prof. G. O. Brohaugh's history of the Hauge's Synod, which commences on page 173 in this volume, contains a discussion on rationalism in Europe in general, and in Norway in particular, which, no doubt, applies to the Swedish clergy as well.—[EDITOR.]

the clergy naturally resisted any and all encroachments upon their field. They had also the civil law on their side. For, ever since the introduction of Lutheranism into Sweden in the early part of the sixteenth century, it had been, and still was, unlawful to worship God in any other form than in accordance with the rites of the established church; nor could religious meetings be legally conducted by other persons than the regular clergy. That such a law could exist among such an intelligent and free people as the Swedes is mainly due to the fact that shortly after the teachings of the great German reformer had become their national religion, strenuous efforts were made to re-establish the Catholic faith among them. To protect the Swedish people from relapsing into Catholicism, the government made it a criminal offense to teach or preach any doctrine except the Lutheran. But the Swedes have always been such devoted Lutherans that for centuries there was little occasion to apply the severe religious laws; nor, perhaps, would they have been applied now, if it had not been for the unwise, not to say fanatical, procedure of some of the dissenters themselves. In Helsingland, for example, the Jansonites publicly burned all religious books except the Bible. Janson was arrested, imprisoned, and escaped to America in 1846, where he became the founder of the well-known Bishop Hill Colony, in Illinois; Scott was mobbed in 1842, the Baptist leader banished from the kingdom in 1851, and more than one of the separatists and revivalists had to suffer longer or shorter imprisonment. It was not until 1873 that the harsh religious laws were abolished in Sweden.

The persecution, however, did not have the desired effect.

Yet, as has been stated before, the Swedes have always been, and are, very devoted Lutherans. Any other form of worship finds little favor with them, consequently the Methodists, the Baptists, and all other dissenters from the established Lutheran church, have, on the whole, not been very successful; while the Mission movement within the state church itself has exercised a great influence.

This movement, which began about 1840-50, was a spiritual awakening within the Lutheran church. It sprang, as has often been the case in all ages and in all countries in regard to religious and social reforms, from the lower stratum of society. The regular clergy and upper circles generally kept aloof, often opposed the whole movement. It was the laymen who commenced to read and interpret the Bible for themselves. It was a continuation among the Swedes of the spiritual awakening which had been originated in Norway by Hans Nilsen Hauge half a century before. It was the strong individuality of the Northmen, who had drenched in blood the classical civilization of Rome and western European Christendom, and sealed with their blood on the battlefield of Lützen the cause of Reformation, that in religious matters asserted their rights as freemen.

In the middle of this century *Fosterlandsstiftelsen* was organized in Sweden by C. O. Rosenius and others. Rosenius had previously co-operated with George Scott, and had conducted revival meetings in different parts of the kingdom. He was also editor of *Pietisten*, a religious paper which has to this day exercised quite an influence in religious matters. The object of *Fosterlandsstiftelsen*, which was composed mostly of laymen although a few of the regular Lutheran clergymen also belonged, was to conduct a religious revival movement within the state church. For this purpose piously inclined laymen were sent to every part of the realm, where they held religious meetings among the farmers and laboring people, and distributed devotional literature. These meetings resembled very much an ordinary Pietistic prayer meeting, and were called *Läsaremöten* (Reading-meetings) or *Missionsmöten* (Missionmeetings); those who participated were at first called *Läsare* (Readers), later *Missionsvänner* (Mission Friends). After a while, however, Dr. P. Waldenström—an ordained Lutheran minister and professor in one of the colleges of Sweden, who, after the death of Rosenius, had become the leader of the Mission movement, and is now well-known as a preacher and author, having also for a number of years been a member of the Swedish Parliament—withdrew from *Fosterlandsstiftelsen*. In 1878 he together with others organized *Svenska Missionsförbundet*, an independent organization, which a large proportion of the Mission Friends joined. Others remained with *Fosterlandsstiftelsen*. The former society has, in 1900, about 100,000 members, supports a theological seminary, and conducts missionary work in foreign countries.

Although several Mission Friends had emigrated before 1868, it was not until that year that C. O. Björk and J. M. Sanngren began at Swede Bend, Boone county, Iowa, and in Chicago, respectively, to gather together the Mission folks. At the former place an organization may be said to have been effected July 4, 1868, which was the first society of its kind in America; but similar societies in a short time sprang up in different parts of the country. The ministers and lay-men of some of these churches met at Keokuk, Iowa, in 1873, and organized the Swedish Evangelical Lutheran Mission Synod, of which Sanngren became president. A similar or-ganization, The Swedish Evangelical Lutheran Ansgary Synod, was effected in 1874; Prof. C. Anderson being the chief promoter. Both these synods called themselves Luther-an, and their constitutions contained the Augsburg Confes-sion; yet the tendency of Dr. P. Waldenström was the pre-dominent feature. As is well known Waldenström differed from the Lutheran Church in regard to the doctrine of atone-ment, mode of worship, and church government. For awhile they both prospered. The Ansgary Synod started a school in Knoxville, Ill. In 1876-77 the Mission Synod, which was the truest specimen of the Mission movement in Sweden, received great accession in membership. In 1884-85, however, they both ceased to exist.[1] At the dissolution each of them numbered about 35 ministers and 4,000 members.

In 1885 several of those who had formerly been connected with the Ansgary and Mission synods organized the Swed-ish Evangelical Mission Covenant of America. This organi-zation has—like the *Svenska Missionsforbundet* in Sweden, which it resembles in name, religious belief and practice, and government, although they are not officially connected—no formulated creed; the Bible being the only authority. Each congregation manages completely its own affairs, resembling

---

1 It is claimed that the dissolution was partly caused by the fact that most of the members of the two synods objected to requiring people to subscribe to the Augsburg Confession before they could become members of the congregations.— [EDITOR.]

in this respect the Congregationalists.[1] The different congregations do not allow any person to join them except those who confess that they are converted and are willing to live a Christian life, resembling in this respect, as well as in mode of worship, the Methodists. According to the statistics of the year ending 1899, the Swedish Evangelical Mission Covenant of America has about 135 congregations, 12,000 communicants, and church property valued at $500,-000; but there are at least twice as many Swedish Mission Friends in this country, who have independent church societies not officially connected with the Covenant. The organization has had a school of their own since 1891, supports missions in China and Alaska, and several papers are published in the interest of the work.

---

1 In fact the Swedish Mission Friends in this country had, for a couple of years, a school in Chicago in connection with the Congregational theological seminary; and many of the ministers claim to be Congregationalists, being admitted and considered as such at the yearly meetings of that organization.—[EDITOR.

Historical Review of the Swedish Lutheran Augustana Synod.

— BY —

REV. C. J. PETRI.

In 1638 the Swedes founded a colony on the banks of Delaware River. The same year these colonists erected, where Philadelphia now stands, the first Lutheran church building in America. Ever since, Swedish immigrants have settled in this country, but up to the year 1840 they were few and came at irregular intervals, and both religiously and socially became completely intermixed with other nationalities. From this time on immigration became regular, but it was not heavy, nor was its direction definite till about 1850, when it assumed immense proportions, and poured in a steady stream into the states and territories of the North-west. During this early period, when the life of the immigrants was chiefly migratory, religious affairs were naturally in a similar unorganized and unsettled condition.

In 1850 Prof. L. P. Esbjörn, the father of the Swedish-American Lutheran church, organized congregations at Andover, Moline, and Galesburg, Ill. But two years previous a Swedish Lutheran church had been organized at New Sweden, Iowa.* On Sept. 18, 1851, The Synod of Northern Illinois was organized, which shortly afterwards effected a connection with the General Synod. Esbjörn and some Norwegians had been invited to unite their congregations in forming the new body. They accepted. But Esbjörn, who was sent by the Swedes as one of their delegates, did not reach Cedarville, Ill., where the conference was held, until Sept. 19th, when the constitution had already been adopted. Most of the American members believed in the *New-Lutheranism*, a less strict Lutheranism, which accepted the Altered Ausburg Confession. The constitution of the Synod of Northern Illinois contained the following sentence in regard to faith: "This synod regards the Word of God as the only infallible rule of faith and practice, and the Augsburg Confession as containing a summary of the fundamental doctrines of the Christian religion, mainly correct." Esbjörn was no disciple of the New-Lutheranism, but he believed in union, thinking that people holding different views in religious matters could co-operate together in Christian fellowship. He joined, but insisted on having a reservation for himself and his congregations in the records in regard to the article of faith, which was granted. In a short time many Scandinavian immigrants and some ministers arrived, who organized churches in different parts of the country, and Esbjörn became the Scandinavian professor at the seminary of the Northern Illinois Synod, in Springfield, 1858. It had been deemed necessary, in order to attend to the religious needs of the Scandinavians to educate in this country men of their own nationalities, as a sufficient number of clergymen

*For a more detailed discussion of this church, see **Rev. M. F. Hokanson's** biography in Vol. II, p. 212.—EDITOR.

could not be secured from home.[1] But Esbjörn could not
agree with the president of the seminary, who adhered to the
New-Lutheranism, and in 1860 he resigned his position. In
order to carry on the work among the many arriving im-
migrants, the Scandinavians had special conferences, namely :
The Chicago conference which was composed of Swedes and
Norwegians; the Mississippi conference, Swedes; and the
Minnesota conference, mostly Swedes.

On account of the existing difference in views in regard
to the Augsburg Confession, and also owing to differences
in language between the various elements composing the
Northern Illinois Synod, the Swedes and Norwegians met, in
the month of April, 1860, in Chicago, for the purpose of establishing a new synod. As a result of this meeting, what is
now called the Swedish Lutheran Augustana Synod was organized, June 5, 1860, at a meeting on Jefferson Prairie, Wis.
Dr. T. N. Hasselquist was elected as the first president, and
served for several years in that office. The name *Augustana*
was adopted at the instance of Dr. E. Norelius. At this meeting 49 congregations were represented by 27 ministers and
15 lay-delegates. These were, of course, not all Swedes, some
were Norwegians, and the meeting was held in a Norwegian
church at Jefferson Prairie, near Clinton, Wis. Swedes and
Norwegians were united in one synod, and hence the original
and incorporated name of the organization was the Scandi-

---

[1] It should be observed that although several ordained Lutheran clergymen
from Sweden have, during the whole immigration period, settled in this country
and become pastors of Swedish-American Lutheran churches, yet the Swedish
Lutherans in America and Sweden have not been, nor are, officially connected with
each other. But the Augustana Synod and the Lutheran church in Sweden have
always been on the most friendly terms. The synod considers herself as a daughter
of the mother church in Sweden, and is so regarded by her.—[EDITOR.

navian Evangelical Lutheran Augustana Synod of North America; it was not until 1894 that the word "Scandinavian" was dropped. According to their own statistics of 1860, 49 congregations, with 4,967 communicants, and 27 clergymen united to form the Scandinavian Synod. Of these, 17 clergymen, 36 congregations, and 3,747 communicants were Swedes. The union of the Swedes and Norwegians continued until 1870, when the latter, on account of the difference in the languages, withdrew and organized themselves into a separate organization. This was considered a wise movement, and since that time a strong and zealous work has been carried on by the different Scandinavian Lutherans. The Augustana Synod has been a member of the General Council of the Evangelical Lutheran Church in America [2] from the beginning of the Council, which met in its first regular convention at Fort Wayne, Ind., Nov. 20-26, 1867. It is at present one of the largest synods belonging to the Council.

From the very beginning the Swedish Lutherans have taken great interest in educational work. Every congregation within the Augustana Synod endeavors to maintain good parochial schools and energetic Sunday schools. Higher education has received a hearty support, and the success and progress of the Augustana Synod in this country must be said to have depended in no little degree upon the early and great enthusiasm toward higher education, which made itself manifest among the Swedes. No sooner had the venerable "fathers" of our synod, such men as Prof. L. P. Esbjörn,

---

[2] The General Council, like the General Synod and similar organizations, is composed of several Lutheran synods which have united for the purpose of advising each other. The Council has no authority over the synods, congregations, or individuals.—[EDITOR.

Dr. T. N. Hasselquist, Dr. E. Carlson, Rev. Jonas Swenson, Dr. E. Norelius, etc., begun their church work, than they began to work for the establishment of colleges and schools. The people in the churches were ready and quick to respond. In 1860 the oldest and largest of the Swedish-American colleges, Augustana College and Theological Seminary, was founded at Chicago; moved to Paxton, Ill., in 1863, and permanently located at Rock Island, the same state, in 1875. In 1862 Gustavus Adolphus College, St. Peter, Minn., was founded. Bethany College, Lindsborg, Kan., was founded in 1881. Since then several academies have been organized, namely: Luther Academy, Wahoo, Neb; Hope Academy, Moorhead, Minn.; Emanuel Academy, Minneapolis, Minn.; and in 1893 two more were organized, namely, Martin Luther College, in Chicago, Ill., and Upsala College, in Brooklyn, N. Y. All these institutions are annually attended by 1,500 students, have had a remarkable progress, and have developed themselves in all directions. The 'property of these different institutions is estimated to be worth about $500,000. They have been a source of great blessing and influence to the members of the Augustana Synod. The greatest number of the 450 ministers of the synod and many of the school teachers have received their training at these institutions. Augustana College and Theological Seminary, however, is the only college where a full theological training is given; it is also the only college directly controlled by the Augustana Synod. The other schools are managed, either by some conference within the synod, or by private corporations composed of Swedish Lutherans.

In the work of education the synod has realized the

power and influence of the press. Dr. T. N. Hasselquist started in 1855 the first Swedish newspaper in America, a religious weekly, now called *Augustana*, which is today the largest Swedish weekly church-paper in the world. The synod publishes also Sunday school papers in the Swedish and English languages. The English papers published by the synod proves that the Augustana Synod is awake on the question of language. The Augustana Synod in America does not expect always to use the Swedish language. The time will come when the English language will be commonly used in our churches, and even now most of the young men who enter the ministry have received such an education that they are able to preach in English as well as in Swedish. The aim of the synod is, therefore, to furnish the people with English preachers and Lutheran literature in English. The Lutheran Augustana Book Concern at Rock Island, under the supervision of the synod, is doing a grand and noble work in sending forth good Lutheran literature in the Swedish and English lauguages.

In 1860 the first Swedish Lutheran orphans' home in America was established by Dr. E. Norelius, in Vasa, Goodhue county, Minn. At present the synod supports six orphans' homes and three hospitals. The value of the property of these institutions is put at $350,000. At the orphans' homes 300 orphans are supported and educated annually. A deaconess institute is also maintained at Omaha, Neb.

The synod is at present divided into eight conferences, viz.: The Illinois, Minnesota, Iowa, Kansas, New York, Nebraska, California, and Columbia. Each conference carries on its special misssion work within its own territory.

AUGUSTANA COLLEGE, ROCK ISLAND, ILL.

GUSTAVUS ADOLPHUS COLLEGE, ST. PETER, MINN.

The missionary work in territories outside the conferences is carried on by the synod through its general board of missions. At present this board superintends the mission work in Utah, gives aid to churches in Florida, Maine, and on the Pacific Coast. The Church Extension Society has been organized within the synod, the duty of which is to assist small and weak congregations in building churches. The aim of the mission has been to gather the thousands of Swedes in this country around the Word of God; with this object in view, many large congregations have, during the 50 years past, been organized and maintained. The synod also supports a special immigrant mission in New York City. In Chicago the immigrant mission is carried on by the Illinois conference.

Since the organization of the synod numerous churches have been organized so that Augustana Synod churches are today to be found in almost every state and territory within the United States and in different parts of Canada. The synod, according to the statistics of the year ending 1899, numbers about 900 congregations, with 200,000 members, of which 115,000 are communicant members. The value of the church property owned by these churches is by a moderate estimate considered to be $4,200,000, and it may safely be said that during the past 40 years the people of the Augustana Synod have used no less than $12,000,000 in building and supporting churches and carrying on missionary work. Adding then thereto the amounts raised for schools, colleges, the theological seminary, orphans' homes, and hospitals, it becomes clear to every unbiased observer that the Augustana Synod has shown itself as an active and wide awake institution, well deserving the confidence of the Swedes in America and the love of all Christian people.

The synod has always without fear and with fervent devotion defended the pure Lutheranism in theory and practice, planted itself on the foundation of a pure Gospel as set forth in the Unaltered Augsburg Confession, has carefully guarded the pulpit and the altar, has taken a firm stand against secret societies and questionable practises, and has as a result, without doubt, made some enemies; yet, by the blessing of God, the synod has carried on a noble and successful work and is today, by far, the leading and most influential religious body among the Swedes of America.

The history of the Augustana Synod during the past forty years shows what can be done by a united effort. The Swedish Lutherans have been a unit from the beginning. No strifes and contentions of any serious nature have existed among the people. The members of the synod have been surrounded by God's favor and united in a true faith, zealously doing their work with a sacrificing love. The synod has had a glorious past but it expects a more glorious future. Long live the Augustana Synod!

Historical Review of the United Norwegian Lutheran Church of America.

—BY—

KNUTE GJERSET, Ph. D.

The higher unity of soul and spirit did not exist among the Norwegian Lutherans at the time the immigration to America commenced, a fact for which we have the best evidence in the movement originated by Hauge. The church of Norway was itself in the throes of a bitter conflict between two widely different tendencies, which, when they were transferred to American soil, only assumed more definite shape and expression. These tendencies merit a brief attention, since they have had such marked effects upon the religious life of the Norwegian people in America.

Hans Nilsen Hauge was a poor, but talented and pious country lad, springing from the yeomanry of Norway. Through pure religious zeal he began to preach to the people of the neighborhood, not any new doctrine, but the teachings of the state church. His voice was raised against the godlessness and unbelief which had seized both clergy and

225-7

lay people by the introduction of rationalism. He denounced the worldliness and extravagance of the ministers
of the state church, and urged the people to repent. A revival movement sprang up, which soon spread over the entire country. A strong religious zeal, which was often mistaken for fanaticism, characterized the followers of Hauge.
They forbade the wearing of any ornaments. Even works
of art in the home were classed among the vanities. They
held that any one who felt an inner calling had a right to
preach, without any regulation or interference by the church.
In severity of life, as well as in religious practice, they much
resembled the Puritans in England. Even after a reaction
against rationalism had begun in the state church, and the
ministers within it were characterized by zeal and devotion
in Christian life, as well as by purity of doctrine, this movement went on. The state church, however, which looked
upon the movement as a revolt against its authority, now
tried to put a stop to it. Hauge was imprisoned and his followers suffered many hardships. But this procedure only
increased the bitterness of the struggle and put new hindrances in the way of understanding and reconciliation.
When the two parties met on American soil, where there was
no compulsion or pressure, the chasm which divided them
merely widened. Elling Eielsen, who arrived in this country
in 1839, was the first preacher of the Gospel to the Norwegian settlers. Eielsen was a faithful disciple of Hauge, and
already in 1846 he and his followers organized what they
called The Evangelical Lutheran Church in America, the first
church organization among the Norwegians in this country.
As emigration continued to increase, several ordained minis-

ters came over. They attempted to come to an understanding with Elling, and several meetings were held for the purpose, but no results could be reached. The old differences soon made themselves manifest. The entirely different views in regard to church life, as well as to internal and external church organization, represented by the two parties, made it impossible for them to come to an agreement. Moreover, the differences in education, in mode of life, and in general training of the representatives of the two tendencies, also laid hindrances in the way, as they found it difficult, much on that account, to really understand and appreciate even each others better qualities.   Union was, of course, impossible. The ministers who came from Norway then organized the Norwegian Lutheran Synod in 1853.

But everything did not work smoothly in the Evangelical Lutheran Church in America, established by Elling Eielsen and his followers. Elling conspicuously lacked all talents of an organizer. The constitution which they had adopted was deficient in many important respects, so that there was often no real connection between the congregations. Dissatisfaction with the condition of things was general, and Elling, who was pre-eminently an evangelist, was unable to remedy it.   Consequently the clergymen, Paul Anderson and Ole Andrewson, left Elling's church and effected a temporary union with the Frankean Lutheran Synod of New York, until a Norwegian synod could be organized in the West. After a short time these ministers again left the Frankean Synod and joined the Northern Illinois Synod with which they were connected till 1860.   To this synod belonged also a number of Swedish ministers and congregations.   On the 5th of June of the last named year the clergymen, Paul Anderson, Ole Andrewson, O. J. Hatlestad, and others, Norwegians; and Hasselquist, Carlson, Esbjörn, and others, Swedes, met on Jefferson Prairie to consider the organization of a Scandinavian synod. The Scandinavian ministers and congregations in the Northern Illinois Synod now left that church and organized the Scandinavian Evangelical Lutheran Augustana Synod, consisting of both Swedish and Norwegian ministers and congregations. According to their own statistics of 1861, 60 congregations, with 5,600 communicant members, and 32 clergymen belonged to the new body. Of these, 11 clergymen, 17 congregations, and 1,400 communicants were Norwegians. The synod erected a school for educating young men for the ministry, at Paxton, Ill. This school, which consisted of both a theological and a collegiate department, had for some time only two professors, and was financially largely supported by the people of Sweden. The synod grew rapidly, and it was found necessary to have a Norwegian professor at Paxton. A call was extended to Rev. A. Weenaas, of Norway, who accepted, and entered upon his duties as professor of theology in the seminary at Paxton in 1868. Weenaas, however, soon grew dissatisfied with his new surroundings and urged upon the Norwegians to erect a school of their own. In 1869 the Norwegian wing of the Scandinavian Lutheran Augustana Synod, following the wish of Prof. Weenaas, bought a school building at Marshal, Wis., where work was begun in the fall, with Prof. Weenaas as president, and the Norwegian students who now moved thither from Paxton.

The difference in language had always been a serious

difficulty within the synod, and in 1870 it was thought best, on account of this difficulty, for the Norwegians and Swedes to separate. The Norwegians then withdrew and organized the Norwegian-Danish Augustana Synod, while the Swedish branch of the old synod continued under the old name. The two organizations, however, were on the friendliest of terms, and promised to co-operate and aid each other as far as possible. Shortly after the Norwegian-Danish Augustana Synod was organized, certain leading professors and ministers within it began to negotiate a union with Rev. C. L. Clausen, who a few years previous, with the congregations in his charge, had left the Norwegian Synod, because of the controversy regarding slavery, or the condition of life servitude. In order to effect this union with Clausen, and his, at that time, quite large congregations, a few ministers and lay delegates at a meeting in St. Ansgar, Iowa, resolved, without asking the congregations, to dissolve the Norwegian-Danish Augustana Synod and reorganize it under a new name. A new organization was effected, called The Norwegian-Danish Evangelical Lutheran Conference, of which Rev. C. L. Clausen was elected president. But this action was not favorably received by all the people of the Norwegian-Danish Augustana Synod. At a church meeting on Jefferson Prairie in the fall of the same year the synod declared the St. Ansgar resolutions null and void. This led to a division of the synod; about half of the congregations and their ministers leaving it and joining the Conference. Among those who thus seceded from the Augustana Synod was also Prof. Weenaas, of the seminary at Marshall, together with a majority of the students. This was a hard blow to the Augus-

tana Synod.   There was a heavy debt on the school building; Prof. Weenaas and the students were gone, besides so
many of the congregations whose financial aid had been
counted on.   The school at Marshall was now able to continue work only in the academic department. This, however,
was of no direct benefit to the synod, and involved considerable expense; consequently attempts were again made to
put the school into condition for educating ministers.   Rev.
D. Lysnes was chosen professor and president, and with his
arrival a new epoch began in the history of the school.   The
theological department again resumed its work; the number
of students increased rapidly, and the debt on the school
buildings was paid.   In 1881 the school was moved to Beloit,
Iowa, where 20 acres of land and commodious buildings had
been secured.   The college department was afterward moved
to Canton, S. D., where buildings to the amount of $8,000
were provided.   The growth of the synod, however, owing
to repeated discouragements, continued to be slow.   According to statistics it comprised, in 1887, 30 ministers, 90 congregations, and 3,500 communicant members.

After the organization of the Conference the school at
Marshall was divided, so that the Conference got the theological department, and the Augustana Synod retained the
academic department.   The theological department was reorganized by the Conference in 1871 into what is now Augsburg Seminary, of which Prof. Weenaas became president. It
was moved to Minneapolis, Minn., in 1872.   The following
year Sven Oftedal, from Norway, became professor at the
seminary, and in 1874 Georg Sverdrup, who two years later
became its president, arrived.   The whole subsequent history

of the institution is closely connected with the energetic efforts of these two men.   The seminary was badly in debt till 1877, when Prof. Oftedal organized committees throughout the congregations of the Conference, who by personal solicitations raised the sum of $18,000, which was more than enough to liquidate the existing debt.   The seminary has been constantly growing, in extent and thoroughness of the courses of study, as well as in numerical strength.   The course of study for ministers is now five years preparatory work, and three years theological training.   In 1891 the seminary had 10 professors and instructors, and 188 students in attendance.   The property, including, besides the seminary buildings, also a dormitory and professor's residence, and the block on which they stand, is valued at $150,000.   The Conference was, undoubtedly, better financially situated than any of the other Norwegian Lutheran bodies.   It was without debts, and had large funds at its disposal.   It enjoyed a steady growth, and exhibited a remarkable vigor in church life.   According to statistics the Conference had, in the year 1887, 101 clergymen, 383 congregations, and 30,000 communicant members.

In 1880 a new church controversy broke out, this time within the Norwegian Synod itself, more serious in character than any of the preceeding.   The controversy first arose in the Missouri Synod between Dr. C. F. W. Walther, of the theological seminary, at St. Louis, Mo., and Dr. F. A. Schmidt, of the theological seminary, at Madison, Wis., regarding the doctrine of election and predestination.   The controversy, involving very fundamental tenets of the Lutheran faith, soon found its way into the Norwegian Synod, which for a number of years had been friendly related to the Missouri Synod. From year to year the struggle grew more intense, involving not only the ministers, but also the lay people in the contest. Discussions were held throughout the Synod at private conferences, and at the yearly synodical meetings, but no agreement was reached. At a church meeting held in Decorah, Iowa, in 1884, each party drafted a statement of their position in the controversy. *Redegjörelsen* (The Explanation) of the Missourians, as the followers of Dr. Walther were called, was signed by 107 ministers. *Bekjendelsen* (The Confession) of the Anti-Missourians, as Dr. Schmidt's followers were called, was signed by 72 ministers, which number was afterward increased to 97. Dr. Schmidt and his followers, who considered the difference in the doctrine of the two contending parties a fundamental one, now established a theological seminary of their own at Northfield, Minn., and here work was begun in the fall of 1886 with Dr. Schmidt and Prof. Böckman as theological professors. This step, however, was not tolerated by the Synod. At the next joint synodical meeting held in Stoughton, Wis., it was condemned as an act of secession and a virtual separation. The Anti-Missourians, however, claimed a right to continue the seminary, and 57 of their ministers signed a protest against the resolutions passed upon them by the meeting, and seceded from the Synod. This step was soon followed by a large number of congregations. According to reliable reports about 100 ministers and over one-third of the congregations left the Norwegian Synod.

These ministers and congregations did not, however, desire to organize themselves into a new permanent church denomination, which would constitute the sixth distinct body among the Norwegian Lutherans in America. They met in Northfield, Minn., in 1886, and effected a temporary organization, known as The Anti-Missourian Brotherhood, of which Rev. L. M. Björn was elected president. It was their purpose and hope to bring about a union with the other Norwegian Lutheran churches, as soon as possible. For this purpose a series of *Fri-Konferenser*, or conferences for a general consideration of the subjects which divided them, were held, in which all the bodies belonging to the Norwegian Lutheran church in this country took part. Six of these conferences were held during the years preceeding and following the organization of the Anti-Missourian Brotherhood; in Roland, Iowa, 1882; Holden, Minn., 1883; St. Ansgar, Iowa, 1884; Chicago, Ill., 1885; Gol, Minn., 1886, and in Willmar, Minn., 1887. These conferences, where discussion was thorough and earnest, and conducted in a brotherly spirit, helped the different parties to come to a better understanding of each others true position, and were largely instrumental in bringing about the union which was soon afterwards effected. The first meeting for the purpose of considering the possibility of union was held by the Anti-Missourians in Minneapolis in February, 1888. Another meeting for the same purpose was held by all the parties, in Scandinavia, Wis., in November, of the same year. At the meeting in Scandinavia the articles of union were adopted for the first time by the denominations which afterward united. They were then submitted for consideration to the congregations, and to each of the organizations in particular. They were approved of by all, not a single congregation raising any objections to the stipulations made. At this same meeting *Opgjör* (Settlement) was also made in regard to the various doctrinal controversies which from time to time had been carried on among the Norwegian Lutherans in America, and an agreement was reached concerning the points in dispute. In the early part of June, 1890, the three organizations, The Norwegian-Danish Conference, The Norwegian Augustana Synod, and The Anti-Missourian Brotherhood, held a meeting in Minneapolis for again to consider the subject of union. At first the organizations held separate meetings. But a strong sentiment in favor of union soon became predominant. They were all tired of the bitter controversies which for so many years had divided into hostile camps those that ought to stand united. On the 13th the delegates, ministers, and professors of the three organizations met in the old Trinity Church, belonging to the Conference, but as this structure was too small to hold the large assembly, they formed in procession and proceeded to the church belonging to the Swedish Augustana Synod, where they organized themselves into The United Norwegian Lutheran Church in America. The articles of union, adopted at the meeting in Scandinavia, Wis., and sanctioned by all the congregations, and by each of the organizations separately, were made the basis of the union. Some of the stipulations in these articles are as follows:

"In order that the contracting parties can organize themselves into a church, they jointly and separately agree to the following stipulations:

"1. The church shall erect and operate one theological seminary.

" 2. This seminary shall be Augsburg Seminary, in Minneapolis.

" 3. The professors at this seminary shall be paid by the interest from a fund.

(*a*) The Augustana Synod shall contribute a fund of $15,000.

(*b*) The Conference shall contribute a fund of $50,000.

(*c*) The Anti-Missourians shall contribute a fund of $50,000.

(*d*) The fund is to consist of cash, or notes drawing interest, or other safe property.

" 4. At said seminary there shall be 5 theological professors.

(*a*) The Anti-Missourians shall employ two theological professors.

(*b*) The Augustana Synod shall employ one theological professor.

(*c*) The Conference shall employ two theological professors.

" 5. The constitution for said seminary shall be drawn up as soon as the union is effected.

" 6. Theological students already admitted to the theological seminaries of the different organizations shall by virtue of this admission be entitled to admission in the new theological seminary.

" 7. The church shall be incorporated as soon as possible.

" 8. To this church shall be transferred all school property—as well real estate as funds—which said organizations may be in possession of, at the time of union.

"9. This real estate shall, when it is transferred to the church, be free from debt.

"10. The preparatory departments at Augsburg Seminary, and at Canton Academy, shall be operated as usual, at least one year after the union is effected. In Beloit, Iowa, the school shall also continue at least one year after the union is effected.

"23. The board of trustees for the respective organizations, such as they have previously been elected by said organizations, shall continue in their office, after the union is effected, until the new church is incorporated, when they shall immediately deed all property, which they hold as board of trustees, to the new corporation."

The part of the contract relating to the transfer of property was fulfilled in due time by the Augustana Synod and the Brotherhood; but Augsburg Seminary, held in trust by its board of trustees, was never transferred according to article eight above.* Within a year after the organization of the United Church a number of newspaper articles began to create a feeling of distrust among the people, and Augsburg Seminary and St. Olaf College were pitted against each other as rival institutions by their most devoted patrons. It was also contended that the United Church had violated the stipulations of its organization by passing the following resolution a couple of days after the date of its origin: "St. Olaf College at Northfield shall be the college of the United Norwegian Lutheran Church." Resolutions of a similar nature were also passed at the annual meeting in 1891, while the college department of Augsburg Seminary was to be

---

* See the articles on the schools and the churches in Minnesota.

maintained "for the time being." This only made the Augsburg faction the less inclined to transfer the property, their stock arguments being, in a nutshell, about as follows: "The founders of Augsburg Seminary intended it to be a theological seminary and a college combined under our board. If it is transferred to the United Church, the college department may be dropped. But that would be contrary to the intention of the founders of the institution: therefore it ought not to be transferred to the United Church." Prof. S. Oftedal, the president of the board, for a long time also contended that the property could not be legally transferred. In this controversy Oftedal was frequently characterized as one who wanted to keep property to which he had no rights; while he and his followers made the countercharge that the United Church intended to violate the agreement on which that association was based. The feeling engendered by this contention waxed quite bitter during the years 1890–93, and when the United Church, at its annual meeting in 1893; decided to abandon the Augsburg buildings in case the property was not deeded over to the United Church in the summer of that year, there was nothing left but to fight to the bitter end. The United Church "removed" its school, thenceforth called the United Church Seminary, from the Augsburg buildings to rented quarters; the Augsburg Publishing House was wrested from the board of trustees of Augsburg Seminary in the spring of 1894, by means of recourse to the courts; legal proceedings were begun in 1896 for the recovery of the Augsburg property; in the fall of 1897 the district court handed down a decision which was favorable to the United Church; in the spring of 1898 this decision was quashed by the state supreme court; the United Church took steps to have the case tried in the court of equity; but in the summer of 1898 the matter was settled out of court by mutual agreement. The main stipulations of this agreement were that the United Church should have the endowment fund, nominally amounting to about $39,-000; and that no more efforts should be made to dislodge the old board of trustees of Augsburg Seminary. Thus ended one of the most memorable struggles in the history of the Norwegian Lutheran churches in America.

The lawyers' fees and other expenses directly connected with the law suit to recover the Augsburg property entailed a total outlay of $11,000 on the part of the United Church. It is easy to appreciate this loss, because it may be expressed in dollars and cents. But it is not so easy to estimate the mental suffering and moral injury caused by the so-called "Augsburg Strife;" and much of the good work done in the United Church during the years 1893–98 was marred by this strife. But no reflection ought to be cast upon the sincerity of the participants, for they believed they were struggling for a good cause, the one party as well as the other.

From 1893 to 1898 the Augsburg faction in the United Church was bent on antagonizing the work of the latter at every point. But the real friends of the United Church, consisting of the people from the Brotherhood, the Augustana Synod and most of the Conference congregations in Iowa, Wisconsin and southern Minnesota—were equal to the occasion. The United Church was never seriously hampered by lack of funds. The treasurer reported to the annual meeting in 1898: "We asked for $13,388 for general expenses, and we received $14,971.55." On Jan. 1. 1897, a dozen congregations were formally expelled, and a number of others withdrew of their own accord.

The whole number of churches served by the 330 ministers who were connected with the United Church in 1900 was 1,100. These churches embraced about 225,000 souls, of whom 125,000 were communicant members. But the whole number of congregations formally belonging was only about 750, which had 100,000 communicant members and 185,000 souls. The reports of the parochial schools showed that on the average almost 30 days were taught in each congregation. The finances were in a healthy condition. The value of the church and school property directly or indirectly controlled by the organization may be put at about $4,000,000.

The Augsburg Publishing House issued about 120,000 books, tracts and other items. *Lutheraneren* and *Luthersk Börneblad* had a combined circulation of 26,000.

In 1899 the United Church owned and controlled a theological seminary, located in Minneapolis, Minn.; St. Olaf College, Northfield, Minn.; Augustana College, Canton, S. D.; a normal school at Madison, Minn.; and an orphans' home at Beloit, Iowa. The institutions mentioned below were either wholly or partly supported by members of the United Church, and several of them were officially connected with that body: Concordia College, Moorhead, Minn.; St. Ansgar Seminary, St. Ansgar, Ia.; Mount Horeb Academy, Mount Horeb, Wis.; Scandinavia Academy, Scandinavia, Wis.; Pleasant View Lutheran College, Ottawa, Ill.; a deaconesses' institute in Chicago; orphans' homes at Lake Park.

Minn., in Chicago, Ill., and at Wittenberg, Wis.; and hospitals at Austin, Crookston and Zumbrota, Minn. Steps have been taken to establish a home for aged people, and to put up new buildings for the theological seminary in or near the Twin Cities.

Missionary work was carried on at several places in southern Madagascar; but since the French took possession of that island the Catholics have somewhat hampered the efforts of the Norwegians. Members of the United Church also contributed quite liberally to the different missions in Asia.

The Augsburg controversy and the withdrawal of the Free Church element subjected the United Church to a great strain. But its honest supporters only rallied the more energetically to her support. At this stage it seems reasonable to anticipate that a body which could not be crippled by passing through such a crisis will be fully able to weather the storms that may rise on her future course, and whatever may happen in the future, the organization of the United Church is the grandest attempt ever made by Norwegian-Americans to neutralize the spirit of religious discord and disintegration among them.

Pages 238-42 were rewritten for the second edition by J. J. Skordalsvold.—EDITOR.

Statistics Regarding the Scandinavians in the United States.

— BY —

O. N. NELSON.

Some one has said that figures never lie. But certainly different statistics on the same subject disagree very much, at least that is the case in regard to the reports of immigration and emigration, by the governments of the United States and the Scandinavian countries. Therefore, I publish, in tables I. and II., all the statistics regarding the Scandinavian immigration and emigration which I have been able to secure. Everything in the United States census which refers to the Scandinavian-Amerians has been compiled in convenient tables, or, when such an arrangement was impossible, the facts have been stated in this article.

But the figures, as given in immigration and emigration reports and in the census, are not altogether correct — far from it — but they are, after all, the nearest approach to the truth which can be had. And if any portion of this book deserves to be studied, it is, perhaps, the following tables; they, for example, contain a good history of the great Scandinavian movements toward the Northwest; they show the proportion of Scandinavian paupers, criminals, idiots, etc., in comparison with other nationalities. In my opinion, however, the Scandinavian statistics, as far as they go, in regard to the Northern immigration into this country, are more reliable than those of the United States.

The United States statistics regarding immigration commenced in 1820. From the close of the Revolutionary War up to 1820 it is estimated that 250,000 immigrants arrived, although the accurate number is not known. Between the years of 1820-68 only the arrival of alien passengers were indicated, no distinction being made between the real immigrants and transient sojourners, but it is estimated that 98 per cent of all the alien passengers remained in this country. Prior to 1868 there was no distinction made between the immigrants from Sweden and Norway; both countries were considered as one. Since 1869 the sex of the immigrants has been recorded by the United States; since 1873, the age; since 1875, the occupation. Immigrants from the British North American possessions and Mexico, comprising about one per cent of the entire immigration into the country, are not included in the United States statistics, from 1885 to 1893 owing to the absence of law providing for the collection of accurate data in regard thereto. The minister of agriculture of the Dominion of Canada reports that during the years of 1885-91 over 500,000 European emigrants arrived at Canadian ports en route for the United States. Of course a large proportion of these immigrants were Scandinavians, but their exact number cannot be ascertained.

It was not until 1869 that there was a law in Norway

which required the taking of accurate data in regard to Norwegian emigration. But from various sources the Norwegian government has secured and published facts in regard to the whole emigration, which, although not very correct, yet on the whole are, perhaps, more reliable than those published by the United States. The Norwegian statistics state that the American statistics in regard to the Norwegian immigration, prior to 1868, are very inaccurate.

The Swedish statistics of emigration date from 1851. In a letter from the statistical bureau of Sweden it is stated that the figures regarding the Swedish emigration to this country are too low up to the year of 1884, and whenever the American statistics are lower, they are still more inaccurate. Since 1884 the Swedish statistics are comparatively correct. While in latter years, even before 1884, the American reports regarding the Swedish immigration are too high, owing to the fact that many thousand Finns, who pass over Gothenburg, are recorded as Swedes. But it must also be remembered that several persons who live in Finland are Swedes by race, and still more so by education and by language.

The Danish statistics regarding emigration began in 1869.

According to the United States statistics, there have arrived from 1820-90 over 15,000,000 immigrants to this country. Most of them have, of course, come from Europe. For example, Germany has supplied about 4,500,000, Ireland 3,500,000, England 2,500,000, the Scandinavian countries 1,250,000, and the immigrants from no other single country have exceeded 500,000. Taking into consideration those who have been omitted from the official reports, it is fair to

estimate that 1,500,000 Scandinavians have settled in the
United States since the country began to be colonized, up to
1900

The Scandinavian emigration began very late.   The Norwegian, which is the earliest, did not exceed 1,000 a year
until 1843, the Swedish not until 1852, and the Danish not
until 1857. The Scandinavian immigration reached its maximum in 1882, when nearly 65,000 Swedes, 30,000 Norwegians, and 12,000 Danes arrived in this country.   Since then
the emigration from all Northern countries has declined.
From 1821-90 the Scandinavian emigrants constituted seven
per cent of the total immigration.   Sixty-two per cent of the
Northern emigrants are male, 65 per cent arrive between the
ages of 15 and 40, 24 per cent are children under 15, and 11
per cent are over 40 years of age. During the years 1881-90,
one person out of 5,914 was a clergyman, one out of every
5,083 a musician, one out of 7,236 a physician and surgeon,
and one out of 3,034 a teacher—in other words, only one
out of 1,017 had a profession, while one out of 12 was a
skilled laborer, and one-half of the Scandinavian emigrants
were either farmers, common laborers, merchants, or servants.

Nor is there any reason to assume that they change their
occupations a great deal when they arrive in this country,
for, according to the United States census of 1870, 1880, 1890,
25 per cent of the Scandinavian-born population were engaged in agriculture, and 50 per cent labored at what was
called "All classes of work."   It is a notable fact that one
out of every four Scandinavian engages in agriculture,
while only one out of six of the native Americans, one out

of seven of the Germans, and one out of twelve of the Irish, follow the same profession.

In 1890 only 32 per cent of the Swedes, 23 per cent of the Danes, and 21 per cent of the Norwegians, in this country lived in cities of over 25,000 inhabitants.

When the first census of the United States was taken, in 1790, there were about four millions of people in the country; in 1830 the population exceeded three times that amount. It was not until 1850 that the foreign elements were taken into account by the census reports. In that year one out of every 1,200 persons was a Scandinavian; in 1860, one out of 435; in 1870, one out of 160; in 1880, one out of 114; and in 1890, one out of 66. But until recently the census did not take into account the children born in this country of Scandinavian parents. In 1880,* however, it was estimated that 635,405 persons in this country, born anywhere in the world, had Scandinavian fathers, but about four thousand less had Scandinavian mothers—these two sums must not be added together, because most of the Scandinavian men and women have married among their own nationalities. About 84 persons out of 100 have both Scandinavian fathers and mothers, 86 have both German fathers and mothers, and 91 have both Irish fathers and mothers. The fact that the Scandinavians inter marry more frequently with other nationalities than either the Germans or the Irish, although less with native Americans, must have a powerful effect in Americanizing the former more quickly than the latter.

In 1880 there were 440,262 Scandinavian-born persons in this country; adding these to those of Scandinavian parentage born in the U. S. must equal 1,000,000. But this re-

---

* The census bulletin enumerating the persons of Scandinavian parentage in the United States for 1890, did not appear until the latter part of 1894, and the result of said report has been tabulated on page 264.

sult is, virtually, also obtained by multiplying 440,262 by 2½. Therefore, if anyone desires to ascertain the exact number of Scandinavians and their children, in proportion to the total population, of any year, state, territory, or city, he can multiply the figures — as found in tables III., IV., V., VI , VII. and VIII., in this volume — by 2½. But the census reports are far from being correct, they omit many persons of all nationalities, and frequently confound foreigners as well as natives; but, as a general thing, they fall below and not above the real number. And, without doubt, the nearest approach to the truth in regard to the number of Danes, Norwegians, Swedes, and their children, in this country, can be had by multiplying the Scandinavian-born — as recorded in the United States census for each year, and in each state, territory, and city — by 3.

According to this method of calculation, one person out of every 25 in the United States was, in 1890, a Scandinavian, either by birth, or by parentage. It is, perhaps, a conservative estimate to assume that there are, in 1900, three millions of Northmen in this country. In several of the Northwestern states they are the controlling power. Two-fifths of the total population in Minnesota are Scandinavians. There are in this country about one-fifth as many Danes as in Denmark, one-third as many Swedes as in Sweden, and one-half as many Norwegians as in Norway.

The United States statistics in regard to the defective population in the country, by nationalities, are very incomplete. In 1870, however, one out of every 670 of the Irish in this country was either deaf and dumb, or blind; one out of 962 of the French; one out of 980 of the English; one out of 1,033 of the native-born Americans; one out of 1,142 òf the British-Americans; one out of 1,480 of the Germans; and one out of 1,810 of the Scandinavians. In the same year one in 197 of the Irish was insane or idiotic, one in 380 of the French, one in 465 of the Germans, one in 584 of the English, one in 672 of the native-born Americans, one in 682 of the Scandinavians, and one in 1,075 of the British-Americans.

In 1880, 1 in 165 of the Spaniards was a prisoner, 1 in 199 of the Chinese, 1 in 207 of the Mexicans, 1 in 260 of the Italians, 1 in 350 of the Irish, 1 in 411 of the Scotch, 1 in 433 of the French, 1 in 456 of the English, 1 in 590 of the British-Americans, 1 in 813 of the Portugese, 1 in 916 of the Russians, 1 in 949 of the native-born Americans and Germans, 1 in 1,033 of the Poles, 1 in 1,173 of the Welsh, 1 in 1,195 of the Belgians, 1 in 1,231 of the Swiss, 1 in 1,383 of the Hollanders, and 1 in 1,539 of the Scandinavians.

The census of 1890, in regard to the defective classes, is very faulty. Yet it appears that one in 132 of the Irish in this country was a pauper, one in 356 of the Germans, one in 387 of the English, one in 690 of the Bohemians, one in 792 of the Scandinavians, and one in 974 of the British-Americans.*

Considering the excellent record of the Scandinavians in regard to crimes and pauperism, the readiness with which they take to farming and become Americanized, the commendable educational and religious training they have received in the North, and it is no wonder that they are by American economists considered to be the best immigrants.

*For a complete discussion of criminality and insanity see pp. 1-22, Vol. II.

About 50 per cent of the Scandinavian emigrants arrive by prepaid passage tickets secured by relatives here. During each year between 1890 and 1900, the postal money orders issued in the United States, payable in the Scandinavian countries, amounted to about $2,250,000, and it is estimated that something like $6,500,000 besides was in one year sent to the North through banks and by other means. During the same period only about $500,000 was annually sent from the North to the United States by means of postal money orders. Of course, part of these sums were settlements for business transactions; yet the United States postoffice reports assert that the excess noted is mainly due to the fact that the immigrants contribute liberally to the support of their friends across the ocean.

It is impossible, however, to arrive at anything like a correct conclusion in regard to what amount of wealth in the shape of presents, prepaid passage tickets, and actual cash which Scandinavian-Americans have transferred from the United States to the North. Smith, in his excellent book, *Emigration and Immigration,* estimates that each immigrant sends to his native country $35, and from 1820–99, according to the United States statistics, not far from 1,500,-000 Northmen have settled in this country. If each of them returned $35, the total sum transferred would amount to $52,500,000.

Each immigrant, however, brings with him a certain sum, which Smith estimates to average from $68 to $100; but no accurate statistics on this subject have ever been published. "It costs," to quote the same authority, "about $562.50 to bring up a child in Europe till

15 years of age, and twice that amount in the United States. But this estimate does not mean the real value of men; they are not valued in dollars and cents. But every immigrant must represent labor capacity, worth at least the value of a slave, which was $800 or $1,000 before the war, but being a free man he may not choose to work. But it is figured that each immigrant is worth $875." Assuming that each Scandinavian immigrant has brought $75, which added to $875, the value of his labor capacity, amounts to $950, and multiplying this by the whole number of immigrants, we find that the Scandinavian countries have sent—or rather permitted to be transfered—to the United States one billion four hundred and fifty million dollars (1,450,000,000) worth of property in the form of human beings and what valuables these have brought with them. Even subtracting the $52,500,000, which have been returned in the shape of prepaid tickets, presents, and cash, it yet leaves the United States in a debt of $1,397,500,000 to the Scandinavian countries.*

The different Scandinavian churches in this country have always exercised a great influence. But it is impossible in this article to give very elaborate statistics in regard to them; nor is it necessary, because this volume contains historical sketches of several of the leading Scandinavian-American church organizations, and each of these sketches deals more or less with the statistics of each denomination. Table X., however, contains some facts in regard to the Scandinavian churches in this country. These facts have mostly been gathered from their own published reports, but in a few cases from the United States census of 1890; and, although they are incomplete, and in some cases inaccurate, they are

---

*According to the immigration report of 1898, the Scandinavian immigrants, who in wealth averaged more than the total European immigrants, had only $29 each.

unquestionably a fair estimate of the strength of the Scandinavian-American churches. Of course, there are other Scandinavian church organizations in this country, besides those enumerated in table X.; but they are small, their union generally loose, and I have been unable to secure any data in regard to them. But I doubt if any one of the church organizations which have been omitted in table X. exceeds 1,000 in membership. Yet there are a great number of Scandinavian churches which are independent, and not connected with any synod, or general organization of several churches; besides, many Scandinavians are members of purely American churches; and it is, perhaps, fair to assume that one-half, or at least one-third, of the Scandinavian-Americans are members of some religious society. During the last fifty years the Scandinavian churches in this country have, no doubt, expended for religious, educational, and charitable purposes, between fifty and one hundred million dollars. Besides the churches, there are in this country many Scandinavian temperance, benevolent, and secret organizations, which have exercised quite an influence, but it has been impossible to secure any statistics in regard to them. It is a notable fact that, although the Swedish population, first and second generations, in this country, exceed, in 1900, the Norwegian by 130,000, yet the different Norwegian-American church organizations have at least 50,000 more communicant members than the Swedish. Strange as it may seem, the various church strifes among the Norwegians appear to have been the main cause of this great difference, because there is no reason to assume that the Swedish people are less religious than the Norwegian.

TABLE I.

SHOWING THE NUMBER OF SCANDINAVIAN PASSENGERS AND IMMIGRANTS, TOGETHER WITH THE TOTAL NUMBER OF ALL ALIEN PASSENGERS AND IMMIGRANTS, ARRIVED IN THE UNITED STATES DURING EACH YEAR FROM 1820-68.

Year.	PASSENGERS AND IMMIGRANTS — ACCORDING TO THE STATISTICS OF THE UNITED STATES.				EMIGRANTS— ACCORDING TO THE STATISTICS OF THE SCANDINAVIAN COUNTRIES.	
	Denmark.	Sweden and Norway.	Total Scandinavians.	Total Aliens.	Norway.	Sweden.
1820............	20	3	23	8,385	....	....
1821............	12	12	24	9,127	1	....
1822............	18	10	28	6,911	....	....
1823............	6	1	7	6,354	....	....
1824............	11	9	20	7,912	....	....
1825............	14	4	18	10,199	53	....
1826............	10	16	26	10,837	....	....
1827............	15	13	28	18,875	....	....
1828............	50	10	60	27,382	....	....
1829......	17	13	30	22,520	....	....
1830.	16	3	19	23,322	....	....
Total '20-30.	189	94	283	152,024	54	....
1831............	23	13	36	22,633	....	....
1832.	21	313	334	60,481	....	....
1833............	173	16	189	58,640	....	....
1834............	24	42	66	65,365	....	....
1835............	37	31	68	45,574	....	....
1836............	416	57	473	76,242	200	....
1837............	109	250	359	79,340	200	....
1838............	52	60	112	38,914	100	....
1839............	56	324	380	68.069	400	....
1840............	152	55	207	84,066	300	....
Total '31-40.	1,063	1,161	2,224	599,124	1,200	....
1841............	31	195	226	80,289	400	....
1842............	35	553	588	104,565	700	....
1843.	29	1,748	1,777	52,496	1,600	....
1844............	25	1,311	1,336	78,615	1,200	....
1845....	54	928	982	114,371	1,100	....
1846............	114	1,916	2,030	154,416	1,300	....
1847.	13	1,307	1,320	234,968	2,600	....
1848......	210	903	1,113	226,527	1,400	....
1849......	8	3,473	3,481	297,024	4,000	....
1850.	20	1,569	1,589	369,980	3,700	....
Total '41-50.	539	13,903	14,442	1,713,251	17,000	....
1851............	14	2,424	2,438	379,466	2,640	934
1852............	3	4,103	4,306	371,603	4,030	3,031
1853............	32	3,364	3,396	368,645	6,050	2,619
1854....	691	3,531	4,222	427,833	5,950	3,980
1855......	528	821	1,349	200,877	1,600	586
1856............	172	1,157	1,330	200,436	3,200	959
1857......	1,035	1,712	2,747	251,306	6,400	1,762
1858............	252	2,430	2,682	123,126	2,500	512
1859............	499	1,091	1,590	121,282	1,800	208
1060............	542	298	840	153,640	1,900	266
Total '51-60	3,749	20,931	24,700	2,598,214	36,070	14,857
1861............	234	616	850	91,918	8,900	1,087
1862............	1,658	892	2,550	91,985	5,250	1,206
1863............	1,492	1,627	3,119	176,282	1,100	1,485
1864............	712	2,249	2,961	193,418	4,300	2,461
1865............	1,149	6,109	7,258	248,120	4,000	3,180
1866............	1,862	12,633	14,495	318,568	15,455	4,466
1867............	1,436	7,055	8,491	315,722	12,829	5,893
1868............	819	11,166	11,985	142,023	13,211	21,472
Total '61-68	9,362	42,357	51,619	1,578,036	65,045	41,250

The United States statistics include only six months of the year 1868, and afterward every statistical year ends June 30.

TABLE II.

SHOWING THE NUMBER OF SCANDINAVIAN IMMIGRANTS, TOGETHER WITH THE TOTAL NUMBER OF ALL ALIEN IMMIGRANTS, ARRIVED IN THE UNITED STATES DURING EACH YEAR FROM 1869-99, AND THE AGGREGATE NUMBER OF IMMIGRANTS FROM 1820-99.

	IMMIGRANTS—ACCORDING TO THE STATISTICS OF THE UNITED STATES, EACH YEAR ENDING JUNE 30.					EMIGRANTS—ACCORDING TO THE STATISTICS OF THE SCANDINAVIAN COUNTRIES.			
Year.	Denmark.	Norway.	Sweden.	Total Scandinavians.	Total Aliens.	Denmark.	Norway.	Sweden.	Total Scandinavians.
1869	3,649	16,068	24,224	43,941	352,768	4,340	18,070	32,050	54,460
1870	4,083	13,216	13,443	30,742	387,203	3,264	14,838	15,430	33,532
1871	2,015	9,418	10,699	22,132	321,350	3,249	12,276	12,985	28,510
1872	3,690	11,421	13,463	28,575	404,806	5,941	13,865	11,838	31,644
1873	4,931	16,247	14,303	35,481	459,803	5,926	10,352	9,486	25,764
1874	3,082	10,384	5,712	19,178	313,339	2,251	4,601	3,380	10,242
1875	2,655	6,093	5,573	14,321	227,498	1,678	4,048	3,591	9,317
1876	1,547	5,173	5,603	12,323	169,986	1,336	4,355	3,702	9,393
1877	1,695	4,588	4,991	11,274	141,857	1,374	3,206	2,921	7,501
1878	2,105	4,759	5,390	12,254	138,469	2,300	4,863	4,242	11,405
1879	3,474	7,345	11,001	21,810	177,826	2,845	7,608	12,761	23,214
1880	6,576	19,895	39,186	65,657	457,257	5,475	20,212	36,263	61,950
Total '69-80	39,502	124,107	153,589	317,698	3,552,162	39,989	118,294	148,699	306,882
1881	9,117	22,705	49,760	81,582	669,431	7,823	25,976	40,620	74,419
1882	11,618	29,101	64,607	105,326	788,992	11,385	28,804	44,359	84,548
1883	10,319	23,398	38,274	71,991	603,322	8,280	22,167	25,678	56,125
1884	9,202	16,974	26,552	52,728	518,592	6,149	14,776	17,664	38,589
1885	6,100	12,356	22,248	40,704	395,046	4,211	13,901	18,222	36,414
1886	6,225	12,759	27,751	46,135	334,203	5,558	15,116	27,913	48,587
1887	8,524	16,269	42,836	67,629	490,109	8,184	20,706	46,252	75,142
1888	8,962	18,264	54,698	81,924	546,889	8,269	21,348	46,561	75,178
1889	8,699	18,390	35,415	57,504	444,427	8,271	12,597	28,529	49,397
1890	9,366	11,370	29,632	50,368	455,302	9,524	10,898	29,487	49,909
Total '81-90	88,132	176,586	391,733	656,490	5,246,413	77,688	186,369	293,285	557,322

TABLE II.—Continued.

Year	IMMIGRANTS—ACCORDING TO THE STATISTICS OF THE UNITED STATES, EACH YEAR ENDING JUNE 30.					EMIGRANTS—ACCORDING TO THE STATISTICS OF THE SCANDINAVIAN COUNTRIES.			
	Denmark.	Norway.	Sweden.	Total Scandinavians.	Total Aliens.	Denmark.	Norway.	Sweden.	Total Scandinavians.
1891	10,659	12,568	36,880	60,107	560,319	9,781	13,249	36,134	59,164
1892	10,593	11,462	43,247	65,302	623,084	9,763	16,814	40,990	67,567
1893	8,779	16,079	38,077	62,935	502,917	8,551	18,690	37,321	64,562
1894	5,581	8,867	18,608	33,056	314,467	3,719	5,591	9,529	18,839
1895	4,244	7,373	15,683	27,300	279,948	3,287	6,153	14,982	24,422
1896	3,167	8,855	21,177	33,199	343,267	2,479	6,584	14,874	23,937
1897	2,095	5,842	13,162	21,089	230,832	1,963	4,580	10,109	16,652
1898	1,946	4,938	12,398	19,282	229,299	2,073	4,805	9,000	15,878
1899	2,650	6,705	12,796	22,191	311,715	2,500	7,000	12,000	21,500
Total '91-99	49,744	85,689	212,028	347,461	3,394,848	44,116	83,466	184,939	312,521
Aggregate 1820-99	192,301		1,222,750	1,415,051	18,830,989	161,793	507,498	683,030	1,352,321

In recent United States reports it is claimed that many persons who visit their native lands are listed as new arrivals when they return to America. During 1896-98 this class of people amounted to about one-fourth of the total Scandinavian immigration. But it is very doubtful if this condition has existed to any great extent in former years. On the contrary, it appears that more actual immigrants have arrived from the North than are recorded.

The figures from the Scandinavian countries for 1899 as well as those from Sweden for 1898 are only approximately correct. Immigration statistics are more fully discussed on pages 243-6 in this volume.

TABLE III.

Showing the number of Scandinavians born in the Scandinavian countries, together with the total population, in each state and territory in the United States—According to the United States census of 1850.

STATES AND TERRITORIES.	Denmark.	Norway.	Sweden.	Total Scandi-navians.	Total Population.
Alabama	18	3	51	72	771,623
Arkansas	7	1	1	9	209,897
California	92	124	162	378	92,597
Connecticut	16	1	13	30	370,792
Delaware	1		2	3	91,512
District of Columbia	6		5	11	51,687
Florida	21	17	33	71	87,445
Georgia	24	6	11	41	906,185
Illinois	93	2,415	1,123	3,631	851,470
Indiana	10	18	16	44	988,416
Iowa	19	361	231	611	192,214
Kentucky	7	18	20	45	982,405
Louisiana	288	64	249	601	517,761
Maine	47	12	55	134	583,169
Maryland	35	10	57	102	583,034
Massachusetts	181	69	253	503	994,514
Michigan	13	110	16	139	397,654
Minnesota Territory	1	7	4	12	6,077
Mississippi	24	8	14	46	606,526
Missouri	55	155	37	247	682,044
New Hampshire	3	2	12	17	317,976
New Jersey	28	4	34	66	489,555
New Mexico Territory	2	2	1	5	61,547
New York	429	392	753	1,574	3,097,394
North Carolina	6		9	15	869,039
Ohio	53	18	55	126	1,980,329
Oregon Territory	2	1	2	5	13,294
Pennsylvania	97	27	133	257	2,311,786
Rhode Island	15	25	17	57	147,545
South Carolina	24	7	29	60	668,507
Tennessee	8		8	16	1,002,717
Texas	49	105	48	202	212,592
Utah Territory	2	32	1	35	11,380
Vermont		8		8	314,120
Virginia	15	5	16	36	1,421,661
Wisconsin	146	8,651	88	8,885	305,391
Total	1,838	12,678	3,559	18,075	23,191,876

TABLE IV.

SHOWING THE NUMBER OF SCANDINAVIANS BORN IN THE SCANDINAVIAN
COUNTRIES, TOGETHER WITH THE TOTAL POPULATION, IN EACH STATE
AND TERRITORY IN THE UNITED STATES—ACCORDING TO THE UNITED
STATES CENSUS OF 1860.

STATES AND TERRITORIES.	Denmark.	Norway.	Sweden.	Total Scandinavians.	Total Population.
Alabama	92	51	155	298	964,201
Arkansas	7	5	25	37	435,450
California	1,328	715	1,405	3,448	379,994
Connecticut	91	22	42	155	460,147
Delaware	5		8	13	112,216
Florida	21	11	31	63	140,424
Georgia	21	13	37	71	1,057,286
Illinois	712	4,891	6,470	12,073	1,711,951
Indiana	109	38	329	476	1,350,428
Iowa	661	5,688	1,465	7,814	674,913
Kansas	70	223	122	415	107,206
Kentucky	44	10	43	97	1,155,684
Louisiana	309	63	193	565	708,002
Maine	59	27	74	160	628,279
Maryland	67	7	48	122	687,049
Massachusetts	213	171	685	1,069	1,231,066
Michigan	192	440	266	898	749,113
Minnesota	170	8,425	3,178	11,773	172,023
Mississippi	31	15	21	67	791,305
Missouri	464	146	239	849	1,182,012
New Hampshire	3	5	20	38	326,073
New Jersey	175	65	88	328	672,035
New York	1,196	539	1,678	3,413	3,880,735
North Carolina	11	4	9	24	992,622
Ohio	164	19	117	300	2,339,511
Oregon	50	43	56	149	52,465
Pennsylvania	234	83	448	765	2,906,215
Rhode Island	10	38	33	81	174,620
South Carolina	38	4	38	80	703,708
Tennessee	32	14	32	78	1,109,801
Texas	150	326	153	629	604,215
Vermont	3		1	4	315,098
Virginia	41	8	57	106	1,596,318
Wisconsin	1,150	21,442	673	23,265	775,881
Colorado Territory	16	12	27	55	34,277
Dakota Territory		129		129	4,837
District of Columbia	5	1	16	22	28,841
Nebraska Territory	150	103	70	323	6,857
Nevada Territory	8	16	41	65	93,516
New Mexico Territory	9	2	3	14	40,273
Utah Territory	1,824	159	196	2,179	11,594
Washington Territory	27	22	33	82	75,080
Total	9,962	43,995	18,625	72,582	31,443,321

TABLE V.

SHOWING THE NUMBER OF SCANDINAVIANS BORN IN THE SCANDINAVIAN COUNTRIES, TOGETHER WITH THE TOTAL POPULATION, IN EACH STATE AND TERRITORY IN THE UNITED STATES—ACCORDING TO THE UNITED STATES CENSUS OF 1870.

STATES AND TERRITORIES.	Denmark.	Norway.	Sweden.	Total Scandinavians.	Total Population.
Alabama	80	21	105	206	996,992
Arkansas	55	19	134	208	484,471
California	1,837	1,000	1,944	4,781	560,247
Connecticut	116	72	323	511	537,454
Delaware	8	....	9	17	125,015
Florida	40	16	30	86	187,748
Georgia	42	14	35	91	1,184,109
Illinois	3,711	11,880	29,979	44,570	2,539,891
Indiana	315	123	2,180	2,618	1,680,637
Iowa	2,827	17,554	10,796	31,177	1,194,020
Kansas	502	588	4,954	6,044	364,399
Kentucky	53	16	112	181	1,321,011
Louisiana	290	76	358	724	726,915
Maine	120	58	91	251	626,915
Maryland	106	17	100	223	780,894
Massachusetts	267	302	1,384	1,953	1,457,351
Michigan	1,354	1,516	2,406	5,276	1,184,059
Minnesota	1,910	35,940	20,987	58,837	439,706
Mississippi	193	78	970	1,241	827,922
Missouri	665	297	2,302	3,264	1,721,295
Nebraska	1,129	506	2,352	3,987	122,993
Nevada	208	80	217	505	42,491
New Hampshire	11	55	42	108	318,300
New Jersey	510	90	554	1,154	⌐906,096
New York	1,698	975	5,522	8,195	4,382,759
North Corolina	8	5	38	51	1,071,361
Ohio	284	64	252	600	2,665,260
Oregon	87	76	205	368	90,923
Pennsylvania	561	115	2,266	2,942	3,521,951
Rhode Island	24	22	106	152	217,353
South Carolina	50	....	60	110	705,606
Tennessee	86	37	349	472	1,258,520
Texas	159	403	364	926	818,579
Vermont	21	34	83	138	330,551
Virginia	23	17	30	70	1,225,163
West Virginia	21	1	5	27	442,014
Wisconsin	5,212	40,046	2,799	48,057	1,054,670
Arizona Territory	19	7	7	33	9,658
Colorado Territory	77	40	180	297	39,864
Dakota Territory	115	1,179	380	1,674	14,181
District of Columbia	29	5	22	56	131,700
Idaho Territory	88	61	91	240	14,999
Montana Territory	95	88	141	324	20,595
New Mexico Territory	15	5	6	26	91,874
Utah Territory	4,957	613	1,790	7,360	86,786
Washington Territory	84	104	158	346	23,955
Wyoming Territory	54	28	109	191	9,118
Total	30,098	114,243	97,327	241,668	38,558,371

In this census nine Danes, three Norwegians, and five Swedes are classified as *Colored.* Of course these persons do not properly belong to the Scandinavian people.

TABLE VI.

SHOWING THE NUMBER OF SCANDINAVIANS BORN IN THE SCANDINAVIAN
COUNTRIES, TOGETHER WITH THE TOTAL POPULATION, IN EACH STATE
AND TERRITORY IN THE UNITED STATES—ACCORDING TO THE UNITED
STATES CENSUS OF 1880

STATES AND TERRITORIES.	Denmark.	Norway.	Sweden.	Total Scandinavians.	Total Population.
Alabama	69	24	119	212	1,262,505
Arkansas	98	33	211	342	802,525
California	3,748	1,765	4,209	9,722	864,694
Colorado	507	354	2,172	3,033	194,327
Connecticut	428	168	2,086	2,682	622,700
Delaware	36	6	71	113	146,608
Florida	259	79	231	569	269,493
Georgia	53	23	138	214	1,542,180
Illinois	6,029	16,970	42,415	65,414	3,077,871
Indiana	583	182	3,121	3,886	1,978,301
Iowa	6,901	21,586	17,559	46,046	1,624,615
Kansas	1,838	1,358	11,207	14,403	996,096
Kentucky	73	21	95	89	1,648,690
Louisiana	285	78	270	633	939,946
Maine	273	99	988	1,360	648,936
Maryland	128	108	177	413	934,943
Massachusetts	576	639	4,756	5,971	1,783,085
Michigan	3,513	3,520	9,412	16,445	1,636,937
Minnesota	6,071	62,521	39,176	107,768	780.773
Mississippi	99	56	302	457	1,131,597
Missouri	970	373	3,174	4,517	2,168,380
Nebraska	4,511	2,010	10,164	16,685	452,402
Nevada	350	119	317	786	62,266
New Hampshire	30	79	131	230	346,991
New Jersey	1,264	229	1,622	3,115	1,131,116
New York	3,145	2,185	11,164	16,494	5,082,871
North Carolina	58	10	24	92	1,399,750
Ohio	642	178	1,186	2,006	3,198,062
Oregon	385	574	983	1,942	174,768
Pennsylvania	945	381	7,557	8,883	4,282,891
Rhode Island	55	56	776	887	276,531
South Carolina	60	5	63	128	995,577
Tennessee	98	25	251	374	1,542,359
Texas	489	880	1,293	2,662	1,591,749
Vermont	35	10	68	113	332,286
Virginia	60	29	49	138	1,512,565
West Virginia	38	3	21	62	618,457
Wisconsin	8,797	49,349	8,138	66,284	1,315,497
Arizona Territory	131	45	106	282	40,440
Dakota Territory	1,447	13,245	3,177	17,869	135,177
District of Columbia	45	19	51	115	177,624
Idaho Territory	586	276	323	1,185	32,610
Montana Territory	190	174	280	644	39,159
New Mexico Territory	23	17	39	79	119,565
Utah Territory	7,791	1,214	3,750	12,755	143,963
Washington Territory	296	580	648	1,524	75,116
Wyoming Territory	188	74	249	511	20,789
Total	64,196	181,729	194,337	440,262	50,155,783

TABLE VII.

SHOWING THE NUMBER OF SCANDINAVIANS BORN IN THE SCANDINAVIAN
COUNTRIES, TOGETHER WITH THE TOTAL POPULATION, IN EACH STATE
AND TERRITORY IN THE UNITED STATES—ACCORDING TO THE UNITED
STATES CENSUS OF 1890.

STATES AND TERRITORIES.	Denmark.	Norway.	Sweden.	Total Scandinavians.	Total Population.
Alabama	71	47	294	412	1,513,017
Arizona Territory	180	59	168	407	59,620
Arkansas	125	60	333	518	1,128,179
California	7,764	3,702	10,923	22,389	1,208,130
Colorado	1,650	893	9,659	12,202	412,198
Connecticut	1,474	523	10,021	12,018	746,258
Delaware	41	14	246	301	168,493
District of Columbia	72	70	128	270	230,392
Florida	105	179	529	813	391,422
Georgia	61	88	191	340	1,837,353
Idaho	1,241	741	1,524	3,506	84,385
Illinois	12,044	30,339	86,514	128,897	3,826,351
Indiana	718	285	4,512	5,515	2,192,404
Iowa	15,519	27,078	30,276	72,873	1,911,896
Kansas	3,136	1,786	17,096	21,998	1,427,096
Kentucky	92	120	184	396	1,858,635
Louisiana	332	136	328	796	1,118,587
Maine	696	311	1,704	2,711	661,086
Maryland	130	164	305	599	1,042,390
Massachusetts	1,512	2,519	18,624	22,655	2,238,943
Michigan	6,335	7,795	27,366	41,496	2,093,889
Minnesota	14,133	101,169	99,913	215,215	1,301,826
Mississippi	90	54	305	449	1,289,600
Missouri	1,333	526	5,602	7,461	2,679,184
Montana	683	1,957	3,771	6,411	132,159
Nebraska	14,345	3,632	28,364	46,341	1,058,910
Nevada	332	69	314	715	45,761
New Hampshire	64	251	1,210	1,425	376,530
New Jersey	2,991	1,317	4,159	8,467	1,444,933
New Mexico Territory	54	42	149	245	153,593
New York	6,238	8,602	28,430	43,270	5,997,853
North Dakota	2,860	25,773	5,583	34,216	182,719
North Carolina	26	13	51	90	1,617,947
Ohio	956	511	2,742	4,209	3,672,316
Oklahoma Territory	37	36	138	211	61,834
Oregon	1,288	2,271	3,774	7,333	313,767
Pennsylvania	2,010	2,238	19,346	23,594	5,258,014
Rhode Island	154	285	3,392	3,831	345,506
South Dakota	4,369	19,257	7,746	31,372	328,808
South Carolina	36	23	60	119	1,151,149
Tennessee	92	41	332	465	1,767,518
Texas	649	1,313	2,806	4,768	2,235,523
Utah Territory	9,023	1,854	5,986	16,863	207,905
Vermont	58	38	870	966	332,422
Virginia	108	102	215	425	1,655,980
Washington	2,807	8,324	10,272	21,413	349,390
West Virginia	44	7	72	123	762,794
Wisconsin	13,885	65,696	20,157	99,738	1,686,880
Wyoming	680	345	1,357	2,382	60,705
Total	132,543	322,665	478,041	933,349	62,622,250

TABLE VIII.

SHOWING THE NUMBER OF SCANDINAVIANS BORN IN THE SCANDINAVIAN COUNTRIES, TOGETHER WITH THE TOTAL POPULATION, IN EVERY CITY IN THE UNION HAVING A POPULATION OF 25,000 OR MORE, AND WHERE THE SCANDINAVIANS EXCEED 1,000—ACCORDING TO THE UNITED STATES CENSUS OF 1890.

CITIES.	Denmark.	Norway.	Sweden.	Total Scandinavians.	Total Population.
Boston, Mass....................	353	861	3,413	4,627	448,477
Brockton, Mass................	18	10	1,282	1,310	27,294
Brooklyn, N. Y................	1,839	4,873	9,325	16,037	806,343
Cambridge, Mass.............	61	226	746	1,033	70.028
Chicago, Ill......	7,087	21,835	43,032	71,954	1,099,850
Denver, Col......................	470	297	3,622	4,389	106,713
Des Moines, Iowa...	227	301	1,952	2,480	50,093
Duluth, Minn...................	301	2,389	4,102	6,792	33,115
Grand Rapids, Mich...... ..	149	128	791	1,068	60,278
Jersey City, N. J......	195	316	558	1,069	163,003
Kansas City, Mo..............	294	119	1,556	1,969	38,316
La Crosse, Wis......	56	2,707	193	2,956	25,009
Milwaukee, Wis.	341	1,821	320	2,482	204,468
Minneapolis, Minn...........	1,542	12,624	19,398	33,564	164,738
New York, N. Y.............. ...	1,495	1,075	7,069	9,739	1,515,301
Oakland, Cal....................	413	242	648	1,303	48,682
Omaha, Neb.....................	4,242	624	6,265	11,131	140,452
Philadelphia, Pa....	704	1,500	1,626	3,830	1,046,964
Portland, Org..............	300	704	1,312	2,316	46,385
Providence, R. I..............	65	163	1,339	1,567	132,146
Salt Lake City, Utah........	1,041	415	1,328	2,784	44,843
San Francisco, Cal..........	1,785	1,396	3,594	6,775	298,997
Seattle, Wash...................	457	1,353	1,525	3,335	42,837
Sioux City, Iowa..............	464	1,758	2,227	4,449	37,806
St. Louis, Mo..................	285	134	876	1,295	451,770
St. Paul, Minn	1,445	3,521	11,787	16,753	133,156
Tacoma, Wash.....	544	1,702	1,983	4,229	36.006
Worcester, Mass..............	64	194	4,558	4,816	84,655

TABLE IX.

SHOWING THE NUMBER AND PLACE OF BIRTH OF THE DEFECTIVE AND CRIMINAL CLASSES IN THIS COUNTRY, TOGETHER WITH THE FOREIGN AND NATIVE BORN POPULATION—ACCORDING TO THE UNITED STATES CENSUS OF 1860, 1870, 1880, AND 1890.

COUNTRIES.	1860.			1870.			1880.		1890.		
	Deaf and Dumb and Blind.	Insane and Idiotic	Population.	Deaf and Dumb and Blind.	Insane and Idiotic	Population.	Prisoners.	Population.	Prisoners.	Paupers.	Population.
Austria	17	6	25,061	18	34	30,508		38,663	195	95	123,271
Belgium	1	15	9,072	13	17	12,555	13	15,535	33	40	22,639
Bohemia				25	70	40,289		85,361	43	174	118,106
British America	194	261	249,970	432	459	493,464	1,215	717,157	2,032	1,006	980,938
China	4	19	35,565	6	40	63,042		104,468	5	4	106,688
Denmark	6	19	9,962	2	32	30,098		64,196	124	120	132,543
England	345	606	433,494	564	950	555,046	1,453	664,160	2,998	2,344	969,092
France	82	183	109,870	121	306	116,402	247	106,971	518	486	113,174
Germany	389	1,484	1,276,075	1,149	3,631	1,690,533	2,270	1,966,742	4,993	7,814	2,784,894
Holland	11	25	28,281	20	63	46,802	42	58,090	84	154	81,828
Hungary				5	3	3,737		11,526	131	154	62,435
Ireland	1,117	3,469	1,611,304	1,771	6,002	1,885,827	5,309	1,854,571	14,592	16,210	1,871,509
Italy	2	14	10,518	17	37	17,157	170	44,230	604	158	182,580
Mexico	45	30	27,466	51	65	42,435	330	68,399	741	51	77,853
Norway	21	38	43,995	75	203	114,243		181,729	243	398	322,665
Poland	4	8	7,298	14	7	14,436	47	48,551	169	238	147,440
Portugal	2	8	4,116	3	15	4,542	10	8,138	18	27	15,996
Russia	4	8	3,160		7	4,644	39	35,722	191	68	182,644
Scotland	89	47	108,518	98	244	140,835	414	170,136	998	696	242,231
Spain	6	8	4,244	6	14	3,764	31	5,121	50	16	6,185
Sweden	14	34	18,625	62	119	97,327		194,337	387	684	478,041
Switzerland	63	91	53,327	121	190	75,153	69	88,621	192	327	104,069
United States	19,750	33,343	23,353,386	31,912	49,087	32,991,142	45,802	43,475,840			53,372,703
Wales	35	67	45,763	63	106	74,533	71	83,302	171	295	100,079
Total Population in the U. S.			31,443,421			38,558,371		50,155,783			62,622,250

The number of prisoners born in Denmack, Norway and Sweden is not given separately for the year of 1880, but together they all had 286.

TABLE X.

COMMUNICANTS, MEMBERS, CONGREGATIONS, AND VALUE OF PROPERTY OF SCANDINAVIAN-AMERICAN CHURCHES.

	About when the work began.	1860 Communicants	1860 Congregations	1870 Communicants	1870 Members	1870 Congregations	1880 Communicants	1880 Members	1880 Congregations	1890 Communicants	1890 Members	1890 Congregations	1900 Communicants	1900 Members	1900 Congregations	1900 Value of all Church and School Property
United Nor. Church	1848	4,230	43	19,355	33,304	137	45,997	80,617	364	83,500	152,200	830	125,000	225,000	1,100	$ 4,000,000
Swedish Aug. Synod	1843	10,000	115	35,000	60,000	300	69,420	127,255	593	84,563	145,503	637	115,000	200,000	900	5,000,000
Norwegian Synod	1843									52,000	94,000	525	70,000	125,000	800	3,000,000
Nor. Free Church	1852	250	5										25,000	40,000	300	1,000,000
Swedish Baptists	1852			3,000	5,000	15	5,000	5,000	57	12,172	12,172	202	18,000	30,000	310	800,000
Hauge's Synod	1839			3,500	3,500	40	6,000	11,000	85	13,000	22,500	185	16,000	21,500	230	600,000
Swedish Methodists	1845				800		5,000	5,000		10,000	10,000	90	15,000	16,000	170	980,000
Swedish Free Mission	1868												12,000	15,000	400	500,000
Sw. Mission Covenant	1868									9,000	9,000	90	10,000	16,000	155	500,000
United Danish Church	1871												10,000	12,000	140	500,000
Danish Luth. Church	1880												8,000	16,000	115	300,000
Nor.-Dan. Methodists	1850			1,500	1,500		3,000	5,000	70	6,000	10,000	70	7,000	13,000	80	250,000
Scan. Congregationalists	1884												5,000	5,000	100	400,000
Dan.-Nor. Baptists	1856						1,700	1,700	25	3,000	3,000	45	3,500	6,000	80	300,000
Icelandic Luth. Church	1879									4,500	4,500		3,000	4,500	28	110,000
Swedish Episcopalians	1849												3,000	3,000	25	50,000
Scan. Adventists	1855												1,500	3,000	30	75,000
Scan. Salvationists	1887												800	1,700	55	25,000
Scan. Moravians	1849												500	1,500	15	5,000
E. Eielsen's "Samfund"	1839						2,500	2,500	40				500	800	10	15,000
Scan. Unitarians	1882												400	400	5	10,000
Scan. Disc. of Christ	1888												200	200	6	10,000
Total													468,400	751,550	5,054	$17,895,000

Most of the Scandinavian-American church statistics, excepting those of the Augustana Synod, are very defective. The Methodists seem to put too high value upon their church property, and the Danish-Norwegian Lutherans ignore that topic altogether. It was reported in 1899 that 16,000 souls belonged to 75 congregations and 50 mission places of the Danish Lutheran Church; and the Swedish Episcopalians appear to average 180 communicants per congregation, although the American Episcopal Church as a whole only averages 110 communicants per congregation; in such cases it was deemed fair to reduce the figures somewhat. Prof. G Sverdrup has estimated the strength of the Nor. Lutheran Free Church, and Rev. N. Wickstrom that of the Swedish Free Mission; none of these factions publish any statistics. The statistics of every Norwegian and Danish Lutheran church association include all congregations served by its ministers whether such congregations belong to the association or not. Six-sevenths of the Scandinavian Congregationalists have been under the influence of the Swedish Mission Friends and are Swedes. Most of the Icelandic Lutherans reside in Canada. The figures given in regard to the Scandinavian Adventists are almost entirely guess work, and it was not even deemed wise to guess how many Scandinavians belong to the Mormon sect and to some other denominations

TABLE XI.

SHOWING THE NUMBER OF PERSONS IN THE UNITED STATES HAVING SCANDI-
NAVIAN PARENTS; BUT THE PERSONS ENUMERATED BELOW MAY HAVE BEEN
BORN IN SCANDINAVIA, AMERICA, OR ANYWHERE ELSE—ACCORDING TO
THE UNITED STATES CENSUS OF 1890, PUBLISHED IN 1894.

STATES AND TERRITORIES.	Denmark	Norway	Sweden	Total Scandi-navians.	
Alabama	143	76	423	642	
Arizona	411	93	273	777	
Arkansas	229	102	586	917	
California	11,863	5,421	15,248	32,532	
Colorado	2,515	1,299	12,975	16,789	
Connecticut	2,018	543	13,378	15,939	
Delaware	58	16	388	462	
District of Columbia	137	82	215	434	
Florida	179	272	833	1,284	
Georgia	111	115	337	563	
Idaho	2,665	1,313	2,332	6,310	
Illinois	17,090	48,091	131,966	197,147	
Indiana	1,200	478	7,910	9,588	
Iowa	25,240	59,822	52,171	137,233	
Kansas	5,581	3,444	31,492	40,517	
Kentucky	162	43	477	682	
Louisiana	536	240	698	1,474	
Maine	1,099	433	2,546	4,078	
Maryland	230	253	496	979	
Massachusetts	2,057	3,082	24,664	29,803	
Michigan	10,180	11,451	37,941	59,572	
Minnesota	22,182	195,764	155,089	373,035	
Mississippi	184	113	526	823	
Missouri	2,470	948	9,537	12,955	
Montana	1,014	2,662	4,465	8,141	
Nebraska	22,267	6,997	47,318	76,582	
Nevada	558	92	421	1,071	
New Hampshire	82	355	1,418	1,855	
New Jersey	4,339	1,530	5,739	11,608	
New Mexico	93	71	215	379	
New York	8,182	9,444	39,768	57,394	
North Dakota	4,032	47,877	7,974	59,853	
North Carolina	45	15	88	148	
Ohio	1,487	659	4,875	7,021	
Oklahoma	67	92	219	378	
Oregon	1,967	3,267	5,235	10,469	
Pennsylvania	2,677	1,458	27,840	31,975	
Rhode Island	142	310	4,227	4,679	
South Dakota	7,199	38,897	12,233	58,329	
South Carolina	71	29	143	243	
Tennessee	159	76	591	826	
Texas	1,216	2,526	4,655	8,397	
Utah	19,736	3,247	10,321	33,304	
Vermont	79	38	947	1,064	
Virginia	129	139	299	567	
Washington	3,949	11,591	12,868	28,408	
West Virginia	50	9	137	196	
Wisconsin	23,882	130,737	29,993	184,612	
Wyoming	1,074	519	1,910	3,533	
Total	213,036	596,131	726,430	1,535,597	

From the above it appears that my estimation, as stated on pages 247-8, of the number of Scandinavians, first and second generation, is too high. But by observing in many places and states the number of Scandinavians who are born in this country, and by comparing them with the same class of other nationalities, I am convinced that the figures in this table are too low. The persons in this country of Irish or German parentage are nearly three times as numerous, according to the U. S. census, as those in America who were born in Ireland or in Germany. And although the emigration from those countries is older than that from the North, yet the proportionate increase of the population of the Scandinavians in the U. S., in comparison with the Irish and the Germans, seems to be too low. No doubt there are today (1900) about twice as many Scandinavians in America as this table indicates. For total population in 1890, see page 280.

TABLE XII.

SHOWING THE NUMBER OF SCANDINAVIANS BORN IN THE SCANDINAVIAN
COUNTRIES, TOGETHER WITH THE TOTAL POPULATION, IN EACH STATE AND
TERRITORY IN THE U. S.—ACCORDING TO THE U. S. CENSUS OF 1900.

STATES AND TERRITORIES.	Denmark.	Norway.	Sweden.	Total Scandinavians.	Total Population.
Alabama	96	159	488	743	1,828,697
Alaska	260	1,243	1,445	2,948	63,592
Arizona	199	123	342	664	122,931
Arkansas	135	54	355	544	1,311,564
California	9,040	5,060	14,549	28,649	1,485,053
Colorado	2,050	1,149	10,765	13,964	539,700
Connecticut	2,249	709	16,164	19,122	908,420
Delaware	43	49	302	394	184,735
District of Columbia	88	101	234	423	278,718
Florida	204	235	561	1,000	528,542
Georgia	88	155	204	447	2,216,331
Hawaii	72	198	140	410	154,001
Idaho	1,626	1,173	2,822	5,621	161,772
Illinois	15,686	29,979	99,147	144,812	4,821 550
Indiana	783	384	4,673	5,840	2,516,462
Indian Territory	33	31	88	152	392,060
Iowa	17,102	25,634	29,875	72,611	2,231,853
Kansas	2,914	1,477	15,144	19,535	1,470,495
Kentucky	77	34	222	333	2,147,174
Louisiana	216	189	359	764	1,381,625
Maine	886	509	1,935	3,330	694,466
Maryland	177	246	347	770	1,188,044
Massachusetts	2,470	3,335	32,192	37,997	2,805,346
Michigan	6,390	7,582	26,956	40,928	2,420,982
Minnesota	16,299	104,895	115,476	236,670	1,751,394
Mississippi	86	74	303	463	1,551,270
Missouri	1,510	530	5,692	7,732	3,106,665
Montana	1,041	3,354	5,346	9,741	243,329
Nebraska	12,531	2,883	24,693	40,107	1,666,300
Nevada	339	50	278	667	42,335
New Hampshire	75	295	2,032	2,402	411,588
New Jersey	3,899	2,296	7,337	13,532	1,883,669
New Mexico	57	33	244	334	195 310
New York	8,746	12,601	42,708	64,055	7,268,894
North Carolina	36	21	68	125	1,893,810
North Dakota	3,953	30,206	8,419	42,578	319,146
Ohio	1,468	639	3,951	6,058	4,157,545
Oklahoma	226	118	494	838	398,331
Oregon	1,663	2,789	4,555	9,007	413,536
Pennsylvania	2,531	1,393	24,130	28,054	6,302,115
Rhode Island	268	342	6,072	6,682	428,556
South Carolina	55	49	65	169	1,340,316
South Dakota	5,038	19,788	8,647	33,473	401,570
Tennessee	117	141	337	595	2,020,616
Texas	1,089	1,356	4,388	6,833	3,048,710
Utah	9,132	2,128	7,025	18,285	276,749
Vermont	225	54	1,020	1,299	343,641
Virginia	128	123	218	469	1,854,184
Washington	3,626	9,891	12,737	26,254	518 103
West Virginia	60	19	132	211	958,800
Wisconsin	16,171	61,575	26,196	103,942	2,069,042
Wyoming	884	378	1.727	2,989	92,531
Total	154,137	337,829	573,599	1,065,565	76,303,387

All the 18 columns of figures forming the basis of the figures given in this and the
following table in regard to the Scandinavians were incorrectly added in the U. S.
Census Reports, Vol. I., making the sums in ev ry column a trifle too high. But in a
private letter from the census department to the author it is claimed that 2,102 Sca di-
navian-b rn persons in the military and naval service stationed abroad are included in
the total sums, alth ugh not mentioned at all in the Census Reports.

As tables XII, XIII, XIV, and XV were not included in the copyright of 1899, a special
copyright was applied for in 1902; and about 2,000 copies of the History, second edition,
do not contain said tables.

TABLE XIII.

SHOWING THE NUMBER OF PERSONS IN THE U. S. HAVING SCANDINAVIAN PARENTS; BUT THE PERSONS ENUMERATED BELOW MAY HAVE BEEN BORN IN SCANDINAVIA, AMERICA, OR ANYWHERE ELSE—ACCORDING TO THE U. S. CENSUS OF 1900.

STATES AND TERRITORIES.	Both parents born in specified countries; or one parent born as specified and one parent native. *			One parent born as specified and one parent born in some other country outside of the U. S.†		
	Denmark	Norway	Sweden	Denmark	Norway	Sweden
Alabama	237	375	1,002	71	54	126
Alaska	343	1,454	1,678	26	73	78
Arizona	538	228	605	93	70	103
Arkansas	332	133	827	51	22	51
California	16,438	8,536	23,747	3,655	1,912	3,609
Colorado	3,847	2,096	18,866	753	578	1,212
Connecticut	3,703	1,083	26,561	759	373	1,232
Delaware	73	59	515	9	15	28
District of Columbia	168	195	362	44	33	68
Florida	378	558	1,136	85	76	179
Georgia	188	277	490	36	50	59
Hawaii	106	370	199	38	83	38
Idaho	4,710	2,767	5,522	900	508	776
Illinois	27,298	59,954	200,058	6,302	7,697	10,055
Indiana	1,709	852	9,915	300	213	603
Indian Territory	80	115	220	11	10	12
Iowa	36,156	71,170	64,580	4,122	3,117	3,830
Kansas	6,687	3,731	35,221	1,005	608	1,320
Kentucky	166	88	491	39	27	98
Louisiana	632	441	826	260	98	249
Maine	1,549	833	3,528	339	235	404
Maryland	345	442	611	144	115	236
Massachusetts	3,363	5,069	49,601	1,293	1,535	3,385
Michigan	12,911	14,091	49,783	2,143	3,842	5,114
Minnesota	32,923	257,959	226,018	5,729	18,350	17,912
Mississippi	231	211	766	35	32	75
Missouri	3,469	1,301	12,169	828	360	1,051
Montana	1,873	5,688	8,219	340	711	850
Nebraska	26,422	7,228	54,301	3,111	1,506	3,010
Nevada	746	95	435	153	36	110
New Hampshire	130	504	2,989	46	121	197
New Jersey	6,723	3,518	11,709	1,656	771	1,840
New Mexico	129	109	446	49	14	60
New York	13,636	18,928	67,037	4,128	3,607	7,228
North Carolina	74	44	166	12	4	32
North Dakota	7,139	72,012	14,602	975	3,432	2,902
Ohio	2,764	1,174	7,256	590	269	811
Oklahoma	582	350	1,290	45	71	96
Oregon	3,319	5,567	8,273	733	975	1,241
Pennsylvania	4,286	2,254	44,777	1,137	698	2,226
Rhode Island	365	502	9,323	107	186	398
South Carolina	134	86	125	18	16	29
South Dakota	10,450	51,199	17,167	1,308	2,810	2,337
Tennessee	220	383	743	69	21	68
Texas	2,362	3,406	9,299	641	551	887
Utah	24,753	4,557	14,580	5,262	1,957	3,846
Vermont	174	93	1,601	35	53	108
Virginia	251	282	395	42	19	60
Washington	6,576	18,824	21,371	1,145	2,235	2,539
West Virginia	117	46	216	38	8	36
Wisconsin	33,794	155,125	48,815	4,261	8,995	7,073
Wyoming	1,815	727	3,155	290	141	281
Total	307,913	787,089	1,083,587	55,255	69,293	90,168

* Nearly all the few native parents referred to here are of Scandinavian extraction.
† About three-fifths of this class of people are the offspring of the intermarriage of Danes, Norwegians, and Swedes.

TABLE XIV.

Showing the number of Scandinavians born in the Scandinavian countries, together with the total population, in every city in the Union having a population of 25,000 or more, and where the Scandinavians exceed 1,000*—According to the U. S. Census of 1900.

CITIES.	Denmark.	Norway.	Sweden.	Total Scandi-navians.	Total Population.
Boston, Mass...................	675	1,145	5,541	7,361	560,892
Bridgeport, Conn..............	350	76	1,349	1,775	70,996
Brockton, Mass................	33	18	1,973	2,024	40,063
Buffalo, N. Y..................	148	185	743	1,076	352,387
Cambridge, Mass..............	130	227	1,584	1,941	91,886
Chicago, Ill....................	10,166	22,011	48,836	81,013	1,698,575
Cleveland, Ohio...............	373	249	1,000	1,622	381,768
Council Bluffs, Iowa.	1,109	79	314	1,502	25,802
Denver, Colo ···	573	344	3,376	4,293	133,859
Des Moines, Iowa..............	240	296	1,907	2,443	62,139
Duluth, Minn.	296	2,655	5,047	7,998	52,969
Erie, Pa......................	120	22	591	733	52,733
Grand Rapids, Mich...........	230	115	912	1,257	87,565
Hartford, Conn................	506	37	1,714	2,257	79,850
Jersey City, N. J..............	319	647	899	1,865	206,433
Joliet, Ill.....................	28	94	951	1,073	29,353
Kansas City, Kans............	182	37	811	1,030	51,418
Kansas City, Mo.....	241	100	1,869	2,210	163,752
La Crosse, Wis................	64	2,023	141	2,228	28,895
Lincoln, Neb..................	178	83	427	688	40,169
Los Angeles, Cal..............	239	163	808	1,210	102,479
Lynn, Mass.	19	42	812	873	68,513
McKeesport, Pa................	19	8	1,283	1,310	34,227
Malden, Mass.................	29	55	617	701	33,664
Manchester, N. H.............	11	19	962	992	56,987
Milwaukee, Wis	514	1,702	659	2,875	285,315
Minneapolis, Minn.............	1,473	11,532	20,035	33,040	202,718
New Britain, Conn............	16	30	1,811	1,857	25,998
New Haven, Conn	234	119	1,376	1,729	108,027
New York, N. Y...............	5,621	11,387	28,320	45,328	3,437,202
Oakland, Cal.	571	344	994	1,909	66,960
Omaha, Neb	2,430	312	3,968	6,710	102,555
Peoria, Ill....................	39	11	528	578	56,100
Philadelphia, Pa..............	934	692	2,143	3,769	1,293,697
Pittsburg, Pa..................	38	63	1,072	1,173	321,616
Portland, Ore.................	414	850	1,711	2,975	90,426
Providence, R. I..............	109	228	2,775	3,112	175,597
Racine, Wis...................	2,815	675	311	3,801	29,102
Rockford, Ill..................	102	129	6,690	6,921	31,051
St. Louis, Mo.................	390	172	1,116	1,678	575,238
St. Paul, Minn................	1,206	2,900	9,852	13,958	163,065
Salt Lake City, Utah..........	965	502	1,687	3,154	53,531
San Francisco, Cal............	2,171	2,172	5,248	9,591	342,782
Seattle, Wash.	641	1,642	2,379	4,662	80,671
Sioux City, Iowa..............	369	1,054	1,460	2,883	33,111
South Bend, Ind...............	70	49	549	668	35,999
Spokane, Wash................	200	570	1,168	1,938	36,848
Superior, Wis.................	236	2,026	2,854	5,116	31,091
Tacoma, Wash.................	352	1,474	1,603	3,429	37,714
Topeka, Kans.................	20	37	575	632	33,608
Worcester, Mass...............	153	269	7,542	7,964	118,421

*In order to retain in this table the same cities as in table XV, which deals with the Scandinavian-Americans in the first and second generations, a few places are enumerated here that have not a Scandinavian-born population of one thousand.

TABLE XV.

SHOWING THE NUMBER OF PERSONS HAVING SCANDINAVIAN PARENTS EVERY CITY IN THE UNION HAVING A POPULATION OF 25,000 OR MORE, AND WHERE THE POPULATION OF ONE OF THE SCANDINAVIAN NATIONALITIES EXCEEDS 1,000; BUT THE PERSONS ENUMERATED BELOW MAY HAVE BEEN BORN IN SCANDINAVIA, AMERICA, OR ANYWHERE ELSE—ACCORDING TO THE U. S. CENSUS OF 1900.

CITIES.	Both parents born in specified countries; or one parent born as specified and one parent native. *			One parent born as specified and one parent born in some other country outside of the U. S. *		
	Denmark	Norway	Sweden	Denmark	Norway	Sweden
Boston, Mass.	978	1,639	7,979	218	500	979
Bridgeport, Conn.	512	108	2,017	120	27	100
Brockton, Mass.	42	23	3,263	32	17	96
Buffalo, N. Y.	266	338	1,282	107	82	189
Cambridge, Mass.	178	339	2,347	60	66	144
Chicago, Ill.	16,563	41,055	100,176	4,328	5,852	6,707
Cleveland, Ohio.	676	378	1,606	116	85	229
Council Bluffs, Iowa.	2,270	153	616	147	30	105
Denver, Colo.	941	571	5,929	242	207	375
Des Moines, Iowa.	451	597	3,778	82	121	182
Duluth, Minn.	477	4,909	8,393	148	659	715
Erie, Pa.	176	24	1,023	45	17	79
Grand Rapids, Mich.	411	216	1,649	67	49	102
Hartford, Conn.	784	64	2,447	100	18	79
Jersey City, N. J.	572	1,034	1,566	247	194	358
Joliet, Ill.	44	187	1,689	14	39	58
Kansas City, Kans.	358	80	1,581	60	18	95
Kansas City, Mo.	436	215	3,544	105	35	216
La Crosse, Wis.	141	5,002	287	46	223	96
Lincoln, Neb.	348	175	1,190	28	35	81
Los Angeles, Cal.	481	329	1,427	103	176	188
Lynn, Mass.	36	63	1,195	14	22	63
McKeesport, Pa.	30	8	2,491	8	20	57
Malden, Mass.	36	81	1,010	39	30	62
Manchester, N. H.	12	43	1,354	12	7	27
Milwaukee, Wis.	1,020	3,848	1,265	247	425	326
Minneapolis, Minn.	2,442	22,183	35,741	621	2,373	2,380
New Britain, Conn.	22	38	2,980	4	15	30
New Haven, Conn.	378	173	2,203	103	55	175
New York, N. Y.	8,457	16,950	42,050	2,926	3,091	5,592
Oakland, Cal.	1,004	708	1,731	266	161	278
Omaha, Neb.	4,399	525	7,367	567	264	487
Peoria, Ill.	80	27	1,074	21	2	57
Philadelphia, Pa.	1,520	1,062	3,271	457	303	648
Pittsburg, Pa.	65	94	1,779	15	15	103
Portland, Ore.	732	1,522	2,884	301	296	479
Providence, R. I.	134	346	4,128	57	139	217
Racine, Wis.	5,300	1,329	501	331	311	184
Rockford, Ill.	130	255	12,434	57	94	157
St. Louis, Mo.	781	341	2,119	309	155	335
St. Paul, Minn.	2,231	6,144	18,796	468	1,050	1,320
Salt Lake City, Utah.	2,033	896	3,100	776	394	721
San Francisco, Cal.	3,394	3,114	7,662	904	593	1,287
Seattle, Wash.	1,059	2,778	3,543	157	271	317
Sioux City, Iowa.	729	2,182	2,844	107	208	206
South Bend, Ind.	111	89	1,093	10	13	25
Spokane, Wash.	325	1,111	1,953	48	122	186
Superior, Wis.	409	3,720	4,817	77	337	327
Tacoma, Wash.	631	2,666	2,697	126	297	309
Topeka, Kans.	45	71	1,181	18	20	35
Worcester, Mass.	218	347	11,879	64	139	248

* See foot-notes under table XIII, page 264c.

BIBLIOGRAPHY

—OF THE—

Scandinavian-American Historical Literature of the Nineteenth Century.

—BY—

O. N. NELSON.

It has been the aim to enumerate in these notes all of the most important books, pamphlets, church reports, and magazine articles which relate to the Scandinavian-American historical literature of the nineteenth century. In order to make the collection as complete as possible, all the leading libraries in Illinois, Iowa, Minnesota, and Wisconsin, as well as some in the Scandinavian countries, have been consulted; a thorough search has been made of a large number of book stores and publishing houses, both in Europe and in this country, and even private libraries have been ransacked. But all these establishments together do not by any means contain all the matters enumerated in this list. There is not a public library in the world that has a fairly complete collection of Scandinavian-American historical literature. The Royal Library in Stockholm and the Angustana College Library in Rock Island have a large number of books, etc., in relation to Swedish-Americans, and Luther College in Decorah has begun to collect materials in regard to the Norwegians. But even these collections are defective. Consequently this bibliography has been compiled from various sources. The voluminous "Sabin's Dictionary of Books" has been carefully examined; and for several years back, I have corresponded with hundreds of Scandinavian-American writers and book collectors. As a result of all this, I have collected in my private library a large number of books and pamphlets, written by Scandinavian-Americans, on various subjects. But even my collection, although very comprehensive, does not contain all the works enumerated in this bibliography.

Besides the books, pamphlets, church annuals, etc., which are mentioned in this list, a large number of emigration reports, school catalogues, legislative manuals, county histories, newspapers, and statistics of various kinds have been consulted in the preparation of the first and second volumes. All the volumes of the U. S. Census from 1790 to 1890, and several state census reports of the Northwestern states, have been carefully examined. But it is, of course, impossible to enumerate all of it here. Hundreds of Scandinavian-American newspapers have been published during the last fifty years, and most of them have contained more or less matter of an historical nature. I have searched the files of several of the most important of such publications, and collected some valuable newspaper articles. Most journals in the North and many English papers

265

in America have at one time or another referred to the Scandinavian-Americans. Millions of private letters have passed between the Scandinavian countries and the United States, and many of them have been valuable historical documents. Evidently, it is beyond the power of mortals to enumerate all historical materials in regard to the Scandinavian-Americans, and I have, rightly or wrongly, limited the list to books, pamphlets, magazine articles, and church reports.

Often it is difficult to determine whether a book is historical, theological, poetical, or simply the product of some crank or stupid fanatic. Nor has it always been possible for me to scrutinize all of the materials enumerated in this bibliography, and I am undecided whether I have sinned most by commission or by omission in this connection. Considering the various church disputes which have been carried on among the Norwegian-Americans, it was deemed wise to include some productions which can hardly be called historical. In fact, some of these so abound in truth and falsehood, personal abuse and religious bombast, as to deserve to be classified as "insane or malicious" literature. The Danes and Swedes have issued less of this class of brain product. The Swedish-Americans can boast of a fairly solid historical literature, which in point of quality excels by far that of the other two nationalities put together. Some works of fiction often paint the social life and customs of a people with a brilliancy and a clearness which surpass most historical productions. In this line of literature the Norwegian-Americans have produced some masterpieces, but none of them have been enumerated in this connection.

It has been deemed unnecessary, in this connection, to deal with the bibliographies regarding the discovery of America by the Northmen and the Swedish settlement on the Delaware River, because the two articles on these subjects have been published in this volume only to make the Scandinavian-American history complete; otherwise the main object of this work is to relate the story of the Scandinavians in the United States in the nineteenth century. Besides, P. B. Watson has published, in the fourth edition of Prof. R. B. Anderson's "America not Discovered by Columbus," a very complete bibliography regarding the Northmen's discovery of America, and Marie A. Brown, in her work, "The Icelandic Discoverers of America," treats the same subject; while the fourth volume of the "Narrative and Critical History of America" contains a very extensive bibliography regarding the Swedish settlement on the Delaware River, by Prof. G. B. Keen.

In the preparation of this work, the following authorities have mainly been relied upon in regard to the history of the Vikings and the history of the Scandinavian countries: Odhner's "Sveriges, Norges och Danmarks Historia"; Geijer's "Svenska Folkets Historia"; Montelius's "Sveriges Historia"; Sars's "Udsigt over den Norske Historie"; Boyesen's "Story of Norway"; Worsaae's "Danes and Norwegians in England, Scotland, and Ireland"; Gibbon's "Roman Empire"; Green's "History of the English People"; Frederiksen's articles in "Scandinavia"; Cornelius's "Svenska Kyrkans Historia."

Pages 267-76 were electrotyped for the first edition, and it was not deemed necessary to rearrange them, although a few publications enumerated there might have been omitted. The rest of this bibliography treats of works omitted in the first edition, which appeared in 1893, and of publications issued since that time.

1841. Om Amerika samt om Emigrant-Föreningen i Stockholm. Stockholm, Sweden.

"Intended to furnish Swedish emigrants with the necessary information about the United States. It contains also a short historical introduction in which the fate of the Swedish settlements in North America is related."

1846. Reise blandt de Norske Emigranter i de Forenede Nordamerikanske Fristater. Rev. J. W. Dietrichson, Stavanger, Norway.

1847. Erik Jansismen i Nord Amerika.

This little pamphlet is an anonymous account given forth as "Bref från en af Utvandrarne," and is in reality a most violent attack upon the beliefs of Janson and his methods in conducting the party of emigrants.

1848. Beretning om de Norske Setlere i Amerika. C. Rudolf, Bergen, Norway.

1851. Nogle Ord fra Praedikestolen i Amerika og Norge. Rev. J. W. Dietrichson, Stavanger, Norway.

1851. Jenny Lind in America. C. J. Rosenberg, New York City.

1853. The Homes of the New World; Impressions of America. Fredrika Bremer, New York City.

These two volumes are mostly made up of letters, written by the authoress during her visit to America, in 1849-52, and contain some information regarding the early Swedish pioneers in this country, as well as descriptions of the places she visited.

1853. Geografisk Politisk Beskrivelse over de Forenede Nordamerikanske Stater, i saerdeleshed for Emigranter. J. Bollin, Kristiania, Norway.

1862. Minnen. Rev. Gustaf Unonius, Stockholm, Sweden.

This work is bound in two large volumes. Rev. Unonius came from Sweden to the Northwest in 1841; remained in America for seventeen years, then returned to Sweden. His work is, perhaps, the best and the most admirable description of the early pioneer life that has yet been published in the Swedish language.

1865. Protocoll och Handlingar rörande Prestmötet i Upsala år 1865. Upsala, Sweden.

> This volume contains a lecture delivered by Prof. L. P. Esbjörn, at the conference of the Swedish Lutheran clergy, held in Upsala in 1865, in which he gives a good historical review of the early Swedish-American Lutheran Church. The lecture is also published in "Korsbaneret" for 1885.

1865. The Emigration from Europe during the present century; its Causes and Effects. A. Jorgensen, Quebec, Canada.

> Translated from Norwegian statistics and reports, and from extracts of other authorities.

1866. The Bergen Family; or the Descendants of Hans Hansen Bergen. T. G. Bergen, New York City.

> This volume gives a complete biography of H. H. Bergen, a Norwegian, who came to America in 1633 and settled in New Amsterdam. His name has probably been identified with the supposed Norwegian settlement at Bergen, N. J., in 1624, which is referred to in *Nordmaendene i Amerika*, by Knud Langeland, but undoubtedly never existed.

1867. Syv Foredrag over de Kirkelige Forholde blandt de Norske i America. Rev. H. A. Preus, Kristiania, Norway.

> Containing a great deal of valuable information in regard to the early history of the Norwegian-American Lutheran churches.

1869. Det Skandinaviske Regiments Historie. J. A. Johnson, La Crosse, Wis.

> This volume is one of the first histories of the famous Fifteenth Wisconsin Regiment, besides it contains biographies of the leading officers in the regiment.

1868-70. Skandinavisk Billedmagazin. Madison, Wis.

> This magazine contains, among other things, quite an extensive account of the first Norwegian settlements in Wisconsin and Illinois, as well as a history of the early Norwegian emigration; written by Prof. Svein Nilsson.

1872. Beskrifning öfver America. Alex Nilsson, Gothenburg, Sweden.

> A pamphlet containing some valuable information in regard to emigration, being, in fact, only an emigration guide-book.

.1874. Två År i Amerika (1872-1874). Hugo Nisbeth, Stockholm, Sweden.

> This volume contains descriptions, by the author, who was a newspaper correspondent traveling through the country, of several Swedish settlements, especially in the Northwest and in California.

1876. Fra Amerika. V. C. S. Topsöe, Copenhagen, Denmark.

> The author traveled through the United States, describes the country, and sometimes refers to the Scandinavian-Americans, especially the Danes.

1876. Wisconsinismen belyst ved Historiske Kjendsgjerninger. Prof. A. Weenaas, Chicago, Ill.

> This book contains a lengthy discussion of the different theological questions which have divided the Norwegian-American Lutherans. The work is rather an attack upon the teachings of some of the ministers of the Norwegian Synod, and was answered by Rev. H. A. Preus in his book, *Professorerne Oftedals og Weenaas's Wisconsinisme betragtet i Sandhedens Lys.*

1876. Professorerne Oftedals og Weenaas's Wisconsinisme betragtet i Sandhedens Lys. Rev. H. A. Preus, Decorah, Iowa.

> This is an answer to Prof. A. Weenaas' book, *Wisconsinismen*, and defends the teachings of the Norwegian Synod and discusses the different theological questions which have divided the Norwegian-American Lutherans.

1877. History of Henry County, Ill. Chicago, Ill.

> This book contains a concise history of Bishop Hill Colony.

1879. Svenskarne i St. Croix-dalen, Minnesota. Robert Gronberger, Minneapolis, Minn.

> A small pamphlet containing a good description of the early Swedish settlements in Washington and Chisago counties, where the first Swedish settlements in Minnesota was made. It also contains a long biography of Jacob Falstrom. Gronberger maintains that Oscar Roos, who came to Minnesota in 1850, was the first Swedish settler in the state; but Rev. E. Norelius, in his great and valuable work, *De Svenska Luterska Församlingarnas och Svenskarnes Historia i Amerika*, asserts that the first Swedish settlement occured in 1851. But in a letter to the editor of this work, Roos affirms Gronberger's statement.

1880. Genom Den Stora Vestern. J. Stadling, Stockholm, Sweden.

> This volume contains a very good description, especially of the Pacific Coast and the West, where the author traveled through. He was very friendly towards America, but the work contains little or nothing in regard to Scandinavian-American history.

1880. Svenskarne i Illinois. Capt. Eric Johnson and C. F. Peterson, Chicago.

> This book is one of the largest and most reliable Swedish-American histories. It contains descriptions of the different Swedish settlements in Illinois, and biographies and pictures of hundreds of Swedes in that state. It also contains some new matter in regard to the Swedish settlement on Delaware River. It is the oldest, and among the best authorities on the Swedish settlement at Bishop Hill. The work is well written and impartial.

1882. Svenka Nationaliteten i Förenta Staterna. Tancred Boissy, Gothenburg, Sweden.

> A small pamphlet containing information in regard to the social, religious, and economical conditions of the Swedes in the United States. The main value of the work is the fact that the author looks at most things from a purely Swedish standpoint.

1883. Ole Bull. Sara C. Bull, Boston, Mass

> This volume contains a biography of Ole Bull and a short mention of his Norwegian colony in Pennsylvania.

1883. Elling Eielsens Liv og Virksomhed. Revs. Chr. O. Brohaugh and I. Eisteinsen, Chicago, Ill.

> This book contains a complete biography of Rev. E. Eielsen, giving a good review of the religious conditions in Norway and among the early Norwegian settlers in this country in his time. It contains also much valuable information in regard to Hauge's Synod, Norwegian-American Lutheran church disputes, and in regard to the hardships of the early pioneers.

1884. Amerika; Seet Fra et Landbosstandpunkt. H. Andreasen, Copenhagen, Denmark.

> The author traveled through this country, described it, and sometimes refers to the Scandinavian-Americans, especially the Danes.

1884. Det Femtende Wisconsin Regiments Historie og

Virksomhed Under Borgerkrigen. P. G. Dietrichson, Chicago, Ill.

A small pamphlet containing a history of the Fifteenth Wisconsin, or Scandinavian, Regiment, and a list of all the persons who were enlisted in the regiment.

1885. Rockfords Svenskar. Geo. Kaedeng, Chicago, Ill.

A pamphlet containing a sketch of the Swedes and their biographies in Rockford and of the business enterprises in which they are engaged.

1883–86. Scandinavia. Chicago, Ill.

This magazine contains several lengthy and important articles on Scandinavan-American history. The last two numbers of 1886 contain historical information about and biographies of the Scandinavians in St. Paul and Minneapolis, Minn. This Magazine, published and edited by N. C. Frederiksen, was among the best literary productions in the English language that has yet been attempted by the Scandinavian-Americans.

1886. Svenska Tidningar och Tidskrifter utgifna inom Nord Amerikas Förenta Stater. Bernhard Lundstedt, Stockholm, Sweden.

This work is very valuable and was published under the direction of the Royal Library of Sweden. It contains a complete history of all of the Swedish newspapers and periodicals that have been, and are, published in the United States.

1886. The History of the Baptist Mission. Rev. G. W. Hervey, St, Louis, Mo.

This volume contains a history of the Baptists in Denmark, Norway, and Sweden, and refers to the Swedish Baptists in this conntry.

1887. The Scandinavians in the United States. Dr. Albert Shaw.

This article, published in *The Chautauquan* in Dec., 1887, contains a great deal of valuable statistics regarding the Scandinavian-Americans, as well as other information. The calm and judicious views of the writer, regarding the topic of the paper, make it of great value.

1887. Historiske Meddelelser om den Norske Augustana Synode. Rev. O. J. Hatlestad, Decorah, Iowa.

This volume contains not only a history of the Norwegian Augustana Synod, but also touches upon the history of the other Norwegian-American Lutheran churches, as well as on the settlements. It is the most complete Norwegian-American history that has yet appeared.

1887.   Scandinavian Studies in the United States.   Daniel Kilham Dodge.

> This article, published in *Science* in May, 1887, contains a good, but rather incomplete, historical review of the studies of the Scandinavian languages in American and Scandinavian-American colleges and universities.   Prof. J. P. Uhler, in a letter published in the same magazine shortly after, adds some new facts on the subject.

1887.   Appletons' Cyclopedia of American Biography. James Grant Wilson and John Fiske, New York City.

> This great and valuable work contains a few biographies of Scandinavian-Americans.

1888.   Two Hundred and Fiftieth Anniversary of the First Swedish Settlement in America.   Col. Hans Mattson, Minneapolis, Minn.

> Containing nothing new, except a letter from the Hon. T. F. Bayard, in which he acknowledges that one of his ancestors, on the maternal side, was a Swede.

1888.   Praedikener over Kirke-Aarets Evangelier holdte of Prester i den Norske Synode i Amerika.   Rev. Einar Wulfsberg, Decorah, Iowa.

> This volume contains several sermons and a few short biographies of ministers of the Norwegian Synod.

1888.   Norwegian Emigration.   Prof. H. H. Boyesen.

> This article was published in *American*, in 1888.

1888.   Den Evanglisk-Lutherske Kirkes Historie i Amerika.   Rev. R. Andersen, Brooklyn, N. Y.

> This volume contains a history of all the American Lutheran churches, as well as biographies of some of the Swedish-American Lutheran ministers in the seventeenth and eighteenth centuries.   The last ten pages contain a brief historical review of the Scandinavian-American Lutheran churches.

1888.   The "Foreign Element" in New York City.   Geo. J. Mason.

> This article, published in *Harper's Weekly*, Sept. 1, 1888, contains some information regarding the Scandinavians in the United States, especially in New York City.

1889. History of Utah. H. H. **Bancroft,** San Francisco, Cal.

The sixteenth chapter and foot-notes on page 411 contain some matters regarding the Scandinavian immigration to Utah.

1889. Den Norske Indvandring til 1850 og Skandinaverne i Amerikas Politik. Johs. B. Wist, Madison, Wis.

A small pamphlet containing a good history of the Danish and Norwegian immigration, and of the Norwegian settlement in Texas.

1889. Nordmaendene i Amerika. Knud Langeland, Chicago, Ill.

This work contains some valuable information in regard to the Norwegian immigration, the first settlements, and the early Norwegian-American press; but, on the whole, it is more of an autobiography of Knud Langeland than a history of the Norwegians. The author is unquestionably mistaken when he asserts that a Norwegian colony existed at Bergen, N. J., in 1624; but for a full discussion on this point consult O. N. Nelson's article on *Hans Hansen Bergen,* published in *The North,* Dec. 21, 1892, and in *Nordvesten* about the same time. A brief statement of the facts regarding this point is also made on page 35 in this volume.

1887-90. Norges Laeger i det Nittende Aarhundrede. Dr. F. C. Kjaer, Kristiania, Norway.

Contains biographies of the Norwegian physicians of the 19th century, some of whom now reside in this country.

1890. Norsemen in the United States. Rev. Kristofer Janson.

In this article, published in *The Cosmopolitan* in October, 1890, the author makes some assertions in regard to Norwegian-American history which hardly coincide with the actual facts; yet his discussion is valuable, both from a literary and historical standpoint.

1890. The Norwegico-Danish M. E. Church in America.

A small pamphlet containing some valuable information in regard to the early history of the Norwegian-Danish Methodist Church in this country. No date or place of publication is mentioned, the author's name does not appear. But the work was written by Rev. A. Haagensen, of Chicago, and, perhaps, published in 1890.

1890. American Lutheran Biographies. Rev. J. C. Jensson, Milwaukee, Wis.

A large volume containing biographies of over 350 Lutheran-American ministers, a large proportion of whom are Scandinavians. As a work of

reference it is very valuable, throwing much light upon the church history
of the different Scandinavian-American Lutheran denominations.

1890. Emigration and Immigration. R. M. Smith, New York City.

This volume contains a very able discussion upon the immigration
question, and frequently refers to the Scandinavian immigrants.

1890. Life of John Ericsson. W. C. Church, New York City.

This work, bound in two volumes, contains a complete biography of
John Ericsson, the greatest Scandinavian-American.

1890. The Swedes in America. Rev. C. A. Swensson, Topeka, Kan.

A lecture published in pamphlet form.

1890. De Svenska Luterska Församlingarnas och Svenskarnes Historia i Amerika. Rev. E. Norelius, D. D., Rock Island, Ill.

This is a large volume containing an extensive history of the Swedish-
American Lutheran Church, and biographies of the ministers, as well as
a history of the different Swedish settlements, from the earliest time of the
immigration in the nineteenth century up to 1860. The work, on the whole,
is fairly accurate, intensely Lutheran, but not bigoted. The author is, no
doubt, mistaken when he asserts that the first Swedish settlement in Minnesota occured in 1851. Both Robert Gronberger, in his *Svenskarne i St.
Croix-dalen, Minnesota*, and Oscar Roos, who was the first Swedish settler in the state, contradict him. Norelius's description of the early settlements is especially excellent and vivid.

1890. Pastor S. Newmans Sjelfbiografi. Rev. S. B. Newman, Chicago, Ill.

This volume contains an autobiography of the author, as well as a great
deal of valuable information in regard to the history of the Swedish Methodist Church in this country.

1890. Det Norske Luther-College. Rev. J. Th. Ylvisaker, Decorah, Iowa.

Contains a history of Luther College, at Decorah, Iowa., and biographies of the professors and instructors connected with the institution

1890. The Lutherans in America. Rev. E. J. Wolf, D. D.
New York City.

This volume contains short, but quite good historical sketches of the different Scandinavian-American Lutheran organizations, including the Swedish Lutherans on the banks of the Delaware River in the seventeenth century.

1890. Genom Norra Amerikas Förenta Stater. P. Waldenström, Stockholm, Sweden.

A large volume containing a chapter relating to the Swedes in America, giving some good specimens of the Swedish-American language. The author is unfriendly towards America, and the work as a whole is very unreliable.

1890. Svensk-Amerikanska Poeter. Ernst Skarstedt, Minneapolis, Minn.

This volume contains biographies and pictures of eighteen Swedish-American poets, together with well selected specimens of their poetical productions. From a literary standpoint, it is one of the best Swedish-American compilations; from a historical standpoint, it shows the tendency and mode of thought of the Swedes in this country, and gives some good examples of the Americanization of the Swedish language. Especially is *Det Nya Modersmålet*, by H. Stockenstrom, an excellent illustration of Swedish-Americanism.

1890. Oregon och Washington. Ernst Skarstedt, Portland, Ore.

This volume contains a great deal of information in regard to the history of the Scandinavian settlements, churches, and societies in Oregon and Washington, as well as biographies of about a hundred Northmen in those states. The work is very reliable.

1891. United Scandinavian Singers of America Souvenir. Harry Randall, Minneapolis, Minn.

A small pamphlet containing a short history of the organization, and biographies and half-tone pictures of some of its leading members.

1890–91. Minnen. English translation: The Story of an Emigrant. Col. Hans Mattson, Lund, Sweden; and St. Paul, Minn.

This volume is not a mere autobiography of the author, which, however, forms the principal part of the work, but as he was one of the early Swedish pioneers in this country, being for years one of the leading Scandinavian-Americans, his work contains much valuable information in regard to Scandinavian-American history. The Swedish edition is the best and most complete, although the last chapter of the English edition contains certain statistical information in regard to the Scandinavian-Americans which is not contained in the Swedish.

1892. The Scandinavians in the United States. Prof. H. H. Boyesen.

In this article, published in *The North American Review* in Nov., 1892, the author, among other things, criticises the Scandinavians for their clannishness. But the article contains also much valuable information in regard to the Northmen.

1892. Scandinavians in the Northwest. Prof. Kendric C. Babcock.

This article, published in *The Forum* in September, 1892, contains valuable information in regard to the Scandinavian-American population, especially in regard to statistics. The author being a native Amer can, his opinions about the Northmen have a specific value.

1892. The Bishop Hill Colony. Dr. M. A. Mikkelsen, Baltimore, Md.

This pamphlet is the most complete history on the subject that has yet appeared. It contains also a discussion of the religious movement in Helsingland, which finally caused the colonists to emigrate.

1892. Augustana College Album. Rock Island, Ill.

A pamphlet containing a history of the school, and biographies of all the professors and instructors who have been, or are, connected with the institution, together with several half-tone pictures.

1892. Ett Hundra År.; En Återblick på det Nittonde Seklet. C. F. Peterson, Chicago, Ill.

A large volume. Only the 6th chapter is devoted to the Swedish immigration and biographies of noted Swedish-Americans.

1892. Sweden and the Swedes. Hon. W. W. Thomas, Chicago, Ill.

The last two chapters contain some original matter in regard to Sweden's commerce with the United States, the Swedish settlement on Delaware River, the Swedes in America in the nineteenth century, and a report of John Ericsson's funeral.

1839. Sandfärdig Beretning om Amerika. Ole Rynning, Kristiania, Norway.

This little volume was the first book which was published in the Norwegian language in regard to America. It was extensively read, and created quite a sensation which resulted in a heavy emigration from Norway to this country in the early forties.

1844. Veiviser for Norske Emigranter. J. R. Reiersen, Kristiania, Norway.

It is mainly an emigration guide, although the first part of the work contains some valuable matters in regard to the early Norwegians in this country.

1846-. Beretning om Hauges Norsk Ev. Luth. Synode.

It is doubtful if any statistics were issued, or even kept, before the reorganization of the synod in 1875. Since that date annual reports, more or less imperfect, have been printed.

1849. Wägledning för Emigranter. Theodor Schytte, Stockholm, Sweden.

This is an emigrant guide, but contains also a description of the condition of the Scandinavian settlements in America.

1851. Wälkomst-Helsning till den Swenska, Norska och Danska Emigranten. Rev. L. P. Esbjörn, New York.

Every evidence seems to indicate that this four-paged pamphlet was the first Swedish publication printed in America in the nineteenth century. It contains religious advice to the Scandinavian immigrants, with directions how to reach the Swedish settlements in Illinois. Four thousand copies were published.

1851-60. Minutes of the Evangelical Lutheran Synod of Northern Illinois.

These reports contain statistics and other informations concerning the Swedish and Norwegian congregations connected with this organization.

1852. Scandinavians in the Northwest. Rev. W. M. Reynolds, D. D.

This article was published in the "Evangelical Review."

1853. The Mission of the Lutheran Church in America. Rev. S. W. Harkey, Springfield, Ill.

This pamphlet refers to the Scandinavians in connection with church work.

1853–. Beretning om det Ordentlige Synode-möde af Synoden for den Norsk-Evang.-Luth. Kirke i Amerika.

It does not appear that any regular church statistics were published by the Norwegian Synod until about 1863, and it is to be regretted that this conservative organization has not issued any first-class reports. All other Norwegian and Danish Lutherans appear to have modeled their statistics after those of the Norwegian Synod, at least as to defects and omissions. Consequently, none of them keep any record of the value of church property, and omit many other things of importance. All the reports of the Norwegian and Danish Lutherans are poorly classified and badly summed up.

1853-55. Bref om Amerika till Hemmavarande Landsmän. C. E. O. Svalander, Halmstad, Sweden.

It was published in two parts, and intended as an emigrant guide-book.

1854. Protocoll, Hållet vid ett Gemensamt Möte af Chicago och Mississippi Evang. Lutherska Conferensen i Chicago.

This is the first church report published in the Swedish language in America in the nineteenth century. It may be of interest to many people that in this pamphlet of a dozen pages, some space is devoted to the discussion of temperance.

1855–. Kirkelig Maanedstidende and Evangelisk Luthersk Kirketidende. Decorah, Iowa.

The last mentioned magazine is a continuation of the first, both being the official organs of the Norwegian Synod. It contains a vast amount of historical data concerning all the Scandinavian-American churches, especially as long as it was issued only monthly or semi-monthly.

1860–. Protokoll af Skandinaviska Ev. Lutherska Augustana Synoden.

This was the official name of the annual reports of the Augustana Synod for over thirty years. The statistical tables in the reports of this organization have always been and are master productions, covering every subject of church work, and having, perhaps, no superior in the world in the line of perfect statistics. Other matters of importance are also included in these publications. Rev. Erland Carlsson was the man who first systematized this work.

1862. Forhandlinger paa det 3die Skandinaviske Kirke-möde i Kristiania 29-31 Juli, 1861.

It contains a lecture delivered by Rev. O. C. T. Andren about the Augustana Synod.

1863. Her Fremträder atter en Skare af Troende Själe. Kristiania, Norway.

This little work contains a number of letters endorsing the missionary labor of Elling Eielsen. The general bombast of the contents resembles the recommendations of a much advertised patent medicine.

1865. Amerika og de Danskes Liv Herovre. Rev. L. Jörgensen. Copenhagen, Denmark.

This pamphlet is virtually valueless.

1867. Hvad Jeg Oplevede under de Sex Förste Aar af Min Virksomhed i Amerika. Rev. C. I. P. Pedersen, Madison, Wis.

The author gives an extensive review of the Norwegian Lutheran church disputes in Chicago during 1861-67.

1867. Skandinaverne i de Forenede Stater og Canada. Johan Schröder, La Crosse, Wis.

It is intended as an emigrant guide, but refers also to the Scandinavian settlements in the United States and Canada.

1868. Historisk Fremstilling. Madison, Wis.

This pamphlet contains a history of the disputes concerning the slavery question which was agitated among the Norwegian Lutherans in 1861-8, especially by Rev. C. L. Clausen and some Norwegian Synod ministers. It was published under the auspices of the church council of the synod, and called forth Clausen's book "Gjenmäle."

1869. Gjenmäle. Rev. C. L. Clausen, Chicago, Ill.

In this work the author defends himself in regard to his position on the slavery question, on which he could not agree with the majority of the ministers of the Norwegian Synod.

1870. Ev. Lutherska Augustana Synoden i Nord-Amerika och dess Mission. Rev. E. Norelius, Lund, Sweden.

A very concise and impartial history of the Augustana Synod. In many respects it is superior to the larger work by the same author.

1870. Märkelige Tildragelser. Rev. T. A. Torgerson, La Crosse, Wis.

It deals only with some local church disputes.

1870-89.   Beretning om den Norsk-Dansk Evang. Luth. Konferentse.

Most of these reports are, like those of other Norwegian Lutherans, rather defective.

1871.   En Rejse i Amerika.   Rev. A. C. L. Grove-Rasmussen, Odense, Denmark.

The author traveled in this country in the interest of "Udvalget," Denmark, and the above is a report of his investigation, which led to the establishment of Lutheran missionary work among the Danes in this country.

1872-.   Referat af Forhandlingerne ved Frikonferenser og Fällesmöder.

A number of reports have been published in regard to meetings held by the various Norwegian-American Lutheran church associations for the purpose of uniting them or discussing certain subjects.   Such reports have been issued concerning conferences held at Rock Prairie, Wis., 1872; St. Ansgar, Iowa, 1881; Decorah, Iowa, 1884; Chicago, Ill., 1885; Willmar, Minn., 1887 and 1892; Lanesboro, Minn., 1897; Austin, Minn., 1899, and no doubt at other places.

1873.   Anteckningar från en Svensk Emigrants Vistelse i Amerika 1871-72.   J. E. Wennström, Upsala, Sweden.

1874.   Aaben Erkläring.   A. Weenaas and S. Oftedal, Minneapolis, Minn.

This is one of the fiercest attacks upon the Norwegian Synod imaginable, being virtually a declaration of war, and it called forth numerous replies. Weenaas, in his book "Wisconsinismen," withdrew his name from it; but Oftedal never took back a single word in it.

1875.   Tale ved Femti-Aarsfesten for den Norske Udvandring til Amerika.   Prof. R. B. Anderson, Chicago, Ill.

This small pamphlet contains very little concerning the Norwegian emigration.

1875-9.   Kvartal-Skrift for den Norsk Lutherske Kirke i Amerika.   G. Sverdrup and S. Oftedal, Minneapolis, Minn.

This magazine contains some valuable articles in regard to the various Norwegian-American Lutheran churches.

1876.   Vore Kirkelige Modstanderes Vaaben.   Rev. V. Koren, Decorah, Iowa.

It cites quotations from A. Weenaas's book "Wisconsinismen," as well as comments on them.

. **1876.** Vor Tids Muhamed. John Ahmanson, Omaha, Neb.

The first two chapters contain a brief history of the beginning of Mormonism in Denmark and Norway, and the immigration of some Scandinavians to Utah in 1856.

1876. Om Absolutionen. Rev. N. C. Ylvisaker, Bergen, Norway.

This pamphlet contains short definitions of the subject by various Norwegian-Americans.

1876. Reseminnen från Amerika. C. J. N., Kristinehamn, Sweden.

The author, Rev. C. J. Nyvall, who traveled in this country in 1875, refers to the religious condition among the Swedes in the United States.

1876-93. Protokoll af Metodist Episkopal Kyrkans Nordvestra Svenska Årskonferens.

These reports of the Swedish Methodists in this country are fairly well prepared and quite complete. No statistics, however, are compiled concerning the annual appropriations which the Swedish-American Methodists have for many years received from the American Methodists, sometimes amounting to over $30,000 in one year. Complete information on this point may be found in the annual reports of the Missionary Society of the Methodist Episcopal Church. In comparison with other denominations, the Swedish Methodists value their church property too high. Since the division of the conference in 1893, their statistics have been very unsatisfactory. But for most purposes, the reports of the Missionary Society can be safely consulted.

1876-94. Nordisk Familjebok. Konversationslexikon och Realencyklopedi. Stockholm, Sweden.

This masterly cyclopedia in eighteen volumes contains biographies of some Scandinavian-Americans, especially such as have returned and settled in Scandinavia. The article on emigration, "Utvandring," is one of the ablest on that subject that has ever appeared in any language, and is superior to those on the same subject in the English and American cyclopedias. It is boldly asserted that the early Scandinavian emigrants were mostly adventurers, unsuccessful individuals, and criminals; but it is admitted that in later years the emigrants are the cream of the middle and working classes. In 1896 an addition to the original work was issued.

1877. Från Nya Verlden. Ernst Beckman, Stockholm Sweden.

Only a few pages refer to Swedish-Americans, and none of it is of any great importance.

1878. Minnen. Rev. J. A. Edgren, Chicago, Ill.
It contains an interesting autobiography of the author, as well as other matters of interest, especially to Swedish-American Baptists.

1878. De Kirkelige Partier blandt vort Folk i Amerika. Rev. V. Koren, Decorah, Iowa.
A pamphlet giving an excellent review of the various Norwegian Lutheran church organizations in this country.

1878. Om Splittelse i Kirken. Decorah, Iowa.
In this pamphlet the predestination question is discussed.

1878. Missourisynoden og den Norske Synode. Rev. O. Asperheim, Brooklyn, N. Y.
This work was written, apparently, for the purpose of showing that the Norwegian Synod has been wrong in most of its disputes with other Lutheran organizations. But it contains also some other matters of historical value.

1879. Trende Breve. De Forest, Wis.
It deals with the schism of Hauge's Synod and Elling Eielsen in 1875.

1879. Falskt Vidnesbyrd af Prof. A. Weenaas. Rev. B. J. Muus, Decorah, Iowa.
In this pamphlet the author defends the teachings of the Norwegian Synod against the attacks of Prof. Weenaas.

1880. Om den Lutherske Kirke i Amerika. Rev. P. Andersen, Chicago, Ill.
This pamphlet refers mostly to the Norwegian Augustana Synod.

1880–. Korsbaneret. Edited by various Augustana Synod clergymen, Rock Island, Ill.
This annual publication is very valuable, containing an immense amount of historical and biographical information concerning the Augustana Synod and its men.

1880–. Protokol af den Norsk- Danske Methodist Aars-konference.
These reports are fairly well prepared and quite complete. But no statistics are compiled concerning the annual appropriations which the Norwegian-Danish Methodists in this country have for many years received from the American Methodists, sometimes amounting to over $20,000 in one year. Complete

information on this subject, as well as on many others, can be secured by consulting the annual reports of the Missionary Society of the Methodist Episcopal Church. In comparison with other denominations, the Norwegian-Danish Methodists value their church property too high.

1881. Naadevalg-Striden. Prof. F. A. Schmidt, Chicago, Ill.
It contains lectures on predestination, and some historical facts concerning the Norwegian Lutherans during the great predestination controversy.

1881. Celebration of the Decennial Anniversary of the Founding of New Sweden in Maine. Portland, Me.
It contains a review of the Swedish colony in Maine, founded in 1870 by W W. Thomas, U. S. Minister to Sweden-Norway.

1881-2. I Amerika. C. E. H. Gestrin, Stockholm, Sweden.
The author resided in this country for twelve years, and refers to the Swedish-Americans.

1882. The Scandinavian Immigration. Rev. W. K. Frick.
This article appeared in "The Lutheran Church Review" for Jan. and April, 1882, and deals with the Northmen principally from a religious and statistical standpoint.

1882. Mormonismen. Rev. J. Telleen.
This small pamphlet refers very briefly to the Scandinavian Mormons.

1882. Fri Menighed i Fri Kirke. Svar paa de 30's Erklæring. Prof. Georg Sverdrup, Minneapolis, Minn.
This pamphlet advocates individual and congregational liberty as against high church principles and practices.

1883. Forhandlinger ved Synodalkonferensen i Chicago.
Most of the report is devoted to the position of Prof. F. A. Schmidt in regard to the predestination question.

1883. Amerikanska Studier. Ernst Beckman, Stockholm, Sweden.
It is composed of two parts, one referring to the Swedes in America, and the other describing the press in the U. S.

1883. Föredrag om Amerika. Isidor Kjellberg, Stockholm, Sweden.

A small pamphlet referring to Swedish-American conditions.

1884. Emigrantmissionen. Rev. R. Andersen, Brooklyn, N. Y.

As an emigrant guide, and as a treatise on the Lutheran work among the Danish immigrants, it is considered to be quite valuable.

1884. Den Gamle og Nye Retning. Rev. J. A. Bergh, Chicago, Ill.

This pamphlet is a protest against the free, new, or loose tendency within the · Norwegian-Danish Lutheran Conference.

1884. Betragtninger og Meddelelser fra Amerika. Rev. P. C. Trandberg, Minneapolis, Minn.

It is virtually an autobiography.

1884-96. Beretning om det Danske Evangeliske Lutherske Kirkesamfund.

These reports do not contain any statistics until 1892, but after that time they are fairly complete.

1885. Bidrag till Utvandringsfrågan. Gustav Sundbärg, Upsala, Sweden.

This large volume is a statistical compilation in regard to the emigration from Sweden, a subject on which the author is recognized as a high authority.

1885-. Svenska Ev. Missions-Förbundets Årsberättelse.

The statistics of the Swedish Mission Covenant of America are undoubtedly among the worst in Christendom. Up to 1895 unsuccessful attempts were made to include in the annual reports the ordinary church statistics, but since that date only the number of ministers and congregations have been mentioned, the former being about twice as numerous as the latter.

1886. Minne. Rock Island, Ill.

This pamphlet contains orations and poems in Swedish, English, German, Latin, and Greek, all delivered in honor of Dr. T. N. Hasselquist on his seventy-first birthday.

1886. Svenska Kyrkans Historia efter Reformationen. C. A. Cornelius, Stockholm, Sweden.

The second volume of this valuable work contains a history of Eric Janson's sect and of the Augustana Synod, and refers to many other matters in connection with the Swedish emigration.

1886. Hvad Jeg Vil. Rev. P. C. Trandberg, Chicago, Ill.
It is a general harangue about himself, the Lutherans, and the Congregationalists.

1887. Fra mit Besög blandt Mormonerne. Rev. Andreas Mortensen, Kristiania, Norway.
The latter part of the book refers to the Scandinavian Mormons.

1887. Skal der Blive Fred? Rev. H. Halvorsen, Chicago.
This pamphlet treats of the disputes in regard to predestination

1888-9. Beretning om det Antimissouriske Broderskab.
These reports do not contain any statistics at all, and apparently are of little value.

1888-. Statistik öfver Svenska Baptist Församlingarna.
These reports of the Swedish-American Baptists are fairly well prepared and quite complete. No statistics, however, are compiled concerning the annual appropriations which the Swedish Baptists in this country for many years have received from the American Baptists, sometimes amounting to about $25,000 in one year. Some information on this point can be secured in the annual reports of the American Baptist Home Mission Society.

1889. Vitus Bering. Peter Lauridsen, translated by Prof. Julius E. Olson, Chicago, Ill.
This is a biography of the great Danish explorer, the discoverer of Bering Strait, who was in the service of Peter the Great.

1889. Address. Rev. C. A. Swensson, Topeka, Kan.
This pamphlet refers to the Swedish-American institutions of learning.

1889. Minnesotas Historia. Robert Grönberger, Minneapolis, Minn.
This volume contains nothing in regard to Scandinavian-American history, except biographies and pictures of about sixty Scandinavians in Minnesota.

1889. Ett Halfår i Nya Verlden. Alexandra Gripenberg, Helsingfors, Finland.
The authoress was a delegate to the international woman's congress at Washington, D. C., in 1888, and afterwards traveled extensively through the United States, visiting and describing some of the Finnish and Swedish settlements, especially in Pennsylvania and California.

1890.   Vid Hemmets Härd.   Rev. C. A. Swensson, Chicago, Ill.

This immense volume is, like most of Swensson's productions, virtually valueless to an historian, often being incorrect and misleading. The same is true of his books "I Sverige" (1890), "Förgät Mig Ej" (1893), and "Again in Sweden" (1898). Yet they may be consulted, as several subjects relating to Swedish-American history are referred to.

1890.   Minnen från en Färd genom Amerika.   Axel E. Lindvall, Karlskrona, Sweden.

The author traveled through this country, and refers to the Swedish-Americans.

1890.   Frugter fra Northfield-Skolen, og lidt fra Augsburg Seminar.   M. Shirley, Minneapolis, Minn.

This pamphlet is a mass of rambling and bitter tirades against some prominent members of the United Church.

1890.   Mindeblade eller Otte Aar i Amerika.   Rev. A. Weenaas, Volden, Norway.

The author gives an historical review of the religious condition of the Norwegian-Americans during 1868-76, especially in regard to the separation of the Swedes and Norwegians in the Augustana Synod and the formation of the Norwegian-Danish Conference.

1890.   Afskeden og dens Grunde.   Rev. P. C. Trandberg, Chicago, Ill.

It contains something concerning the work of the Congregationalists among the Scandinavians in America.

1890.   Festtaler.   Chicago, Ill.

This pamphlet contains the speeches delivered at the dedication of Luther College in 1890.

1890.   Hvad den Norske Synode Har Villet og fremdeles Vil.   Rev. V. Koren, Decorah, Iowa.

This pamphlet contains the main principles of what the Norwegian Synod teaches.

1890-.   Beretning om den Forenede Norsk Lutherske Kirke i Amerika.

The statistical tables in the reports of the United Church treat of about half as many topics as those of the Augustana Synod, but the former occupy almost twice as much space as the latter. In half a dozen different places, the various subjects have been tablulated in alphabetic order according to the names of the pastors, covering nearly 150 pages. All of which could easily have been put under two headings, thereby saving much space. Besides, on account of the statistics being classified on a single basis, it is very difficult to find any information in regard to a certain congregation if the name of the officiating clergyman is not known. To ascertain the strength of the United Church in a given state would require as much labor as to search in a waste-basket for a pin. Many of the ministers report as members all the children they have baptized, notwithstanding that the parents do not belong to the church, and that some of these children will never attend any service. In fact it is impossible to tell the strength of the United Church until their methods of keeping statistics have been thoroughly reformed.

1891. Amerika. K. Zilliacus, Chicago, Ill.
This is only an emigration guide, full of patent medicine advertisements.

1891. Svenskarne i Minnesota. Axel A. Ahlroth, St. Paul, Minn.
Two small pamphlets, containing historical matter regarding several of the Swedish settlements in Minnesota. The work is unreliable. The writer has quoted several pages from "Svenskarne i St. Croix-dalen, Minnesota," by Robert Gronberger, without crediting the latter, or in any way indicating that it is not the writer's own production.

1891. Den Stora Skilnaden emellan Svenska Statskyrkan och Augustana Synoden. Rev. O. A. Toffteen, Minneapolis, Minn.
This pamphlet contains a general harangue about the merit of the Apostolic Succession and the shortcomings of the Augustana Synod.

1891. Hand-Book of Lutheranism. Rev. J. D. Roth, Utica, N. Y.
It refers to the Scandinavian-American Lutherans.

1891. En Sommer i Amerika. Anton Nielsen, Odense, Denmark.
Only a few pages in the beginning of this small book refer to the Danish-Americans.

1892. Svenskhet i Amerika. Prof. D. Nyvall, Minneapolis, Minn.
A small pamphlet referring to various matters concerning Swedish-Americans.

1892.   Amerika-bok.   Isidor Kjellberg, Linköping, Sweden.

The author traveled in this country, and his pamphlet refers briefly to some Swedish-American affairs.

1892. Valda Skrifter. John A. Enander, LL. D., Chicago, Ill.

This volume contains some historical information regarding the Swedish-Americans, especially in regard to the Swedish-American press.

1892. Brydninger i den Forenede Kirke.   Rev. K. B. Birkeland, Minneapolis, Minn.

It is written from the standpoint of a Free Church man, and contains a history of the disputes in the United Church up to the time of the publication of the book.

1892.   Geschichte der Lutherischen Kirche in Amerika. Prof. A. L. Graebner, St. Louis, Mo.

It refers to the Scandinavian-American Lutherans.

1892-3.   Återblick öfver den Fria Missionsverksamheten bland Svenskarne i Amerika.   Rev. C. M. Youngquist.

This valuable article, giving a complete history of the Swedish Mission movement in this country, was published in "Hem-Missionären" in 1892-3.

1892-5.   The Alumnus, or the Augustana Journal. Rock Island, Ill.

This magazine, when issued monthly, contained some valuable matters in regard to the Augustana Synod and its men.

1893. Jubel-Album.   Revs. C. A. Swensson and L. G. Abrahamson, Chicago, Ill.

This large volume contains some valuable historical matters concerning the Augustana Synod. It has been severely criticised by some of the leading men of said organization.

1893.   Lutherans in All Lands. Rev. J. N. Lenker, A. M., Milwaukee, Wis.

Contains a great deal of valuable historical and statistical matter in regard to the Scandinavian Lutherans in all countries.

1893. Courts of Conciliation. Nicolay Grevstad.
Only the last part of this excellent article, published in "The Atlantic Monthly," November, 1893, relates to the Norwegians in America.

1893. Kort Uddrag af den Norske Synodes Historie. Rev. Jacob Aall Ottesen, Decorah, Iowa.
A small pamphlet, but contains a fairly complete history of the Norwegian Synod.

1893. Blik paa Amerikanske Forhold. H. I. S. Astrup, Kristiania, Norway.
A small work of little importance.

1893. Augsburgs Historie. Rev. C. Saugstad, Minneapolis, Minn.
It contains a brief history of Augsburg Seminary,

1893. A History of the Evangelical Lutheran Church in the United States. Rev. H. E. Jacobs, New York.
It refers to the Scandinavian Lutheran associations in this country.

1893–. Beretning om Augsburgs Venner and Frikirken.
In these reports no attempt has been made in regard to statistics, excepting that everything is avoided that might give a clue to the strength of the organization.

1894. En Emigrants Resa. A. G. Carlsson, Chicago, Ill.
The author's observations are narrated, but the pamphlet is of little value.

1894. Är Episkopalkyrkans Mission bland Våra Landsmän i Amerika Berättigad? Dr. C. A. Blomgren, Rock Island, Ill.
This pamphlet is a protest against the attempt of the Episcopalians to proselyte among the Swedes.

1894. Hemlandstoner. K. H. Gez. von Scheele, Stockholm, Sweden.
It contains many valuable facts concerning the Augustana Synod and the Swedish-Americans.

1894. Bland Svenskar och Yankees. Hj. Cassel, Stockholm, Sweden.
The author, being a newspaper editor and spending much of his time among

20

the Swedes in St. Paul, Minn., has painted in fine colors the virtues and faults of the people he came in contact with. Ernst Skarstedt says: "This author has given a better description of the religious, social, and political conditions of the Swedes; residing in the American cities than any other writer."

1894. Minde fra Jubelfesterne paa Koshkonong. Decorah, Iowa.

This volume gives much information about the Norwegian Synod, especially in regard to its work in Wisconsin. In it is published Rev. A. Bredesen's address, containing, besides other matters, an excellent summing up of the peculiar social conditions prevalent among the Norwegian pioneers.

1894. A Norwegian-American College. Prof. Andrew Estrem.

This article, published in "The Midland Monthly," June, 1894, contains a good history of Luther College.

1894. Det Femtende Regiment. O. A. Buslett, Decorah, Iowa.

This is the most extensive historical and biographical work on the Scandinavian Regiment that has yet appeared. But it is not compiled with the best care and judgment.

1894. Den Norsk-Danske Methodismes Historie. Paa Begge Sider Havet. Rev. A. Haagensen, Chicago, Ill.

It is supposed to be a complete history of the Norwegian-Danish Methodist churches, but a large portion of the book is, virtually, only a reproduction of the annual church reports of the Norwegian-Danish Methodists in this country. Consequently, it is not a critical or carefully prepared production.

1894. Thomas Brown's Scandinavian Newspaper Directory. H. O. Oppedale, Chicago, Ill.

It contains quite an extensive historical review of several Scandinavian-American newspapers, as well as some other matters. Some of the informations, however, are not very reliable.

1894. Den Forenede Kirke. Rev. T. H. Dahl, Stoughton, Wis.

It is written from the standpoint of the "majority," and contains a history of the disputes in the United Church up to the time of the publication of the book.

1894. The Norwegians in the United States. Nils P. Haugen, Washington, D. C.

This speech, containing some valuable hints, was delivered at the World's Fair in Chicago, in 1893.

1894. Redegjörelse for Mine Anker mod Prof. H. Bergsland. Rev. O. S. Meland, Red Wing, Minn.

The object of this pamphlet is to prove Prof. Bergsland's incapacity, and God is called upon to witness the assertions. Personal spite and religious bombast are the predominant features of this publication.

1894-8. Legal documents in regard to Augsburg Seminary vs. the United Norwegian Church, Minneapolis, Minn.

This collection includes various published briefs and decisions, some of which give a minute history of some of the Norwegian Lutheran associations and of Augsburg Seminary.

1895. Den Norsk-Lutherske Kirkes Grundläggelse i Amerika. Rev. S. M. Krogness, Kristiania, Norway.

This article was published in "Luthersk Kirketidende" for January 26th, 1895, and appears to be quite valuable.

1895. Gjensvar til Pastor Melands *Redegjörelse*. Prof. H. H. Bergsland, Red Wing, Minn.

This is an answer to Rev. O. S. Meland's attack upon the author.

1895. The First Chapter of Norwegian Immigration (1821-1840). Prof. R. B. Anderson, Madison, Wis.

The main value of this volume consists of a somewhat minute information in regard to the doings of each individual of the Sloop party and his or her descendants. A large portion of the work is virtually a translation of Prof. Svein Nilsson's articles, published in "Billed-Magazin" in 1868-70. The optimistic view which the author takes of the Sloop party is hardly, it seems, warranted by facts. From an historical and literary point of view, the book is lacking in generalization, and an unexpectedly large amount of space is devoted to the author himself and his relatives.

1895. Metodismen i Sverige. Rev. T. M. Erikson, Stockholm, Sweden.

This volume refers also to the Swedish Methodists in this country.

1895. Svenska Metodismen i Amerika. N. M. Liljegren, N. O. Westergreen, och C. G. Wallenius, Chicago, Ill.

This is quite a large volume, and gives a detailed account of nearly all Swedish-American Methodist congregations and clergymen. If the work had been better generalized, it would have been more valuable. As has already been stated on pages 209-10 in this volume, the authors have no authority for asserting that Dr. C. M. Wrangel was a Methodist.

1895. Enskilda Skrifter af Pastor A. A. Swärd. Ernst Skarstedt, San Francisco, Cal.

This pamphlet contains some brilliant expressions concerning the merits and shortcomings of some of the Swedish-American poets.

1896. The Scandinavian Contingent. Prof. K. C. Babcock.

This article was published in "The Atlantic Monthly," May, 1896, and is well written, but contains nothing new concerning the Scandinavians.

1896. Afholdssagens Historie. Prof. J. L. Nydahl, Minneapolis, Minn.

The author does not pretend to give a full history of the Scandinavian-American temperance movement, yet about one-sixth of the volume is devoted to that subject.

1896. Amerika i Vor Tid. Carl W. Möller, Helsingör, Denmark.

It is only a large emigration guide.

1896. Knute Nelson. L. A. Stenholt, Minneapolis, Minn.

It contains an extensive biography of Knute Nelson, which the author claims is based upon the authority of Knute Nelson himself.

1896. Immigration. Knute Nelson, Washington, D. C.

This speech, delivered in the United States Senate, contains some valuable hints in regard to immigration in general.

1896. Samfunds Haandbog. Rev. J. C. Jensson, Minneapolis, Minn.

This volume enumerates the institutions connected, directly or indirectly, with the United Norwegian Lutheran Church.

1896. A History of the Danes in America. John H. Bille, Madison, Wis.

This pamphlet is rather incomplete and sometimes unfair; but at the same time it is very valuable, being the only work of its kind, containing also a bibliography.

1896. Nödvendige Bemärkninger. H. Hjertaas and H. H. Bergsland, Red Wing, Minn.

It is one of those numerous Norwegian pamphlets dealing with theological and personal disputes.

1896. Bihang till Minnen. Rev. Gustaf Unonius, Stockholm, Sweden.

This pamphlet is a reply to some of the statements made by Rev. E. Norelius in his large history of the Swedish Lutherans in America. Unonius accuses the latter author of unfairness, partiality, and misrepresentation. In the first number of "Tidskrift," 1898, Norelius answers Unonius, and the two old men, both on the brink of eternity, shake their fists at each other across the Atlantic ocean.

1896-. Beretning om den Forenede Danske Evangelisk-Lutherske Kirke.

The statistics of this organization are very incomplete and badly generalized

1897. Fra Amerika. Henrik Cavling, Copenhagen, Denmark.

These two large volumes were written in haste by a Danish editor who traveled in this country. From an historical standpoint, the work is more conspicuous for its faults than for its merits. Nor do the hundred odd pages in the second volume, dealing with the Norwegians in America and written by P. Groth, Ph. D., appear to be any better. The latter writer has translated several of our biographies of Scandinavians in Minnesota, without giving us proper credit. A Swedish translation by Petrus Hedberg was published in Stockholm, in 1898.

1897. Det Norske Luther College. Prof. Gisle Bothne, Decorah, Iowa.

Only a small portion of this volume of nearly 500 pages is an original production, the remaining part of the book being a reprint of some catalogues and other works. Apparently, this publication has not been prepared with care and good judgment, although the author, who is considered to be a man of ability, has been working on it for over ten years. Only fourteen pages are devoted to the biography of Prof. L. Larsen, who for over a third of a century has been the soul of Luther College, and nine-tenths of the biography relates to the celebration of his twenty-five years' jubilee, in 1884; but some twenty pages are devoted to men who have been connected with the institution only for a few years. The author quotes liberally from the expressions of different individuals, but not a single one of Prof. Larsen's utterances has been mentioned, and virtually no clue is given in regard to the trials, triumphs, and make-up of this important man,

who, it seems, should be treated at considerable length in a history of an institution of which he has been the chief man ever since it was founded.

1897-. Valkyrian. New York.

This excellent magazine, published by O. K. Johansen and edited by E.
Sundell, contains several articles, in relation to the Swedish-Americans, of great
historical and literary value.

1897. Våra Pennfäktare. Ernst Skarstedt, San Francisco, Cal.

This volume contains biographies of nearly all the Swedish-American editors
and writers, living and dead, with specimens of their productions. It is virtually
the only attempt ever made to produce a history of the Swedish-American literature, a subject on which the author is undoubtedly the highest authority. The
introductory chapter, especially, gives an excellent and masterly summing up of
the Swedish-American literature.

1898. Pennteckningar och Reseskildningar. F. A. Lindstrand, Chicago, Ill.

It contains some sketches in regard to Swedish-American history.

1898. Svenskarne i Worcester, 1868-98. Hj. Nilson and Eric Knutson, Worcester, Mass.

Contains an historical and biographical review of the Swedes in Worcester.

1898. Red Wing Seminarium. M. G. Hanson og H. H. Elstad, Red Wing, Minn.

This pamphlet contains a brief and good history of the school of Hauge's
Synod.

1898. Norge i Amerika. L. A. Stenholt, Minneapolis, Minn.

The presentation is somewhat original, but otherwise no new historical matters have been produced.

1898. Kort Udsigt over det Lutherske Kirkearbeide blandt Nordmändene i Amerika. Prof. Th. Bothne, Chicago, Ill.

This is the first attempt ever made to write a critical history of the different
Norwegian-American Lutheran organizations. Considering the many strifes
which have divided the Norwegian-American Lutherdom into different factions,
in which some of the ablest minds and some of the most stupid simpletons have
participated, it is doubtful if any mortal ever can rightly interpret the pas-

sions and motives of all the men who have fought these theological battles; and the author, as he says himself, is not even a theologian. The constant harangue against the official class of Norway is out of place in a church history; and the baneful influence which this class has, according to the author, exercised upon Norwegian-American church affairs, is undoubtedly much exaggerated. Everything considered, it is no wonder that the book has been severely criticised, even by men who can speak with authority, and many errors have been pointed out. Yet the work appears to have been written in a manly and fearless spirit, and deserves to be carefully studied by persons who are interested in Norwegian-American church history.

1898–. Tidskrift. Edited by Dr. E. Norelius, Rock Island, Ill.

The reproduction of historical documents in relation to Swedish-Lutheran congregations, which existed before the Augustana Synod was organized, in 1860, appears to be the main object of this magazine, although the first number contains a lengthy discussion in regard to Rev. G. Unonius.

1898. History of the Swedish Baptists in Sweden and America. Capt. Gustavus W. Schroeder, New York.

This is the first work of the kind that has appeared so far, but only about one-fifth of the book deals with the Swedish Baptists. Throughout most of the remaining 250 pages the author carps at the religious, political, and social conditions of the Swedish people.

1898. Från Canada. Rev. Svante Udden, Rock Island, Ill.

This pamphlet gives a history of the work of the Swedish Lutherans in Canada.

1898. Sverige i Amerika. C. F. Peterson, Chicago, Ill.

This large volume is more of a history of civilization in regard to the Swedish-Americans than a history of facts, being about the only attempt ever made in that line. It contains also a number of biographies and some statistical tables; the latter, however, are not very accurate. Most of the chapters dealing with Swedish-American churches, schools, language, press, arts, political influence, etc., constitute a masterly and original presentation of those subjects.

Autobiography of Rev. A. Cedarholm.

This is a small pamphlet translated from the Swedish language into English, by Mrs. Caroline Cedarholm. It contains no date or place of publication. Rev. A. Cedarholm appears to have been one of the early Swedish Methodist missionaries, both in the American Northwest and in Sweden. The work is written in the most unsystematic manner imaginable, and as a specimen of religious enthusiasm and fanaticism it is valuable.

Historical Review of the Scandinavians in Minnesota.

—BY—

O. N. NELSON.

Minnesota occupies the exact center of the North American continent, being located midway between the Atlantic and Pacific oceans, and between Hudson Bay and the Gulf of Mexico. In area it is the ninth state in the Union, containing about 84,000 square miles, or nearly fifty-four million acres, being half as large as Sweden and six times the size of Denmark. There are, it is estimated, ten thousand lakes in the state, and nearly four million acres of land is covered with water. Minnesota has numerous rivers and water-courses which drain the country, make navigation practicable, and furnish power for manufacturing purposes. One of the world's greatest rivers, the Mississippi, rises in the northern part of Minnesota. The natural resources of the state are great and various, mineral and timber abound, the soil is rich and productive, the scenery is beautiful and diversified.

I. PIONEERS AND SETTLEMENTS.

It may be said that the history of Minnesota commenced

yesterday. About 200 years ago the Jesuits visited the state, but at the beginning of the nineteenth century not a single settlement of the whites existed. In 1823 the first steamboat ascended the Mississippi as far as Fort Snelling, which was just then built; yet, for years after, the savage Indians were, virtually, the sole occupiers of the land on which now over one and a half million civilized people dwell. In 1850 there were only 6,000 inhabitants in the state.

But if the history is brief, the development has been rapid, and the Scandinavians have, during the whole period, been powerful agents in developing the natural resources and promoting the intellectual and religious welfare of the state. The marvelous material development of the state is largely due to the industrious Scandinavian immigrants. Their great love and fitness for farming, their frugality and energy, have subdued a wilderness and made it inhabitable for civilized people. It is true that the Northmen have been the greatest gainers themselves, for as a general thing they arrived poor, while they now often live in wealth and splendor. Yet a state, or a nation as a whole, is always benefited by the prosperity of its citizens. And an American educator, who has made special study of the Scandinavians in the Northwest, believes that he can prove that in counties where many Scandinavians have settled, a more rapid material development has occurred than in counties occupied by other nationalities. His conclusion is perhaps correct. At any rate, the state and the coming generations are under great obligations to the Northern immigrants, who by struggle, hard toil, suffering, and self-sacrifice laid the material, social, political, intellectual, and religious foundations of the State of Minnesota; and who, when the Civil War threatened to destroy the nation, enlisted in the defense of the Union and of human freedom.

As it is utterly impossible to give the full facts concerning all the Scandinavian settlements, or even of one-half of them, only a few of the earliest will be mentioned. At the end of this article, however, the population of each county has been enumerated, which may be of some value in tracing the migratory movements. But it is to be regretted that the state census reports for 1865 and 1885 did not enumerate the various nationalities in the different counties of Minnesota, and most of the national census reports are also defective in this respect.

DANISH. The man who established the first bank in Minnesota, in 1853, was a Dane, Dr. C. W. W. Borup, who settled permanently in St. Paul, in 1848, although he undoubtedly had been in the state years before that time, having been in the far West before 1830. The well-known Rev. C. L. Clausen is said to have visited that part of Minnesota where St. Cloud now is located, in company with a dozen Norwegians, in 1850. The biographies of both these important men can be found in this volume. But no Danish settlement seems to have been started in the state very early, as in 1850, according to the United States census, there were only one Dane in Minnesota, and 170 ten years later. Since 1880, however, their number has materially increased, and in 1900 there were in the neighborhood of 40,000 Danish-born or having Danish parents within the state.

NORWEGIAN. It is claimed that several Norwegians

settled below St. Paul on both sides of the Mississippi river
in 1851. In 1852 and 1853, however, the Norwegians commenced to settle in Houston and Fillmore counties, and
Tosten Johnson and Hans Valder were among the very first
Norwegian settlers in Minnesota. According to the United
States census, there were, in 1850, seven Norwegians in the
state, and they numbered nearly 10,000 ten years later.
Since they have greatly increased, and undoubtedly have
exercised a greater power and influence in the commercial
and public affairs of the state than any other single foreign
nationality. In several counties they are the controlling
element in regard to business, politics, and society. South
of an imaginary line drawn due west from the Twin Cities,
there is hardly a single city or village of over 500 inhabitants in which there is not some Norwegian merchant or
business man. With some exceptions, especially in the districts lying between Minneapolis and Willmar and between
St. Paul and Duluth, where the Swedes greatly predominate,
this is also true of other portions of the state. There must
be at least 300,000 Norwegians of the first and second generations residing in Minnesota in 1900.

SWEDISH. One of the first pioneers and Protestant missionaries among the Indians in Minnesota was a Swede,
Jacob Falstrom, who came to the state before 1819,
in which year Fort Snelling was established; and, although
he did little or nothing in promoting civilization because he
had degenerated into savagery himself, yet he was a noted
character. He was the *first* Northman in the Northwest.
The first Swedish settlement in the state was commenced
at Marine, Washington county, in 1850, by Oscar Roos and

two other Swedes. Dr. E. Norelius, in his great work, *De Svenska Luterska Församlingarnas och Svenskarnes Historia i Amerika,* asserts that the first Swedish settlers arrived in 1851; this, however, is a mistake. Both Roos himself and *Svenskarne i St. Croix-dalen, Minnesota*—the latter is a small but excellent pamphlet by Robert Gronberger—contradict Norelius. By settlers, in this connection, we refer especially to those who either located in certain places in company with other Northmen, or tried to form Scandinavian colonies there. Falstrom and Borup were traders and adventurers, not settlers.

It may be of interest to notice that a family from the neighborhood of Motala, Sweden, made a trip exclusively by boats from that place to Taylor's Falls as early as 1850–51, making one of the most remarkable journeys ever performed by a Scandinavian immigrant in the nineteenth century. It took eight weeks to cross from Gothenburg to New Orleans, and when the party reached St. Louis they were destitute and starving, but at this juncture they met the famous Jenny Lind, who assisted them so they could proceed to their destination.

In no state in the Union, with the probable exception of Illinois, have the Swedes played such an important part as they have done in Minnesota. This they have done mostly because they have been more numerous than the Swedes in any other state. According to the United States census there were four Swedes in Minnesota in 1850, twenty years later they numbered over twenty thousand, and in 1900 there must be at least 280,000 Swedes of the first and second generations in the state. Excepting the Germans,

the Swedish-born people in the state are more numerous
than any other foreign-born nationality, but the Norwegians
outnumber them by about 20,000 when both the first and
second generations are taken into account.

II. CAUSES OF IMMIGRATION TO MINNESOTA.

It is impossible to determine the causes which have been
operative in directing the Northern immigration to Minnesota. The great resources of agriculture, timber, and mining; the varied and beautiful scenery—all of which resemble
the resources and scenes of the North—might have had something to do with the movement. The climate of Minnesota,
on the other hand, is extremely dry, and often severe, while
the climate of the Scandinavian countries, on the whole, is
moist and temperate; consequently that could be no inducement. But the chief reason has been, perhaps, the same as
that which directed the movement towards the Northwest
in general, namely, the Scandinavian immigration on a large
scale and the opening of the state for settlement occurred
about the same time. Then add the great impulse and the
direction which the early Scandinavian pioneers gave to the
whole movement, and the question is undoubtedly solved.
Such well-known pioneers as Col. H. Mattson and Rev. E.
Norelius have done a great deal in directing the Swedish
immigration towards the state. The Danish-Norwegian-
American historical literature is very limited, in comparison
with the Swedish, consequently it is no easy task, on account
of lack of materials, to determine who were the real leaders
in directing the Norwegian immigration into the state.
F. S. Christensen undoubtedly did much to draw the atten-

tion of the Danes towards Minnesota. But the honor and
credit of settling the state with a good class of people does
not belong exclusively to one or a few, but to hundreds and
thousands of Scandinavian immigrants who induced their
relatives and friends to join them.

III. The Civil and Spanish Wars.

At the outbreak of the Civil War, Colonel Hans Mattson
organized, in Goodhue county, Company D, which became
part of the Third Regiment of Minnesota. This company,
containing about 100 men, was composed exclusively of
Scandinavians. Not a single one of them had been drafted,
nor did any of them desert. But the Northmen who enlisted in that company are small in number in comparison
with the total number of Scandinavians from the state who
fought against the Rebellion. According to the *Annual
Report of the Adjutant-General of the State of
Minnesota,* published in 1866, not less than 1,500 Northmen from the state participated in the defense of the Union,
and fought against the enslavement of men. Of these,
about 25 were Danes, 800 Norwegians, and 675 Swedes.
As the Norwegians were more than twice as numerous in
the state at that time as the Swedes, it is evident that the
latter nationality enlisted in much greater proportion than
the former. In numerous instances the nativity of the soldiers is omitted; and it is not easy to count correctly all the
names in such publications; hence it is fair to estimate that
2,000 Scandinavians from Minnesota enlisted under the
Stars and Stripes. According to the United States census of
1860, Minnesota had a population of 172,000. Twenty-

three thousand soldiers, or one-eighth of the total population of the state, enlisted under the Union flag; while at the same time one out of every six Scandinavians in Minnesota, as well as in Wisconsin, fought for his adopted country.

The state of Minnesota has the distinguished honor of having offered the first volunteer regiment to the federal government and of having enlisted the first volunteer soldier in the United States. The Scandinavians in the state flew to arms at the very beginning of hostities. Nearly fifty Northmen served in the First Regiment, and more than three times that number fought in connection with the Second Regiment, in which A. R. Skaro, a Norwegian, was captain of Company E. But excepting him and Col. H. Mattson, not a single Scandinavian from Minnesota rose to the position even of captaincy, although several held minor commands.

Attempts were made in Minnesota, chiefly through the efforts of Christian Brandt, to muster into service a full-fledged Scandinavian regiment at the outbreak of the Spanish War in 1898, but the regiment was not accepted by the authorities, and the undertaking came to naught. About ninety Danes, five hundred Swedes and Norwegians, equally divided between the two nationalities, and a few Icelanders enlisted in the four volunteer regiments which the state furnished. Many other persons born in this country of Scandinavian parents also participated, but their number cannot be ascertained. One person out of every three hundred in the state enlisted against the Spaniards, and about one out of every four hundred of the Scandinavian-born individuals was engaged in that occupation. Minnesota supplied 5,313 soldiers, among whom were some influential Northmen, notably John Lind, afterwards governor of the state.

IV. POLITICAL INFLUENCE.

The Northmen have always exercised a great influence upon the political affairs of the state. They have often been able to run politics according to their own sweet will, not because they have specially excelled in intelligence or political sagacity, but on account of their numerical strength. There is no reason to assume that they, on an average, are brighter than the Northmen in other portions of the Union; yet most states might safely try to manage their politics without much regard to the Scandinavian-Americans. In Minnesota such an attempt would wreck any party or politician; and the real or supposed hostility to the Scandinavians on the part of the Republican candidate for governor in 1898, was one of the causes which defeated him by over 20,000 votes, although the rest of the state ticket went Republican by about 40,000 majority. Many of the Scandinavian politicians in the state are very ordinary mortals. Some of them cannot write a correct letter either in their own language or in English. It applies to the Scandinavians, as well as to the other nationalities, of course, including the native Americans, what a member of the state legislature said on the floor of the house of representatives: "The first I came here I wondered how I got here, but the longer I stay the more I wonder how the rest of you got here." For it is certainly a surprise to some of the Scandinavian politicians themselves and to everybody else "how they got there." There are only a few of the 255

21

Scandinavians who have represented their districts in the two bodies of the state legislature that have had more than a common school education—some of them have not even had that—although many of them are men of more than ordinary ability. For several years past the so-called leader of the house of representatives has been J. F. Jacobson, of Lac Qui Parle county, a coarse-grained, boisterous, uneducated, bankrupt individual, who "among his colleagues was feared rather than trusted." In later years, however, there has been considerable improvement in regard to the Scandinavian legislators.

We, of course, do not in any sense intend to say or indicate that the Scandinavian politicians in Minnesota have not been, both in regard to educational qualifications and in regard to natural abilities, equal to any other politicians in the state. On the contrary, they have, perhaps, been superior to many others, especially as they have had experience in more than one country, which ought to have a tendency to make a person broad-minded. And certainly some of them have made a most excellent record during their political career, and their names are inseparably connected with the history of the state and nation. Others, again, have received the highest scholastic training both in the North and here.

Minnesota was organized as a territory in 1849, and a state constitution was adopted in 1857. During that time not a single Scandinavian was elected to any of the territorial legislative bodies. Rev. P. A. Cederstam, a Swedish Lutheran minister, was the only Northman who sat in the constitutional convention and signed the constitution of

Minnesota. But the Norwegians were not much behind the
Swedes in regard to Minnesota legislation. For in 1857–8,
Hans Hanson and T. G. Fladeland—both Norwegians—
were in the state legislature, being, therefore, the first Scandinavian law-makers in Minnesota. Since over 255 descendants of the Vikings have exhibited their wisdom or ignorance in the arena of the capitol. Of these, 5 were Danes,
170 Norwegians, and 80 Swedes. Some of them, however,
have been re-elected several times. In some years, one out
of every six of the representatives and senators was a
Northman. But the Scandinavian population in the state
constitutes two-fifths of the total, consequently they were
not represented according to their due proportion. The
Norwegians have been more numerous in the state, their
immigration is older, they settle more in the country districts, and they take a greater interest in politics than the
Swedes; that is, no doubt, the reasons why they have had a
larger representation. Today (1900) the Germans-born
persons outnumber by far the Norwegians, and the Swedes
nearly equal them; but taking the history of the state as a
whole, the Norwegians have wielded a more powerful political influence than the Swedes and Germans put together.
L, J. Stark, in 1865, was the first Swede who served in the
state legislature. Soren Listoe, being the first Dane, entered
ten years later. J. Lindall, Ole Peterson, and A. Railson
were in the state senate in 1872, being, therefore, the first
Northmen who represented their districts in that body.

There are many counties in the state which have for
years elected Scandinavian county officials, and in some
counties all the officials are Northmen. In a lecture de-

livered in 1897, Prof. D. Magnus said: 'Today the Scandinavians in Minnesota hold 338 county offices, and if we count 16 offices to a county, there is enough of them to fill every office in 21 counties. In 18 counties they hold the office of county superintendent of public instruction; in 26, that of auditor; in 33, that of register of deeds; and in 36, nearly one-half of all the counties in the state, that of treasurer.' There is enough of Scandinavian officials in Minnesota to govern a fair-sized kingdom in Europe.

As has been related, they have ever since the state constitution was adopted been well represented in the two legislative bodies. But it was not until 1869 that any of them was elected to a state office. F. S. Christensen seems to have conceived the idea, and commenced to agitate the same in his paper, in 1869, which resulted in calling a Scandinavian convention at which Col. Hans Mattson was nominated for secretary of state, being shortly after endorsed by the Republicans, and was elected in 1869. At the Republican state convention where Col. Mattson was nominated he made the following speech, in which he undoubtedly echoed the sentiments of the majority of Scandinavians at that time as well as today: "The time does not admit of any extensive remarks upon my part, yet so much has been said lately regarding the Scandinavian element that the subject, perhaps, requires an explanation from me; and as the chosen representative of the Scandinavian people of this state in the present campaign, I am authorized to express their views, and I do so from a thorough knowledge of them. It is true that we have left our beloved land; we have strewn the last flowers upon the graves of our forefathers, and have come here to stay, come here to live, come here to die. We are not a clannish people, nor do we desire to build up a Scandinavian nationality in your midst. You have known us here for many years; you have seen us come among you unacquainted with your language and your customs, and yet I know that you will bear me witness how readily and fraternally we have mingled with you, learned your language and adopted your ways, and how naturally our children grow up as Americans, side by side with yours. We have been cordially received in this great West by your own pioneers, and have become prosperous and happy. Yes, we love this great country of freedom, and we wish to be and remain Americans."

Col. Mattson was, of course, elected secretary of state, being, therefore, the first Scandinavian state official in Minnesota, and was re-elected eight years later. Besides him, John S. Irgens and Frederick P. Brown, both Norwegians, and Albert Berg, a Swede, have been elected to the same position. The following Scandinavians have also held high official positions in the state: for example, Charles Kittelson was elected treasurer in 1879; A. E. Rice, lieutenant-governor in 1886; Adolph Biermann, auditor in 1890; and Knute Nelson and John Lind, governors in 1892 and 1898, respectively. Knute Nelson was re-elected in 1894, but resigned the following year when he was elected to the United States senate.

It will thus be seen that the Scandinavians have held nearly all the important state offices, and generally filled them with credit. But it will also be observed that the

positions they have been elected to have not required any
special training or high scholastic educational qualifications; natural abilities and experience could fill the bill.
While, for example, the offices of attorney-general, superintendent of public instruction, and chief and associate
justices of the supreme court, which require the highest
college and professional training, have never been held by
any Northmen. They have men in the state who could fill
these places, yet so far they have failed to do so. Knute
Nelson, who was elected in 1882, has the honor of being the
first Scandinavian who sat in the United States Congress,
and John Lind, who was elected in 1886, is the first and
only Swede who has ever been elected to that body.
Both these men have represented their constituencies well,
and have been an honor to the race from which they sprung.
Since, Kittel Halvorson and H. E. Boen, both Norwegians,
have also been elected to Congress.

Most of the Scandinavians in Minnesota, as well as in
other states, have been and are Republicans, yet no party
has a mortgage on them, for some of their best educated
men belong to the Democratic, People's, or Prohibition
parties.

It is not our purpose in this article, nor in this volume
for that matter, to advocate any theory of Scandinavism,
yet it is an historical fact that the Danes, Norwegians, and
Swedes in this state have always been on very intimate
terms with each other. In some states the three nationalities live at sword's point. In Minnesota, on the contrary,
they join hands in nearly all great social, financial, political,
and religious undertakings. Many social affairs on a large

scale are neither Swedish, Norwegian, nor Danish, but
Scandinavian. At the Republican national convention in
Minneapolis, in 1892, all the Northmen of all political parties organized a Scandinavian club in order to entertain
their visiting countrymen. It is true that petty strifes and
jealousies sometimes occur between them, but, on the whole,
the Danes, Norwegians, and Swedes in Minnesota consider
themselves to be closely related and to have common interests. A forcible illustration of this was had in 1896,
when John Lind ran for governor on the fusion ticket. He
received by far more Norwegian votes than Swedish, even
in Norwegian Republican counties, as compared with Swedish Republican counties. Many Norwegian Republicans,
no doubt, voted for Lind partly because they admired the
man, and partly because they desired to return a favor to
the Swedes, who had always stood by the Norwegian
Republican candidates.

V. OCCUPATION.

Of course, most of Minnesota's Scandinavians have been
and are common laborers, servants, and farmers. Yet
today there is not a single learned profession in which they
cannot be found, and in some they have distinguished themselves and become famous both in this country and abroad.
Some of the Northmen in the state do business amounting
to millions of dollars annually, and pay out thousands of
dollars every year in taxes. There are Scandinavian business men in nearly every fair-sized city and village in the
state, and hundreds of lawyers and physicians of Scandinavian extraction, especially Norwegian, practice their pro-

fessions in Minnesota. Literarily the Northmen in Minnesota are well supplied. About thirty Scandinavian weekly newspapers, a few monthly publications, and several books are published in the state. Some of the Scandinavian editors and writers in the state are famous in the literary world, both in this country and in Europe. Over one-fourth of all the Scandinavian-American newspapers and periodicals are published in Minnesota. Here the Northmen have had intellectual advantages and connections with their native lands which their countrymen in many other parts of the Union have never enjoyed. They have had the pleasure to hear and come in contact with some of the greatest and noblest men and women that the North has ever produced. For example, Fredrika Bremer, Ole Bull, Björnstjerne Björnson, Kristina Nilsson, P. Waldenström, and Bishop K. von Scheele visited the state in 1850, 1877, 1880, 1884, 1889, and 1893, respectively.

VI. Statistics.

According to the census of 1850, there were twelve Scandinavians in Minnesota. That is, one out of every fifty persons was born in the North. In 1860 one out of every seventeen persons in the state was born in the Scandinavian countries; in 1870 and 1880 one out of seven; and in 1890 one out of six. But taking into consideration those who have Scandinavian parents, two-fifths of the entire population of the state are Northmen. Today (1900) there are in Minnesota about 620,000 Scandinavian-born or having Scandinavian parents. No state in the Union has such a great number or large proportion; in fact, nearly one-fourth of all the Northmen in the United States reside in Minnesota, which has seven Scandinavians to each square mile, while Norway has only thirteen persons to the square mile. There are more Northmen who reside in Minneapolis than in any other city in the world, save Copenhagen, Stockholm, Kristiania, Gothenburg, and Chicago. Taking into consideration only the first and second generations, there are about 40,000 Danes, 300,000 Norwegians, and 280,000 Swedes in the state. In most cases a fair estimate of the Scandinavian-American population of the first and second generations may be obtained by multiplying the number of Scandinavian-born by 2½. In Minnesota, however, this is not exactly true in regard to the Swedes and Norwegians. According to the United States census of 1890, each of these nationalities in the state numbered about 100,000 persons born in the old country, but counting also those who had Norwegian parents, the number was 195,764, against 155,-089 Swedish-born or having Swedish parents. Considering the omission which all census reports are guilty of, and the increase of population since 1890, it is undoubtedly a conservative estimate to add about 100,000 to each of the two nationalities. The greater number of persons born in this country of Norwegian parents, in comparison with the same class among the Swedes, is due mostly to the earlier immigration of the former people; and this fact is one of the main causes why the Norwegians in the Northwest have been able to exercise a greater influence than the Swedes in the public affairs. A large proportion, probably a majority, of the leading public and professional men among the Norwegians in this state and elsewhere were born in this

country of Norwegian parents who were able to give their
sons a good start in life. The second generation of the
Swedes in the state are just beginning to come to the front.
Ten years ago they were virtually an unknown quantity as
far as political and professional activity is concerned.
According to the state census of 1895, there were 16,143
Danish-born persons residing in Minnesota; 107,319 Nor-
wegian-born; and 119,554 Swedish-born. No statistics or
even estimates can be given in regard to Scandinavians of
the third generation which, especially among the Norwegians, is quite numerous. A fourth generation of Scandinavian-Americans cannot be said to exist yet. According
to the state census of 1895, there resided in Minnesota
7,652 Finns and 457 Icelanders. Most of the former nationality have settled in the northern part of the state, especially in St. Louis county, where nearly half of the total
number lived. Of course, a large proportion of these Finns
are virtually Swedes. Nearly all the Icelanders in Minnesota seem to reside in Lyon and Lincoln counties. But as
an illustration of the defectiveness of statistics, it may be
mentioned that although about fifty or sixty Icelanders live
in Minneapolis, no one is put down for that place in the
state census of 1895.

TABLE XII.

SHOWING THE NUMBER OF SCANDINAVIANS BORN IN THE SCANDINAVIAN
COUNTRIES, AND THE TOTAL POPULATION IN EACH COUNTY OF MIN-
NESOTA.

COUNTIES.	U. S. CENSUS OF 1860.	STATE CENSUS OF 1875.				STATE CENSUS OF 1895.			
	TOTAL POPULATION.	DENMARK.	NORWAY.	SWEDEN.	TOTAL POPULATION.	DENMARK.	NORWAY.	SWEDEN.	TOTAL POPULATION.
Aitkin..............	2	1	1	11	205	13	257	953	5.224
Anoka.............	2,106	4	123	304	5,709	99	315	1,215	11,181
Becker....	386	14	570	195	2,256	85	1,616	883	13,725
Beltrami...........						8	225	36	1,364
Benton....	627	.....	22	23	1,974	14	127	380	7,793
Big Stone........			76	43	3(5	99	607	657	7,477
Blue Earth........	4,803	108	798	452	20,942	253	969	951	32,295
Brown	2,339	319	629	114	9,815	392	781	187	18,431
Carlton............	51	6	22	114	495	41	295	1,146	7,458
Carver.............	5,106	11	72	1,312	13,033	10	53	1,127	17,567
Cass...............	150	5	.....	.....	239	21	133	283	3,425
Chippewa......		16	1,140	193	2,977	70	2,054	696	10,805
Chisago	1,743	40	25	2,369	6,046	48	90	4,780	13,118
Clay...............		9	367	53	1,451	83	3,186	1,341	15,154
Cook...............					215	....	103	52	427
Cottonwood......	12	29	420	61	2,870	242	931	253	10,187
Crow Wing........	269	9	28	48	1,031	157	511	850	11,561
Dakota............	9,093	20	530	365	17,360	211	398	787	21,345
Dodge.............	3,797	151	1,168	32	10,045	267	1,065	81	12,753
Douglas......	195	104	942	960	6,319	258	1,434	2,824	16,942
Faribault..	1,335	39	1,018	29	11,131	209	1,191	228	20,139
Fillmore..\........	13,542	66	6,753	67	28,337	60	4,098	57	28,599
Freeborn..........	3,367	801	3,004	81	13,189	1,945	2,647	365	21,138
Goodhue..........	8,977	84	5,192	3,856	28,500	116	3,513	3,731	32,268
Grant..............		7	474	124	1,191	46	1,754	922	7,987
Hennepin	12,849	153	2,263	2,676	48,725	1,917	12,762	22,480	217,798
Houston...........	6,645	29	2,922	257	16,566	7	1,779	238	15,556
Hubbard...........						5	26	55	2,447
Isanti	284	9	14	2,006	3,901	12	52	4,346	10,195
Itasca.............	51	.....	.....	.....		10	72	210	3,965
Jackson...........	181	21	900	47	3,506	250	1,194	257	12,324
Kanabec...........	30	.....	.....		311	3	35	1,423	2,714
Kandiyohi.........	76	126	1,910	1,719	8,083	328	2,452	3,009	16,322
Kittson............			.....	.....		36	571	1,851	6,289
Lac qui Parle.....		.....	579	6	1,428	71	2,873	482	12,687
Lake......	248	.....	3	.....	161	19	143	581	2,211
Le Sueur..........	5,318	8	31	79	13,237	8	60	336	20,915
Lincoln............		4	95	11	412	820	590	205	7,196
Lyon..............		9	394	7	2,543	196	1,065	478	12,425
McLeod.......	1,286	117	246	93	8,651	610	155	182	19,134
Marshall....... ...		.....	.....	.....		73	1,907	2,596	12,072
Martin.............	151	14	120	74	3,738	148	243	822	13,981
Meeker..	928	96	551	1,454	8 626	268	664	3,311	17,389
Mille Lacs........	73	6	64	5	1,300	27	119	877	5,129

TABLE XII.—Continued.

COUNTIES.	U. S. CENSUS OF 1860. Total Population.	STATE CENSUS OF 1875. Denmark.	Norway.	Sweden.	Total Population.	STATE CENSUS OF 1895. Denmark.	Norway.	Sweden.	Total Population.
Morrison	618	87	16	14	2,722	172	376	1,457	19,163
Mower	3,217	118	2,209	88	13,682	370	1,874	237	21,546
Murray	29	....	229	112	1,329	78	852	654	9,322
Nicollet	3,773	14	1,038	1,377	11,525	61	491	1,540	14,299
Nobles	35	2	162	131	2,750	61	372	781	11,905
Norman	....	....	....	....	....	18	4.388	317	13,470
Olmsted	9,524	136	1,064	49	20,946	302	743	86	22,316
Otter Tail	240	124	2,619	618	9,174	321	5,740	2,763	39,453
Pine	92	1	7	102	795	44	228	1,951	8,631
Pipestone	....	....	....	....	....	116	322	123	7,115
Polk	240	4	369	27	937	257	8,048	2,625	39,209
Pope	....	1	1,388	321	4,078	64	2,618	721	11,607
Ramsey	12,150	159	565	1,437	36,333	1,412	3,087	10,665	147,537
Redwood	....	110	186	78	2,982	509	568	377	13,533
Renville	245	18	1,594	431	6,876	158	1,820	1,?47	21,818
Rice	7,543	40	1,366	85	20,622	182	1,399	315	26,837
Rock	....	19	389	10	1,861	65	1,137	79	8,597
Roseau	....	....	....	....	....	1	861	676	3,493
St. Louis	406	62	223	310	3,517	372	4,199	9,013	78,575
Scott	4,595	3	227	212	12,394	37	243	124	15,035
Sherburne	723	53	124	187	3,018	183	392	720	7,137
Sibley	3,609	2	166	494	8,884	37	135	1,131	16,436
Stearns	4,505	66	367	110	17,797	154	755	559	39,925
Steele	2,863	312	660	33	10,739	755	542	45	15,798
Stevens	....	2	208	54	786	35	800	411	6,543
Swift	....	12	807	202	2,269	56	1,847	840	11,846
Todd	430	3	263	83	3,818	48	981	923	17,674
Traverse	....	....	28	....	100	26	185	983	6,064
Wabasha	7,228	6	240	509	17,296	11	129	534	18,587
Wadena	....	....	15	....	210	13	221	213	6,076
Waseca	2,601	16	680	219	9,994	43	634	309	14,713
Washington	6,123	77	159	1,607	14,751	296	461	3,230	27,417
Watonwan	....	30	721	381	4,024	57	1,168	856	10,262
Wilkin	40	11	126	33	528	32	851	221	6,200
Winona	9,208	114	870	183	27,385	116	514	173	37,134
Wright	3,729	14	171	1,564	13,775	40	346	3,016	27,653
Yellow Medicine	....	1	1,033	58	2,484	43	2,394	503	12,581
Total	172,023	4,052	53,766	30,507	597,407	16,143	107,319	119,554	1,574,619

Historical Review of the Scandinavian Schools in Minnesota.

—BY—

J. J. SKORDALSVOLD.

The state of Minnesota is not lacking in higher institutions of learning. On the contrary, time and again academies and colleges have been equipped for efficient work long before students could be secured in sufficient numbers to form good-sized classes. And pupils of Scandinavian stock are welcome at all kinds of schools. Yet the Scandinavians of the state have made and are still making strenuous efforts to build up and equip schools of their own, which must necessarily compete with other private and public institutions of the same kind.

The earliest Scandinavian schools were started by Lutheran church people for the purpose of educating ministers, and teachers for parochial schools; and three-fourths of those which have survived the ordeal of competition are still controlled by men who support this work for the sake of keeping their countrymen within the fold of the church of their forefathers, and of making them, if possible, better and nobler American citizens than it is supposed they would have been if those particular educational advantages had not been offered to them. The great bulk of the work performed at this class of schools is of a decidedly secular nature. But in many cases the secular branches are taught mainly in order to secure attendance in our age of commercialism. In the course of the last few years some business colleges have been started by young Scandinavians as business enterprises pure and simple. These have had even greater odds than the former to contend against, and some of them have expired after a short and troublous career.

No less than a score of educational institutions in Minnesota are owned and controlled by Scandinavians. About one-half of the whole number devote more or less time to Hebrew or the classical languages, and a majority of them offer business courses. Over two thousand young persons have graduated from these institutions during the last quarter of the nineteenth century, and nearly one-third of them completed a theological course in Lutheran seminaries. Today (1900) about 160 professors and teachers are engaged in teaching over 3,000 students who attend Scandinavian schools in the state. These institutions represent a value of about half a million dollars.

A large majority of the students were born in America, but over ninety per cent of them are of Scandinavian extraction. The Scandinavian languages are losing ground from year to year in these schools, and in most of them English is used almost exclusively in daily intercourse. It is worthy of note that very many young Americans of Scandinavian stock will rather attend schools managed by Scandinavians than other schools even when the latter are better equipped:

they feel more at home among their own kinsmen. As a rule, those who attend schools managed by Scandinavian church people learn to take life seriously, and in after life they are found to be the strong men and women of their communities. The more ambitious ones continue their studies in the state university or some university in the East, and a few of them will round off their education in Europe.

None can be more fond of American liberty than are the Scandinavians, none can be more ardently devoted to the essentials of American civilization. And yet it must be admitted that their leading minds do not take kindly to the idea of being unconditionaliy swallowed up and losing their identity in the new nation, to the up-building of which they contribute such a great share. They believe they furnish good timber for this nation; they also believe they ought to have something to say about the construction of it. This sentiment has found its loftiest expression in their schools.

The clergy, especially that of the Norwegian Synod and the Augustana Synod, have worked hard and persistently for regular parochial schools, and the result is that such schools are taught at least two months a year in most of the congregations. They are generally located in public school houses or church buildings, and are taught when the public schools are closed. Quite a number of congregations have built parochial school houses, especially in the southern part of the state, and in certain parts of Goodhue county, for instance, they are about as numerous as the public school houses.

A few words must also be said about the relation of the

Scandinavians to other schools in the state. One of the first concerns of a Scandinavian after he has settled on a piece of land is to provide some sort of schooling for his children; and no matter how seriously he may take religious affairs, an English common school education is apt to find great favor with him. He wants a cheap teacher, however, and he is generally in favor of as short terms as possible. About one-half of the pupils of the public schools of Minneapolis are of Scandinavian blood.

SWEDISH. Gustavus Adolphus College, in St. Peter, practically dates from 1862. In that year Rev. E. Norelius started a school in Red Wing, but the next year it was removed to East Union, Carver county, and named St. Ansgar's Academy. In 1874 twenty-three prominent members of the Minnesota Conference formed a corporation for the purpose of establishing and maintaining "an institution of learning and instruction in the arts and sciences," and in the course of the next two years a suitable building was put up in St. Peter. In 1876 the academy mentioned above was removed into the new building. From that time the school has been known as Gustavus Adolphus College, and it is supported and controlled by the Minnesota Conference of the Swedish Lutheran Augustana Synod. The growth of it has been steady and vigorous, and for years past it has ranked with the best colleges of the Northwest. It comprises college, academic, commercial, musical and normal departments. The main object of the school is to give young people "a thorough liberal education, based upon and permeated by the principles of Christianity as confessed by the Lutheran Church," and some aspect of the Bible or of the history of the church receives marked attention in every class. "A musical atmosphere pervades the entire institution," says the catalogue, and great efforts have been put forth to make the conservatory of music correspond to the fastidious demands of a musical race. The library contains 9,000 volumes; the specimens in the museum number several thousand; and the laboratory is well supplied with chemical, physical, mathematical and astronomical apparatuses. The Minnesota Conference has always treated this college generously, and the faculty has been a strong one. And yet the high standing of the institution is very largely due to the eminent fitness of Prof. M. Wahlstrom as president, which position he has held since 1881. There are sixteen professors and instructors, several of whom hold doctors' degrees from the leading universities of Sweden and this country. About 220 students have graduated from the college, and the Augustana Theological Seminary at Rock Island, Ill., draws some of its best material from this source. The attendance is about 300, more than one-fourth of whom are ladies. The campus, which is twenty-five acres in extent, commands a fine view of the surrounding country. There are six college buildings, the largest one of which is a massive structure of Kasota stone. The current expenses amount to about $18,000 a year, and the value of the college property is $75,000.

The Northwestern Collegiate and Business Institute, in Minneapolis, was established by Rev. E. A. Skogsbergh, in 1885, and he has been closely connected with the school since that time. At present it is owned and operated by a corporation, the most of whose members are co-operating

22

with the Swedish Mission Covenant. For years past the annual enrolment has been about 150. There are from eight to ten instructors, and the school offers four courses of study.

Crookston College, in the city after which it is named, was established in 1896, without capital, and it is owned by private parties. Its catalogue offers about ten courses of study, and the work is carried on by as many instructors. In later years the attendance has been not far from 300. The college property is worth at least $7,500.

Hope Academy was founded at Moorhead in 1888 by the Red River Valley District of the Minnesota Conference of the Swedish Augustana Synod, and was discontinued in 1896. The faculty consisted of five members, and the school offered the same number of departments. The enrolment for the last year of its existence was 84.

Emanuel Academy was founded in Minneapolis in 1888 by members of the Augustana Synod, and was discontinued in 1892. Five instructors were employed in the course of the last year of its existence, and the enrolment for that year was 91.

NORWEGIAN. Augsburg Seminary, in Minneapolis, has passed through many vicissitudes. The Norwegian members of the Scandinavian Augustana Synod decided to establish a theological seminary of their own in 1869, and this was located at Marshall, Wis. It was named Augsburg Seminary, though, in the words of its first president, "many may have desired a name of a more Northern origin." A building originally erected for school purposes was bought for $4,000, and the work was begun under favorable auspices. But a part of those Norwegians who were in the

deal organized themselves into a new association, the Norwegian-Danish Evangelical Lutheran Conference, in 1870,
and the professors and students left the building almost to
a man and continued their work in connection with the new
association. The class was crowded into Cooper's Hall, the
dimensions of which were 18x10 feet and eight feet to the
ceiling. In the winter of 1870–71 there were two professors
and about a score of students, and they were all contending
against grim poverty and other odds of an equally serious
nature. In 1872 the school was removed to its present
location, Rev. O. Paulson having been instrumental in
securing grounds and erecting a suitable building. Indeed,
his efforts in this respect have justified his friends in calling
him "the father of Augsburg." Prof. A. Weenaas was the
president of the seminary from the start to the spring of
1876. He was an able man, and his main strength lay in
his ability to arouse fanatical enthusiasm in his associates—
he was a typical Norwegian-American chieftain in religious
warfare. The removal to Minneapolis marks an era of
expansion, not only of Augsburg Seminary, but of the Conference as well. Since 1873 Prof. Sven Oftedal has occupied
a chair of theology, and Prof. G. Sverdrup has served as
president since 1876. For a quarter of a century these two
men have made Augsburg Seminary the great storm centre
of the Norwegian Lutheran church in America, and their
work is of such character that it may yet take decades
before the historian can put it in its true light. It may be
said even at this stage, however, that they aim at the
greatest possible simplification of religious doctrines; congregational independence; and a vigorous religious life in

the individual. During the seventies the seminary was loaded down with debt, but Prof. Oftedal succeeded in raising $18,000 for the liquidation of it. During the years 1890–93 the seminary was operated under the auspices of the United Church, and it was officially regarded as the theological seminary of said association. But as the board of trustees failed to transfer the property to the United Church, the latter "removed" its seminary from the Augsburg buildings into rented quarters in the summer of 1893. Those who remained at Augsburg, and their friends, on the contrary, have always maintained that at this critical moment the United Church simply withdrew from Augsburg and started a "new" seminary of its own. In the course of time the Augsburg faction was organized into the Free Church, and the controversy between this body and the United Church about the ownership of the Augsburg Seminary property aroused great bitterness, and many harsh words were used. The matter was fought in the courts from 1,896 to 1898, which involved a combined expenditure of about $17,000. In the summer of 1898 the case was settled by mutual agreement to the effect that the Augsburg Seminary corporation should keep the property, while an endowment fund amounting to about $39,000 was to be turned over to the United Church. Legally, the seminary is owned and controlled by a corporation. There are eight professors, and the seminary offers three departments, namely, a preparatory, a classical and a theological. About 260 students have been graduated from the theological, and 120 from the classical department. The annual enrolment is about 200. The present value of the property is $60,000.

Red Wing Seminary is the college and theological seminary of Hauge's Evangelical Lutheran Synod. This institution was located in Red Wing and at its present quarters largely through the prompt and timely action of a single man, H. M. Sande. From the middle of the fifties to the latter part of the seventies, several attempts to establish a permanent seminary were made in said synod, but without success. In the fall of 1877 Sande was advised that the building now used by Red Wing Seminary could be bought for $10,000, though it had cost about $20,000. He and a few of the leading men of the synod felt confident that the synod would buy the property, and in order to prevent it from passing into other hands before the synod was able to take the necessary formal steps to make a purchase, he bought the property at his own risk Jan. 8, 1878. As soon as possible the synod endorsed his action, and March 1, 1878, the property was deeded to the synod. The seminary was publicly opened Sept. 17, 1879, with Rev. I. Eisteinsen as president. Prof. G. O. Brohough has been teaching in the school since its opening, excepting the years 1893–95. No president has been retained for any great length of time, and seven different men have served in that capacity since the seminary was opened. There are two departments, a theological and a preparatory; and the former is in charge of three professors, the latter of four. The work has been hampered by frequent changes in the faculty; but the school has turned out a large number of able and fearless men who generally are a power for good in their spheres of action. Over one hundred young men have graduated from the preparatory, and about eighty from the theological department. Over seventy of the latter have entered the ministry of the Gospel. Graduates from the preparatory department may enter the State University without examination. The total annual enrolment is from 140 to 150. Some money has been raised for a new dormitory, which will be named after H. M. Sande. The value of the property is $20,000.

St. Olaf College, at Northfield, was originally called St. Olaf's School. Rev. B. J. Muus may justly be called the father of this institution, for he was the soul and backbone of the movement which resulted in its establishment. A number of prominent members of the Norwegian Synod held a meeting in Northfield Nov. 6, 1874, and adopted articles of incorporation for the school, and this was finally opened Jan. 8, 1875, in a frame building formerly used as a public school house. The school was removed into quarters of its own in the fall of 1878. To begin with, it was only an academy; but in 1886 a college department was added. The languages predominate in the collegiate department, and even Hebrew is taught in the classical courses. The college was originally owned and controlled by a corporation, most of whose members joined the United Church in 1890, and in 1899 the ownership and control of the institution were formally transferred to the United Church, the articles of incorporation being amended so as to substitute this body for the old corporation. Prof. Th. N. Mohn served as president from 1875 to 1899, and at the latter date Rev. J. N. Kildahl was elected to succeed him. The faculty is composed of a dozen members. For a number of years Prof. H. T. Ytterboe devoted his whole time to his duties as financial secretary, and his success in collecting voluntary contributions to the college was very great. About 55 persons have graduated from the collegiate, 220 from the academic department. The attendance was steadily decreasing for years, the enrolment for 1891–92 being 184; that of 1897–98, 113. The property of the college is valued at $40,000.

Luther Seminary, the theological seminary of the Norwegian Evangelical Lutheran Synod, was established in 1876, at Madison, Wis., where it remained until 1888. During this period Prof. F. A. Schmidt and Prof. H. G. Stub successively served as president of the institution. The work carried on here during the eighties was marred by doctrinal controversies, in which Prof. Schmidt was the central figure, and in 1886 only seven students were in attendance. Nevertheless, over fifty young men were graduated from the seminary while it was located at Madison. In 1888 the seminary was removed to Minneapolis, where the school building of Our Savior's Church served as temporary quarters during the winter of 1888–89. In the fall of the latter year it was removed to Robbinsdale, where it was located in a magnificent building erected for the purpose at a cost of $30,000. This building was destroyed by fire Jan. 11, 1895, and for the next four years the work of the seminary was carried on in a frame building in Robbinsdale, which formerly had been used as a hotel. With admirable determination the synod secured new grounds at Hamline, St. Paul, on which a building was put up at a cost of $60,000, and the seminary has been located there since the fall of 1899. The seminary offered only a practical course during the years 1876–78, but a theoretical course

was added at the latter date. At first only two professors
were employed, but for a number of years past the faculty
has consisted of four professors. Prof. J. B. Frich has
served as president since 1888. This seminary in one respect
holds a unique position, being the only Scandinavian-American institution of learning which educates ministers, but
which has no other department connected with it as a
feeder to the theological department. The main reason
given for this isolation is, that it is not desirable that
young men should be kept constantly under the influence of
the same mind or minds from the time they enter college until they enter the ministry—it would stunt their
mental development and make them caricatures of some
favorite teacher or teachers. The whole number of graduates up to date is about 225, and the attendanec is about
45. The value of the seminary property is at least $80,000.

The United Church Seminary, Minneapolis. In 1886 the
Anti-Missourians established a theological class in connection with St. Olaf College, at Northfield, Minn.; but when
the Anti-Missourians, in 1890, joined two other associations in organizing the United Church, the professors, M. O.
Böckman and F. A. Schmidt, removed from Northfield to
Augsburg Seminary, Minneapolis, which institution was to
be the theological seminary of the United Church. But
as the old board of trustees of Augsburg Seminary failed
to transfer the property, the United Church "removed" its
seminary and located it in rented quarters at the corner of
Franklin and Twenty-sixth avenues south, Minneapolis.
This occurred in 1893, and since that year the institution
has been known by its present name. Prof. M. O. Böckman

has served as president since 1893. There are nine professors and instructors, and the annual enrolment is about 200. The number of graduates* is about 150 from the theological, and 40 from the classical department. In 1899 the United Church resolved to discontinue the college department in the spring of 1900, leaving the school a theological seminary pure and simple. At the same time it was also resolved to secure permanent grounds and to erect buildings for the seminary in or near the Twin Cities.

The United Norwegian Lutheran Church, at the time of its organization in Minneapolis, in 1890, resolved to establish a teachers' seminary. Accordingly, the Normal School of said church association was built at Madison, Minn. The dedication of the first building took place Nov. 10, 1892, and ever since that date the work at the school has been carried on with great regularity. The school is managed by a board of regents and a board of trustees elected by the annual meetings of the United Church. As indicated by the name, "the aim of the school is to qualify young men and women for teachers in our public schools and in the Norwegian parochial schools." Only two courses, a preparatory and a normal, are offered, and English and Norwegian are the only languages meddled with. On the whole, the program of this school is comparatively modest, and perhaps for that very reason its attendance has been growing rather slowly. But the work is done thoroughly and enthusiastically, and as a power for good this institution stands high. For years the work has been performed

---

* For the years 1891-93 the graduates of the United Church Seminary, as given by its catalogue, are the same as those given by the catalogue of Augsburg Seminary.

by five instructors, under the able and popular leadership of Prof. O. Lokensgaard, and the annual enrolment is about 120. The value of the main building is $26,000, and a dormitory has just been erected at a cost of $10,000.

The Willmar Seminary, at Willmar, has been in operation since the fall of 1883. It was established through the efforts of members of the Norwegian Synod, and it is owned by a corporation which was organized in 1882 and reorganized in 1890. The school offers five courses; but these actually embrace more than some schools parading twice that number of courses in their catalogues. There are eight professors and instructors. H. S. Hilleboe, who for a long series of years held the position of president, deserves special mention because he was the chief instrument in building up the school. In the early nineties the attendance reached almost 400; but hard times and competition reduced it very materially. The annual enrolment now averages about 225, and it is on the increase. The whole number of graduates is about 160. The cost of the establishment is $20,000, and it now affords class-room accommodation for 500 students.

The Lutheran Ladies' Seminary, at Red Wing, is the only Norwegian school of its kind in America. From the start it has been owned and operated by a corporation whose members belong to the Norwegian Synod. A dozen persons are connected with the school as instructors, and it offers seven courses of study, four of which cover five years each. The number of branches taught is great, ranging from cooking and dressmaking to German, French and Latin. The corporation has made strenuous efforts to render the school a first-class institution of learning, and its career since it was established, in 1894, has been encouraging. The discipline is very strict. The attendance for the first year in the history of the seminary was 57, but in the course of time this number has more than doubled. The seminary building is a noble structure, and large enough to accommodate 150 students. "The seminary grounds are unsurpassed," and occupy eighteen acres. The whole property is worth $80,000.

Luther Academy, at Albert Lea, was opened in the fall of 1888. It was established and is still owned and controlled by a corporation within the Norwegian Synod. "Luther Academy aims to build up character and manhood on Christian principles," and "religious instruction is given a prominent place among the branches taught." The school offers six branches of study, and the class work is conducted by an equal number of instructors. The whole number of graduates up to date is over one hundred, and the annual enrolment is from 150 to 200. The main building is a large, fine brick structure, and the value of the whole property is $25,000.

Concordia College, at Moorhead, has been in operation since 1891. It is owned and managed by a corporation within the United Church, and its chief aim is to educate teachers for public and parochial schools. It offers classical, normal, business, music and domestic industry courses, and the number of instructors is from six to twelve. The average annual enrolment is about 250, and the whole number of graduates up to date is nearly 100. The value of the property is $40,000.

The Park Region Luther College, in Fergus Falls, was opened in 1892. It was established by ministers and laymen of the Norwegian Synod and is controlled by a corporation. The school offers a commercial and an academic course, and the studies are especially adapted to the needs of those who intend to teach public and parochial schools. There are six professors and instructors; the whole number of graduates from the school is about 60; and the annual enrolment is almost 200.

Glenwood Academy, at Glenwood, has been in operation since 1894. It is owned and managed by a corporation composed wholly of members of the Norwegian Synod. The school offers only four courses of study, but each one is quite comprehensive, and the work is thorough. The annual enrolment is about 100. The property belonging to the school is worth $8,000.

The Minnesota Normal School and Business College is located in Minneapolis. It was established in 1896. In 1899 its proprietors bought the Minneapolis Normal College, which institution was opened at Crookston, Minn., in 1893, but was removed to Minneapolis in 1894. The consolidation of the two schools raised the attendance of the former to about 400. The catalogue offers almost a dozen different courses of study, and the faculty numbers almost a score of professors and instructors.

The Southern Minnesota Normal College, at Austin, was started at Kenyon, Minn., in 1895, and was removed to its present location in 1897. The enrolment for the year 1897-98 was 207, and since that time the attendance has materially increased. The corps of professors and instructors numbers ten, more than half of whom devote their whole time to the work in the school. There are about ten different courses of study; and the value of the property belonging to the institution is $7,000.

Wraaman's Academy has been in operation in South Minneapolis since 1890. Its enrolment never reached 100, and the present attendance is about 20.

Northwestern Free Church Mission School has been at Belgrade since 1897. Its aim is religious edification and instruction, and its attendance is about 50.

DANISH. The Danebod High School, at Tyler, is an adaptation, on American soil, of the unique Danish institutions known for the past fifty years as "the people's high schools." Accordingly, the students at Danebod may choose any study they please; there are no examinations; no degrees are conferred; only practical and character-building branches are taught; and the boys attend in winter, the girls in summer. The school dates from 1888, and is owned by a corporation; but the buildings are rented by A. Bobjerg, the principal. The enrolment is about 60. The property of the school is worth $5,000.

The above account includes all Scandinavian schools of any account in this state; but we have intentionally left out several defunct schools which we did not consider to be of such importance as to deserve mention in this work.

OTHER INSTITUTIONS. The attendance at the four state normal schools is about 3;000. Of this number, about 525, or 18 per cent, are evidently of Scandinavian parentage. It is estimated that 40 per cent of the population of the state are of Scandinavian stock; hence the Scandinavians do not furnish quite one-half of their natural share of the attendance at the Minnesota state normal schools. Only thirteen per cent of the university students are of Scandinavian extraction; but they constitute forty per cent of the attendance at the agricultural school connected with the university. The former percentage is surprisingly low. But this is not due to any interference from the Scandinavian schools. In fact, the latter seem to serve as feeders to the university. The main cause is the general disinclination of the rich Scandinavian farmers to keep their children in a purely secular school which requires the student to toil on for years and years before his education is finally finished, and which even at the best does not offer any highway to wealth or honor. This statement is indirectly substantiated by the fact that a very large proportion of this class of students have to fight their way single-handed through their university course. Prof. O. J. Breda for a number of years occupied the chair of Scandinavian languages and literatures at the State University, and his acknowledged scholarship made him one of the strongest men at that institution. In 1899 he removed to Norway, and J. S. Carlson, an able educator, succeeded him. The number of Scandinavian professors and instructors in the state institutions is strikingly small. At Carleton College, Northfield, a Scandinavian department has been in operation since 1885, and twenty per cent of the students at that college are of Scandinavian stock. Prof. D. Magnus is at the head of the Scandinavian department, and through his efforts many of his young countrymen and countrywomen have been induced to attend this college.

Historical Review of the Scandinavian Churches in Minnnesota.

—BY—

O. N. NELSON AND J. J. SKORDALSVOLD.

The Scandinavians have been powerful agents in promoting the intellectual and religious welfare of the people of the state of Minncsota. One of the first pioneers and Protestant missionaries among the Indians in Minnesota was a Swede, Jacob Falstrom, who came to the state before Fort Snelling was established, in 1819; and, although he did little or nothing in promoting civilization because he had degenerated into savagery himself, yet he was a noted character. He was the *first* Northman in the Northwest. Since that time some other Scandinavians have endeavored to Christianize the savage as well as the civilized natives of the North Star State. But the main effort of the majority of the religiously inclined Northmen has been directed towards maintaining and promoting the religious principles among their own people. In this respect they have been so successful that in 1900 there were in the neighborhood of 1,600 Scandinavian congregations in the state, with an aggregate membership, including the children, of nearly two

hundred and fifty thousand. That is, over one-third of the
Minnesota Scandinavians belong to some leading religious
association. But several thousand Northmen are members
of purely American churches, and some even associate themselves religiously with other nationalities, for example, with
the German Lutherans, and a very few have joined the
Irish Catholics. This class of people together with those
who do not belong to any church, but yet attend regularly
a certain place of worship, would probably increase the
number of church-going Scandinavians in the state to
about half a million, or over two-thirds of their total number. There are about 1,100 church edifices; and the value
of these buildings, parsonages, schools, and other institutions owned and controlled by the Northmen in the state in
the interest of religion, education, and benevolence seems to
be nearly $4,000,000.

The great bulk of the religious work has been and is
done by the Lutherans. Out of the 250,000 Northmen in
the state who are church members, about 215,000 belong
to the Lutheran associations. They control all the important Scandinavian schools, and own six hospitals and
four orphans' homes. Many attempts have been made by the
different American denominations to do missionary work
among the Scandinavians in the state. More money has
been expended and more brain-work wasted for this purpose
in Minnesota, especially in the Twin Cities, than in any
other state in the Union. American Baptists, Methodists,
Episcopalians, Congregationalists, Adventists, Presbyterians, Unitarians, and others have endeavored to convert the
Scandinavians to their respective creeds. Some of them have

succeeded fairly well, but hardly, it seems, in proportion to the expenditure. The Methodist Missionary Society, for example, has paid out about $50,000 annually for a number of years to the Scandinavian Methodists in the United States. Of course, Minnesota has received a large share of these appropriations. Besides, wealthy Methodists have assisted poor churches in their neighborhoods; yet, in spite of all this, there were only about 3,000 Scandinavian Methodists in the state in 1900. Other denominations have also been very generous; but, with the probable exception of the Baptists, have not been any more successful. A Scandinavian Unitarian church in Minneapolis has received over $25,000 from the Americans during the last sixteen years, and for several years past each member of this church has cost the Americans over $15.00 a year. A Scandinavian Presbyterian church cost the American Presbyterians about $1,000 a year for half a dozen years, or nearly $100 annually for each communicant. In pursuing missionary work among a people who all have received at least the rudiments of a Christian training, proselyting can hardly be avoided even by conscientious men, and some of the so-called missionaries have been merely unscrupulous adventurers. The noblest religious zeal and the basest methods of proselyting have been practiced in order to regenerate the Scandinavians in this state, or to change their religious belief. But in spite of the fact that neither money, devotion, nor moral scruples have been spared, yet the result has not been very great. The main causes of this meagerness in results are the conservatism of the Scandinavians and their devotion to the Lutheran faith. Many Northmen, both

23

church members and outsiders, also feel it as a humiliation that they should be treated as fit subjects for missionary work the same as are the savages of Africa. Nor should it be overlooked in this connection that the Scandinavians are very fond of self-government in religious as well as in political matters. And when the zealous devotees or paid emissaries have tried to convert to their views Lutheran church members of good standing, the Lutherans have sometimes publicly denounced such practice. They have maintained that as independent and self-sustaining church organizations, they were entitled to the considerations and courtecies which are supposed to be practiced among the different denominations. As good American citizens and orderly Christians, the Scandinavian-American Lutherans have opposed to the bitter end all attempts to make their countrymen the tail end of any sect; and they have always believed, justly or unjustly, that they could take care of their religious instruction and promote their Americanization in as satisfactory manner as anyone else, if not a little better. With the Americans, and to a certain extent among the Scandinavians, religious selfishness and national bigotry have apparently played a part in all this activity. Yet it is to be hoped that Christian zeal has in the main prompted the contending parties to such energetic exertions, and as the Northmen stand as victors in the field, little complaint is nowadays heard from them. The other parties have paid out large sums of money, and some continue to do so yet, and all have received valuable lessons of experience.

The typical Norwegian of the nineteenth century is restless and impatient. On his native soil he has given vent to this restlessness and impatience through his national politics; in America, partly through his church work. Indeed, no set of emigrants of the nineteenth century have carried on such extensive and persistent church controversies among themselves as have the Norwegians and their descendants from the time of the exodus of the Sloop folks down to our day. Singularly enough, however, the contentions of the church members, instead of scaring away outsiders, have actually attracted them. Accordingly, though the Norwegians, as a nationality, are not naturally more religious than other Indo-Europeans, those of them who have landed upon our shore during the past sixty years enjoy the unique distinction of having joined some church in larger numbers, proportionately, than any other immigrants of the same period. The Norwegian Lutherans in the state for thirty-five years past have been engaged in mutual controversies of different kinds. Many of them—in fact the most of them—have at one time or another deplored this internecine warfare and protested that it would destroy the church. But on the whole it has actually stimulated the church work, and close observation has convinced us that if there had been peace instead of war, the Norwegian Lutherans in the state would have numbered several thousand less than they do now. It may not seem pious to say so, but many a worldly-minded Viking has become so interested in the fight that he has joined the faction with which he sympathized in order to assist in beating the opposing faction. Thus, what might be supposed to keep the Norwegians out of the church has actually drawn them into it.

THE UNITED NORWEGIAN LUTHERAN CHURCH.   The
Minnesota contingent of the United Church came from three
sources.   The Anti-Missourian Brotherhood deserves to be
treated first because its former adherents now constitute
the mainstay of the United Church in this state.   Up to the
middle of the eighties the Brotherhood was an integral part
of the Norwegian Synod.   The people that formed the
Brotherhood deprived the synod of some of its largest
and most prosperous congregations in Minnesota, notably
those in Goodhue county, which locality for twenty years
had been the great stronghold of the synod in the state.
About 80 Minnesota congregations belonging to the
Brotherhood became a part of the United Church in 1890.
The whole number of souls belonging to these congregations and some fifteen others served by nearly forty Brotherhood ministers who joined the United Church was about
28,000.   The corporation controlling St. Olaf College at
Northfield, consisted mainly of adherents of the Brotherhood, and the latter operated a theological class in connection with the college from 1886 to 1890.   At the organization of the United Church this class and its two professors
were transferred to Augsburg Seminary, which was then to
be regarded as the theological seminary of the United
Church.   Nearly all of the Brotherhood congregations have
remained true to the United Church during a decade of
trials and tribulations.

The Norwegian-Danish Lutheran Conference was the
most vigorous and energetic of the three organizations that
formed the United Church.   The leading pioneers of the
Conference in Minnesota were the Revs. O. Paulson and

T. H. Dahl, who obtained footholds in Minneapolis and elsewhere at the close of the sixties. The career of the Conference during the years of 1870-90 was an unbroken series of victories, and though the internal strifes at times were quite bitter, the losing faction, represented by certain congregations in the southern part of this state and in Iowa, never withdrew from the association. From Minnesota the Conference contributed about forty ministers and 170 congregations to the United Church. One hundred and forty of these congregations actually joined the association, and the aggregate number of souls belonging to all of them was about 27,500. It will thus be seen that the Conference and the Brotherhood furnished an equal number of ministers and practically an equal number of souls to the United Church from this state; but the former had almost twice as many congregations as the latter.

The Augustana Synod was by far the smallest of the three associations that were merged into the United Church. The oldest congregation of the Augustana Synod in Minnesota was organized by Rev. P. Asbjörnsen, June 8, 1857, at Newburg, and this was one of the oldest Norwegian Lutheran churches in the state. The growth of this synod was checked by the organization of the Conference within its ranks, and it required great courage to keep up the organization in the face of its powerful rivals. In this state the United Church received from the Augustana Synod eleven congregations which embraced over 2,000 souls, and three ministers.

The state of Minnesota contributed to the United Church, in 1890, about 275 congregations, 45 of which, however, did not formally join the association, but were served by ministers who did so; and the whole number of souls embraced by the movement was between 55,000 and 60,000. During the years 1890-93 the membership increased materially, chiefly by the admission of new congregations, and the parochial reports of the United Church for the year 1893 give the names of more than 350 congregations in the state. But that has been the highest mark so far. The internal struggles which seemed to shake the very foundations of the association during the years 1893-98 retarded the growth of the body as a whole, and in this state the number of congregations dropped from about 355 in 1893 to 285 in 1898. In 1900 the total number of souls belonging to the United Church in the state was not quite 65,000. The people of this association have manifested a commendable zeal for higher education, and they support four important schools, four hospitals, and one orphans' home in the state. There are about 230 church buildings, and the value of the property owned either by the United Church or by its congregations in the state was about $850,000 in 1900.

THE LUTHERAN FREE CHURCH. This association is a resuscitation of a certain faction of the Norwegian-Danish Evangelical Lutheran Conference, which in 1890 became a part of the United Church. During the years 1890-93 two contending factions arose within the United Church, and when this body, in the summer of 1893, took practical steps to "remove" its theological seminary from the Augsburg Seminary buildings, the "Friends of Augsburg" held an informal meeting and resolved to rally around their favorite institution. At this stage they were often called simply "the minority," and their opponents "the majority." After the summer of 1893 there could be no co-operation between the two factions. "The minority" held regular annual meetings of their own, calling themselves "the Friends of Augsburg" from 1893 to 1896, and the Lutheran Free Church from June 12, 1897. The Free Church has its stronghold in the northern part of Minnesota and in North Dakota, while the most of the old Conference people living elsewhere remain in the United Church. The leaders of the Free Church are an exceedingly aggressive set of men, and opposition only seems to spur them on to greater activity. And they have actually endeavored to accomplish something new under the sun. This endeavor is embodied in the Practical Rules of the Free Church, § 6, which grants any member of any Lutheran church the right to vote at the annual meetings of the Free Church, provided he or she endorses the principles and rules of said body, and promises to co-operate with it. Augsburg Seminary is the heart and soul of the movement. This is not accidental; for while the other Lutheran church organizations have started schools in different parts of the country, the leading Augsburg minds have given but scant encouragement to such endeavors outside their own institution. The watchword of the Free Church is congregational independence and individual edification. Being yet in its formative period, it has neglected its statistics. According to the estimates of Prof. Georg Sverdrup, the Free Church contains altogether in the United States about 40,000 souls, 25,000 of whom are communicants, and these are organized into about 300 local churches. According to the same authority

the association owns property to the value of about
$1,000,000. The Free Church has about two-thirds of its
strength in Minnesota. The Free Church people have
always contributed liberally to the work carried on by the
association. The annual contributions in this state in 1898
aggregated about $15,000; and the chief items of expendi-
ture of the Free Church were $5,500 to foreign missions,
$4,000 to Augsburg Seminary, and $2,500 to home
missions. The Norwegian Lutheran Deaconesses' Institute
in Minneapolis is largely supported by Free Church people.
Most of the congregations have church buildings of their
own, but there are comparatively few parsonages.

HAUGE'S SYNOD. This association, originally called the
Evangelical Lutheran Church of America, for years had its
stronghold in Wisconsin. But during the fifties and sixties
its center of population moved westward, and in 1876,
thirty years after its organization, more than one-half of its
congregations were located west of the Mississippi river.
The organization received its present name and its "new
constitution" at the annual meeting of 1875, which was
held June 5-13, at Arendahl, Minn. Since the establishment
of the theological seminary and college of the synod in Red
Wing, in 1879, this state has been the chief scene of activity
within the synod. In 1900 about 40 out of a total of 100
ministers and professors resided in Minnesota; and about
65 out of a total of 230 congregations are located in the
same state. The whole synod consists of about 18,000
communicants and 30,000 souls, and almost exactly one-
third of them reside in Minnesota. The growth of this body
is healthy and steady, its membership having almost

doubled during the past fifteen years. Of the 155 church buildings belonging to the synod, fully one-third are located in Minnesota—Elling Eielsen and a few others kept up a separate organization from the middle of the seventies, abiding by the "old constitution," and they are represented by three congregations in this state.

SWEDISH MISSION. The oldest congregation belonging to the Mission Covenant in the state was organized at Salem, Olmsted county, in 1870. About half a dozen others were organized during the seventies. The development of the covenant was most rapid during the eighties, and since that time its stronghold has been in the Twin Cities. The statistics of the covenant are very defective in this state as elsewhere, and the figures given do not indicate the work actually carried on. There are about 30 congregations formally belonging to the covenant, and they have an aggregate membership of about 5,000, counting the children. There are over 50 ministers, or about two for each congregation. But a large number of these men have received no theological training whatever, and several support themselves mainly by manual labor. Most of the congregations have church buildings of their own. One of them, the Minneapolis Tabernacle, has a seating capacity of 3,000, and is worth $35,000. The value of all the church property in the state exceeds $100,000. The only institution of learning connected with the covenant in the state is the Northwestern Collegiate and Business Institute, which is located in the Minneapolis Tabernacle. The 30 congregations contribute on the average about $1,000 each to the different branches of work performed by the congregations and the covenant—The Free Mission people, according to the estimates of Rev. N. Wickstrom, are represented by about 130 churches, which have a communicant membership of about 3,900, and church property valued at $65,000. The Scandinavian Congregationalists, who are mostly Swedish Mission Friends, have about 100 congregations and 7,000 communicants in the United States, and they are well represented in Minnesota.

BAPTISTS.   The first Swedish Baptist church in the state was organized by Rev. F. O. Nilsson in Houston, Aug. 18, 1853, with a membership of nine.   By the year 1860 there were eight churches with 162 members.   The Minnesota conference dates from the year 1858, and its growth since its organization has been steady and healthy.   In 1900 it consisted of 80 churches, which are cared for by 50 pastors. The number of communicants is about 5,500.   One-fourth of the members reside in the Twin Cities.   There are about 60 church edifices valued at $140,000.

Fifteen Danish Baptists organized a congregation Oct. 11, 1863, at Clark's Grove, Freeborn county, and this is the oldest Danish organization of its kind west of the Mississippi.   Several other Danish Baptist congregations were started in the southern part of the state during the next few years, and in the eighties Norwegian Baptist congregations grew up in the Twin Cities.   The Norwegian and Danish Baptists of Minnesota and Iowa formed the Western conference in 1883; but this was divided along the state line eight years later, the Minnesota conference having been organized May 30, 1891, at Stillwater.   In 1900 a score of congregations belong to the conference, and the number of com-

municants is about 1,400. There are twelve preachers, and
the value of the property owned by the congregations is
$35,000.

METHODISTS. Two Norwegian girls who were members of a Norwegian Methodist congregration at Washington Prairie, Iowa, came to St. Paul in the course of the
years 1851–53, and they were doubtless the pioneers of the
Scandinavian Methodist churches in the state. The first
movement crystallized in the organization of a Scandinavian church in St. Paul, in 1853. The movement made but
little progress during the next ten years, but in the early
sixties several new congregations were started. Up to 1877
the Norwegian Minnesota conference worked in connection
with the American conferences, but since that date the Norwegian Methodists of several Northwestern states, including Minnesota, have managed their affairs somewhat inde-
pendently. In 1900 there are about 40 congregations in the
state, which are served by twenty odd ministers, and an
epual number of local preachers. The total number of
communicant members is 1,400. The value of the 30 church
buildings and the 15 parsonages has been put at $83,000.

Since 1893 the Swedish Methodist churches in Minnesota have constituted a part of the Northern Mission Conference. In 1900 there are 35 congregations in the state.
Their total membership is about 1,600, and about 2,000
children attend their 40 Sunday schools. Nearly every
congregation has a church building, and the aggregate
value of the church buildings and the parsonages is put at
$115,000. There are over 20 regular ministers and about a
dozen local preachers.—It should be observed that the

Methodists generally put a high value on their church property. Often it is estimated, in their reports, to be worth twice as much as another denomination would rate similar possessions. But it was deemed best to retain their own figures.

DANISH LUTHERANS. The United Danish Evangelical Lutheran Church, which was organized in Minneapolis, in 1896, has about a score of congregations in this state in 1900. The total number of persons connected with them is about 3,000. Some twenty children are cared for at an orphans' home in Albert Lea.—The Danish Evangelical Lutheran Church had seven congregations in the state in 1899, and the number of souls connected with these was a little over 1,600. The Danebod high school, at Tyler, is operated in connection with the latter association.

ICELANDIC LUTHERANS. The Icelandic Evangelical Lutheran Church of America was organized the 25th of January, 1885. A very large proportion of the members, about 3,500 communicants and 6,000 souls, reside in Canada; yet about 650 persons belong to the four congregations in the state, all located in Lincoln and Lyon counties. The church property is estimated to be worth $9,000 The religious work among the Icelanders in said places was begun in 1879 by Rev. J. Bjarnason, and for some time a newspaper, *Kennarinn*, has been published in the interest of the church at Minneota, by Rev. B. B. Jonsson.

UNITARIANS. Several Norwegian Unitarian churches were started during the eighties in Minnesota and Wisconsin by Kristofer Janson. But the movement has made no progress during the past ten years, and the bona fide membership of the four congregations in the state is not quite 300. The Nazareth congregation in Minneapolis has a church building worth $8,000. A Swedish Unitarian church in Minneapolis was discontinued several years ago.

EPISCOPALIANS. A Swedish Episcopal congregation was organized in Minneapolis, in 1892, by Rev. O. A. Toffteen, and since that time the Episcopalian propaganda has been pushed with considerable energy among the Swedes. In 1899 there were nine congregations in the state, and they had a total membership of about 1,500, including 1,000 communicants.

Nearly all the great denominations not treated above under separate heads have at one time or another carried on missionary work among the Scandinavians of the state. The Adventists, Universalists, Presbyterians, and Disciples of Christ are all represented by Scandinavian congregations; but their following is not strong numerically, and the work is spasmodic rather than systematic. The Salvation Army has a considerable following among the Scandinavians, and they are organized into a number of vigorous corps. The total membership in the state is several hundred.

Historical Review of the Minnesota District of the Norwegian Synod.

—BY—

REV. JOHN HALVORSON.

The Minnesota District of the Norwegian Synod did not receive its separate organization and officers until 1876; but its history goes back to settlements and churches founded by Norwegian immigrants and pastors during the latter days of the territory. The first Norwegian clergyman who visited the settlers in the present Minnesota District was N. Brandt, of Rock Prairie, Wis., who arrived at Red Wing in June, 1855. Together with a companion, he visited on foot his newly arrived countrymen in other portions of Goodhue county. During the summer of 1856 some of the settlers organized a Lutheran congregation and secured 100 acres of land for church purposes, the present Holden parsonage.* In September of the same year they were visited by Rev. H. A. Stub, of Coon Prairie, Wis., who conducted several meetings and assisted them in framing a constitu-

*See "Söger Hjem," by Rev. B. J. Muus, p. 133. If the author is correct, then this seems to have been the first Norwegian Lutheran church organization in the state of Minnesota. No clergyman appears to have been present when the church was organized.

tion and issuing a call for a pastor. The minutes of the
meeting were subscribed to by 72 voting members, and the
letter authorizing the church council of the synod to call a
pastor for them was signed by four trustees, namely, Knut
K. Finseth, Kjostel G. Naeseth, Halvor Olsen Huset, and
Christopher Lockrem.   In 1857 Rev. Munch and Prof.
Larsen visited the settlements in Goodhue county.   The
latter preached six days in succession to large audiences,
many following him from place to place.   During one week
in June he baptized 100 children, of which 33 were baptized
at one service near Nestrand, Rice county, and 14 were con-
firmed at this place.   The next year he preached in St. Paul,
Stillwater, Carver, St. Peter, Mankato, and other places.
At one time, after a fourteen days' journey, mostly afoot,
Prof. Larsen—who resided in Pierce county, Wis.—came to
Knut Finseth sorefooted, his shoes being entirely worn out.
Finseth sent to Kenyon for shoes; but as no small number
of men's shoes could be found there, a pair of ladies' shoes
was procured, and in these Goodhue county was traversed.
Rev. A. C. Preus also visited the pioneers who were under
Prof. Larsen's charge up to 1859, when B. J. Muus, from
Norway, who had been called by the church council, arrived
in November, and became the first resident pastor of the
Norwegian Synod within the present Minnesota District.
Up to this time some of the settlements were visited only
once a year by a synod clergyman, as the ministers were
few in number and most of them resided hundreds of miles
from the outposts in Minnesota. Rev. P. A. Rasmussen,
residing at Lisbon, Ill., but not belonging to the synod, had
charge of a congregation in Goodhue county for some years;

but as he became a member of the synod in 1862, his parishioners the following year joined the churches tended by Rev. Muus. In 1859-60 a parsonage was built for Rev. Muus, and in the latter year a church building was erected. In 1860 the first subscription for Luther College was made, amounting to $603, contributed by forty-two church members in Goodhue county. According to the statement of Rev. Muus, about $10,000 was contributed by the churches of his charge to higher institutions of learning during the first twenty-five years of his ministry. This shows the zeal and love for God's word and His kingdom among the early settlers. In 1862, June 12-20, the synod held its annual meeting in the East Holden church, when the congregation was formally accepted as a member of the synod.

The Indian outbreak in 1862 drove the settlers of Kandiyohi and other western counties eastward, many taking refuge in the older settlements in Rice and Goodhue counties, and for about three years immigration to the western parts of the state virtually ceased; but when peace and quiet was restored the settlers returned. In 1863 Thomas Johnsen was ordained, and took charge of churches in Nicollet and other western counties, thus relieving Rev. Muus, who up to this time had served all the congregations as far west as Norway Lake and as far south as Blue Earth and Waseca counties. Rev. Johnsen for several years visited the Norwegian settlements extending from Emmet county, Iowa, to Douglas county, Minn., a distance of about 300 miles. Many of the congregations could be reached only twice a year; but the people were glad to hear the Word of God, to have marriage rites properly performed, to have their chil-

24

dren baptized, and to partake of the Lord's Supper. Any further pastoral care of the souls was impossible, but the pioneers waited patiently and hoped the time would arrive when they could have a pastor located in their midst. The great need of pastoral visits is seen from the number of infant baptisms.   On a journey through Meeker and Kandiyohi counties, in 1867, Rev. Johnsen baptized 55 children in three days, and nearly 200 during the year.   Rev. Muus and Rev. N. Quammen, the latter having settled in Dakota county in 1866, baptized in 1867 about 250 and 100 infants, respectively.   Before 1868 synod congregations had been organized in all the counties in the state where many Norwegians had settled, even in counties bordering on the Dakota line, for example, Yellow Medicine.   At that time the Norwegian immigration to Minnesota was very large, and great demands were made for permanent pastors.   N. Th. Ylvisaker, a well-known lay-preacher from Norway, arrived in 1868, was ordained, took charge of churches in and around Red Wing, and organized, in 1869, the first synod congregation in Minneapolis, Our Savior's church. Four of the fourteen men who were ordained in 1869 located in Minnesota the same year, namely, J. A. Thorsen, Olmsted county; L. J. Markhus, Norway Lake; Peter Reque, Pope county; and O. Norman, St. Paul.   The last mentioned, especially, made long missionary journeys in the northwestern part of the state; and Otter Tail county, in particular, became a promising field for church work.   Rev. A. Jakobsen, traveling on skis, visited Kandiyohi county before 1867; and two years later Rev. N. Brandt, vice-president of the synod, made an extensive trip of three months, and preached in nearly every corner of the state where a few Norwegians could be gathered together. In 1870 Rev. H. A. Preus, the president of the synod, visited nine pastors and sixteen churches in Minnesota, going as far west as Pope county. These visits of the chief officers of the synod show the care and supervision exercised by them in the mission work and resulted in the organizing of several congregations and consequent calling of pastors, who settled in the new field. According to the parochial reports of 1869, Minnesota had 39 churches and 13 pastors; but some of the congregations covered whole counties, thickly settled by Norwegians.

One of the greatest missionaries of the Norwegian Synod, Rev. L. Carlsen, commenced to work in Douglas and Grant counties in 1872. After a few years of earnest labor and extensive travel, he removed to San Francisco, Cal., then to Australia; but returned to the United States later on. Rev. K. Björgo settled in Becker county in 1872, and became the first missionary of the synod in the Red River Valley on the Minnesota side. At the same time Rev. J. Hellestvedt commenced work at Sheyenne river, N. D,, being the first pastor west of the Red river. A great immigration to the Red River Valley took place in the early seventies. Rev. B. Harstad located at Mayville in 1874, and did a grand work in founding churches on the wide prairies of Dakota. Later on Rev. O. H. Aaberg was called to Grand Forks county, and took charge of the immigrants as far west as Devils Lake. Numerous churches were organized on both sides of the Red river, especially in the vicinity of Crookston and Grafton. Even as far north as Pembina, where some Icelanders had formed a settlement, the synod pursued its labor by securing Thorlakson, an Icelandic minister, to attend to the spiritual needs of his countrymen.

At the annual meeting in Decorah, Iowa, in 1876, it was found expedient to divide the synod into three districts, so that the people of each section of the country might have a better opportunity to attend to and become acquainted with the increasing work of the church. The Minnesota District did not include the southern tier of counties in Minnesota, but it extended clear to the Pacific ocean. But in 1893 the territory west of the Rocky Mountains was organized into the Pacific District. The Minnesota District was the smallest of the three in regard to church members, the poorest in regard to wealth; but it offered the greatest missionary field and had the best prospect of growth. Missionaries were in demand, and one clergyman preached at twenty-one places. It took him several weeks to make the circuit. During the whole history of the district, the main work has been to gather the scattered Norwegian settlers into congregations, to preach to them the Word of God, and to have them partake of the sacraments of Jesus Christ. The missionary work is superintended by a board of three members, and the president of the district is ex-officio chairman.

Rev. B. J. Muus was chosen president of the district in 1876; Rev. N. Th. Ylvisaker, vice-president; O. K. Finseth, lay member of the church counsil; Rev. H. G. Stub, secretary; and H. G. Rasmussen, treasurer. Rev. Muus was president of the district for seven years. He was a leading spirit, a powerful character, an organizer; but unyielding and harsh in dealing with human frailties. He was a pioneer in educational work, and through his efforts a Lutheran academy was started at the Holden parsonage about the year 1868. Only two terms were taught; but in 1874 Muus and a few others founded what is now St. Olaf College, at Northfield, thereby demonstrating that a higher institution of learning could be established and maintained by the Norwegian Lutherans in spite of a number of similar institutions supported by the state or by private people of other nationalities.

When the controversy on predestination started in 1880, many of the pastors and church members of the district were for some time in doubt which party to join. Rev. Muus sided against the synod, and soon became the acknowledged leader of the opposition in the state; this, together with troubles of a personal nature, was the main reason for his defeat as president of the district in 1883, when Rev. B. Harstad was elected to succeed him. During the turbulent times when the predestination controversy was raging, the meetings and discussions of the district resembled very much the proceedings of a Polish parliament. At the meeting of the synod in Minneapolis, in 1884, the two parties were so evenly divided that hardly any resolutions could be passed. Prof. Larsen was elected editor of *Kirketidende* by a majority of one vote; and the opposition endeavored to prevent the ordination of those theological candidates from Luther Seminary who sided with the Missouri Synod. At the meeting of the district at Norway Lake, in 1885, Rev. Muus refused to recognize Rev. Harstad as president, and boldly advocated that pastors who taught the tenets of the Missouri Synod should be deposed from their pulpits. Some congregations ousted their pastors, in some instances legal suits followed in regard to the possession of church property, and it may be said that terror and anarchy reigned supreme in the district for a while. Nowhere was the struggle more bitter and determined than in the two large congregations at Norway Lake. By large majorities both of them deposed, in 1886, their pastor, L. J. Markhus, who sided with the Missouri Synod; but the minority, consisting of about 50 families protested, declared the deposition of Rev. Markhus unconstitutional and a violation of the by-laws, and by main force entered the church buildings which the opposition had without authority closed against them. The majority, however, carried Rev. Markhus bodily out of the churches, and he soon died a broken-down man. The minority tried to retain the parsonage, but were sued for the possession of the same. The lawsuit continued for four years, went to the supreme court of Minnesota, and the minority was forced to give up all the property and pay damages and costs. But the Norwegian Synod, at its annual meeting at Stoughton, Wis., in 1887, endorsed the position of the minority. As a result of the predestination controversy, fully one-third of the church members in the district left the synod. Almost the whole of Goodhue county, with its large congregations, and all of the Red River Valley north of Goose river, seceded. In several places, however, the synod people organized new congregations and built new church edifices, having generally lost all they had paid to the old buildings. In other places again the synod congregations remained untouched, for example, in Minneapolis, St. Paul, Sacred Heart, Fergus Falls, Benson, Glenwood, etc. In some instances people left the synod and joined other Lutheran associations or organized independent congregations.

Of late years, however, the district has enjoyed a rapid growth, partly, herhaps, on account of the split in the United Norwegian Church, and today it is stronger than it has ever been. The strongholds of the district are the country churches, especially those of Olmsted, Otter Tail, Pope, Renville, and Chippewa counties in Minnesota, and those in Traill and Cass counties in North Dakota. A number of churches have in recent years also been added to the synod in Polk, Marshall, Kittson, Todd, and Mille Lacs counties in Minnesota. According to the synodical report for 1899, the Minnesota District contained nearly 350 congregations, served by 100 pastors. The number of souls was about 50,000, with 30,000 communicants. Nearly 3,000 infants were baptized in one year, and over 7,000 services held. One hundred school teachers, some of whom were theological students, instructed the children in religion in the parochial schools. At the synodical meeting held at Spring Grove, Minn., June 15–21, 1899, it was reported that during the past year fourteen new clergymen had taken up the work in the district, while only three had moved out, and one who had formerly seceded repented of his errors; nine churches had been dedicated; and nine new congregations, principally from the northern parts of the state, applied for membership. A farm of 160 acres and suitable buildings have lately been secured in Norman county, Minn., where a new orphans' home has been started, of which Rev. H. A. Blegen is superintendent.

A large number of academies and other higher institutions of learning, treated of more fully in another portion of this volume, are controlled by members of the Minnesota District, which shows the interest taken in education.

Since 1892 Rev. K. Björgo has been president of the district, and since 1898 has devoted all his time to the duties as president, having no regular congregation under his charge.   The president receives an annual salary of $1,200 and free house.   His responsibilities are great, and he constantly travels from place to place in the district, encouraging and instructing pastors and people in the right use of the privileges God has given the church, as well as seeing that harmony and order prevail.

While the Wisconsin and Iowa districts contain more of the old pioneers, both of the clergy and the lay members, the Minnesota District is known for its youthful spirit, energy, and impatience of restraint. But the districts work together in brotherly love and Christian fellowship.

Historical Review of the Minnesota Conference of the Augustana Synod.

—BY—

REV. C. J. PETRI.

The Minnesota Conference was organized two years before the Augustana Synod, in Centre City, Minn., on the 8th of October, 1858. The organizers were Revs. E. Norelius, P. Beckman, P. Carlson and J. P. C. Boren. The lay-delegates were Håkan Svedberg, Centre City; Daniel Nelson, Marine; Ole Paulson, Carver; Hans C. Björklund, Ruseby. The conference numbered on the day of its organization five ministers, and thirteen congregations with 900 communicant members. The thirteen congregations of the conference were all, except one at Stockholm, Wis., located in the state of Minnesota, namely, at Centre City, Marine, St. Paul, Vasa, Red Wing, Cannon River, St. Peter, Scandian Grove, Spring Garden, Union, Götaholm and Vista. Within the conference were five church buildings, the first having been built in Red Wing, in 1856. During the first year of its existence the expenses of the conference amounted to about $1,500. The pioneers of the conference started out, from the first meeting of the conference, full of hope

361

and courage in their missionary work. In fact it was then and is now the hopeful missionary work that gave and still gives to the Minnesota Conference its character and success. Speaking of the first meeting of the conference in 1858, Dr. Norelius, about forty years later, says: "I have been present at many meetings since then, and I have seen greater gatherings of people, but I have never witnessed such deeply felt interest, such sincerity and so much enthusiasm as I saw at this our first meeting. The movement was not only new to us, but the Spirit of God was mighty in our churches. The meeting was filled with a holy inspiration and spiritual power. Our souls were embued with a joyful courage. When we had succeeded in organizing our forces, we felt that we had made a great progress. We heeded no difficulties, everything seemed to us possible."

Part of the minutes of this first meeting reads as follows: "Services were held every afternoon, and on Sunday two services were held. The church was always filled with attentive hearers. The members of the conference were cordially and royally entertained, and many of our dear countrymen will long cherish the memory of this meeting. On Sunday a collection for the treasury of the conference was taken, amounting to $5.09." The Swedish-Lutherans in Minnesota were united and ready to take up the missionary work for the temporal and spiritual welfare of the Swedes in the Northwest. They have during the past forty years not only taken an active part in the work of the Swedish-Lutheran church throughout the United States, but also and especially labored with faithfulness and sacrifice for the advancement of the material and spiritual interests amongst the hundreds of Swedish settlements in Minnesota, the Dakotas and Wisconsin. At a very early date in the history of the conference efforts were put forth for the promotion of higher education. The people of Minnesota felt it to be their duty to have in their midst an institution of learning, and in 1862 a beginning was made by the establishment of a school which today is Gustavus Adolphus College, in St. Peter, one of the leading educational institutions in the Northwest. A few years later, in 1865, Dr. Norelius began the work of caring for orphans, and so was established the orphans' home at Vasa, Minn., which is today supported by the conference. This institution, where on the average 50 children are annually cared for, has been very liberally supported, although the misfortunes of the institution has tried the liberality of the people; once the home was destroyed in a tornado and once by fire. This institution is governed by a board of trustees elected by the conference. In harmony with this work of mercy, the conference has also maintained a hospital, the Bethesda Hospital, in St. Paul. This institution was established in 1881 and is today one of the best equipped hospitals in the Northwest. These institutions are indications of the united and faithful work and consecration of the Swedish-Lutherans in Minnesota. Much has been done, but much more could have been done had not the conference had its hands full with missionary efforts; congregations had to be organized; churches and parsonages had to be built, and schools established. Realizing the fact that they are in America, and that they and their children must naturally more and more make use of the language of the country, the Swedish-Lutherans in the eighties began to establish English churches under the auspices of the conference. But owing to the large immigration, and also to the opposition the Lutherans encountered on the part of other missionary efforts made by those who labored for the tearing asunder of the Lutheran churches, the conference had its hands full in taking care of its own churches, and the English work was somewhat neglected.

The conference is now stronger than ever, having been faithful in its defense of the doctrines and practices of the Lutheran church. The conference today, after more than forty years of zealous work, numbers nearly 140 ministers, 340 congregations with a total membership of 70,000, out of whom 40,000 are communicant members. There are within the conference about 275 church buildings and 100 parsonages, valued at more than one million dollars. In one year the parochial schools had an attendance of 7,132 scholars, and the Sunday schools 13,536.

In order more effectively to carry on the work, the conference is divided into 15 mission districts, viz: Chisago district with 22 congregations; St. Paul, 18; Goodhue, 20; N. Minnesota Valley, 20; Pacific, 35; St. Croix Valley, 24; Alexandria, 27; S. Minnesota Valley, 19; N. E. Dakota, 16; Big Stone, 22; Lake Superior, 28; Central, 13; James River, 12; Red River, 33; Mississippi, 15; and Canada Mission, 10. With such an arrangement the different parts of the conference fill their mission in their special field and at the same time present to the world one undivided and strong Lutheran church among the thousands of Swedish-Americans in promising Northwest.

Biographies of Scandinavians in Minnesota.

Aaker, Lars K., state senator and pioneer—Alexandria— born 19 Sept., 1825, in Lardal, Telemarken, Norway; died 1895. He graduated from Hviteseid normal school; emigrated to the U. S. at the age of twenty; settled in Dane county, Wis., where he taught school for a while; then farmed, and moved to Goodhue county, Minn., in 1857. Here he took a claim; was elected to the state legislature at the time of the outbreak of the Civil War, but enlisted in the Third Minnesota Volunteer Infantry, and was commissioned first lieutenant in company D, which was composed of Scandinavian soldiers, with Col. H. Mattson as captain. He served in Kentucky and in Tennessee, but, on account of ill health, resigned in 1862. Aaker represented his district in the legislature in 1859, 1860, 1862, 1867, 1869, and was state senator in 1881. He lived on his farm in Goodhue county until 1869; then moved to Alexandria, where for six years he was register of the U. S. land office, and engaged in general merchandise for nine years; was receiver of the U. S. land office in Crookston in 1884–93. Aaker was one of the first Scandinavian legislators in the state, an active Repub-

365

lican, and a delegate to the first convention of the party held in Wisconsin in 1856. He was widely and favorably known throughout the whole Northwest; was married twice, and had children by both wives.

Almen, Louis G., clergyman—Balaton—born 30 March, 1846, in Tössö, Dalsland, Sweden. At the age of twenty-four he emigrated to this country; worked at first as a common laborer; was a railroad contractor in Minnesota and Wisconsin for a couple of years; and after having attended Augustana College, Rock Island, Ill., for three years, he graduated from the theological department of this institution in 1876. His first charge was at Beaver, Iroquois county, Ill.; but after having remained there for about three years, he became for one year a traveling missionary in Yellow Medicine and Lac qui Parle counties, Minnesota; then accepted a call to New London, and settled at his present place in 1893. For over twelve years he was editor of the church and temperance departments of *Skaffaren*—the semi-official organ of the Swedish Lutheran Minnesota Conference. For a long time he has been the most ardent temperance advocate of any of the ministers of his denomination in the state of Minnesota, and is one of the ablest parliamentarians in the conference. Almen was married to Alice C. Johnson in 1876; they have several children living.

Anderson, Abel, clergyman and educator—Montevideo —born 5 Dec., 1847, in Dane county, Wis. His mother's ancestors had been officers in the Norwegian army for several generations; in 1830 she married Björn Anderson, a farmer's son and a Quaker, but a marriage between the

daughter of an officer and a farmer was in those days, and
to a certain extent is yet, looked upon with great disfavor;
besides, the young couple had not only sinned against the
social rank, but, what was worse still, Anderson did not
belong to the state church, the Lutheran. To avoid all
social and religious unpleasantness, they emigrated to the
U. S. in 1836; lived a year in Rochester, N. Y., and four years
in Illinois; settled in Wisconsin in 1841, being therefore
among the very earliest Scandinavian immigrants in this
country. Abel Anderson, who is a brother to the well-
known Prof. R. B. Anderson, attended Albion Academy two years and the University of Wisconsin for a
couple of years; graduated from Luther College, Decorah,
Iowa, in 1872, and two years later completed his theological studies at Concordia Seminary, St. Louis, Mo.
From 1874–87 he had charge of a church belonging to the
Norwegian Evangelical Lutheran Synod at Muskegon,
Mich., being also school inspector for several years; took
active part in politics; was a delegate to the Republican
national convention which nominated Blaine for president
in 1884, being one of the first Scandinavians in this country
who was a delegate to a national convention of this party;
was a candidate for representative to the state legislature
twice, but his party being in the minority, was defeated
both times. Anderson came to Appleton, Minn., in 1887,
and settled in Montevideo the following year, having
charge of churches at both places. He has been instructor
in ancient and modern languages, in which he is considered
to be quite proficient, at Windom Institute, and was one of
its trustees. He has contributed frequently to the *Chicago*

Tribune and other papers, both in the Norwegian and the English language. In 1874 he was married to Mary Olson, of Cambridge, Wis. Anderson has two brothers who are married to two of his wife's sisters. They have several children living, of whom two daughters have studied at Carleton College, Northfield, Minn.

Anderson, Berndt, journalist—St. Paul—born 2 Aug., 1840, in Lund, Sweden. After having completed a course at the University of Lund, he was employed in the department of the interior, Stockholm, from 1865–73, then went abroad, studying the natural sciences in Denmark and Germany. In 1880 he emigrated to this country, and has most of the time since been editor-in-chief of *Skaffaren*— the latter being the organ of the Minnesota Conference of the Swedish Lutheran church, and advocating Republican principles. The predominant features of Anderson's writings are clearness and learning. In 1893 he was appointed dairy and food commissioner by Governor Nelson, being the first Swede in Minnesota who was ever appointed chief of a state department, and was re-appointed twice. At the time of his appointment certain individuals seemed to think that it was not wise to appoint to such responsible position any one except a practical farmer—in most cases the male members of the farming community have neither a practical nor a theoretical knowledge of how cheese and butter are made. It did not, however, take long before Anderson proved that he was the right man for the place, and soon became a terror to the oleomargarine dealers, several of whom he successfully prosecuted. On account of his thorough scientific knowledge of dairy products and his

BERNDT ANDERSON, ST. PAUL.

PROF. H. H. BERGSLAND, RED WING.

REV. L. M. BIORN, ZUMBROTA.

C. BRANDT, ST. PAUL.

C. L. BRUSLETTEN, KENYON

conscientious attention to the duties imposed upon him, he did much to raise the standard of Minnesota cheese and butter; and certainly was one of the ablest dairy and food commissioners the state ever had. Anderson has for several years taken a very active part in politics and has been a delegate to many Republican local and state conventions. He is married and has grown children.

Anderson, Daniel, state legislator—Cambridge—born 3 Feb., 1842, in Hassela, Helsingland, Sweden. He came with his parents directly from Sweden to Chisago Lake, Minn., in 1851. They moved to Freeborn county in 1857. At the outbreak of the Civil War, Anderson joined the Tenth Minnesota Infantry, fought at Tupelo, Miss., and served in the army for three years. He came to Isanti county in 1868 and was elected county auditor the same year; since he has been county surveyor, county commissioner, and judge of probate. He was a member of the state legislature in 1873, 1875–77, 1879, and 1889. Anderson is a plain, unassuming man, who has hardly a common school education, though Col. Mattson taught him how to drive oxen. In the legislative manuals he was always styled "laborer;" yet he is considered to have been one of the most influential Scandinavian legislators in the state. He has gone through all the adversities of pioneer life. Anderson is a life-long Republican, and was married in 1869.

Arctander, J. W., lawyer—Minneapolis—born 2 Oct., 1849, in Stockholm, Sweden. His father, who belonged to one of the oldest families of Norway, was for some years a professor in Sweden, but returned to his native land in 1854. Young Arctander received a college education in

25

Skien, graduated with honors from the University of Norway, was a journalist for a while, but his radical views
brought him into trouble, and he became a political exile
and emigrated to America in 1870. For a couple of years
he was connected with a Norwegian paper in Chicago, where
he also studied law, and was admitted to the bar in Minnesota, in 1874. For about ten years he practiced law at
Willmar, and has been located in Minneapolis since 1886.
Arctander has a great reputation as a criminal lawyer, and
has been very successful in handling personal damage cases.
He is author of *Practical Handbook of Laws of Minnesota*, published in the Norwegian language in 1876, and
thoroughly revised and published in Norwegian and Swedish
twenty years later. He has also translated Henrik Ibsen's
play, *The Masterbuilder*, into English. The 17th of May,
1897, a magnificent statue of the famous Norwegian violinist, Ole Bull, was put up in the main park of Minneapolis,
mostly through the untiring energy and self-sacrifice of
Arctander. For about two years he spoke, wrote, stormed,
until his efforts were crowned with success; and in connection with the Ole Bull statue—the only statue in the public
parks of Minneapolis—Arctander's name will long be
remembered with gratitude throughout the Northwest. In
1898 he made a great stir by publicly announcing that he had
been converted to God, although he at the time was a member of the American Methodist Church, which he had joined
in 1897 and which is supposed to accept as members only
such persons as profess to have been converted.

Arosin, O. H., county treasurer—St. Paul—born 14
May, 1861, in Stockholm, Sweden. He received a high

school education in his native city; learnt the printer's trade; emigrated to America in 1879, coming directly to St. Paul; was connected with the Swedish paper *Skaffaren* for a couple of years; started a jeweler store in 1883; worked in the postoffice in 1883-7; was elected assemblyman in 1894, being re-elected two years later, and served as president of the assembly for two years; and was elected county treasurer in 1898 by a small majority. During all these years of public activity, Arosin has retained his jeweler store. He is a member of the English Lutheran church; affiliates with the Republican party; belongs to the orders of Free Masons and Odd Fellows; was married to Laura Nelson, of St. Paul, in 1891, by whom he has a couple of children.

Askeland, Hallward Tobias, librarian and musician—Minneapolis—born 30 Nov., 1860, in Stavanger, Norway. He completed a course in the Latin school of his native city; emigrated in 1875, coming directly to Minneapolis; graduated from the literary department of Augsburg Seminary in 1882; taught music for a few years; was editor of *Felt-Raabet,* the first Norwegian prohibition paper published in Minnesota, from 1886—89, but the paper ceased; and he has ever since 1889 been librarian of the Franklin Avenue branch of the public library. Askeland takes great interest in music and literature, and for several years was organist of the Norwegian Lutheran Trinity Church, and secretary of what is now the Minnesota Total Abstinence Association. In 1883 he was married to Julia Skallerud of Minneapolis. They have several children.

Bendeke, Karl, physician and surgeon—Minneapolis—

born 1841, in Kristiania, Norway.   After going through the
regular old country college course, he was admitted to the
University of Norway as a student in 1859.   He studied
medicine there from 1863–68, when he was appointed surgeon on board an emigrant vessel which brought him to
this country.   He settled first in Chicago, where he practiced
his profession for two years; moved to Minnesota in 1870;
located in Minneapolis in 1875, where he has since resided.
Bendeke has at different times visited foreign medical institutions for the purpose of extending his studies in certain
specialties, principally diseases of the eye and ear.   In 1877
he visited the eye clinics of London and Paris; in 1881
attended the New York Eye and Ear Infirmary for three
months, and in 1891 spent about the same length of time at
the university clinics of Berlin, Germany, where he studied
the most modern methods of research and treatment in the
various branches of medicine and surgery.   His professional
skill in conjunction with his long residence in the country
has naturally given him a reputation as one of the leading
Scandinavian physicians of the Northwest.   In 1869 he was
married to Josephine Fauske, of Bergen, Norway.   They
have one daughter, who is an accomplished violinist.

   Bennet, C. C., merchant—Minneapolis—born 1847, in
Malmö, Sweden.   He is the son of Baron Wilhelm Bennet,
who was an officer in the Swedish army.   Young Bennet received a good education; went to Copenhagen, Denmark, at
the age of fifteen, to learn the furrier's trade; emigrated to
Montreal, Canada, in 1867, where he worked at his trade
for over a year; then traveled through several of the Eastern
states, but returned to Montreal to become a member and

manager of a fur company. In 1877 he went to Omaha,
Neb., and opened a wholesale house in furs; but as the business proved unprofitable, he moved shortly afterwards to
Minneapolis, where he has ever since been engaged in his
trade. Always taking an active interest in the social life of
his countrymen, Bennet has several times been president of
the Swedish society Norden. He has been a prominent
speaker at many important Scandinavian festivals and
other great gatherings. He was the chief promoter in
organizing, in 1888, Battery B of the First Battalion, which
is composed mostly of Swedes; Bennet—generally known
as Captain Bennet—has been commander of the battery
ever since its organization. In 1874 he was married to a
Canadian lady. They have grown children.

Berg, Albert, secretary of State—Centre City—born 25
June, 1861, in Centre City, Minn. His parents were among
the early Swedish settlers at Chisago Lake. He attended
Carleton College, Northfield, in 1876–78; then studied at
Gustavus Adolphus College, St. Peter, for a couple of years.
Berg traveled as a salesman through the Western states for
four years, then taught school for three years, was elected
register of deeds of Chisago county in 1886, and was
re-elected two years later. He was a delegate to the Republican national convention at Minneapolis in 1892, and at
the state convention that year was a strong candidate for
secretary of state. In 1894 he was elected secretary of
state, and has since been re-elected twice. Berg. is a
Lutheran, quite a good singer, and is married.

Bergsland, H. H., educator—Red Wing—born 23 Jan.,
1858, in Fillmore county, Minn. His father emigrated from

Telemarken, Norway, to the United States in 1846, and his mother came from the same place a few years later. They settled in Fillmore county a couple of years before he was born. After having received a common school education, young Bergsland entered Red Wing Seminary in 1880, and graduated from the theological department of this institution five years later; then attended a theological school in Kristiania, Norway, for two years, after which he accepted the position of theological professor in Red Wing Seminary. From 1889 to 1897 Bergsland was president of this institution, but at the latter date he again became theological professor. In 1895 he published a small pamphlet in answer to the fanatical attack made upon him by Rev. O. S. Meland. In 1887 he was married to Anna L. Thompson, of Fillmore county, Minn.

Biermann, Adolph, state auditor—Rochester—born 19 Nov., 1842, in Kristiania, Norway. Biermann emigrated to America at the age of nineteen and at once entered the Union army, enlisting in company I of the Twenty-fourth Wisconsin Volunteers, serving till the close of the war, and participating in the battles of Perrysville, Ky., and Murfreesboro, Tenn. In 1866 Biermann made a visit to Norway, and upon his return settled at Rochester. He was elected county auditor of Olmsted county in 1874, which position he held till 1880. In 1875 and 1882 he was placed in nomination by the Democratic party as secretary of state; in 1884, as representative to Congress; in 1883, as candidate for governor. He was defeated. In 1885 he was appointed collector of internal revenue for Minnesota by President Cleveland. In 1890 he was elected, on the Democratic ticket, to the office of state auditor, but after having served one term was defeated for the same position in 1894. Biermann is still a bachelor.

Biörn, Ludvig Marinus, clergyman—Zumbrota—born 7 Sept., 1835, in Moss, Norway.   His father was a minister in the state church of Norway, and some of his ancestors held high military and ecclesiastical positions in Slesvig. Biörn became a student at the University of Norway in 1855, graduating as cand. theol. in 1861.   The following year he emigrated to America, being called as pastor by the congregation of the Norwegian Synod in Manitowoc county, Wis.   Here Biörn met with all the hardships incident to pioneer life.   The war, too, added to the difficulty; company F of the Fifteenth Wisconsin Regiment was mostly taken from his congregation.   In 1879 he removed to Goodhue county, Minn., to the congregations of Land and Minneola.   Biörn was one of the leaders of the Anti-Missourians in the great predestination controversy, and when, after the division of the synod, the United Church was organized out of three Norwegian Lutheran denominations, Biörn became the vice-president of the new body. *The North,* in 1893, says: "Biörn has a frank, honest, prepossessing face.   He is a thoroughbred gentleman, a popular preacher, an able writer, and last but not least, there is a vein of true poetry in his psychical make-up which has found expression in a number of poems, two or three of which are gems of their kind."   One of his sons is practicing law in St. Paul.

Björgo, K., clergyman—Red Wing—born 2 Oct., 1847, in Voss, Bergen stift, Norway.   He came to the United States

in his infancy; graduated from Luther College, Decorah,
Iowa, in 1870, and three years later completed his theologi-
cal studies at Concordia Seminary, St. Lôuis, Mo.; was
pastor of several churches at and around Lake Park, Becker
county, Minn., for about fifteen years, and accepted a call to
Red Wing in 1888. Björgo was elected president of the
Minnesota District of the Norwegian Evangelical Lutheran
Synod in 1891, and has been one of the chief promoters in
establishing the Young Ladies' Lutheran Seminary at Red
Wing—the only Scandinavian institution of its kind in
America. He was married to Ingeborg Lien, of Decorah,
Iowa, in 1876; they have several children.

Böckman, Marcus Olaus, clergyman and educator—
Minneapolis—born 9 Jan., 1849, in Langesund, Kristiansand stift, Norway. His father was receiver of customs at
Ekersund, where young Böckman received his early school
training, and after having completed the course at Aars and
Voss' Latin school, Kristiania, he graduated with high honors from the theological department of the University of
Norway in 1874, was ordained and accepted a call from a
congregation in Goodhue county, Minn., the following year,
remaining there for eleven years. Rev. J. C. Jensson, in
American Lutheran Biographies, says: ' When the
great controversy concerning election and conversion arose
in the Norwegian Synod, Böckman took part with the Anti-
Missourians and became one of the leaders in opposing the
Missourians. In 1886 the Anti-Missourian faction established a theological seminary of their own at Northfield,
Minn., and Böckman was called to fill one of the chairs at
this institution. From 1887-90 he was one of the editors

DR. KARL BENDEKE, MINNEAPOLIS.

A. E. BOYESEN, ST. PAUL.

of *Lutherske Vidnesbyrd*, the church paper of the Anti-Missourians. In 1890 Böckman became a member of the faculty of Augsburg Seminary. He is a bright scholar and one of the most eloquent Norwegian preachers in this country.' Since 1893 he has served as president of the United Church Seminary. Böckman has been married twice, and has several children.

Boeckmann, Eduard, physician and surgeon—St. Paul—born 25 March, 1849, in Östre Toten, Hamar stift, Norway. His father was an officer in the army, and later became postmaster at Moss. Young Boeckmann received a careful college education; graduated from the medical department of the University of Norway in 1874; visited Copenhagen, Utrecht, Paris, and Heidelberg, for the purpose of studying the diseases of the eye; practiced his profession in Bergen for ten years, meanwhile visiting the United States three times and practicing medicine at shorter periods in different parts of this country. He came to America first in 1882; has crossed the Atlantic Ocean over twenty times; and located permanently in St. Paul in 1886, where he has ever since resided. Boeckmann at first became noted as a specialist of the diseases of the eye, but has since engaged in every branch of medical practice and surgical operations—in all of which he has, by general consent, become skillful. He was married to Anne Sophie Dorothea Gill, of Bergen, in 1875; they have children.

Boen, Haldor E., congressman—Fergus Falls—born 2 Jan., 1851, in Söndre Aurdal, Valders, Norway. At the age of seventeen he left his native country and came to Mower county, Minn., but settled in Otter Tail county three years

later. Here he worked in the county auditor's office for
a while, taught in the public schools for five years, and was
an active agitator of the Farmers' Alliance and People's
party movement. In 1880 he was county commissioner,
and for a number of years acted as deputy sheriff. During
the years of 1885–89 he was a member of the executive committee of the state Alliance. He was elected, on the Republican ticket, register of deeds of Otter Tail county in 1888,
and re-elected on the Alliance ticket two years later. In
1892 the People's party nominated him for Congress, and
he was elected by a very small majority; but was defeated
in 1894. Boen introduced a number of radical bills while in
Congress, and succeeded in getting one measure through.
The *Boen Law* provides that criminal cases in the U. S.
courts must be tried in the district where the offense was
committed. Boen does not seem to possess the educational
qualifications or the mental and moral make-up to properly
fill the high position to which he was elected. Since 1895 he
has been editor and publisher of the *Fergus Falls Globe*.
In 1874 he was married to Margit G. Brekke; they have
several children.

Borup, Charles William W., pioneer—St. Paul—born 10
Dec., 1806, in Copenhagen, Denmark; died in 1859. At the
age of twenty-one he came to the United States, remained
in New York for about a year, then went to Lake Superior,
and, as an Indian trader, entered the service of the American fur company, of which concern he finally became the
chief agent, residing at La Pointe for several years. Borup
moved to St. Paul in 1849, and four years later he, in connection with his brother-in-law, Charles H. Oakes, organ-

ized the first bank in the territory of Minnesota. As an illustration of the banking capacity in those early days, it may be mentioned that, for lack of funds, the banking concern was unable to pay a check of $130 which a customer desired to get cashed. But Borup soon improved the banking business, and became the best financier in the territory. It is claimed that his parents and ancestors were prominent people, and that he received a careful education in Denmark, graduating as a physician, but never practiced the profession. It is not known what caused him to sacrifice his high standing and bright future in his native country. Here he endured the hardships of a Western pioneer, associating for years a great deal with the Indians; he, like many other early pioneers, married a woman who had Indian blood in her veins, by whom he had many children. One of his sons became a captain in the United States army; his daughters, who are claimed to have been very handsome, were all married to men of prominence. Borup was not only the first banker in Minnesota, he was also the first consul who represented a Scandinavian country in Minnesota, and donated a lot in St. Paul to the Methodists, in 1853, on condition that a Scandinavian church should be built thereon, and this was the first Scandinavian religious organization in the state. His son, Theo. Borup, is a leading business man in St. Paul.

Boyesen, Alf E., lawyer—St. Paul—born 21 April, 1857, in Kristiania, Norway. His father was a captain in the Norwegian army, and he is a brother to the well-known author Hjalmar Hjort Boyesen. At the age of thirteen Boyesen emigrated to this country, attended Urbana University, Urbana, Ohio, for four years; studied law a short time with his brother I. K. Boyesen in Chicago; was admitted to the bar in Minneapolis, Minn., where he also had studied in private offices, in 1880; practiced his profession in Fargo, N. D., for seven years; moved to St. Paul in 1887; in 1890 entered into partnership with M. D. Munn and N. M. Thygeson; and formed a partnership with P. J. McLaughlin in 1897. Few law firms in St. Paul have a larger practice than the one of which Boyesen is a member, and Boyesen himself had an extensive practice in North Dakota, and is now recognized as one of the leading Scandinavian attorneys in the Northwest. In 1883 he was married to Florence Knapp, a daughter of Frederick M. Knapp, of Racine, Wis.

Brandt, Christian, journalist—St. Paul—born 28 Jan., 1853, in Vestre Slidre, Valders, Norway. His ancestors came from Germany to Denmark, and moved from there to Norway at the fall of the Struense and Brandt's administration. He received a college and military education in Kristiania, was appointed second lieutenant in the army at the age of twenty-one, went to Germany the following year to study civil engineering at the polytechnic school in Aachen, and emigrated to the United States in 1876. His intention was to engage in civil engineering, but failing to find employment, he became for two years city editor of *Daglig Skandinaven* in Chicago; was assistant editor of *Faedrelandet og Emigranten,* La Crosse, Wis., for a couple of years; bought *Red River Posten,* which was published in Fargo, N. D., but sold it the following year; became editor-in-chief of *Nordvesten* in 1881, and later publisher. From 1887–89 he was inspector general of the National Guard of Minnesota, with the rank of brigadier-general. In 1890 he was appointed deputy collector of internal revenue; started the Norwegian newspaper, *Heimdal,* the following year, but sold it in 1893. He was for two years assistant editor of *Minneapolis Tidende,* and returned in the spring of 1897 to *Nordvesten,* of which paper he at present is editor-in-chief. During the war with Spain Brandt organized a Scandinavian regiment, of which he was elected colonel, but it was not called into service. He was the first to advocate the election of two Scandinavians to state offices, which resulted in the election of Col. H. Mattson as secretary of state and A. E. Rice as lieutenant-governor, in 1886. In 1878 he was married to Bessie Sörenson, of Chicago; they have children.

Breda, O. J., educator—Minneapolis—born 29 Apr., 1853, in Horten, Norway. He received a classical education; graduated from the University of Norway; proceeded to this country in 1873; graduated from Concordia Theological Seminary, of St. Louis, in 1875; accepted a call to St. Paul, but soon embraced the opportunity offered him to fill a professor's chair in Luther College. Before entering upon his new duties, however, he returned to Noway, where for two years he busied himself with philological studies, and from 1879 to 1882 did very creditable work as professor of Latin and Norwegian in Luther College. After another year's study in Norway he received a call to the professorship of Scandinavian languages just then established in the University of Minnesota. A leave of absence of one year was improved in further fitting himself for his new duties, which he assumed in the fall of 1884. The chair of Scandinavian languages, or "Scandinavian language," as the intelligent lawmakers had styled the study thus first raised to the dignity of a professorship in Minnesota, for some time called for but little attention, and Breda assisted regularly at teaching Latin, his ability and learning being generally acknowledged.   In 1899 he resigned and returned to his native land. He was married in 1886 in Horten, Norway, to Emilie Braarud. They have no children.

Brohough, G. O., educator—Red Wing—born in Eidsvold, Norway. He came to Red Wing in his early boyhood, where he attended the city public schools. At an early age he entered the State Normal School at River Falls, Wis. After graduating from this institution he taught several terms in the public schools. Not finding his thirst for knowledge satisfied, he entered the state university at Minneapolis, graduating with the class of 1889. Since then he took a course in the law department of his alma mater, receiving the degree of LL. B. in 1892. During his senior year he received a prize offered by the American Institute of Civics for the best thesis on economics. For several years he has been professor at the Red Wing Seminary. Brohough was superintendent of the public schools of Red Wing for some time. His brother, Chr. O. Brohough, came to America in 1869, and has since been pastor of Hauge's Synod congregations in Red Wing, Chicago, and the Twin Cities. He has published several books, among which may be mentioned: *Vaegteren, Sangbog for Söndagsskolen, Elling Eielsens Liv og Virksomhed, Guitar Laere,* etc.

Brown, Fred P., secretary of state—Blue Earth City—

born 12 Aug., 1838, in Kobbervig, Kristiansand stift, Norway. His grand-father was Bishop Nordahl Brun. At the age of nine Brown went to sea as a cabin boy, and for nine years led the hard and hazardous life of a sailor. In 1854 he emigrated to America, settling in Dane county, Wis. In 1862 he moved to Rochester, Minn., and located at Blue Earth City, his present home, in the year following. Brown was register of deeds of Faribault county for eighteen years. In 1890 he was elected secretary of state on the Republican ticket, and re-elected two years later. He is married, and has several children.

Brusletten, C. L., legislator—Kenyon—born 2 Sept., 1853, in Hallingdal, Norway. He came to America with his parents in 1858, settling in the neighborhood of his present home. He attended the district school in winter and worked on the farm in summer. In 1879 he graduated from the Northwestern Business College at Madison, Wis., and since that time has been engaged in the mercantile business. Brusletten was postmaster at Kenyon for eight years and held many of the most important offices of his township and village. The farmers' elevator at Kenyon was built largely through his efforts, and he has served as treasurer of this and as vice-president of the Citizen's State Bank of Kenyon, since those institutions were established. He also owns a large and valuable farm in Kenyon, and has farms in other places in the Northwest. He was elected to a seat in the lower branch of the state legislature in 1896, and re-elected to the same position in 1898. His legislative record was creditable.

Cappelen, F. W., engineer—Minneapolis—born 31 Oct.,

1857, in Drammen, Norway. He received his early education in Fredrikstad, and came out at the head of his class.
Having completed a course and graduated at a technical
school in Örebro, Sweden, he continued his studies at the
polytechnic institute in Dresden, Germany, and was the
first Norwegian who distinguished himself at a final
examination in that institution. In 1880 he emigrated to
America; was appointed assistant engineer on the Northern
Pacific R. R., in Montana, and bridge engineer on the same
road in 1883. At the latter date he removed to Minneapolis, and from 1886 to 1892 served as bridge engineer of
the city of Minneapolis. By this time he was generally
admitted to rank among the leading engineers of the Northwest, and he was appointed city engineer, which position
he held for half a dozen years. The most noteworthy monu_
ments to his engineering skill are the Northern Pacific
railroad bridge near the state university of Minnesota and
the reservoirs of the public waterworks of Minneapolis.
His wife is of German birth; they have several sons.

   Carlsen, L. A. K., clergyman—Brandon—born 6 Nov.,
1842, in Trondhjem, Norway. His father was pastor in the
state church of Norway. Young Carlsen was educated in
his native city and at the University of Norway; accepted a
call from a couple of Norwegian Synod congregations in
Douglas and Grant counties, Minn., in 1872; was called to
San Francisco, Cal., in 1877, and to Sydney, Melbourne,
and other places in Australia, in 1879; returned to Douglas
county in 1887; made another trip to Australia, visiting the
Hawaii Islands and New Zealand, in 1890; and was again
called to take charge of the missionary work among the

PROF. J. S. CARLSON, MINNEAPOLIS.

H. J. GJERTSEN, MINNEAPOLIS.

Norwegians in those distant colonies, but for some time has been located at Great Falls, Montana. Carlsen is considered to be one of the greatest missionaries in the Norwegian Synod.

Carlson, Johan S., educator—Minneapolis—born 8 Nov., 1857, in Frödinge, Småland, Sweden. He came with his parents to the United States when he was quite young, and was brought up on the farm. After having attended Gustavus Adolphus College, St. Peter, Minn., for a couple of years, he graduated from Augustana College, Rock Island, Ill., in 1885; then studied for two years at the University of Upsala, Sweden, and completed the course for candidate of philosophy at that institution in 1887. The same year he accepted a call to Gustavus Adolphus college as assistant professor of English and mathematics; was elected professor of history and philosophy of that institution the following year, which position he occupied for ten years, and in which capacity he made an excellent record. Augustana College conferred the degree of Master of Arts upon Carlson in 1889, and in 1894 he again went to Sweden and completed the course for doctor of philosophy, which degree was conferred upon him by the famous University of Upsala in 1895, his thesis being *Om Filosofien i Amerika*. He was elected editor-in-chief of *Minnesota Stats Tidning,* the semi-official organ of the Swedish Lutheran Minnesota Conference, in 1898, and the next year he was called to the State University as professor of Scandinavian languages and literatures. Carlson is a member of the American Academy of Political and Social Science as well as of the American Statistical Association. He

26

was Republican presidential elector in 1892, has stumped the state for his party, is considered to be one of the best Swedish public speakers in the land, writes able editorial articles, and is a prominent member of the Swedish Lutheran church, having for years been one of the leading lay-delegates at the annual meetings of said organization. In 1890 he was married to Maria M. Anderson, of Carver, Minn. They have four children.

Christensen, Ferdinand Sneedorff, vice-consul for Denmark and banker—Rush City—born 18 April, 1837, in Copenhagen, Denmark; died 1896. He received a college education in his native country, wrote some poems in his younger days, and participated in the Danish war with Germany in 1864. Christensen came to the U. S. in 1866, stopped in Chicago for two years, then moved to Rochester, Minn. Here he commenced the publication of *Nordisk Folkeblad,* which was one of the first Danish-Norwegian newspapers in Minnesota, and Christensen was the first Scandinavian in the state who commenced to agitate the election of a Scandinavian state official, which resulted in the nomination and election of Col. Hans Mattson as secretary of state in 1869. Christensen became land agent for the St. Paul and Duluth Railroad company, and moved to Rush City in 1870. In 1882 he started the Bank of Rush City. He was assistant secretary of state from 1880–82, was appointed vice-consul for Denmark in 1883, represented his district in the state legislature in 1878, and held various local offices. Christensen, who for years was the most prominent Dane in Minnesota, had, on his arrival in this country, to endure the usual hardships common to all immi-

grants, and for some time he earned his bread by blacking
stoves for a hardware store in Chicago.   In 1869 he was
married to Zelma A. Willard, who survives him.

Clausen, Claus Lauritz, clergyman and pioneer—Austin
—born 3 Nov., 1820, on the island of Aerö, Fyen stift, Denmark; died in Paulsbo, Wash., 1892.   His father, who kept
a country store, intended to let his son study law.   And
young Clausen at the age of fifteen, after he had received a
good common school education and some instruction in the
German language, commenced to study law in the office of
one of the officials, where he remained for three years.   But
the legal principles soon tired Clausen; and, being very religious, he decided to become a missionary of the Gospel.   For
two years he studied theology under private instruction,
but, being poor, he was compelled to seek employment as a
tutor.   In 1841 he visited Norway, and soon decided to go
to Zululand, South Africa, to preach for the natives.   But
the reputation of his missionary zeal had been circulated to
the Norwegian settlement at Muskego, Racine county, Wis.
These people felt the need of a preacher and a teacher, especially were they anxious to have their young children
instructed in the religion and language of their fathers.
They called Clausen.   He accepted.   And, after having
returned to Denmark and married there, he, in company
with his bride, arrived at Muskego, Wis., in 1843.   Shortly
after his arrival he was examined by a couple of German
Lutheran ministers, was ordained Oct. 18, and organized
what is generally supposed to be the first Scandinavian
Lutheran church in America, since the Swedish settlement at
Delaware River in the seventeenth century.   This, however,

is a mistake. For three or four years previously to Clausen's arrival, Elling Eielsen had built a log meeting house at Fox River, Ill. This may be called the first Norwegian church building and church organization in the U. S., and Eielsen was ordained by a Lutheran minister fifteen days before Clausen. On the other hand it must be admitted that Eielsen was not friendly towards any attempts to effect solid church organizations, and seems to have ridiculed ordained clergymen both before and after his own ordination. He certainly had not the educational qualifications which a Lutheran pastor is supposed to possess, and virtually remained during his whole life an itinerant lay-preacher. In 1844 Rev. J. W. C. Dietrichson arrived at Muskego from Norway; he was a disciple of Bishop Grundtvig and succeeded, at least for a while, in convincing Clausen to his views. But Dietrichson's Grundtvigianism terrified Eielsen and the friends of Hauge. In 1851 A. C. Preus, H. C. Stub, and C. L. Clausen met at Rock Prairie, Wis.,—Dietrichson being in Europe at the time—and organized the Norwegian Synod. Clausen was elected president of the synod. The constitution of this organization, which it was claimed contained too much leaven of Grundvigianism, was revoked the following year; Clausen objected to the change and desired the leaven to remain. But in later years Clausen changed his views on this subject. When *Emigranten*, which was one of the first Norwegian newspapers in this country, was started in 1851, Clausen became its editor, remaining in that position, however, only a short time, as his ill-health compelled him to go farther West. For several years after his arrival to this country, his lungs had been in a bad condition. To restore his health he, in 1852, withdrew from the regular ministry, went to Iowa, and located at St. Ansgar, Mitchell county, where soon a prosperous Norwegian settlement sprang up. For a number of years Clausen was engaged in farming and business ventures of various kinds, as well as in politics. Having regained his health and again entered the ministry, he, in June, 1861, attended the annual meeting of the Norwegian Synod, held at Rock Prairie, Wis., and upon application was admitted to membership. At this meeting, a declaration from the ministers in regard to slavery having been called for, the following resolution, agreed to by all the ministers, Clausen included, was offered: "Although, according to the Word of God, it is not a sin *per se* to hold slaves; yet slavery is *per se* an evil and a punishment from God, and we condemn all the abuses and sins connected with it, and, when our ministerial duties demand it, and when Christian love and wisdom require it, we will work for its abolition." This resolution on "slavery *per se*" (in itself) was afterwards supplemented by two other statements, both well known, to-wit: "No Christian can be a pro-slavery man," and " 'American slavery', or slavery as constituted by American laws and customs, was *per se* sinful and abominable." Clausen, however, soon publicly withdrew his consent from the resolution of 1861, and declared that slavery is a sin *per se,* that is in every case and under all circumstances; but, being the only one that did so, and dissenting on other important questions, he decided to leave the synod in 1868, asserting that the majority of its ministers were too narrow-minded. No other of the many Norwegian-American church

disputes has been so thoroughly debated and generally mis-
understood as has the slavery question. The Norwegian
Synod has never to this day receded from the position it
took in 1861; but the majority of the Norwegian lay-people,
practically all of whom were strong sympathizers with the
Northern cause, have always failed to comprehend the real
attitude of the synod on this topic. Consequently Clausen
had the popular side of the argument, as he denounced,
principally, the evils of the American slavery, while the
leaders of the synod maintained and tried to prove from the
New Testament that the condition of servitude is not sinful
per se. In regard to the attitude of Clausen and the Norwegian Synod on the slavery question a great deal can be
learnt by reading Clausen's book, *Gjenmäle,* and *Historisk
Fremstilling* by the synod church council. The former
work, especially, is a master production. At the outbreak
of the Civil War Clausen enlisted in the Fifteenth Wisconsin
Regiment—better known as the Scandinavian Regiment—
under the brave Col. H. C. Heg; was appointed chaplain,
but his poor health compelled him to resign in 1862. In
1870 he became one of the organizers of the Norwegian-
Danish Evangelical Lutheran Conference, and was its president for the first two years, then he resigned. In 1856–57
he represented his district in the legislature of Iowa; took a
trip to Norway in 1867, being at the same time appointed
by the governor of Iowa as commissioner of the state to
the exposition in Paris, France. After having resided in
Iowa for nineteen years, he moved to Virginia, then to
Philadelphia, where he preached for one year; accepted a
call to Austin, Minn., 1878; spent the last few years of his

eventful life with his son at Paulsbo, Wash., where he died. He is buried at Austin. Jensson, in *American Lutheran Biographies,* says of Clausen: "Since his arrival at Muskego, in 1843, Rev. Clausen's name is woven into the principal events of the history of the Norwegian Lutherans of this country, down to recent years. Zealously and faithfully he administered to the spiritual wants of the pioneers, travelling continually between the small and scattering settlements throughout the Northwest." He was married to Martha F. Rasmussen, of Langeland, Denmark, in 1842, by whom he had one son. She died in 1846; since he married Mrs. Birgitte I. Pedersen. One of his sons is practicing law at Austin, and is one of the leading lay-members of the United Norwegian Church.

Clausen, Peter, artist—Minneapolis—born 1830, in Denmark. 'At an early age he evinced marked artistic ability, and at the age of thirteen years was apprenticed to a fresco painter and decorator, at the same time studying drawing at Ringsted. After serving his time he went to Copenhagen, studying two years at the Royal Art Academy, receiving a diploma for excellence in ornamentation, model figure drawing, and oil painting. While decorating the Royal Palace in Stockholm, Sweden, he attended the Royal Academy of Arts in that city, receiving a diploma from the Antique school. He afterwards devoted several years to scene painting, finally coming to the United States in 1866. Shortly after his arrival here his services were secured to decorate the First Universalist Church in Minneapolis, Minn., and many churches, public buildings, and private edifices in that city bear evidences of his skill.

Every summer Clausen devotes a portion of his time to
studying natural scenery. Among his studies from nature
the most remarkable is the picture of St. Anthony falls,
including both sides of the island, painted in 1869. His
large paintings of the Yellowstone Park and the Great
Northwest have placed him high in the rank of scenic artists
in this country. He is an active member of Dania Society,
and of some secret organizations.'

Colberg, A. P. J., journalist—St. Paul—born 19 Aug.,
1854, in Bitterna, Vestergötland, Sweden. At the age of
sixteen he came with a brother and a sister to this country;
they settled in Carver county, Minn., where he for a while
worked as a common laborer, and later, after having entered
college, taught and preached during vacations. Colberg
attended Gustavus Adolphus College, St. Peter, Minn., for
two years, and studied at Augustana College, Rock Island,
Ill., for four years. In 1886 he became associate editor and
business manager of what is now called *Minnesota Stats
Tidning*, the oldest Swedish newspaper in Minnesota,
having been established in 1877; it has always been the
organ of the Swedish Lutheran Conference of Minnesota,
but is owned by private individuals; since Colberg became
manager its circulation has been doubled and is now about
15,000. Colberg is a prominent member of the Swedish
Lutheran church, and has held several important offices in
the same. In 1886 he was married to Anna E. Nelson, of
Nicollet county, a daughter of Andrew Nelson, who is one
of the wealthiest Swedish farmers in the country; they have
several children.

Darelius, August B., lawyer and legislator—Minneapolis

DR. J. G. SKARO, MINNEAPOLIS.

REV. M. F. GJERTSEN, MINNEAPOLIS.　　REV. J. C. JENSSON, AUSTIN.

REV. J. J. KILDSIG, ALBERT LEA.　PROF. T. S. REIMESTAD, MINNEAPOLIS.

—born 3 July, 1859, in Skölvened, Vestergötland, Sweden. He came to the United States in 1873, "to acquire freedom of action, liberty of thought, and independence in life." At first he worked on farms, then clerked in stores, kept books, was interested in a grocery business for two years, graduated from the law department of the University of Michigan in 1889, and was elected to the state legislature of Minnesota in 1890. In the house of representatives he was the author of the bill which repealed the obnoxious struck jury law, and secured the passage of the same. Darelius has resided in Minneapolis since 1876. He is a Democrat, and was nominated by his party for judge of probate in 1898, but was defeated with the rest of the ticket. He is one of the trustees and secretary of the Swedish hospital, and has a very large practice. In 1894 he was married to Tillie Anderson of Minneapolis.

Eggen, J. Mueller, clergyman and author—Lyle—born 20 Apr., 1841, near Trondhjem, Norway. He clerked in Trondhjem for his uncle for some time, at the same time taking private instruction with the view of entering the University of Norway, where he, after having spent a couple of years in Tromsö, attended lectures for two years. Afterwards he taught languages in Bergen for a short time, prepared himself for the stage, and appeared in a number of theatrical performances. He studied at a seminary for one year; established a high school in Tryssil, of which he was principal for several years. In 1865 he accepted a call to take charge of a Norwegian high school in this country, but after his arrival he changed his mind and entered the theological department of Augustana College, Paxton,

Ill., graduating the following year. Eggen preached at Racine and vicinity, Wis., for about five years; had charge of a congregation at Luther Valley, Wis., from 1871-82; and has ever since been pastor in Mower county, Minn. He belonged to the Scandinavian Augustana Synod, of which he was secretary for some time, until the Conference was organized in 1870, when he joined that body, which became part of the United Norwegian Lutheran Church in 1890. For nine years he was secretary of the Conference, served as vice-president for two years, and was elected president in 1886, but on account of ill health declined to accept the position. He was one of the organizers of the United Church, and became its missionary secretary, a position he had also occupied in the Conference. Eggen has written considerably for the Norwegian-American press, as well as several books. He uses a flowery language, but there is not much depth to his literary productions. In 1858 he was married to Henrietta Rossow; they have several children.

Engstrom, Augustus Ericson, educator—Cannon Falls —born 22 March, 1851, in Vestergötland, Sweden. His ancestors on his father's side came from Germany to Sweden at the time of Gustavus Adolphus. At the age of eighteen young Engstrom emigrated to this country; worked his own way through Carleton College, Northfield, Minn., from which institution he graduated in 1878, and of which he has been one of the trustees since 1890. Ever since his graduation he has been principal of the high school at Cannon Falls; was elected superintendent of schools of Goodhue county in 1882, and has been re-elected ever since without opposition; was elected president of the state association of county superintendents in 1889; was elected president of the Minnesota state teachers' reading circle in 1892, at the same time being appointed chairman of the state committee on common school exhibits at the World's Columbian Exposition. He ranks as one of the ablest school superintendent in the state. In 1880 Engstrom was married to Mary A. Conley, of Burlington, Iowa; they have several children.

Falstrom, Jacob, pioneer—Afton—born 25 July, 1793 or 1795, in Stockholm, Sweden; died 1859. His father is said to have been a wealthy merchant, but the young man left home at the age of twelve or fourteen years and sailed with his uncle. Of the six or seven different authorities which have been consulted in regard to Falstrom, there are not two that agree. Some maintain that he lost his way in London, England, and, being unable to find his uncle's ship, took passage for North America; others again assert that his uncle was cruel to him, and that he, on that account, ran away, intending to return to Sweden, but instead was landed in Canada, where he soon became acquainted with the Indians, whose habits and modes of life he adopted. He seems to have arrived in Minnesota, at least, before 1819, being employed by the American fur company to trade with the Indians around Lake Superior. He spoke French and several Indian languages, married an Indian woman, by whom he had several children, some of whom now live in Washington county, Minn., and in nearly every respect lived and acted as the aborigines. In later years he became very religious, and for a long time acted as a kind of Methodist missionary among the Indians. He took a claim in Washington county in 1837. Falstrom was unquestionably the first Scandinavian in Minnesota, but unlike his contemporary Northman, Borup, he exercised no influence upon the affairs of the state. The former simply degenerated into savagery, while the latter rose above his surroundings.

Felland, Ole G., educator—Northfield—born 10 Oct., 1853, in Koshkonong, Dane county, Wis. His parents came from Telemarken, Norway, in 1846, and settled on the farm where he was born. Young Felland graduated from Luther College in 1874, being one of the first who received the degree of B. A. of this institution. Afterwards he studied, for two years, the classical and German languages at the Northwestern University, Watertown, Wis., and received the degree of A. M. of this institution in 1892; and becoming interested in theology he commenced to study this branch of knowledge at Concordia Seminary, St. Louis, Mo., completing his course there in 1879. Then he had charge of the Norwegian Lutheran churches at Kasson and Rochester, Minn., for a couple of years, and became a teacher in St. Olaf College in 1881. Felland has taught English, Norwegian, German, Latin, Greek, Hebrew, history, and botany. At the time of the controversy on predestination, in 1880, he sided with the Anti-Missourians and joined the United Church in 1890. In 1888 Felland visited England, France, Germany, Denmark, and Norway. He was married in 1883 to Thea Johanna Midboe, of Vernon, Minn.; they have several children.

Fjelde, Jacob, sculptor—Minneapolis—born 10 April, 1859, in Aalesund, Norway; died 1896. One of his ancestors married, in 1750, a daughter of a French Huguenot family; his father was a wood carver, and Fjelde worked at this trade until he was eighteen years of age. He studied sculpture with Bergslien, in Kristiania, for about a year and a half; studied nearly three years at the Royal Academy, Copenhagen, Denmark, and spent two years in Rome, studying the classical masterpieces. Before emigrating to this country in 1887, he produced *The Boy and the Cats, Spring,* and other figures, besides a bust of Henrik Ibsen, etc.— all of which received favorable comments of the Scandinavian and the Roman press, and of art critics. Most of his early productions are preserved in the museums of Bergen and Kristiania. Fjelde, during his residence in Minneapolis, made busts, both in marble and in bronze, of some of the best known Scandinavians and Americans in the country, and such works as his statues, *The Reading Woman,* in the Minneapolis Public Library, and the *Gettysburg Monument*—both in bronze—have gained a national reputation. Fjelde's works have received high commendation of the critics and of the public, and the *Ole Bull* statue, in the main park of Minneapolis, is undoubtedly his greatest work. In 1888 he was married to Margarita Madsen, of Copenhagen, Denmark.

Fliesburg, Oscar Alf., physician and poet — Minneapolis—born 5 April, 1851, in Småland, Sweden. His grandfather was a German who settled in Sweden in the eighteenth century; his father was an officer in the Swedish navy. Fliesburg studied a few years at a college in Kalmar; graduated as a pharmacist in 1869; followed his profession for a few years in Stockholm, Gothenburg, and other places in

Sweden; visited most of the European countries, as well as parts of Africa and South America; arrived in the United States in 1874; has clerked in drug stores in New York, Baltimore, Chicago, St. Louis, and in different places in Minnesota, besides having traveled through nearly every state in the Union. Fliesburg studied medicine at spare times for several years, passed his medical examination before the Minnesota state medical board in 1883, and graduated from the College of Physicians and Surgeons, Chicago, in 1885; practiced his profession in Hudson, Wis., for three years, then resided in St. Paul for several years, and settled in Minneapolis in 1894. Here he took an active part in the establishment of the Swedish hospital in 1898, and has built up a large practice. Fliesburg devotes part of his time to literary pursuits, having published several poems in *Svenska Folkets Tidning, Valkyrian*, and *Svea,* etc., besides writing on medical questions for American journals. In 1893 he, in connection with Lewis P. Johnson, published in the English language *Cristoforo Colon,* a lengthy epic poem dealing with the discovery of America by Columbus; and in 1899 he issued *Vildrosor och Tistlar,* a large volume of over 300 pages, which is a collection of the author's poems, much of which had previously appeared in some Swedish newspapers. If the critics are to be relied upon, Fliesburg is a poetical genius, whose fault in poesy is said, by some of his critics, to consist in ignoring strict poetical rules and not adhering strictly to the severe grammatical construction of the Swedish language, permitting himself more freedom than is usually allowed. Consequently, his productions have been highly praised and severely criticised.

It is generally admitted, however, that his conceptions are sublime, perhaps too much so to be properly understood. In 1879 he was married to Mina Birgitta Opsahl, of Chicago; she died in 1880, and in 1889 he was married to Brita Sundkvist, of St. Paul.

Fosmark, O. N., clergyman—Fergus Falls—born 17 Nov., 1853, in Columbia county, Wis. His parents came from Norway to the United States in 1845. He graduated from Luther College in 1875, and completed his theological studies at Concordia Seminary three years later; and has ever since been pastor of a church belonging to the Norwegian Synod in Furgus Falls, and is also president of Park Region Luther College. In 1879 Fosmark was married to Sarah Norman, of Otter Tail county, Minn. They have several children.

Fosnes, C. A., lawyer and legislator—Montevideo—born 2 July, 1862, in Gloppen, Bergen stift, Norway. At the age of four he came with his parents to this country; they settled in Winona county, Minn., but moved to Faribault county two years later. Fosnes received a common school education, attended the state normal school at Winona for two years, and studied law in a private office in Winona. Since 1884 he has practiced his profession in Montevideo, and was the Prohibition candidate for Congress in 1888. He has been a member of the school board in his district, and city attorney and mayor. In 1897 and 1899 he served in the state legislature, having been elected on the Fusion ticket, although he is independent in politics. Fosnes made an excellent record as a legislator, and was especially successful in defeating several pernicious bills. If his party had been in the majority instead of in the minority some of the highly deserving measures which he tried to pass would undoubtedly have been enacted. He is a Freemason and a member of the I. O. O. F., and was married to Sarah Arneson, of Montevideo, in 1883. They have children.

Foss, H. A., journalist and author—Minneapolis—born 25 Nov., 1851, in Modum, Norway. He enjoyed a common school and commercial education; came to America in 1877; worked on farms in Minnesota and wrote some for Norwegian newspapers; settled at Portland, N. D., where he was postmaster in 1885–87; published and edited *Normanden* at Grand Forks, N. D., in 1887–92; removed to Minneapolis in 1893; and has since spent his time in editing a weekly, *Nye Normanden*, owned partly by himself. Foss was a Prohibitionist in the eighties and took active part in the anti-saloon campaign in North Dakota; but for the past ten years he has been a radical Populist, his campaign editorials being choice samples of the so-called "calamity howling" of the reform press of the early nineties. In 1892 he was candidate for congress on the People's party ticket in North Dakota. Foss has written several books, some of which are very popular, and five of them have been re-published in Norway. He was married to Inga O. Fjeld in 1886; they have several children.

Foss, Louis O., legislator—Wendell—born 1854, in Portage, Wis. His parents were Norwegians, and he received a common school education at Portage; removed to Minnesota in 1879; has been engaged in farming since that date in Grant county; was justice of the peace for

DR. O. A. FLIESBURG, MINNEAPOLIS.

DR. OLOF SOHLBERG, ST. PAUL.

COL. HANS MATTSON, MINNEAPOLIS.

A. SODERSTROM, MINNEAPOLIS.

twelve years, town clerk for ten years, and judge of probate for eight years; has been a member of the lower branch of the legislature since 1894, being elected on the Republican ticket. In the legislature of 1899 he was looked upon as one of the most combative members of his house. He is the head of a family.

Fremling, John, clergyman—Vasa—born 21 June, 1842, in Främmestad, Vestergötland, Sweden. After having received a high school education in Skara, Fremling for two years attended the Lyceum in Upsala, and had decided to become a minister of the Gospel in his native country; but in 1870 Prof. Hasselquist, who had just returned to Sweden for the purpose of securing young men to enter the Swedish-American ministry, induced him to emigrate to the United States. Before he was ordained, however, he studied one year at Augustana College, Paxton, Ill. From 1871-82 Fremling had charge of the Swedish Lutheran church in Sabylund, Wis.; was pastor in Welch, Minn., for five years, and at Fish Lake for two; and came to Vasa in 1889. He was president of the Minnesota Conference in 1883-87 and has held the same position since 1897. When Fremling was thirty years of age he was married to Emelia A. Edholm, a sister of A. E. Edholm, of Stillwater. They have one child.

Frich, Johannes Bjerch, educator and clergyman—Hamline—born 15 July, 1835, in Nannestad, Romerike, Norway. He is the son of G. J. Frich, pastor in the state church of Norway. After having finished his Latin school course at Kristiania, he entered the University of Norway and was graduated as theol. cand. in 1861. The following year Frich

27

was ordained minister, and in the summer of the same year emigrated to America to take charge of twelve congregations belonging to the Norwegian Synod, and located in La Crosse, Trempealeau, and Jackson counties in Wisconsin; served as minister for twenty-six years; was for a number of yea's secretary of the synod; became president of the Eastern District in 1876, which position he held till 1888. He was then called as professor of theology at Luther Seminary, of which institution he is now president. In 1894-9 he was vice-president of the Norwegian Synod. Frich was married to Caroline Nilsen in 1862. They have several children.

Gausta, Herbjorn N., artist—Minneapolis—born 1854, in Telemarken, Norway. He came with his parents to the U. S. in 1867; attended Luther College for three years; then went to Europe, and for seven years studied painting in Kristiania, Norway, and Munich, Germany; returned to America in 1882; lived in Chicago, Madison, La Crosse, and Decorah, until 1887, when he went to Italy, Germany, and his native country. Gausta has resided in Minneapolis since 1889 and has made portrait paintings of some of the best known people in the United States. Prof. Breda said of him: "He does not know how to advertise or put himself forward; but he is one of the best Scandinavian artists in this country; his landscapes are beautiful, original, and natural." *The Literary Northwest* for January, 1893, in speaking about Minneapolis artists, refers to Gausta as follows: "He is an admirable figure painter and also strong in landscape."

Gjertsen, Henry J., lawyer—Minneapolis—born 8 Oct., 1861, near Tromsö, Norway. Gjertsen came to this country when six years of age, living with his parents on their farm at Lake Amelia, Minn., and attending the common school during the winter months until he was fifteen. When seventeen he requested his parents to permit him to go to college, and his father finally consented to let him go to the Red Wing Seminary, where he completed the six years' course in the collegiate department. In the last year of his college course he determined to enter the legal profession, and already began the study of law privately before leaving the seminary. He continued the study of law and was admitted to the bar at the age of twenty-three. While studying law Gjertsen was employed in a number of small cases, one of which as a test case was appealed by his opponent to the supreme court, Gjertsen thus receiving the distinction of being acknowledged attorney of record in the supreme court before he was admitted to the bar. Since his admission to practice Gjertsen has conducted a general law business in Minneapolis, where he has built up a wide-spread and lucrative practice, having also successively conducted a number of important cases before the higher courts. He has, within the last few years, with ability conducted cases against railroad companies and other corporations before the United States courts. He has also been admitted to practice before the United States Supreme Court at Washington. He has several times been a delegate to state conventions, served as a member of different Republican county committees, and was appointed a member of the charter commission of Minneapolis in 1897. For many years he has edited the legal departments of *Skandinaven*, *Minneapolis Daglig Tidende*, and *Svenska Ameri-*

kanska Posten. In 1897 he published a hand book of
American law in Norwegian and Swedish, which received
much praise by the press and the critics.   In 1899 Gov.
Lind appointed him inspector general of the state militia,
with the rank of brigadier general.   At the age of twenty-
one Gjertsen was married to Gretchen Goebel, a German
lady.   They have one child.

Gjertsen, Melchior Falk, clergyman—Minneapolis—born
19 Feb., 1847, in Amle, Bergen stift, Norway.   Gjertsen
had passed several classes in the Latin school at Bergen
when he emigrated with his parents to America in 1864.
Shortly after their arrival the family came west, and young
Gjertsen found employment in Milwaukee.   It was his desire
to enter the commercial life, but a severe illness made him
change his plans, and, according to his father's wishes, he
began to study for the ministry.   He entered the Augustana
College and Seminary at Paxton, Ill., from which institution he graduated in 1868.   The same year Gjertsen was
ordained minister of the Gospel and took charge of the congregation at Leland, Ill., where he remained for four years.
He then moved to Stoughton, Wis., where he was pastor for
nine years.   He has since resided in Minneapolis, where he is
minister of a church now belonging to the Norwegian Free
Church.   In 1870 Gjertsen was a delegate to the meeting
which organized the Norwegian-Danish Conference, to
which organization he belonged till the establishment of the
United Church, and in 1873 he was sent as a delegate to the
general meeting of the Norwegian missionary society held
in Drammen, Norway.   He published a volume of songs
called *Hjemlandssange.*   Gjertsen is a very active worker

in the field of education, of temperance, of charity, etc. He was one of the organizers of the Associated Charities of Minneapolis, as well as of the first stable temperance society among the Norwegians in Minneapolis, the Norwegian Y. M. C. A., and deaconess' home. In 1889 he was elected member of the Minneapolis board of education, of which body he was secretary and president. Gjertsen did some excellent work while serving on the board. In 1869 he was married to Sarah Mosey; they have several children.

Grinager, Mons, soldier—Minneapolis—born 7 Oct., 1832, in Hadeland, Harmar stift, Norway; died 1889. His father was a well-to-do farmer, who gave his son a fair education. At the age of twenty-one he came to this country, directly to St. Paul, but moved to Decorah the following year, where he was in the mercantile business for three years. In 1857 he took a claim in Freeborn county, Minn., and at the outbreak of the Civil War enlisted in the Fifteenth Wisconsin Regiment, better known as the Scandinavian Regiment, in which he became captain. At the battle of Stone River he was severely wounded and had to retire from the army for a while. After the close of the war he returned to his farm; held various local offices; was revenue assessor for some time of the first district of Minnesota, which included twenty-nine counties; was register of the U. S. land office in Worthington from 1874-82; settled in Minneapolis in 1886, where he was vice-president of Scandia Bank; owned also several farms in Freeborn county, and had commercial relations in Dakota. Grinager was the Republican nominee for state treasurer in 1873, defeated;

was one of the presidential electors in 1888, and served as vice-president for Minnesota of the Republican national league for a few years. His son Alex Grinager is quite a noted artist.

Grindeland, Andrew, lawyer and state senator—Warren—born 20 Nov., 1856, in Winnesheik county, Iowa. His parents were from Voss, Norway. He received an academic education in Decorah, Iowa; taught in the public schools of Iowa and in Dodge county, Minn., for a while; graduated from the law department of the University of Iowa in 1882, and has ever since practiced his profession in Warren. Here he has been a member of the city council, judge of the probate court, chairman of the school board, and has held various other offices; was one of the founders of the Grand Forks College; assisted in organizing the State Bank of Warren, of which he is one of the directors. Grindeland has taken an active part in every political campaign ever since Knute Nelson ran for Congress; he is a Republican and a member of the Norwegian Synod. For four years he was a member of the State Normal school board, and was elected to the state senate in 1898, being one of the most active men of the session in 1899. In 1882 he was married to Ingrid Frode, of Winnesheik county, Iowa; they have several children.

Gronberger, Robert, humorist and writer—Forest Lake —born 2 Oct., 1840, in Kalmar, Sweden. He received a college education in his native city. In 1869 he emigrated to the U. S.; lived in Wisconsin for three years; then moved to St. Paul, and remained there until 1877, when he settled at Forest Lake. Gronberger is a Democrat and has been assessor of the town for twenty years. He is not married, and seems to stick to his bachelorship with a certain degree of stubbornness; no wonder he claims to have had "plenty of adversities, but of successes, none, so far." It is not, however, as a politician or as an unsuccessful lover that Gronberger has become noted, but as a humorous writer. Everyone who knows anything about the Swedish-American literature, knows also *Myself*—that is Gronberger. For under this nom de plume he has for many years contributed a large number of correspondences and humorous sketches to *Minnesota Stats Tidning*, *Svenska Amerikanaren*, *Svenska Folkets Tidning*, and other Swedish papers. Besides, he is the author of three Swedish books, *Svenskarne i St. Croixdalen, Minn.*, and *Minnesotas Historia* and *Kalle Fröjdelin*—the latter is a novel, written in a natural and agreeable vein of humor. Gronberger has devoted much time to the study of Swedish-American history. *Svenskarne i St. Croixdalen, Minnesota,* is the best and most correct history of the Swedes in that part of the country that has yet been published. In it he describes the first Swedish settlement in Minnesota with more exactness than any other author.

Guttersen, G., legislator—Lake Crystal—born 13 May, 1859, in Grover, Winona county, Minn. His father came from Telemarken; his mother from Stavanger, Norway. Guttersen received a common school education, and completed a course at the Mankato normal school in 1884. He taught school about four years; was engaged in farming until 1895; and after that date was manager of a corporation, running a store and creamery at Butternut. Guttersen has held a number of minor positions of trust in his locality, including that of postmaster.   In 1889 he was elected engrossing clerk of the house of representatives of the state legislature, and in 1892 and 1894 was elected to a seat in the same body.   In 1896 he declined the nomination for the same position, but was again elected in 1898, receiving a phenomenally large majority and being the only man in his county who served three terms in the state legislature. Guttersen is a Republican and a member of the United Church.   He was married to Alma Pettersen, of Butternut, in 1889; they have children.

Halgren, C. G., state legislator — Watertown — born 1840, in Ulricehamn, Vestergötland, Sweden.   He received a common school education in his native country; emigrated to the United States at the age of fourteen; settled with his parents at Fulton, Ill., where he served a four years' apprenticeship at the printer's trade; and came to Carver county, Minn., in 1858.   At the outbreak of the Civil War he enlisted as a private in company B of Ninth Minnesota Volunteer Infantry, and served until the close of the war; was postmaster from 1877–85 in Watertown, where he also has a drug store; was elected to the lower branch of the state legislature in 1880, 1882, and 1888.   Halgren is a Republican, is married, and has a son practicing medicine at Watertown.

Halvorson, John, clergyman—Minneapolis—born 4 Dec., 1861, in Stavanger, Norway.   He came with his parents to the United States at the age of nine; graduated from Luther College at the age of nineteen; studied one year at the German Northwestern University, Watertown, Wis., and gra-

PROF. D. MAGNUS, NORTHFIELD.

C. A. FOSNES, MONTEVIDEO.

A. GRINDELAND, WARREN.

PROF. O. LOKENSGAARD, MADISON.

R. E. THOMPSON, PRESTON.

duated from this institution in 1881; then studied theology both at Concordia Seminary and Luther Seminary, and was ordained in 1884. He served as assistant pastor at Mayville, N. D., for a couple of years; then had charge of the church at Norway Lake, Minn., for four years, and accepted the call of the Zion Church, Minneapolis, in 1890. Halvorson belongs to the Norwegian Synod, but is an ardent advocate of the use of the English language, and believes in the future of the Lutheran church in this country only when it retains our fathers' faith and uses our children's language. He was English lecturer at Luther Seminary from 1890 to 1894. During his missionary work, both in Dakota and at Norway Lake, he quite frequently preached in English, being also a contributor to several English theological periodicals, as well as Norwegian. In 1889 he was married to Bertha Glesne, of Norway Lake, who was the first child of European parents born in the settlement. They have several children.

Halvorson, Kittel, congressman—Belgrade—born 15 Dec., 1846, in Hjertdal, Telemarken, Norway. He came with his parents to the U. S. when he was an infant of only two years of age; they settled in Wisconsin, where young Halvorson attended the common schools. At the outbreak of the Civil War he enlisted in company C, First Wisconsin Heavy Artillery, and served until the close of the war; then settled on a homestead in Stearns county, Minn., where he has been engaged in farming, stock raising, and dealing in agricultural implements. Halvorson was elected to the United States Congress in 1890 by the Farmers' Alliance and the Prohibitionists, but was by no means successful as a lawmaker.

He frankly acknowledged his incapacity by the following utterance just before election: "I do not think I am the proper man to send to Congress; but if you elect me anyway, I assure you that I shall do my best." He is a Lutheran, takes interest in the temperance movement, has a family, and represented his district in the state legislature in 1887.

Hanson, Oesten, clergyman—Aspelund—born 8 July, 1836, in Norway; died 4 Aug. 1898. At the age of fifteen he emigrated with his parents to this country; they settled in Wisconsin, but moved to Goodhue county, Minn., in 1856. Here young Hanson was ordained in 1861, and served the same congregation until his death. In 1875–6 he was president of Hauge's Synod, was its vice-president for about twenty years, was president of the board of regents of Red Wing Seminary for several years, and was again elected president of the synod in 1887. His son, M. G. Hanson, was born 11 July, 1853; graduated from Red Wing Seminary in 1884; had charge of congregations in St. Paul for eight years; was located at Grand Forks, N. D., for six years; became principal of Red Wing Seminary in 1898; and was elected president of Hauge's Synod the same year, and re-elected in 1899. He is married and has children.

Hilleboe, H. S., educator—Benson—born 28 Oct., 1858, in Roche-a-Cree, Adams county, Wis. His father and grand parents came from Norway to the United States in 1853. Young Hilleboe worked on the farm and attended the district school till the age of sixteen; then taught some in the public schools. In the fall of 1875 he entered Luther College, from which he was graduated in 1881. In 1886 he received the degree of master of arts from that institution.

During his college days and after his graduation he taught in the public schools and occasionally in the parochial schools. In 1884 he began to teach in Willmar Seminary, and during the years 1886–99 he was eminently successful as principal of that institution. At the latter date he was appointed superintendent of the public schools of Benson. Hilleboe is one of the most aggressive Prohibitionists in the state, and was nominated for governor by his party in 1894. He was married in 1887 to Antonilla Thykesen, of Calmar, Iowa.

Hobe, E. H., Swedish-Norwegian vice-consul—St. Paul—born 27 Feb., 1860, in Risör, Norway. While yet a boy, Hobe took up his residence with his uncle at Tvedestrand, where he received a good school training, and having completed his studies here he was employed in a ship brokerage house in the city of Arendal. Already in his early years Hobe gave evidence of a marked business ability, so that at the age of seventeen he was employed as head clerk in one of the large wholesale and retail establishments in that city. In 1879 he went to Copenhagen, Denmark, where he studied for some time at the noted Gruner's business college, and upon his return to Norway became bookkeeper for a large wholesale house in Kristiania. Having finished the required military duties, Hobe emigrated to America in 1883, coming directly to St. Paul, Minn., where he began his career as clerk in the business department of the paper *Nordvesten*. His ability, however, was soon noticed, and after a short time Hobe became associate editor. In this capacity he served for about two years, when he opened up business as dealer and broker in real estate. In 1887 Hobe made a trip to Europe, visiting, among other places, Copenhagen, Denmark, where he was married to Johanna Mueller. Upon his return to America, Sahlgaard, then Swedish-Norwegian vice-consul in St. Paul, and the owner of an extensive business, invited Hobe to become his partner. Hobe accepted, and shortly before Sahlgaard's death bought out the latter's interest in the business. Under his management it has since grown to be one of the largest land dealing firms in St. Paul. In 1893 Hobe was appointed Sahlgaard's successor as Swedish-Norwegian vice-consul, in which capacity he has done some excellent work, and ranks today as one of the leading Scandinavian business men in the Northwest.

Hoegh, Knut, physician and surgeon — Minneapolis — born 15 April, 1844, in Kaafjord, Tromsö sift, Norway. After being graduated from the Latin school of Trondhjem, Hoegh entered the University of Norway, and graduated from the medical department in 1869. Shortly after his graduation he emigrated to America, coming to La Crosse, Wis., where he followed his profession till 1889, when he moved to Minneapolis. While in La Crosse Hoegh built, in 1871, a private hospital to facilitate the treatment of the many patients from far and near who sought his professional aid. In 1880 he went to New York City to pursue some special studies in his profession, and in 1887 he went to England and Germany, where he made a special study of surgery. Hoegh has been a member of many medical associations, and of the Minnesota board of health, being appointed to the latter position by Gov. Nelson. He was also a member of the health commission of the state of Wisconsin, and a member of the board of inspectors of the insane asylum of the same state. Hoegh was married in 1870 to Anna Dorthea Moen; they have children.

Holt, Andrew, lawyer—Minneapolis—born 20 May, 1855, in East Union, Carver county, Minn. His parents were among the early Swedish settlers; they came to this country in 1853. He received a Swedish education at Gustavus Adolphus College; graduated from the University of Minnesota in 1880, being the first Scandinavian who completed a course at this institution. He studied law in Glencoe, and commenced to practice in Minneapolis in 1882, being shortly after admitted as a member of the firm Ueland & Holt. He is one of the organizers of St. John's English Lutheran Church; is an advocate of temperance, but affiliates with the Republican party. In the summer of 1894 Knute Nelson appointed him judge of the municipal court of Minneapolis, and in the fall of that year he was elected to the same position. In 1885 Holt was married to Hilda C. Turnquist, and they have children.

Husher, Ferdinand A., journalist and state legislator—Minneapolis—born 16 June, 1825, in Viborg, Denmark; died 1895. His father was for a number of years collector of customs, and afterwards an actor. While very young Husher removed to Norway, entering the university there, and graduating in 1845. From 1851-64 he held various positions, and for the five years following was assistant pastor at Nissedal, but emigrated to America in 1869, going to La Crosse, Wis., where he became assistant editor of *Faedrelandet og Emigranten.* From 1873-75 Husher became editor and part owner of *Budstikken,* Minneapolis; was register of the U. S. land office at La Crosse from 1878–83; became managing editor, and later also proprietor of the first-named paper, with which he removed to Minneapolis in 1886.   In 1888 Husher was elected member of the state legislature of Minnesota, but resigned when, in 1890, he was appointed U. S. consul at St. Thomas, Ontario, Canada.   From 1879–84 Husher was a member of the Republican state central committee in Wisconsin, and in 1884 was presidential elector at large for the same state. After his return from Canada, in 1894, he went to Grand Forks, N. D., to assume editorial charge of *Normanden.*

Jackson, Andrew, clergyman—Rush Point—born 11 Feb., 1828, in Valla, Bohus län, Sweden.   He studied in a college for six or seven years, and taught in private families; became a sailor; emigrated to this country in 1852; worked in saw mills on Hudson River for five years; and took a claim in Kandiyohi county, Minn., in 1858.   After having studied in Chicago for a couple of years he was ordained in 1861, and took charge of Swedish Lutheran congregations in Kandiyohi county until 1862, when he together with the settlers was driven away from their homes by the Indians. Jackson taught the first public school in Meeker county, and when a Swedish school, which later became Gustavus Adolphus College, was opened at Carver in 1863, be became principal of that institution, a position he retained until the school was moved to St. Peter in 1876.   For twenty-five years he had charge of churches in Carver county, moved to St. Paul in 1890, and has since been pastor at Rush Point. Jackson was married in 1863, his wife died in 1875, and in 1877 he was married the second time.   His son J. A. Jackson was born 17 July, 1868, in Carver county, Minn.; graduated fron Gustavus Adolphus College in 1891 and from the iaw department of the state university in 1893; and since the latter date has been practicing law in St. Paul, having for years been the only Swedish attorney in that city.   In 1898 Jackson was elected to the state legislature, and worked hard and faithfully, especially as chairman of the committee on public buildings, and as a result of his labor the new capitol will, undoubtedly, be completed in 1903 instead of in 1910.   He is a member of the Swedish Lutheran church and a Republican.

Jacobson, Jacob F., state legislator—Madison—born 13 Jan., 1849, in Hjelmeland, Kristiansand stift, Norway.   At the age of seven he came with his parents to this country; they settled in Fayette county, Iowa, where young Jacobson worked on his father's farm until 1871, when he moved to Lac qui Parle county, Minn., and commenced to deal in agricultural implements, and he claimed in 1892 to do an annual business of $75,000.   But he failed a couple of years later, and it is said that he settled up his troubles in a sort of a private way; some of his creditors receiving ten cents on the dollar, and others about fifty cents on the dollar. From 1873–79 he was county auditor, has served in the lower branch of the state legislature since 1889, was a delegate to the Republican national convention at Minneapolis in 1892, and has held several local offices.   He is a member of Hauge's Synod, and takes a very active part in the social, financial, and political affairs of the community and of the state, being an ardent temperance advocate and a Republican, who often addresses public meetings in the interest of his party.   But his oratorical qualifications consist mostly

in his strong lungs. Both in his conversation and in his
speeches he yells to the top of his voice. He seldom knows
when silence would be wisdom. These peculiarities of
Jacobson have had a great deal to do with his success in
public life, for it has been asserted that many people in Lac
qui Parle county vote for him simply because he is such a
good advertisement for the county, being always, of course,
referred to in the legislature as "the gentleman from Lac
qui Parle." Such mention of a new community has a tendency to raise the value of real estate. Yet he must be a man
of ability, since he has been the recognized leader in the legislature for some years. Many of the measures he has
advocated have been wise, and his tactics are shrewd.
The St. Paul Dispatch cartooned him in 1899 as "the
red dragon of Lac qui Parle;" and it cannot be denied that
on account of his rudeness and brutal treatment of other
people's opinions and honesty, he is "feared rather than
trusted." Jacobson was married in 1873, and his wife died
in 1879; married again in 1883, and became a widower four
years later; married the third time in 1889. He has had
children by all his wives.

Jaeger, Luth, journalist—Minneapolis—born 4 Aug.,
1851, near Arendal, Norway. He received a classical education; was admitted to the University of Norway in 1870,
but after having studied for one year at that institution, he
emigrated to this country at the age of twenty; clerked in
Madison and La Crosse, Wis., from 1871–76; was connected
with a Norwegian weekly paper, *Norden,* in Chicago, one
year; became editor of *Budstikken,* Minneapolis, Minn., in
1879, a position which he held for about eight years; and

E. H. HOBE, ST. PAUL.

SOREN LISTOE, ST. PAUL.

the next four years he was deputy collector of internal revenue. Jaeger was in the real estate business in Minneapolis for a short time and lived in New Mexico during part of one year. In 1886 the Democratic party nominated him for secretary of state, but with the rest of the ticket he was defeated. In 1890 he was elected a member of the board of education, in which work he took great interest and rendered valuable services. He was one of the founders of *The North* in 1889, remaining in editorial charge of the paper until its discontinuance in 1894. *The North* was a weekly journal published in the English language and devoted to the interests of the Scandinavians as citizens of the United States. As such it became the repository for much valuable information, while ably and forcibly preaching the need of a more rigid and intense Americanization of the foreign-born than the latter themselves usually think desirable. Jaeger is a clear and forcible writer, uninfluenced by any political, religious, or national prejudices. He unquestionably ranks among the very best Scandinavian-American writers. His opinions on the leading questions of the day, as published in *The North*, were extensively quoted by the Scandinavian-American press. By the native Americans and foreign-Americans, not Scandinavians, *The North* was considered the representative organ of Scandinavian-American opinions. To the leading journalists in Stockholm, Copenhagen, and Kristiania, Jaeger's name is very familiar. He was for several years an officer in the Security Savings and Loan Association, his connection with this now defunct corporation being severed under circumstances alike creditable to him as an official and man. In 1897 Jaeger was appointed

28

receiver of the Scandia Bank of Minneapolis and is also engaged in the real estate, loaning, and insurance business. In 1883 he was married to Nanny Mattson, only daughter of the well-known Col. Hans Mattson, a lady who takes great interest in educational affairs and charitable institutions. They have three boys.

Janson, Kristofer N., clergyman and author—Minneapolis—born 5 May, 1841, in Bergen, Norway. His father was a business man and American consul at Bergen; his mother was a daughter of Bishop Neumann, who was bishop of Bergen stift. After having completed the course at the Latin school of his native city, Janson entered the University of Norway, and graduated from this institution, with the highest honor, as a theological candidate. During his university career, as well as afterwards, he was the leader of a movement, having in view the re-placing of the Danish-Norwegian language and literature which was forced upon the Norwegian people at their connection with Denmark in the fourteenth century. He devoted himself to private teaching, and was one of the promoters in founding people's high schools in Gudbrandsdalen and other places, for the purpose of raising the intellectual level of the peasants. He wrote extensively, both poetry and novels, and it is generally considered that he produced his best literary works during his younger days. In 1882 he accepted a call to become minister of a liberal society in Minneapolis, and organized Unitarian churches among his countrymen in Minneapolis, in Brown and Otter Tail counties, Minnesota, and at Hudson, Wis. Janson took active part in all movements in the nature of social reforms and intellectual improvements. After his emigration to this country he returned to Europe and visited Italy, France, Germany, Holland, the Faroe Islands, Iceland, and the Scandinavian countries. It is generally acknowledged that *Han og Ho* and *Den Bergtekne* are the best of his numerous literary productions. The latter has been translated into English under the title *The Spellbound Fiddler*. His experiences as a minister in the Northwest have been described in *Praeriens Saga*. In 1868 Janson was married to Drude Krog, a daughter of a Lutheran minister; they had seven children, and two of their sons are practicing physicians. Mrs. Janson not only assisted her husband in his literary endeavors, but also produced original literary works of her own, for example: *En Saloon-Keepers Datter,* etc. With all his brilliancy, however, Janson did not seem to be well-balanced. He became a Spiritualist, returned to Noway in 1894, was divorced, and married a medium.

Jensson, Jens Christian, clergyman and author—Austin—born 25 March, 1859, in Sandnes, Kristiansand stift, Norway. He came to America in 1862 with his parents, who first settled in Neenah, Wis. Later they moved to Fillmore county, Minn. Having availed himself of the educational facilities offered by the common and high schools of that neighborhood, he attended for two years the theological school conducted by the Norwegian Augustana Synod near Decorah, Iowa. In 1876 he entered the academy, then located at Marshall Wis., where he remained until 1880. His theological course he completed at the Philadelphia Lutheran Theological Seminary in 1882. Since his ordination to the ministry in 1880, he has also done some work in connection with the post-graduate course of the Chicago Lutheran Seminary. Jensson has served Norwegian Lutheran churches in the following places: At Wiota, Iowa, a few months; at Leland, Ill., from 1882 to 1885; in Milwaukee, Wis., from 1885 to 1890; and at Clinton, Wis., from 1885 to 1899, settling at his present place in the latter year. From 1886 to 1890 he served as secretary of the Norwegian Augustana Synod; and since 1894 as secretary of the United Church. In 1890 Jensson published *American Lutheran Biographies.* This is a bulky volume of 900 pages, and is, perhaps, the largest original literary work published in English by a Scandinavian-American. As a work of reference it is very valuable, throwing much light upon the church history of the different Lutheran denominations in this country, including, of course, the Scandinavian organizations. In 1896 he collected and edited *Samfunds Haandbog.* This work enumerates and describes all the different missionary, charitable, and educational institutions, etc., which were controlled or owned by members of the United Church, or which were in any way directly or indirectly connected with that organization. He was married in 1879 to Rosa Andrina Thompson, of Marshall, Wis. They have children.

Jensvold, John, lawyer—Duluth—born 25 March, 1857, in Albany, Wis. His parents were among the first Norwegians in this country, coming here as children. Brought up on a farm he received his education in the public schools; at the State Normal school, Winona; in Luther College, Decorah; and in the law department of the State University of Iowa, from which he graduated in 1880. He practiced his profession in Iowa until 1888, and since at Duluth, where he ranks as one of the leading lawyers, and occupies a prominent position in political and social circles. He was married in 1888 to Lena Darrah, of Dubuque, Iowa.

Johnsen, Thomas, clergyman—Norseland—born 27 April, 1837, in Valders, Norway. He is the youngest of nine children, and lost his parents at an early age. At the age of fourteen he came with three of his brothers to the United States, and for some years was engaged in farming, then entered Concordia College, St. Louis, Mo., and graduated from the theological department of this institution in 1863. Since he has been located at his present place in Nicollet county, as pastor of Norwegian Synod congregations. For several years Johnsen had charge of a large missionary field in Minnesota, including Blue Earth, Faribault, Brown, Watonwan, Jackson, Carver, McLeod, Renville, Meeker, Kandiyohi, Stearns, Pope, Douglas, Chippewa, Yellow Medicine counties. Some of his charges were about 300 miles apart, and could be visited only once or twice a year. He has done more, perhaps, than any other man to build up Norwegian Synod congregations in the state, and was one of the most prominent Norwegian Lutheran pioneer clergymen in the Northwest. In 1863 he married Maren E. C. Sahlgaard. She died in 1898, leaving three children.

Johnson, C. J., lumber manufacturer — Minneapolis — born 12 Sept., 1849, in Hofmantorp, Småland, Sweden. He received a common school education; came to America in 1869, stopping for a short time at Vasa, Minn.; proceeded to Stillwater, where he worked in a saw mill; removed to

Minneapolis in 1870, where he worked in saw mills and lumber yards and clerked in a store; completed a course in the high school and attended the state university; was engaged in the retail lumber business, in company with C. A. Smith, at Evansville and other places, living at that place in 1879–84; and at the latter date he and Smith started a wholesale and manufacturing lumber business in Minneapolis.   Johnson withdrew from active business in 1899, and the same year he and his family visited Sweden and other European countries.   He is a Republican, a member of the Swedish-Lutheran church, an excellent mechanic, and a great reader, having one of the largest libraries of any Scandinavians in the Northwest.   Johnson was married to Mary S. Craft, of Vestergötland, Sweden, in 1882.   They have three sons.

Johnson, Gustavus, musician — Minneapolis — born 2 Nov., 1856, in Hull, England. His father was a Swede, his mother an English lady.   Johnson was only a child when the family moved to Stockholm, Sweden; here he studied music under the direction of A. Lindström, G. Mankell, Conrad Nordquist, and Prof. Winje.   He left the "Venice of the North" in 1875, and, after a brief stay in the East, came West, appearing in concerts in all the leading cities in Illinois, Wisconsin, Iowa, and Minnesota. Since 1880 Johnson has resided in Minneapolis, is recognized as one of the leading pianists in the Northwest, and in the many concerts in which he performs he always receives the most flattering comments.   As a teacher Johnson ranks among the foremost, his instruction being sought by students from all over the Northwest.   In 1898 he founded a piano school, and next year he established the Johnson School of Music,

Oratory and Dramatic Art, an institution which has a high reputation. He is also highly spoken of as a composer. In 1882 he was married to Caroline F. Winslow, an American lady, of Royalton, Vt. They have one child.

Johnson, Marcus, state senator—Atwater—born 14 July, 1849, in the northern part of Helsingland, Sweden. When an infant of only two years of age he came with his parents to the United States; they settled at Waupaca, Wis., but moved to Kandiyohi county, Minn., five years later, where Johnson has resided ever since. In 1880 he was a delegate to the Republican national convention which met in Chicago and nominated Garfield for president, represented his district in the state legislature in 1883, and served in the state senate during the sessions of 1887–89. In 1890 President Harrison appointed him collector of internal revenues for Minnesota. He is interested in elevators, flouring mills, and other large enterprises in different parts of the state. Johnson is not married.

Johnson, Tosten, pioneer and state senator — Black Hammer—born 21 July, 1834, in Valders, Norway. At the age of twelve he learned the blacksmith's trade; came to this country in 1851; resided for one year in Dane county, Wis.; then settled in Houston county, Minn., where he has ever since been engaged in farming. The first Norwegian settlements in the state seem to have been started in Houston and Fillmore counties in 1852 and 1853, and Johnson and his brother are the first Norwegian settlers in Minnesota that have yet been recorded. He was drafted into the army in 1864, and says that "being discharged at the close of the war without any wounds" is the chief success he has had in life; represented his district in the state legislature during the sessions of 1869, 1871, and 1873: was elected state senator in 1886 and re-elected two years later; and has held various local offices, having been county commissioner for four years and railway postal clerk 1880–85. Johnson is one of the leading and most influential Scandinavians in Houston county. He is a Republican and was married in 1861.

Johnston, L. A., clergyman—St. Paul—born 12 Aug., 1855, in Sugar Grove, Pa. His parents were natives of Hesleby, Småland, Sweden, and came to this country in 1846, being among the earliest Swedish arrivals in the nineteenth century. They first settled at Buffalo, but removed to Sugar Grove two years later. Young Johnston received a common school education; studied music about four years under a private instructor; attended the high school at Sugar Grove for three years; and continued his studies at Augustana College, graduating from the college department in 1879, and from the theological department in 1881. From 1881 to 1886 he was pastor of a Swedish Augustana congregation in Des Moines, Iowa. While located there he was office editor of *Bethania*, a religious bi-monthly, and vice-president of the Iowa Conference for one year. His work at Des Moines was successful, and his congregation erected a $20,000 church building during his stay there. Johnston next removed to Rockford, Ill., where he served the First Lutheran Church, the largest congregation of Augustana Synod, until 1894, and since that year he has been pastor of the First Swedish Lutheran Church of St. Paul. He was vice-president of the Illinois Conference for three years, and n 1894 was elected president of the same body; was a mem-

REV. C. J. PETRI, MINNEAPOLIS.

PROF. M. O. BOCKMAN, MINNEAPOLIS.

REV. C. L. CLAUSEN, AUSTIN.

REV. L. A. JOHNSTON, ST. PAUL.

REV. E. NORELIUS, VASA.

ber of the board of directors of the Augustana Hospital in Chicago for three terms; has been a member of the board of directors of the Augustana Book Concern ever since the synod took charge of it; has been a member of the board of directors of Augustana College since 1893, and chairman of the same for two years; was a member of the board of directors of Gustavus Adolphus College for three years, and chairman of the same for 3 years; and has been a member of the board of directors of the Bethesda Hospital for three years, and chairman for the same length of time. Johnston has often lectured on social, economic, and historical topics, within as well as outside the Augustana Synod; and he prepares his sermons with great care. He was married to Anna S. Lindgren, of Rock Island, Ill., in 1881; they have several children.

Kildahl, J. N., clergyman and educator—Northfield—born 4 Jan., 1857, near Trondhjem, Norway. His father being a school teacher, young Kildahl received a careful Christian training; came with his parents to Goodhue county, Minn., in 1866; was a regular attendant at common and parochial schools; attended Luther College, graduating in 1879; and closed his studies at Luther Seminary, Madison, Wis., in 1882, by passing his theological examinations. He was at once ordained, and served congregations in Goodhue county from 1882 to 1889, excepting one year (1885–86), when he occupied a chair of theology in the Red Wing Seminary. In 1889 he accepted a call from the Bethlehem church in Chicago, which he served during the next ten years. For some years he was secretary of the United Church. In the fall of 1899 he entered upon his duties as president of

St. Olaf College, Northfield. Rev. J. C. Jensson, in his
American Lutheran Biographies, says: "Kildahl's sermons combine the instructive, the rhetorical, the logical, and
the emotional in fair proportions. His genial, generous
spirit, his facility at adapting himself to persons of every
character and condition, and his disposition to identify
himself with them in all their joys, and sorrows, and interests, give him an influence over them which few pastors
possess." Kildahl for years has been a leading mind in the
United Church, and even in the most heated controversies
friend and foe alike would agree that his fair-mindedness is
more than ordinary. He was married to Bertha Söine in
1882; they have children.

Kildsig, Jens Jensen, clergyman—Albert Lea—born 30
Jan., 1856, in Brejning, near Ringköbing, Denmark. He
received a military education at Viborg, having taken the
corporal and sergeant examinations; bought his father's
farm and worked it for a couple of years; emigrated in 1881,
coming directly to Chicago, Ill., where he had a market
garden, but lost all his property by a flood in 1885; and
entered Chicago Theological Seminary, completing his
studies in 1889. He associated himself with the Danish
Evangelical Lutheran Association in America, becoming one
of the leading men in that organization. After his ordination in 1889 he organized a church at Racine, Wis., and was
elected visitor to the northern district in 1891, and the same
year accepted a call to Minneapolis, Minn. He has served
as a member of the board of trustees of Trinity Seminary,
Blair, Neb., as well as treasurer of *Kirke Bladet*. He
returned to his old congregation in Racine in 1895; but the

next year he consented to take charge of the Danish emigrant mission work in New York and Brooklyn, besides serving some congregations in the vicinity, and accepted a call to his present place in 1898. Through the union of the Danish Lutheran churches, Kildsig became a member of the United Danish Lutheran Church in 1896, being the same year appointed district president of the eastern district of the latter organization. Kildsig was married in 1887 to Ane Marie Kristine Mose, a daughter of a well-to-do farmer in Denmark, where he had gone for the purpose of celebrating his marriage.

Kittelson, Charles, state treasurer—Montevideo—born 1837, in Sigdal, Kristiania stift, Norway. He came to this country at the age of thirteen; resided for seven years in Wisconsin; then moved to Albert Lea, Minn., where he resided for several years, and was county treasurer of Free-born county for six terms. At the outbreak of the Civil War he enlisted in the Tenth Minnesota Infantry, was successively promoted to second lieutenant, first lieutenant, and captain of company E of his regiment. In 1872 he was presidential elector; served as state treasuer in 1880–87; was for a few years connected with a couple of banks in St. Paul; moved to Minneapolis in 1890, where he was president of Columbia National Bank until it failed about seven years later; and has since together with a son been operating a flour mill in Montevideo. Kittelson seems to have been out of place as a public servant. His bookkeeping as treasurer of Freeborn county could not be disentangled by experts. Ignorance rather than dishonesty appears to have been his main fault. He is a Republican.

Knatvold, T. V., legislator and banker—Albert Lea—
born 2 Oct., 1853, in Norway. He came to this country
in 1862 with his parents, settling in Freeborn county,
Minn.; received a common school and high school education; and in 1877 engaged in the hardware business at
Albert Lea. Since 1893 he has been engaged in the banking
business. Knatvold served as alderman of the city of
Albert Lea for several years, and was elected mayor in
1893, and re-elected in 1894. In 1890 he was nominated
for state senator by the Republicans, but was defeated by
the combined forces of the other parties. In 1896 he was
elected to that position by a majority of almost one thous-
and, and re-elected in 1898. Knatvold is a Republican, and
belongs to the Norwegian Synod. He is married.

Lagerstrom, R., musician—St. Peter—born 12 June,
1861, in Spring Garden, Minn. His parents came from
Sweden to the U. S. in the early fifties. He commenced to
study music when only four years old; continued his studies
at Northfield, and completed his musical education at the
Royal Conservatory of Music, Stockholm, Sweden, where
he, after three years' attendance, graduated in 1888. Since
he has had charge of the musical department of Gustavus
Adolphus College. In 1890 he received the degree of master
of music of Alfred University, Alfred Center, N. Y., and
two years later the degree of doctor of music was conferred upon him by the Grand Conservatory of Music, New
York. Both degrees were bestowed upon him on the merits
of his compositions. He composed the excellent *Cantata,*
rendered in 1883, at the great celebration of the three
hundredth anniversary of the adoption of the Upsala decree.

Lagerstrom was married to Mary Carlson, of East Union, Minn., in 1888.

Langum, Samuel, state legislator—Preston—born 18 Aug., 1857, in Fillmore county, Minn. His parents were Norwegians. He attended an academy in Wisconsin, the high school of Decorah, Iowa, and Augsburg Seminary, Minneapolis. After having completed his education he returned to Fillmore county, where he taught school for a while; was deputy register of deeds for four years; was elected sheriff in 1881; was warden of the penitentiary at Stillwater for some time; became editor and proprietor of a local newspaper in Preston; was elected to the state legislature in 1892; has been secretary of the state senate for some years. Langum was married to Emma C. McCollum in 1878; they have children.

Liljegren, N. M., clergyman—Minneapolis—born 9 Dec., 1846, in Vemmerlöf, Skåne, Sweden. His parents were farmers, but young Liljegren received a college education in Gothenburg; joined the Methodist church at the age of twenty-two; preached and delivered temperance speeches in different parts of the kingdom until he emigrated in 1886; had charge of a church in Chicago for three years, then moved to Marinette, Wis.; came to Minneapolis in 1890; and later on settled at Aurora, Ill. Liljegren has written some books, contributes regularly to newspapers, is an ardent temperance man and a good speaker. In 1876 he was married to Sofie Witting of Gothenburg. They have children.

Lind, Alfred, physician and surgeon—Minneapolis—born 11 March, 1862, in Tråfvad, Vestergötland, Sweden.

His parents were farmers. He came to America in 1880, and his life since that date has been chiefly that of the indomitable student, as may be seen by a glance at the following record: In 1887 he received the degree of A. B. at Augustana College; that of B. S. in the University of Minnesota in 1889; graduated from the medical department of the same institution in 1891; practiced medicine for two years at Lake Park, Minn.; studied one year at the University of Berlin, Germany, and received the doctor's degree of this institution in 1894; practiced for two years in Minneapolis; studied a few months in New York; completed a one year's course in Gymnastiska Centralinstitutet, Stockholm, Sweden, graduating in 1897; practiced for some time in Minneapolis; and graduated as candidate of medicine from the University of Upsala, Sweden, in 1898, and as physician and surgeon from Karolinska Institutet, Stockholm, Sweden, in 1899. Probably no other Scandinavian-American physician can point to such a record as the above. But Lind has not only obtained a thorough theoretical medical education, but has also been very successful in his practice, and undoubtedly ranks as one of the leading Swedish physicians in this country. For the third time he began to practice his profession in Minneapolis in 1899. He is a member of the Augustana Synod, and affiliates with the Republican party. In 1892 he was married to Hannah Johnson, of Axtell, Neb.; they have a couple of children.

Lind, John, governor—Uew Ulm—born 25 March, 1854, in Kånna, Småland, Sweden. At the age of fourteen Lind came to America, settling in Goodhue county, Minn., where he was obliged from the outset to aid his parents in supporting the family. In the fall of 1868, having been in this country only a few months, he was so unfortunate as to lose his left arm in handling a gun, or rather on account of the stupidity of a surgeon who appears to have made an unnecessary amputation. But with untiring energy and preserverance Lind was still able to make his way with one arm, and at the same time to attend school, so that in 1870 he obtained a teacher's certificate. In 1873 he moved to Sibley county, Minn., and came to New Ulm the year following. From 1875–76 he attended the University of Minnesota. Lind had for some time cherished the idea of entering the legal profession, and with this object in view he devoted himself to the study of law in private, partly by himself and partly in an attorney's office in New Ulm. In 1876 he was admitted to the bar, and opened a law office of his own the year following, when he was also elected superintendent of schools for Brown county, a position he held for two years. In 1881 Lind was appointed receiver in the U. S. land office at Tracy, a position he held till 1885. These duties, however, did not prevent him from continuing in his legal profession, in which his eminent talents soon made him distinguished. But not only did Lind become noted as one of the ablest lawyers in his part of the state, but his great ability in public life, and his excellent qualities as a man soon convinced the people of the state of Minnesota of his eminent fitness for representing their commonwealth in Congress. Consequently, in 1886, he was elected congressman for the second district, and so well did he discharge his duties that he was elected for a second term by an overwhelming majority, while nearly all the other

candidates on the Republican ticket were defeated, a fact
which illustrates Lind's popularity. While in Congress,
Lind introduced and succeeded in passing a great number of
important measures, such as, a bill by which all foreign
books not published in England are admitted to the United
States free of duty, and an amendment to a bill by which
foreigners who serve on United States men-of-war may
become citizens, as well as if they were on land. He also
secured the location and erection of an Indian school at
Pipestone City, a United States court house at Mankato,
and the passage of a law dividing the state into six districts
for holding United States court, instead of one. The two
first mentioned measures are very important to the adopted
citizens, and Lind deserves great credit for having procured
the passage of such wise laws, which have directly greatly
benefited the Scandinavian-Americans. He declined a third
nomination, and intended to devote his whole time to his
personal affairs. But when the silver issue became the pre-
dominent feature of the presidential campaign in 1896, he
sided with the Silverites, and the Fusion forces nominated
him for governor. Lind refused to accept the nomination.
But after having been besieged for about two weeks by a
large number of honest Silverites and some unscrupulous
demogogues, he consented to accommodate them. During a
campaign of much bitterness, he was severely criticized by
most of his former Republican friends, and mistrusted by
many of his new allies. But in spite of this he received
about fifty thousand votes more than his party colleagues,
and came within three thousand votes of being elected, and
many believed that he actually beat his opponent, whose

JOHN LIND, NEW ULM.

L. A. ROSING, CANNON FALLS.

party had controlled the politics of the state for more than a third of a century. Lind's success was remarkable, considering that the majority of the leading men of his own nationality, especially the Swedish Lutheran clergymen, bitterly opposed him. He probably did not receive over twenty-five per cent of the Swedish votes in the state, as most of them are ardent Republicans. He received by far more Norwegian votes than Swedish, even in Norwegian Republican counties, as compared with Swedish Republican counties. Consequently, the result of the election was due more to Lind's popularity and his opponent's weakness than to any other cause or causes. The congressional records show that Lind virtually made the same speeches during the campaign on the silver question, as he had done in Congress a few years before when he was considered a loyal Republican. Yet his standpoint on this issue has made an epoch in the political history of the state of Minnesota. Lind was quarter master in the army during the Spanish War in 1898, and was elected governor the same year, running about 60,000 ahead of his ticket, thus becoming the first Swedish-born governor in the United States, as well as being the only man of that nationality who ever served in Congress. In 1898 the Swedes in general, and the Lutheran clergy in particular, did not oppose him with the same fierceness as in 1896. Yet it is very doubtful if he received a majority of the Swedish votes in the state. All people admit that Lind made an excellent record in Congress. It is not time yet to express an opinion in regard to his executive ability. He has a difficult position to fill, being opposed by a hostile legislature, and surrounded by a hungry crowd of

29

office seekers, and some of his appointments have been
severely criticized even by his own party. Lind is a good
Icelandic scholar, speaks English without a foreign accent,
and is an able orator. He was married in 1879 to Alice
Shepard. They have three children.

Lindholm, A. T., writer and poet—Stillwater—born 9
May, 1835, in Gothenburg, Sweden. He received a college
and commercial education in his native city; emigrated to
the U. S. in 1854; was book keeper in Galva, Ill., for two
years; then moved to Mankato, Minn., where he was cashier of the First National Bank for fifteen years, besides
being deputy collector of internal revenue. In 1871 Lindholm, in company with Col. H. Mattson and H. Sahlgaard,
went into the banking and exchange business in St. Paul,
but seven years later he moved to Stillwater, where he has
resided ever since, being employed as book beeper for different business houses. Both in 1878 and in 1890 he was the
Democratic nominee for secretary of state, but with the
rest of his ticket was defeated. Lindholm is prominent as
a literary man, and especially noted as a skillful translator
from the Scandinavian languages into English. Among other
things he has translated Tegner's *Srea* and *Sång till
Solen*, Runeberg's *Sveaborg* and several of his *Fänrik
Ståls Sägner,* Geijer's *Vikingen,* and many of Isben's
poems. He has also made a successful attempt as a dramatic author in the English language, in which his lengthy
drama, *Demosthenes,* is written. In 1888 he was elected
honorary member of the *Nordiska Literatur-Sällskapet*
of Stockholm, Sweden, an honor which only a few Swedish-
Americans besides Lindholm enjoy. He has been a member

of the board of education of Stillwater, and was married
to Anna Olson, of Mankato, Minn., in 1862.   They have
children.

Listoe, Soren, journalist—St. Paul—born 27 April,
1846, in Copenhagen, Denmark.   His grandfather was a
prominent officer in the Danish army.   Listoe received a
good education through private instruction; came to this
country in 1866 to join his father, who had previously emigrated; was connected with Danish-Norwegian newspapers
in Wisconsin for a couple of years; went to Minneapolis,
and was associate editor of *Nordisk Folkeblad* until
1871; then became mail agent, and settled in Breckenridge.
In 1874 he was elected to the state legislature, being the
first Dane in the state who served in this body.   In 1875
he was appointed register of the U. S. land office at Alexandria, a position which he held for eight yesrs.   For
several years Listoe lived on his farm near Breckenridge;
became editor-in-chief of *Nordvesten*, St. Paul, in 1887;
was appointed U. S. consul at Dusseldorf, Germany, in
1892; but after having remained abroad for one year he
returned to Minnesota, and again took charge of *Nordvesten*.   He was appointed major on the governor's staff
in 1886, and has since served as aid-de-camp to all subsequent governors, having in the meantime been promoted to
the rank of colonel.   Listoe has for years been considered to
be one of the most prominent Danes in the state, and was
appointed by President McKinley U. S. consul at Rotter-
dam, Holland, in 1897.   In 1872 he was married to Hannah
Johnson; they have several children.

Löbeck, Engebret E., temperance lecturer — Farwell —

born 11 Oct., 1864, in Tryssil, Hamar stift, Norway. He emigrated to America in 1867, and spent his boyhood and early manhood on his father's farm near Holmes City, Minn.; "dug on the farm in the day, and read literature in the night"; and, yielding to a yearning for a better education than the common schools could afford, studied successively at Augsburg Seminary, Wraaman's Academy, the State University of Minnesota, all at Minneapolis, and Willmar Seminary. Some years ago he began to lecture on temperance, and so successful did he prove in this line of work that at present he is one of the most popular Scandinavian temperance lecturers in America. His chief points of strength are his evident devotion to the cause which he advocates; his self-forgetting, contagious enthusiasm; his fluency of speech; his tremendous voice; and last, but not least, his magnificent physique. Löbeck frequently contributes both prose and poetry to Norwegian papers, chiefly *Reform* and *Ungdommens Ven.* In 1894 he published a small collection of poems, *Forglemmigei,* the first edition of which was exhausted in a few months, and five years later issued *Billeder fra Dödens Dal,* a temperance and prohibition argument cast in the form of a novel. He is a member of the Swedish Augustana Synod, a "prohibitionist from head to foot," and was president of the Wisconsin Total Abstinence Association in 1896. In 1896 he was married to Martha Nordby, a graduate of the Fargo high school, in North Dakota. They have children.

Lokensgaard, O., clergyman and educator—Madison— born 23 Nov., 1854, in Aal, Kristiania stift, Norway. At the age of three he came with his parents to the United

States; they settled in Rice county, Minn.; but four years later moved to Dakota, remaining there, however, only one year; since 1862 they have resided in Nicollet county, Minn. Lokensgaard graduated from Luther College, Decorah, Iowa, in 1878, and completed his studies at Luther Seminary three years later. Then had charge of a church at Granite Falls, Minn., until 1892, when he became principal of the normal school at Madison, which position he has filled with great credit ever since. Lokensgaard is the most influential Norwegian advocate of total abstinence in the Minnesota valley. In 1881 he was married to Ellen Kravik, of Dane county, Wis.; she died in 1892. In 1894 he was married to Anna Romtvedt, of Cottonwood county, Minn. He has several children.

Lomen, G. J., lawyer and state legislator—St. Paul—born 28 Jan., 1854, near Decorah, Iowa. His parents came from Valders, Norway, in 1850, and settled on a farm in Iowa. Young Lomen attended Luther College for six years, and graduated from the law department of the University of Iowa in 1875; then moved to Caledonia, Houston county, Minn., where he practiced his profession, was clerk of court for eight years, and held various local trusts. In 1885 he located in St. Paul; represented his ward in the state legislature in 1891; was the Republican candidate for municipal judge in 1890, and, with the rest of the ticket, was defeated. Lomen has conducted several important professional cases, and is by general consent considered to be one of the leading lawyers in St. Paul. He is a member of the Norwegian Synod, and was married to Julia E. M. Joys, of Manistee, Mich., in 1878; they have several children.

Lund, E. G., educator — Minneapolis — born 10 Aug., 1852, in Arendal, Norway. Lund came with his parents to Springfield, Ill., in 1853; there they remained four years; then moved to St. Paul, returning to Springfield, however, in 1862. In 1871 he entered the college at Springfield, and after having studied there two years went to Thiel College, Greenville, Pa., from which institution he graduated in 1877. He then began the study of theology at the General Council Theological Seminary, Philadelphia, graduating in 1881. Lund was then ordained for the ministry, and accepted a call to four congregations in Westmoreland county, Pa. In 1883 he accepted a call to the Norwegian-English Lutheran church at Milwaukee, Wis., belonging to the Norwegian Augustana Synod. Two years later he was called to an English Lutheran church at Greensburg, Pa., where he remained for six years. In 1888 he was called to the presidency of Thiel College, but declined. In 1891 the home mission committee of the General Council extended a six months' call to Lund as home missionary at Tacoma, Washington. In 1891 he accepted a call to become English professor of theology at the theological seminary of the United Church. Lund is considered to be one of the foremost men in the United Church, and the degree of doctor of divinity was conferred upon him in 1899 by Wittenberg College, Springfield, Ill., one of the leading English Lutheran institutions in the country. He is said to be the only Norwegian-American Lutheran who has ever received such degree. In 1891 he was married to Anna Hippee, an American lady of Greenville, Pa. They have one daughter.

Lundeen, John August, officer in the U. S. army—

St. Peter—born 6 March, 1848, in Hvetlanda, Småland, Sweden. At the age of five he came with his parents to the U. S.; they settled in Minnesota. Young Lundeen attended the Swedish school in Carver for about a year; studied at Augustana College, Paxton, Ill., in 1865-66, and graduated from the United States Military Academy, West Point, N.Y., in 1873, being the fifth in his class. Since his graduation he has served with his regiment, the Fourth United States Artillery, in various garrisons; for example, in San Francisco, Oregon, Alaska, Virginia, Connecticut, Rhode Island, Boston, Minnesota, Georgia, and Baltimore. From 1876–79 he was professor of military science and tactics, as well as teacher of mathematics and the Swedish language, in the University of Minnesota. From 1887–92 he was assistant professor of mathematics in the United States Military Academy at West Point. It must be remembered that the mathematical instruction in that institution is considered to be the most thorough of any schools in the world, and Lundeen's appointment as instructor in this branch of knowledge was a high recognition of his ability. Besides Lundeen there are only three Scandinavian-born (all Swedes) who have graduated from West Point. He was promoted captain of artillery in 1898 and assigned to the Seventh Artillery, which was then organized at Fort Slocum, N. Y., and commanded Fort Greble, R. I.—a fort that commands the western entrance to Narragansett Bay—during the Spanish-American War. Lundeen is, of course, in appearance, speech, and sentiments, a thorough American, yet he is proud of his Swedish birth and his Scandinavian ancestry, and takes pains to let his nationality be known.

In 1879 he was married to Mary Cutler Johnson, of Minneapolis, Minn. They have two daughters.

Lundholm, Erik Mauritz, physician and surgeon—St. Paul—born 20 June, 1858, in Venjan, Dalarne, Sweden. After having completed his college education at Falun, he entered the medical department of the University of Upsala in 1881, remaining there five years; and then continued his studies at the Karolinska Institutet located in Stockholm, from which he graduated in 1890. It must be remembered that the laws of Sweden require the medical students to take their first examination at one of the universities of Upsala or Lund, the second and third examinations may be taken either at one of the universities or at the Karolinska Institutet in Stockholm; besides, the students must do certain hospital work, and their last hospital work must be done in Stockholm. And the students, to save expense and time, generally complete the first five or six years of their medical studies at one of the universities, and the last four at the Karolinska Institutet. Lundholm also followed this custom. For three summers he served as assistant physician at the springs of Sätra, Vestmanland, and in Djursätra, Vestergötland; then visited the United States in 1888, passed his examination in St. Paul before the state medical board of Minnesota, and returned to Sweden to complete his studies. Since 1891 he has successfully practiced in St. Paul, besides being connected with Bethesda Hospital in St. Paul, having had charge for some years of the gynecalogical and surgical department of this institution, and is recognized as one of the ablest surgeons in the Northwest. Lundholm was married to Anna Olson, of Gestrikland, in 1890. They have children.

P. T. MEGAARDEN, MINNEAPOLIS.

G. F. SUNWALL, MINNEAPOLIS.

Lunnow, Magnus, journalist — Minneapolis — born 25 Sept., 1852, in Broby, Skåne, Sweden.   Lunnow received a college education in Kristianstad, served for some time as private tutor, and emigrated to America in 1874, coming to Canada, where he supported himself as a common laborer, later as a shipping clerk.   In 1878 he accepted a position on the editorial staff of *Svenska Tribunen,* and became managing editor of *Minnesota Stats Tidning* two years later.   After some time Lunnow became editor and part proprietor of *Svenska Folkets Tidning,* in Minneapolis, with which paper he is still connected.   *Svenska Folkets Tidning,* which may be regarded as a continuation of *Minnesota Stats Tidning,* and as the exponent of the progressive and liberal ideas once represented by the latter, has had a marked success, which is largely due to Lunnow's able service.   Lunnow is unmarried.

Magnus, Daniel, educator — Northfield — born 1851, in Vermland, Sweden.   At the age of nineteen he emigrated to this country; graduated from the classical department of Oberlin College, Ohio, in 1881, and from the theological department of that institution three years later; then studied one year in Sweden and Germany, and attended the University of Upsala, Sweden, in 1891–92.   Since 1885 he has been professor in Carleton College, Northfield, being one of the most successful Swedish educators in the state, and through his efforts many young Scandinavians have been induced to attend Carleton College.   Magnus is unmarried.

Mattson, Hans, pioneer and soldier—Minneapolis—born 23 Dec., 1832, in Önnestad, Skåne, Sweden; died 5 March, 1893.   *The North,* at the time of his death, gave the fol-

lowing biography of him: "He received a good education
in Kristianstad; served a year and a half in the Swedish
army as cadet of the artillery. Emigrated in the spring of
1851, arriving at Boston June 29. Suffered the hardships
and disappointments incident to ignorance of the English
language, and inability to perform hard manual labor.
Went West, to Illinois, in 1852, settling the next year in
Minnesota, which henceforth remained his home. Was married in 1855 at Vasa, Goodhue county, Minn., to Cherstin
Peterson, who, with five children, survives him. Quit farming and went into mercantile business, but was caught in
the crisis of 1857. Read law at Red Wing, and was admitted to the bar, but soon gave up practice to become
county auditor of Goodhue county. Commenced to take
active part in politics as a Republican. During the summer
of 1861, organized a company of young Goodhue county
Swedes and Norwegians, with whom, in the fall, he reported
at Fort Snelling; was elected its captain, and went South
with the Third Regiment in Nov. Was promoted to major
the following year; was on his way back after having been
home sick on furlough, when the regiment surrendered at
Murfreesboro. Was made a lieutenant colonel after the
surrender of Vicksburg, and, in April, 1863, was promoted
to colonel, remaining in command of the regiment until
Sept. 16, 1865, when it was mustered out at Fort Snelling,
Minn.. Assisted in establishing *Svenska Amerikanaren*
in Chicago. Was, in 1867, appointed secretary of the Minnesota board of emigration. Returned on his first visit to
Sweden in 1868. Was in 1869 elected secretary of state
for Minnesota, but left before the expiration of his term with

his family for Sweden, as general agent in northern Europe
for the Northern Pacific R. R. Co. Returned to the United
States early in 1876. Was elected a presidential elector the
same year. Helped to establish *Svenska Tribunen*, of
Chicago, having previously commenced the publication of
Minnesota Stats Tidning, at Minneapolis, with which
latter he remained identified until 1881. On July 2, 1881, was
appointed consul general to India. Filled this important
position with great credit for two years, when he returned
home and tendered his resignation. Was appointed manager of a land grant company in New Mexico and
Colorado. In 1886 was elected secretary of state for Minnesota, and re-elected in 1888, serving two terms. In 1887
he organized the Security Savings and Loan Association, of
Minneapolis, whose president he was at the time of his
death. Two years later he formed a company for the publication of *The North*. Was one of the principal promoters,
in 1888, of the 250th anniversary celebration of the landing
of the first Swedish settlers on the Delaware, and collected
the addresses delivered on this occasion in a small *Souvenir*.
In 1891 wrote and published a volume of recollections,
which in the Swedish version is known as *Minnen*, while
the English edition is entitled *The Story of an Emigrant*.
Mattson's knowledge was confined to no particular class of
people. Swedish-Americans naturally looked up to him as
a leader, for he possessed in an eminent degree many of the
requirements of leadership." *Valkyrian* for August, 1897,
says of Mattson: "His character shows us, in general features, the product of the two factors, Swedish birth and
education combined with a long and active life under the

protection of the American flag. Very few Swedish-Americans have led such a romantic life as his. It was rich in sudden changes and new departures; and behind the outlines of this life lay an interesting world which at first sight looks less important, but which in fact is more instructive to him who desires to study it in the light of the spirit of the times in which he most vigorously appeared as the Swedish pioneer in America."

Megaarden, Philip Tollef, sheriff—Minneapolis—born 2 Oct., 1864, in Alamakee county, Iowa. His parents were born in Norway, and his father served three years in the Fourth Iowa Cavalry during the Civil War. Young Megaarden attended public schools in Dickinson county, Iowa, and in Minneapolis, and he has resided in that city since 1877. In 1878 he entered Augsburg Seminary, but the death of his father compelled him to discontinue his college education and enter the everyday battle of life in order to support a number of little brothers and sisters. At first he performed manual labor, but later on he successively held the positions of clerk in a fuel office, bookkeeper, and court officer. Meanwhile he continued his studies as best he could, and often did he pore over his books into the small hours of night. In the course of time he managed to take a course in a business college, and in 1892 completed a three years' course in the law department of the State University, receiving the degree of LL. B. Megaarden was admitted to the bar the same year; completed a post-graduate course in his alma mater the next year, receiving the degree of LL. M.; practiced law for some time; served as chief deputy sheriff of Hennepin county in

1895–96; resumed the practice of law; but on Jan. 1, 1899, entered upon his duties as sheriff of Hennepin county. As deputy sheriff Megaarden made an excellent record, and demonstrated his ability to manage public affairs. Henceforth it was generally admitted that he was one of the leading Scandinavian public men in the city of Minneapolis. He is a rock-ribbed Republican, and belongs to more than a dozen different political clubs and secret organizations, of which may be mentioned the K. of P., the I. O. O. F., the Freemasons, the Elks, the Viking League, the Modern Woodmen, the Red Men, the Modern Samaritans, and Sönner af Norge. He is also secretary of the interstate sheriffs' association. Megaarden was married to Angeline Erickson, of Lake Crystal, Minn., in 1897.

Mohn, Thorbjörn N., educator—Northfield—born 15 July, 1844, in Saude, Nedre Telemarken, Norway. At the age of nine he came with his parents to this country; they settled in Columbia county, Wis., but moved to Dodge county, Minn., in 1860. Young Mohn attended the public schools; worked on his father's farm for some time; graduated from Luther College in 1870; and completed his theological studies at Concordia Theological Seminary three years later. After having been ordained by the president of the Norwegian Synod, he was pastor of congregations in Chicago and St. Paul, and from 1875 to 1899 was president of St. Olaf College, Northfield, Minn. But as soon as the school became the property of the United Church in 1899, he was dispensed with as president, but retained as a teacher. Mohn is considered to be an educator, but was not successful as manager of the school, and the attendance was steadily diminishing during the last decade of his administration. Rev. J. C. Jensson, in *American Lutheran Biographies*, says: 'Mohn has labored faithfully to build up a good school, and was for several years chairman of the ministerial conference of the Norwegian Evangelical Lutheran Synod for the district of Minnesota, and in 1888 he, together with many others, severed his connection with the synod, and effected the organization known as Anti-Missourians, which in 1890 joined in forming the United Norwegian Lutheran Church.' In 1875 he was married to Anna Elizabeth Ringstad, of Decorah, Iowa; they have several children.

Muus, Bernt Julius, clergyman—Norway—born 15 Mar., 1832, in Snaasen, Trondhjem stift, Norway. His father kept a country store; his mother was a daughter of the rector of the parish, Jens Rynning, in whose home Muus was brought up, as his mother died when he was an infant. At the age of seventeen he graduated from the Latin school in Trondhjem; then entered the University of Norway, not knowing exactly whether he should prepare for the ministry or become a civil engineer; but his father's entreaties prevailed, and in 1854 he received his degree as candidate of theology. After having been engaged in teaching, both as tutor for children and as teacher in a couple of schools in Kristiania for five years, Muus in 1859 accepted a call from a Norwegian Lutheran church in Holden, Goodhue county, Minn. Rev. J. C. Jensson, in *American Lutheran Biographies*, says: "The church government kindly allowed him to be ordained without taking the usual minister's oath, which he could not take without conscientious scruples." Having been received as a member of the Norwegian Synod, he commenced his ministerial duties in Goodhue and Rice counties. Muus held meetings in twenty-eight preaching stations scattered throughout Minnesota and the western part of Wisconsin. Most of these stations could be visited only twice a year. In later years, however, he received assistance. When the Minnesota District of the synod was organized in 1876, Muus was elected its president, a position he held for nine years, and was the chief promoter in founding St. Olaf College. Muus had had considerable experience in newspaper work when he came to America, and has written numerous articles for the Norwegian as well as for the Norwegian-American press, besides being the author of a few smaller religious books. He served the same congregation—which is now part of the United Church—ever since his arrival in this country up to 1899, when he returned to Norway. During the predistination controversy he sided with the Anti-Missourians, being for years one of the fiercest opponents of some of the principles advocated by the Norwegian Synod, from which organization he never withdrew, until he was expelled in 1898. He attempted reformation, not revolution. He held a unique position, being both conservative and radical. Yet it seems that his standpoint was more logical than that of his brethren who withdrew from the synod. Rev. John Halvorson says: "Muus was a leading spirit, a powerful character, an organizer; but unyielding and harsh in dealing with human frailties." He was married just before leaving Norway, but his family life was not happy. His wife sued him for cruelty and harsh treatment, in 1880, which resulted in a separation; and although the people at large considered Muus the suffering party, yet he lost much of his influence.

Myran, Ole H., state senator—Ada—born 18 Jan., 1853, in Nore, Numedal, Norway. He received a common school education at his birthplace and in this country; came from Norway with his parents in 1868, stopping one year in Illinois, and settling in Goodhue county, Minn., the following year. He worked on farms around Zumbrota and clerked in that town for years; was engaged in farming on his own account in Lincoln county; and settled at Ada in 1881. Here he kept a hotel for three years, and since the middle of the eighties he has been engaged in the mercantile business. In 1898 he was elected to the senate and served as chairman of the drainage committee. He is a Republican and a member of the Order of Odd Fellows and of the Knights of Pythias. Myran has been married twice, and at present is a widower. He has several children.

Nelson, Andrew, state senator—Litchfield—born 15 Dec., 1829, in Frönnenge, Halland, Sweden. After having received a common school education he emigrated to the U. S. in 1856, and spent the next two years in Galesburg, Ill., working as a common laborer; came to Minnesota in 1858; stayed near Willmar for five years, working on his claim, but the Indians drove him to St. Paul in 1862. The next year he went to Washington county and engaged in farming, staying there about five years; came to Meeker county in 1869, and bought a large farm. In 1871 he engaged in general merchandising in Litchfield, continuing the business until 1876; since then he has been in the banking business most of the time. He was president of Meeker County

KNUTE NELSON, ALEXANDRIA.

LUTH JAEGER, MINNEAPOLIS.

L. O. THORPE, WILLMAR.

REV. F. O. NILSSON, HOUSTON.

VICTOR NILSSON, MINNEAPOLIS.

Bank for a while, has since held the same position in the Bank of Litchfield, and owns considerable property. Nelson represented his district in the state legislature in 1874, and in the state senate in 1875-6; has been county commissioner and member of the city council, and has held various local offices. He is a member of the Swedish Lutheran church, of which he has been a trustee for several years; belongs to the Republican party; was married to Ellen Johnson in 1868.

Nelson, Andrew, legislator—Norseland—born 12 July, 1837, near Kristianstad, Sweden. In 1855 he came with his parents to this country. They settled in Nicollet county, Minn., where Nelson now owns and cultivates several large farms, and is considered to be one of the wealthiest Swedish farmers in Minnesota. Rev. E. Norelius in his history says that Nelson has taken great interest in the Swedish Lutheran church, and been a constant financial contributor to Gustavus Adolphus College. He represented his district in the legislature in the seventies. In 1863 he was married to Carolina Pehrson; they have several children.

Nelson, Knute, United States senator—Alexandria— born 2 Feb., 1843, in Voss, near Bergen, Norway. His parents and their ancestors for generations back belonged to the yeomanry of the country. At the age of three years he lost his father, and a little more than three years later he came with his mother to the U. S., arriving at Chicago in July, 1849. The cholera then raged in the city, in most instances with fatal effect. Nelson was stricken with the dread disease, but was among the few fortunate ones who survived the plague. In 1850 he moved with his mother to Walworth county, Wis., and from there to Dane county,

30

in the same state, in 1853. After having, through considerable obstacles, obtained a fair common school education, he
entered Albion Academy as a student in 1858, and pursued
his studies there till 1861, when he, with a score of school-
mates, enlisted in the 4th Wisconsin Regiment. He
remained in the service as private and non-commissioned
officer till 1864, when he returned and resumed his studies
at the academy, graduating in 1865. He participated with
his regiment in the capture of New Orleans, the first siege of
Vicksburg, the battles of Baton Rouge and Camp Bisland,
and the siege of Port Hudson. In the great charge of this
siege, on the 14th of June, 1863, he was wounded and captured, and remained a prisoner until the place surrendered
on the 9th of July. In 1865 he became a law student in the
office of Senator Wm. F. Vilas, Madison, Wis. He was
admitted to the bar of the circuit court for Dane county in
1867, and immediately entered on the practice of his profession. That year he was elected member of the assembly for
the then second district of Dane county, his home, and was
re-elected in 1868. In 1871 he moved to Alexandria, Douglas county, Minn., where he has ever since been engaged in
farming and practicing law. As a lawyer he has had an
extensive practice in that part of the state. In 1872–74 he
was county attorney for Douglas county, and in 1875–78
he was state senator in the thirty-ninth legislative district,
composed of five counties. In the senate he was instrumental in securing the legislation under which the unfinished
lines of the St. Paul & Pacific Railway were completed. In
1880 he was presidential elector on the Garfield and Arthur
ticket. In the fall of 1882, in a campaign of unparalleled heat

and bitterness, he was elected member of Congress for the fifth district of Minnesota, by a plurality of 4,500 votes. He was re-elected in 1884 by a plurality of 12,500 votes, and in 1886 he was re-elected by an almost unanimous vote. While in Congress he was a member of the committee on Indian affairs, and was especially instrumental in securing the passage of a law for the opening of the Red Lake and other Indian reservations in Minnesota, and for civilizing the Indians, and allotting lands to them in severalty for farming purposes. In Congress he was an ardent tariff reformer not altogether in harmony with his party, even going so far as to vote for the Mills bill. This subjected him to some criticism among the politicians, but the great mass of the people were with him and approved of his independent course. He was a member of the board of regents of the state university from 1882 until 1893, and has taken a deep interest in the welfare and growth of that institution. In 1892 he was unanimously nominated, by acclamation, candidate for governor, of the Republican party, and was elected in November following, by a plurality of 14,620 votes. Nelson made an excellent record as governor, and was again unanimously re-nominated in 1894 and re-elected by a plurality of 60,000 votes. But in January the following year he was elected U. S. senator by the legislature for a term of six years, thus becoming the first Scandinavian who has been chosen to represent his new country in the capacity of senator, governor, and congressman; and Nelson has filled all the positions mentioned with great credit to himself and has been an honor to the state of Minnesota. It may be fair, however, to mention that his election to the U. S. senate did not seem to be popular with a large majority of the people. They wanted him to be their governor, they voted for him as such, and did not desire a substitute to occupy his chair. Nelson's popularity suffered severely, yet the state did not lose anything, for as senator he has worked hard and conscientiously. He is married and has grown children.

Nelson, Peter, state senator—Red Wing—born 14 Apr., 1843, in Skatelöf, Småland, Sweden. He received a common school education in his native country; emigrated to the U. S. at the age of twenty-three; lived in Rockford, Ill., a short time, then moved to Mississippi, where for a few years he was engaged in Oxford as a building contractor and hardware merchant. Since 1873 he has been in the hardware business in Red Wing. Nelson is one of the few Swedes who have joined the Democratic party, of which he is a leading member, and was the party's nominee for secretary of state in 1892, but with the rest of the state ticket was defeated. He was a member of the Democratic central committee for several years. In 1887 he was state senator and secured, among other things, the passage of a bill which provided for the removal of the State Reform School from St. Paul to Red Wing. Nelson married Olivia Olson in 1871. They have grown children.

Neumann, C. F., writer and sign painter—St. Paul—born 17 Jan., 1850, in Jönköping, Sweden. His father was a musical director, a German by birth, who traveled through the Scandinavian countries, but resided otherwise in Denmark, of which country young Neumann's mother was a native. Neumann attended a Latin school in Copenhagen for four years; became a sailor at the age of fourteen and followed this life for three years, visiting both the Arctic and the Tropical regions and most of the European countries; landed in Philadelphia at the age of seventeen, and, having no money, he walked to Chicago, which took him seven weeks. After having worked as a common laborer for a short time he learnt the painting business; started a shop of his own in Chicago, in 1871; located in Minneapolis, in 1880, and here followed his trade for eight years; then moved his business to St. Paul. He was one of the chief men in promoting the building of Dania Hall in Minneapolis. Neumann has contributed quite extensively to the American daily papers in St. Paul and Minneapolis, as well as to the Danish-Norwegian press. He has been married three times, and he had children by all his wives.

Nilsson, F. O., clergyman and pioneer—Houston—born 28 July, 1809, in Värö, Halland, Sweden; died 1881. His mother died when he was seven years of age, and his father, who owned a small farm, was a confirmed drunkard and had to be put under guardianship. Consequently, young Nilsson enjoyed few or no educational advantages, and at the early age of fourteen commenced to earn his own living by learning the shoemaker's trade, and for four years followed his master from house to house assisting him in making shoes. At the age of eighteen he became a sailor, and visited, among other places, also New York, where he deserted his vessel in 1832. A couple of years later a Methodist revivalist converted him, but he continued the life of a sailor until his thirtieth year. It does not appear that Nilsson was dissipated before his conversion, but on the contrary was during his youth rather religiously inclined, which culminated in an intense fear of damnation. In the fall of 1839 he visited his relatives in Sweden. He did not return to America as he had intended, but began to urge people to repent of their sins, wandering on foot from house to house, from village to village. In 1842 the Seamen's Friend Society in New York appointed him missionary for the sailors in Gothenburg, with $100 salary a year. When he was married, in 1844 or 1845, his wages were raised to $175 a year, on which he supported himself and family for a number of years. At times he also visited the surrounding country as well as Norway. Nilsson remained a member of the Lutheran state church up to 1845, although he was arrested a couple of times for breaking the conventicle law. At this time a Swedish-American sailor and Baptist, Capt. G. W. Schroeder, visited Gothenburg and became acquainted with Nilsson. Through Schroeder's influence he began to study the question of infant baptism, and was soon convinced that it was all wrong. As a consequence he went to Hamburg, Germany, in 1847, in order to be immersed by Rev. J. G. Oncken. On his return to Sweden he commenced with great discretion to preach the new doctrine. During the night of Sept. 21, 1848, Nilsson's wife and four other persons, most of whom appear to have been his relatives, were immersed, and the first Swedish Baptist church in the world was at the same time organized in Landa village, Halland. A. P. Förster had been sent from Hamburg to perform the ceremonies. Nilsson was ordained in Hamburg the next spring, when the Baptists in his native land numbered thirty-five persons. Religious toleration was not a virtue or a fashion in Sweden at that time. Nilsson was, in

1850, mobbed, arrested, and condemned to be banished from the kingdom by Göta *hofrätt*, in Jönköping, simply because he had tried to spread the doctrines of the Baptists in his native land. He appeared in person before King Oscar I., and asked him to commute the sentence; then wrote to him to the same effect, at the same time suggesting that it was the duty of the Lutheran clergymen to try to re-convert dissenters to Lutheranism, which had not been properly done in Nilsson's case; and at last appealed to the mercy of the monarch. But nothing availed. He left Sweden July 4, 1851, probably being the last person who had to be a fugitive from that kingdom for the sake of religion. His banishment created a stir in the civilized world, and for a while Sweden was considered to be a land of intolerance and bigotry. The public opinion of the world— that great power before which monarchs and mobs tremble —had undoubtedly a great deal to do in swinging Sweden, at about this time, into line with the most progressive lands in regard to religious liberty. Yet some of the Swedish Lutheran clergymen, who generally have been blamed for all the religious shortcomings in their country, had for years before advocated the utmost religious freedom. Before Nilsson left Sweden he selected leaders for his four small congregations; then visited Copenhagen, Hamburg, London, and Norway. On his return from the latter country he stopped at Gothenburg to take his wife with him, and con-ducted a few meetings in secret, but the police sent him to Denmark. After having remained in Copenhagen a couple of years, he emigrated to America in 1853; preached for some time in Burlington, Iowa; bought land and settled near Houston, Minn., in 1855; and during five years organized seven Swedish Baptist congregations in Minnesota. He was sent, in 1860, by an American Baptist congregation in New York as a missionary to Sweden. On his return he was pardoned by King Carl XV., and soon located in Gothenburg, where for seven years he had charge of the small Baptist congregation in that city. When about sixty years of age, Nilsson returned to America, partly, it seems, because other Baptist clergymen excelled him in learning and ability; but principally because he had by reading some of Theodore Parker's works commenced to doubt the truth of parts of the Bible. Yet for a few years afterwards he was pastor of the Swedish Baptist church at Houston; but his religious doubts were discovered, and most of his former friends deserted him. It has been asserted that he became a rank infidel; this has been denied by the Baptists, who, however, admit that he could not be called an orthodox Christian during the last days of his eventful life, and one of their historians, Rev. A. G. Hall, says that the seed of infidelity had undoubtedly remained in Nilsson's soul ever since his youth as the result of having read Thomas Paine's writings. Nilsson's boldness and combativeness made up for what he lacked in education and talent. He converted many. The Baptists maintain that Nilsson was an honest enthusiast who sacrificed much for his religion; the Lutherans and Methodists who came in contact with him in the Northwest claim that he was a coarse and unscrupulous adventurer who shrank from no means to accomplish his purpose. Both opinions are probably correct, as he appears to have lacked the proper balance-wheel, and flung from

PROF. SVEN OFTEDAL, MINNEAPOLIS.

PROF. GEORG SVERDRUP, MINNEAPOLIS.

one extreme to another, partly because his nature craved excitement.

Nilsson, Victor, author and critic—Minneapolis—born 10 Mar., 1867, in Östra Torp, Skåne, Sweden. His father owned this estate on the southermost point of southwestern Sweden, where Victor was born, but the family resided in Gothenburg from 1870 to 1885. Young Nilsson received a careful college education in the latter city, where his father was a prosperous merchant. The whole family came to America in 1885. He was connected with the editorial staffs of various Swedish papers in the Twin Cities up to 1891, when he was appointed librarian of the East Side Branch of the Minneapolis Public Library. For a number of years he attended lectures in the University of Minnesota, making a thorough study of Romance and Teutonic philology, with Old Norse history, language, and literature as a specialty. In 1897 this institution conferred the degree of doctor of philosophy upon him. His thesis on the occasion was a scientific treatise on *Havamal* in the older Edda, and has been recognized by scholars on both sides of the Atlantic. Nilsson has always been an enthusiastic admirer of Northern culture, especially of all pertaining to literature, art, and music; and on these subjects has contributed many critical articles to the Swedish-American and Anglo-American journals and magazines. He possesses a fine literary judgment; and as a critic probably outranks all other Scandinavian-Americans. His book *Förenta Staternas Presidenter* has been well spoken of; and his history of Sweden, a large volume of nearly 500 pages and published in the English language in 1899, contains a complete history of the Swedish people from the earliest period down to the present time, and the presentation of recent events is especially masterly and critical. He has written a number of short stories, and delivered several lectures in different parts of the country. He was secretary of the executive committee of five for the great Scandinavian singing festival in Minneapolis in 1891. Nilsson has been president of the Orpheus Singing Society; financial secretary of the United Scandinavian Singers of America, and of the American Union of Swedish Singers; and was the official speaker during the concert tour to Sweden, in 1897, of Swedish-American singers, and at the same time visited several other European countries. He is not married. His sister Emma Nilsson has a high reputation as a singer, having for years studied in Berlin, Germany, where she made a successful debut in grand opera in 1884. His younger sister, Mrs. Bertha Nilsson Best, has made quite a reputation as an opera singer.

Norelius, E., clergyman and author—Vasa—born 26 Oct., 1833, in Hassela, Helsingland, Sweden. His parents were pious farmers, who, like most of the Swedish people of the same class in those days, did not believe in any higher education than was necessary for confirmation; but young Norelius succeeded in persuading them to permit him to attend a college in Hudiksvall for a couple of years. He was religiously inclined from his early childhood, and was an enthusiastic believer in the pietism advocated by Rev. F. G. Hedberg, the noted Finnish divine. Without any specific reason or any certain plans for the future, he, at the age of seventeen, emigrated to this country, spending eleven weeks on the ocean. After having landed in New York he proceeded to Chicago, where he met the well-known Swedish pioneer Rev. G. Unonius, who advised him to go to the Episcopal seminary, at Nashota, Wis., and there prepare to enter the Episcopalian ministry. But Norelius was too much of a Lutheran to even dream of any such thing. He concluded, in his perplexity as to what to do and where to go, to seek the advice of the pioneer of the Swedish-American Lutheran ministers, Prof. L. P. Esbjörn, with whom he was not personally acquainted; but he knew that Esbjörn had come to America the year before and settled at Andover, Henry county, Ill. Believing that Esbjörn was the right person to give the best advice, Norelius set out from Chicago to hunt him up, going by canal a hundred miles to La Salle, and footing the rest of the road for some sixty miles to Andover. Here he found Esbjörn living among his countrymen in a primitive way, in great poverty and sickness; but he received Norelius kindly, and advised him to enter Capital University, Columbus, Ohio, where support had been offered to a poor Swedish student who would prepare for the Lutheran ministry. The famous Jenny Lind had also given $1,500 to the school in order that a Swedish professorship might be established there. Esbjörn accompanied Norelius to this institution in the spring of 1851, where the latter spent about five years. For defraying the expenses of the journey from Illinois to Ohio, and for some clothing, Dr. Passavant, of Pittsburg, Pa., sent Norelius twenty-two dollars. His vacations were spent in various ways: for example, working on farms, chopping wood, selling books, teaching, and preaching. During his last vacation he preached and taught school at Chisago Lake, Minn.; previously to this he had done the same thing in Chicago. In 1855 the Evangelical Lutheran Synod of Northern Illinois licensed him to preach for the Swedes in several places in Tippecanoe county, Ind.; but these people had recently arrived from the old country, and were too poor to buy the expensive land in the Eastern states, therefore no permanent Swedish settlement in this part of the country was to be expected. Norelius and another gentleman were delegated to go to Minnesota in search of a suitable place for a settlement; they came to Vasa, Goodhue county, Minn., in 1855—where Col. H. Mattson and his party had already a couple of years before commenced a prosperous Swedish settlement—and Norelius at once organized churches in Red Wing and Vasa, of which he became pastor the following year, when he was ordained. He had to suffer all the inconveniences and trials of a pioneer life; many settlements were founded and churches organized; he had to spend his time more as a traveling missionary than as a settled pastor. In 1858 he was elected county auditor of Goodhue county, but at the same time received an offer to become editor of *Hemlandet,* in Chicago, which he accepted, resigned his pastoral duties, and proceeded to Chicago. In 1859 Norelius, on account of ill health, moved to Attica, Ind., and he took charge of the Swedish Lutheran church there, but the following year accepted a call as a traveling missionary in Minnesota. During this time he passed through many thrilling events, experienced many perils and self-denials, visited—on foot or on horseback—every nook and corner where any Swedes had settled, preached and organized churches in many places. He has undoubtedly sacrificed more in order to elevate his country-men in Minnesota, and has benefited them more than any other Swede. His salary amounted to about $400 a year, out of which he had to pay all his traveling expenses, and at the end of the year he might have saved souls, but nothing of his salary remained. In 1861 he moved from St. Paul, where his family had resided for a year, to Good hue county, and took charge of his old congregations in Red Wing and at Vasa. Ever since his ministerial labor has been chiefly confined to Goodhue county, although he has done some missionary work on the Pacific Coast and in various other parts of the country. His health has been delicate during the greater part of his ministry. Besides his regular work in the ministry, he founded an orphanage at Vasa in 1865, and conducted it himself for eleven years. In 1862 he commenced a private school in Red Wing, which has grown up to be Gustavus Adolphus College, in St. Peter. Norelius was in 1874 elected president of the Augustana Synod, serving in that capacity for seven years, and was elected to the same position in 1899. (Most of the above facts in this biography have been collected from *American Lutheran Biographies*, by Rev. J. C. Jensson). At Red Wing, in 1857, he commenced to publish *Minnesota Posten,* the first Swedish newspaper in Minnesota; the venture was too early, and proved to be a financial failure, and after one year's starveling existence, the paper was united with *Hemlandet* in Chicago, of which Norelius, as before stated, became editor. It may be of interest to note that the first six numbers of *Minnesota Posten* con-

tained the following notice: "Because ready cash in these
times is scarce, the editor will, for the subscription for the
paper, take farm and other products, which will be valued
at market prices," and the last number announces that "the
paper must cease, because many subscribers failed to send
in their subscriptions." In 1872 he started *Lutersk
Kyrkotidning*, which was merged into *Augustana* the
following year. Norelius and P. Sjöblom commenced to
publish *Evangelisk Lutersk Tidskrift* in 1877, but
changed the name to *Skaffaren* the following year. He
has also contributed extensively, especially on religious and
historical subjects, to many Swedish-American journals.
In 1889 he was called to the editorial chair of *Augustana,*
the official paper of the Augustana Synod, published at
Rock Island, Ill., but his ill health compelled him to resign the
following year. He has for a number of years been editor
of *Korsbaneret*, which is an annual published by the
Augustana Synod. Norelius is the author of the following
books: *Salems Sånger* (1859), *Handbok för Sön-
dagsskolan* (1865), *Ev. Luterska Augustana Synoden
i Nord Amerika och dess Mission* (1870), and *De
Svenska Luterska Församlingarnas och Svenskarnes
Historia i Amerika* (1890). Only the first volume of the
last mentioned work, which deals with the Swedes in America from the earliest emigration of the nineteenth century
to 1860, has yet appeared. His history is intensely
Lutheran, somewhat partial, poorly classified, and not
indexed. The author relates his experiences and the experiences of others very minutely, without much attempt to
condense the whole to a scientific historical treaty. The

facts on the whole are fairly correct, except in regard to
the first Swedish settlement in Minnesota, which was not
stated in 1851, as he asserts, but in 1850, when Oscar Roos
and two other Swedes made the first settlement at Marine,
Washington county, which is substantiated both by Roos
himself and in a little excellent pamphlet, *Svenskarne i
St. Croix-dalen, Minnesota* (1879), by Robert Gronberger.* Norelius's description of the natural appearance of
the country in the early days is excellent, but in many
respects his earlier and smaller history is superior to his
later and larger book. All his writings contain a great
deal of wit, humor, and imagination. Col. H. Mattson, in
his admirable book, *Minnen* (1890), refers to Norelius in
the following manner: "In the beginning of the month
of September, 1855, Rev. E. Norelius visited the settlement
(Vasa), and organized a Lutheran church. Thirty-five
years have elapsed since that time, and many of those who
belonged to the first church at Vasa now rest in mother
earth close by the present stately church edifice which still
belongs to the same congregation and is situated only a
short distance from the place where the latter was organ-

---

* In regard to this sentence, which was also in the first edition of this volume, Norelius remarks: "It depends upon what you mean by the word 'settlement.' If it can be
called a settlement where two or three single men, bachelors, make a claim without
making such claim a constant habitation, then of course I do not dispute the priority
of the Marine colony. But if by a settlement is meant a permanent habitation, especially by one or more families, then the Swedish colony at Marine is not older than the
one at Chisago Lake." As I understand it, a settlement may be permanent or temporary, and may be composed of families, bachelors, or old maids. The early arrival in
this state of Oscar Roos and his companions has been mentioned in a few places in this
volume simply because it was deemed to be of considerable historical importance, and
not as a reflection upon Norelius for having failed to refer to those pioneers. The constant reference to this omission on my part is a mistake which can hardly be avoided in
a cyclopedic work like this, and I prefer the repetition of important histerical facts
to the omission of those facts.—EDITOR.

ized.   Rev. Norelius himself lives only a few hundred yards
from the church building.   Thirty-five years have changed
the then cheerful, hopeful young man into a veteran,
crowned with honor, and full of wisdom and experience.
His beneficent influence on the Swedes of Goodhue county
and of the whole Northwest will make his name dear to
coming generations of our people."   Norelius visited his
native land in 1868 for the purpose of improving his health,
but returned in a worse condition.   In 1855 he was married
to Inga C. Peterson, of West Point, Ind., by whom he has
had four sons and one daughter.

Oftedal, Sven, educator—Minneapolis—born 22 March,
1844, in Stavanger, Norway. He graduated from the Latin
school of his native city in 1862; completed his theological
studies at the University of Norway in 1871, having also
devoted much of his time to the study of ancient and modern
languages, literature, and philosophy; studied one year in
Paris, France; traveled through several of the European
countries; and accepted a call as theological professor at
Augsburg Seminary, Minneapolis, in 1873, where he has
since remained.   The great success of the seminary is largely
due to Oftedal's energy and perseverance.   In 1878 he was
elected a member of the board of education, a position he
held for ten years, being president of that body for four
years; and in 1886, when the Minneapolis Public Library
was established, he was elected by the legislature as one of
the chartered members of that library, and has been chairman of the library committee ever since.   In these two capa-
cities he has been able to do more than any other person to
have the Scandinavians in the city recognized by the public

DR. C. J. RINGNELL, MINNEAPOLIS.

O. H. MYRAN, ADA.

C. A. RICE, WILLMAR.

DR. G. P. SANDBERG, ST. PAUL.

J. SHALEEN, LINDSTROM.

at large. He was the originator of the present high school system in Minneapolis and the branch system of the Minneapolis Public Library. Oftedal has taken an active part in temperance and church work, being one of the organizers of the first stable Norwegian temperance society in Minneapolis, and was for years one of the leading men in the Norwegian-Danish Conference. Oftedal occupies a unique position in the history of the Norwegian Lutheran churches in America. Most of the leaders in those churches have at one time or another been engaged in controversies bristling with harsh words. But he alone has time again been in the midst of the fiercest of these battles. Indeed, he has spent years in a perfect calm; but again and again the storm has gathered around that man as around no other Norwegian-American. At some future date he may possibly be taken as the ablest and grandest expounder of that remarkable hatred of conventional restraint which characterized the Norsemen of his time. Even at close range it is not very difficult to see that Oftedal could have spent a life of ease and unruffled honor if he had chosen to devote his magnificent mental gifts to the upbuilding of the existing institutions of the majorities, instead of repeatedly siding with apparently hopeless minorities. His is surely a mind that rebels against power as such; but it aims rather at the destruction of what is conceived as baneful influences than at self-aggrandizement; bitter as it may be at times, it is, after all, more altruistic than egotistic. Oftedal cannot be properly judged until some time after his life-work is completed. He is married, and has grown children.

Olson, C. O. Alexius, lawyer and legislator — Minneapolis—born 5 April, 1872, in Long, Vestergötland, Sweden. At the age of two years he emigrated with his mother to America, coming directly to Minneapolis, where later he attended the public schools, graduating from the North Side High School in 1891; employed his out-of-school hours as carrier on the daily papers, and as clerk in stores and offices; graduated from the academic department of the University of Minnesota in 1895, from the law department in 1896, and in 1897 received the degree of LL.M. from the same institution; was admitted to the bar by the Minnesota supreme court in June, 1896, and has since been engaged in the general practice of law; at the University was actively interested in student affairs, serving successively as class president, editor of *The Ariel* (the students' paper), and as cadet major of the University Battalion; is a member of the general college fraternity Zeta Psi, and of Delta Chi (Law); in 1892 traveled in Europe, visiting Germany, Denmark, Sweden, Norway, and England; during the summer of 1893 was employed at the Chicago World's Fair; is president of the Minneapolis High School Alumni Association, and secretary of the John Ericsson Memorial Association; in religion a Lutheran; in politics a Republican; at the general election in 1898 was elected to the office of representative in the Minnesota state legislature.

Olson, Seaver Elbert, merchant—Minneapolis—born 1846, in Ringsaker, near Hamar, Norway. His boyhood was spent partly in assisting his father in his profession as carpenter, partly at school. From early childhood he showed himself to possess singular abilities. Already at the age of ten he became a teacher and conducted his own little school. Olson came with his parents to this country in 1858, and they settled on a farm near La Crosse, Wis. He attended Beloit College, Wis., for one year; commenced business for himself in Rushford, Minn., in 1867, but the entire stock was destroyed by fire in less than a month after he started. He rebuilt the store and for about three years had a good trade; then entered into partnership with his former employer in La Crosse, Wis.; but three years later the firm was dissolved, and Olson continued in the business until 1878, when he came to Minneapolis, Minn. Here he united himself with N. B. Harwood. They failed in 1880, and Olson was again made penniless, with nothing but an unimpeachable credit and an excellent record as a business man. He next went into partnership with Ingram. This firm was afterwards changed to S. E. Olson & Company, now being one of the largest dry goods establishments in the West, and perhaps the greatest Scandinavian store in the United States, doing an annual business of about $2,000,000. Olson is a stockholder of several banks, is also connected with many other large enterprises, and has a family.

Ostrom, O. N., banker and grain dealer—Minneapolis—born 29 July, 1850, in Åby, near Kristianstad, Sweden; died 1893. He emigrated to America in 1867, staid the first year at Afton, Minn., then went to St. Peter. Being a builder and contractor, he erected here, among other buildings, Gustavus Adolphus College. Ostrom moved to Minneapolis in 1877, and two years later he engaged in the general merchandise and wheat business at Evansville; this large wheat trade compelled him subsequently to build twenty-

five elevators along the Great Northern R. R. In 1882
Ostrom became one of the stockholders and directors of the
First National Bank of Alexandria; the following year he
established the Bank of Evansville, of which he assumed the
management as cashier. Ostrom returned to Minneapolis
in 1887, and, in company with other prominent Swedes, organized the Swedish American Bank, with a capital of one
hundred thousand dollars. In 1889 he organized the Inter-
State Grain company — a half million dollars' concern.
Ostrom was president and manager of the Inter-State Grain
company, and president of the Swedish American Bank. At
the age of twenty he was married to Helena Elg; they have
grown children.

Östlund, O. W., educator—Minneapolis—born 27 Sept.,
1857, in Attica, Ind. His parents were among the earliest
Swedish immigrants in this country; they came from Östergötland. Young Östlund graduated from Augustana College in 1879, and eight years later his alma mater conferred
the degree of master of arts upon him. He studied natural
sciences for two years at the University of Minnesota; has
been entomologist of the natural history survey of Minnesota since 1884, having published numerous reports on his
specialty, and contributes occasionally to some of the leading magazines on scientific subjects. Since 1890 he has
been assistant professor of zoology at the State University;
was entomologist of the State Horticultural Society from
1887-90; is a member of the Davenport Academy of Sciences,
and of the Minneapolis Academy of Science. Östlund is an
active member of the English Lutheran church, having been
one of its trustees for several years. He is unmarried.

Pederson, Knud, legislator—Underwood — born 1844, in Norway.   He came to this state in 1868, and has been engaged in farming in Otter Tail county.   He served as town supervisor, treasurer, and assessor for six years, and as county commissioner for thirteen years.   Since 1896 he has been a member of the house of representatives of the state legislature.   Pederson owes the position last mentioned to the Populist party.   He is a widower.

Petersen, Ole P., clergyman and pioneer—Minneapolis —born 28 April, 1822, in Fredrikstad, Norway.   He became an orphan at the age of six, was brought up by a well-to-do family, was a sailor for a few years, and emigrated to this country in 1843.   He was converted to Methodism by the well-known Swedish pioneer and missionary, O. G. Hedstrom, in 1846; returned to his native land three years later, and was the first who introduced the faith of Methodism in Norway; came back to America in 1850, and the next year commenced to preach among his countrymen in Winnesheik county, Iowa.   With the exception of C. B. Willerup, a Dane, Petersen was the first Methodist minister among the Norwegian pioneers in this country.   He often had to travel on foot during the hot summers and cold winters through the Western states, suffering all the hardships incidental to frontier life.   In 1850 he was married in Norway to Anne Amundsen.   They had two children, and for some years past he has been living with one of them in the East.

Petersen, W. M. H., clergyman and educator—St. Paul —born 26 Nov., 1854, in Ringerike, Norway; died 1899.   He came to this country in 1862, settling with his widowed

mother in Rochester, Minn.; stayed for some time at Pointed
Creek, Iowa; completed courses at Luther College and at
Concordia Seminary, graduating from these institutions in
1875 and 1878, respectively. During the remainder of his
life he served a Norwegian Synod congregation in St. Paul.
Having a strong memory and being an untiring student, he
gradually accumulated a great amouut of well-digested and
carefully systematized knowledge. He was a great specialist. In order to make proper use of this valuable treasure
he was appointed, in 1894, to a chair of theology in Luther
Seminary. But his health began to fail, and in 1898 he
made a trip to Europe in hopes of gaining strength. Petersen prepared his sermons with great care, and some of them
have been preserved in the collection printed by the synod.
He wrote considerably for the official paper of the synod,
and his most noted effort as an author treats of the inspiration of the Bible. He was married to Anna K. Söraas, of
Dodge county, Minn., in 1880; they had six children.

Peterson, Andrew P, state legislator—Cokato—born 7
Sept., 1851, in Sweden. At the age of nine he came with his
parents to this country; they settled in Carver county, Minn.,
where young Peterson received a good common school
education. He was in the mercantile business in Cokato for
a few years, and has since 1880 been the proprietor of a
drug store. Peterson has held various local offices, been
county commissioner of Wright county, and represented his
district in the state legislature in 1877. In 1878 he was
married to Anna S. Anderson, of Minneapolis. They have
children.

Peterson, Frank, clergyman— Minneapolis — born 19

Nov., 1847, in Stockseryd, Östergötland, Sweden. At the age of four he came with his parents to this country; they settled in Rock Island, Ill., and moved to Lansing, Iowa, in 1855, where young Peterson received a good common school education. In 1863, while not yet sixteen years old, he enlisted in the Ninth Iowa Cavalry, which was almost constantly engaged in fighting the Texas Rangers and Quantrell's Band in Missouri, Texas, and Arkansas. So depleted were the ranks of his regiment, that but few remained after the war to return home. After the war he studied one year at a university in Chicago; took a trip to Sweden, in order to improve his health, where he spent a year; taught in the public schools in Iowa and Minnesota for several years; and intended to study law, when he finally concluded to enter the ministry, and accepted a call of the Swedish Baptist church in Worthington, Minn., in 1875. After having remained there for a while, he took charge of a congregation in Chicago; came to Minneapolis in 1881, and for eleven years served the First Swedish Baptist church, which had a great prosperity during his ministry. In 1890 he accepted the appointment as district secretary of the American Baptist Missionary Union, which is one of the strongest missionary societies among Protestants, either in America or on the continent, employing 2,500 workers, scattered throughout twenty nations of the world. This society expends over a million dollars annually. Peterson was a successful teacher, is an able speaker both in Swedish and English, and has collected a great deal of material for a history of the Swedish Baptist church. In 1878 he was married to Emma C. Johnson, of Chicago.

Peterson, James A., lawyer — Minneapolis — born 18 Jan., 1859, in Dodge county, Wis. His parents were Norwegians. He graduated from the literary department of the University of Wisconsin, Madison, Wis., in 1884, and three years later from the law school of the same institution, having made his own way through college by teaching school. Since he completed his education he has been practicing his profession in Minneapolis, being recognized as one of the leading Scandinavian attorneys in the state of Minnesota. In 1893 Peterson was appointed assistant county attorney, and in 1897 and 1898 he served as county attorney. While occupying this position he became a terror to evil-doers; and the ability with which he prosecuted some public officers belonging to his own political party is claimed to have had something to do with his failure to receive the renomination for a second term which had become traditional in that party with regard to certain county officers. Peterson is a Republican. In 1889 Marie Emily Dahle, of Dane county, Wis., who is a graduate of the University of Wisconsin, and was a classmate of Peterson, became his wife. They have children.

Peterson, John, collector of customs—St. Peter—born 6 July, 1841, in Kil, Vermland, Sweden. His parents were farmers, who gave their son a good common school education, and at the age of seventeen he commenced to work in a large factory. Later on he held the position of shipping clerk; was engaged in building at Stockholm and Sundsvall for some time and in constructing railroad stations and bridges during a couple of years; and in 1867-9 was located near Karlstad as superintendent of the construction of

REV. FRANK PETERSON, MINNEAPOLIS.

REV. E. A. SKOGSBERGH, MINNEAPOLIS.

government railroad bridges. In 1869 he emigrated to America, coming directly to St. Peter, and after having worked as a common laborer for a short time, he began, in company with others, operations as a railroad contractor, and for eighteeen years the firm of which he was a member carried on a large business throughout the Northwest. Since he has followed the same occupation on his own responsibility, and has also been interested in banking and farming. Peterson has taken an active part in public affairs. He has been a member of the city council of St. Peter, serving as its president for a couple of years; was a member of the congressional committee of his district for several years; has been a delegate to numerous Republican conventions; was elected to the state senate in 1894; and in 1897 President McKinley appointed him collector of customs. He has also been a member of the board of trustees of the State Hospital for the Insane, having been appointed by Gov. Merriam and Gov. Nelson, and was a member of the board of directors and treasurer of Gustavus Adolphus College for several years. Peterson is a member of the Swedish Lutheran church; and was married in 1873 to Fredrika Elisabeth Lundberg. They have several children.

Peterson, J. W., state senator—Vasa—born 30 Mar., 1838, in Småland, Sweden. At the age of eightcen he came with his parents to this country; they settled in Chisago county, Minn., where young Peterson worked on the family homestead until 1862, when he enlisted in company I of Sixth Minnesota Volunteers. He served against the Indians in Minnesota and Dakota; was promoted to the rank of sergeant; honorably discharged in 1865, and has ever since farmed at Vasa. Peterson was in the state senate during the sessions of 1873–74, in the lower branch of the legislature in 1885, and again in the senate in 1891–93; besides, he has held several local offices. The general opinion is that he is one of the most influential Scandinavian legislators of Minnesota. Peterson is a Republican and a Lutheran, and was married in 1868 to Carrie Johnson, who is twelve years his junior.

Pettersen, Wilhelm Mauritz, educator and poet—Minneapolis—born 17 Dec., 1860, in Mandal, Kristiansand stift, Norway. His father was a sea captain of German extraction, his mother belonged to the old Norwegian farmer stock. After having graduated from Mandal's *middelskole,* he, at the age of fifteen, went to sea; passed a first mate's examination; sailed as second mate, both on Norwegian and American vessels; and came to Minneapolis in 1882. Two years after his arrival he graduated from Augsburg Seminary, Minneapolis; afterwards studied Greek and English literature for a couple of terms at the University of Minnesota; and was appointed professor of history and mathematics of his alma mater in 1889. Pettersen is a poet of considerable repute, having inherited a poetical taste and ability from his mother, who wrote verses occasionally; a volume of his collected Norwegian poems was published in 1891; and a drama, *En Ny Slägt,* appeared in 1895. It is generally admitted that Pettersen has written some excellent poetical productions. He has also considerable experience as a journalist, but his prose writings lack clearness and generalization. He is a member of the Norwegian Lutheran Free Church, is a Democrat, has delivered campaign speeches throughout the state, and has a family.

Petri, Carl J., clergyman—Minneapolis—born 16 June, 1855, in Rockford, Ill. His parents came from Småland, Sweden, to this country in 1852. They settled in Chicago, Ill., but moved to Rockford two years later, where they have resided ever since. Petri received his early education in the parochial and public schools in Rockford. In 1871 he entered Augustana College, Paxton, Ill., from which institution he was graduated in 1877, being therefore a member of the first class sent out from this institution, and has since received the degree of A. M. of his alma mater. He took special interest in languages and history, in which subjects he had the best standing in the college. Petri pursued the study of the English language with a view to become an educator in this branch, and when he came to Minneapolis in 1878, the board of directors of Augustana College advised him to continue his study of English with a view to teach it in that institution. He studied English and Anglo-Saxon at the University of Minnesota for one year; then went to Philadelphia, where he took charge of a Swedish Lutheran congregation; and attended for one year the University of Pennsylvania, taking a special course in history and English, also attending Dr. Krauth's lectures on philosophy. In 1880 he consented to be ordained. He remained in Philadelphia until 1884, when he became professor of history at Gustavus Adolphus College, in which capacity he made an excellent record. In 1888 Petri accepted a call as pastor of the largest Swedish Lutheran congregation in Minneapolis, where he has since resided. He was the originator and one of the chief leaders in the arrangement for the great celebration, in Minneapolis, in 1888, of the 250th anniversary of the landing of the Swedes in America in the 17th century. In 1893 he was one of the chief organizers of the celebration of the 300th anniversary of the Upsala Decree, being also the first one who translated said decree into English. Petri has been vice-president of the Minnesota Conference of the Swedish Augustana Synod for several years, and a member of the board of directors of Gustavus Adolphus College. In 1881 he, with others, started the *Augustana Observer*, the first English church paper among the Swedes in America. He has also been editor of an English Sunday-school paper belonging to the church. He was a member of the advisory council of the religious congress at the World's Fair in Chicago, in 1893; is a member of the Institute of Civics, and took a very active part in starting the Swedish hospital in Minneapolis, in 1898. Petri is a good speaker in both Swedish and English, and as an organizer and manager of church and social affairs, there are few of the ministers within the Augustana Synod that equal him. He was married in 1880 to Christine Andersson, of Dalarne, Sweden; the wedding ceremony being performed in the historical Old Swedes' Church, Philadelphia, Pa. They have several children.

Petri, Gustave A., lawyer—Minneapolis—born 21 Sept., 1863, in Rockford, Ill. His parents came from Småland, Sweden, to Chicago in 1852, and moved to Rockford two years later, where they have resided ever since. He is a brother to Rev. C. J. Petri. He studied at Gustavus Adolphus College, St. Peter, Minn., for a few years; then entered the University of Minnesota, Minneapolis, graduating from the classical department of this institution in 1890, with the degree of A. B., and from the law department three years later, with the degree of LL. B. The year of 1891 he spent on the Pacific Coast, studying law most of the time at Seattle, Wash., in the office of Judge Green, ex-chief justice of the state of Washington. After having completed his legal education, he has successfully practiced his profession in Minneapolis, having won several important cases in the supreme court of the state. Petri is a member of the Swedish Lutheran Church, having taken active part in church and Sunday-school work. Although not a professional politician, he has always taken an active interest in politics, having always affiliated with the Republican party. In 1894 he was married to Ida M. Peterson, of Grove City, Minn., who had formerly attended Gustavus Adolphus College for several years, and studied music at the Royal Conservatory in Stockholm, Sweden, for two years; they have children.

Railson, Andrew, state senator—Norway Lake—born 16 Aug., 1833, in Sigdal, Kristiania stift, Norway. He emigrated to this country at the age of seventeen; worked in the pineries and at other common labor in Green county, Wis., for about five years; visited his native country, and on his return located in Stillwater, Minn., working in the saw mills for a couple of years; then took a claim in Kandiyohi county, being one of the earliest settlers in this part of the country. At the time of the terrible Sioux

Indian outbreak, in 1862, Andrew and his brother Even were among the bravest defenders of life and property; but nevertheless they were driven away from their homes by the fierce Redskins, and did not return until 1865. He has been county treasurer of Kandiyohi county for five years; was receiver of the U. S. land office at Redwood Falls from 1884–87; represented his district in the state legislature in 1871; served in the state senate during the sessions of 1872–73, and has held various local offices. Andrew Railson, Jonas Lindall of Chisago county, and Ole Peterson of Pope county were the first Scandinavians who were elected state senators in Minnesota; but many other Northmen, however, had served in the lower branch of the legislature ever since the state constitution was adopted, in 1857. Railson was again elected to the state legislature in 1892. In 1860 he was married to Bertha Johnson. They have children.

Rast, Gustaf, clergyman — Red Wing — born 13 July, 1857, in Fristad, Vestergötland, Sweden. He emigrated to the U. S. in 1873, after having received a common school education in Sweden; attended the literary department of Augustana College for four years; and graduated from the theological department of this institution in 1884. For nearly three years he had charge of the Swedish Lutheran church at Stockholm, Wis., and has since 1887 been pastor in Red Wing. He has been secretary, vice-president, and treasurer of the Minnesota Conference of the Augustana Synod; served six years on the board of directors of Gustavus Adolphus College, and has held the offices of secretary and president of said board; has during the biggest part of his ministry served in the executive committee of the conference, and always taken an active part in the educational and missionary work of his church. In 1884 he was married to Hanna Anderson, of Princeton, Ill. They have several children.

Reimestad, Theodor S., educator — Minneapolis — born 28 Apr., 1858, at Jäderen, Norway. He received a high school education in his native land; emigrated with his parents to this country in 1872, coming directly to Iowa, where he attended the graded school at Ackley; continued his studies at Augsburg Seminary, Minneapolis, graduating, in 1880, from the college department, and in 1883 from the theological department; was pastor of churches in Dane and Green counties, Wis., for two years; and in 1885 settled down to his life-work, accepting a position as professor at his alma mater, his chief subjects being the history of Norwegian and Danish literature and Latin. Reimestad has for years taken great interest in temperance work, having lectured very extensively on total abstinence and prohibition in the Northwest as well as written considerably on the same subjects. He is also one of the most widely known Scandinavian tenor singers in America, and is instructor in vocal music at the seminary. He was the originator and organizer of the Norwegian Lutheran Singers' Union, being its first president and later on its director-in-chief. He has published *Kampmelodier,* a collection of temperance songs and, in company with Rev. M. F. Gjertsen, *Sangbogen,* a huge collection of religious songs, including some of Reimestad's best efforts as composer and writer of songs. In 1888 he organized the Augsburg Quartette, which devoted four seasons to the cause of total abstinence and prohibition, traveling through several northwestern states; for years was president, and in 1895 secretary, of the Minnesota Total Abstinence Association; and has been president of the Total Abstinence Congress since it was organized. In 1888 the Prohibitionists nominated him for lieutenant-governor. Reimestad has made two noted trips to Norway. In 1895 he went there upon invitation and gave a series of successful temperance concerts in the cities; and in 1898 he, in company with Rev. Gjertsen, spent most of the summer in singing and preaching to large audiences in all the large cities and most of the principal towns.

Rice, Albert E., lieutenant-governor — Willmar — born 1847, in Vinje, Kristiansand stift, Norway. He received a common school education in his native country, emigrated to the U. S. in 1860, and settled in Wisconsin. At the outbreak of the Civil War he enlisted in the famous Fifteenth Wisconsin Regiment of Volunteers, better known as the Scandinavian Regiment; was wounded in his left hand at the battle of New Hope Church; settled in Minneapolis after the war; but moved to Willmar in 1870, to engage in general merchandise; and has later also become interested in banking. Rice represented a Minneapolis district in the state legislature in 1870, served in the state senate during the sessions of 1874–75 and 1878–85, and was lieutenant-governor from 1887–91. Rice was a delegate to the convention in Philadelphia, which nominated Grant for president in 1872, and was appointed a member of the board of regents of the University of Minnesota in 1897. His long and honorable legislative career has largely been devoted to measures opposing railroad and elevator monopolies, for

A. E. RICE, WILLMAR.

PROF. J. B. FRICH, HAMLINE.

REV. T. JOHNSEN, NORSELAND.

PROF. H. G. STUB, HAMLINE.

PROF. J. YLVISAKER, ROBBINSDALE.

the protection of the farmers against the ravages of the grasshoppers, and for the taxation of telegraph and telephone companies. As a parliamentarian, Rice has few, if any, equals in the state. He is a Republican. Rice is married to a Swedish lady, who possesses considerable literary ability. Their son, Cushman A. Rice, was born in Willmar March 15, 1878. He graduated from Willmar high school at the age of sixteen; entered the State University one year later; enlisted as first lieutenant in company D of Fifteenth Minnesota Volunteers at the outbreak of the Spanish War in 1898; was mustered out with his regiment in the spring of 1899; and shortly after President McKinley appointed him first lieutenant, assigning him to the Thirty-fourth U. S. Infantry. Since he has been promoted captain of company M, of the above mentioned regiment, and served in the Philippine Islands since the fall of 1899. Rice is probably the only Scandinavian-American who ever held the high rank of captaincy at the early age of twenty-one.

Ringnell, Carl John, physician and surgeon — Minneapolis—born 3 June, 1864, in Vissefjerda, Småland, Sweden. After having attended school for five years, he, at the age of eighteen, emigrated to this country; attended Gustavus Adolphus College, St. Peter, Minn., for three years, and graduated from the medical department of the University of Minnesota in 1891; has also been studying at the principal hospitals in Europe. Ringnell has gained the confidence of the people and has a very large practice; has been appointed attending physician at the Free Dispensary, which is a part of the University of Minnesota, and the Nurses' Training School; is a member of the Minnesota Medical Society, and

32

of the American Medical Association. In 1896 he took a post graduate course at Tulane University, New Orleans, La., and has traveled extensively in Mexico and Central America. In 1891 he was married to Carrie Morris Wilkins, of New York City, she being a grand niece of Gov. Morris, who was one of the signers of the Declaration of Independence. They have one daughter.

Roos, Oscar, pioneer and county official—Taylor's Falls —born 1827, in Skara, Sweden; died 1896. He crossed the Atlantic ocean in 1850, being therefore one of the earliest Swedish emigrants in this country. He lived the first summer at Rock Island, Ill. In October, 1850, he, together with two other Swedes, and upon the advice of the well-known Rev. Unonius, moved to Minnesota and took a claim where Marine, Washington county, is now located. This was the first Scandinavian settlement in the state. After having resided at Marine and worked in the pineries for ten years, Roos in 1860 moved to Taylor's Falls. He was register of deeds of Chisago county from 1860–70, receiver of the U. S. land office from 1870–75, and county treasurer from 1875–83. He has always taken an active part in public affairs and been deeply interested in everything pertaining to the welfare of Chisago county, in which he was the first Scandinavian who held an office, as well as the first Scandinavian settler. Roos was married to Hanna Swanstrom in 1870.

Rosing, August G., secretary of the Minnesota Scandinavian Relief Association of Red Wing—Red Wing—born 1 Sept., 1822, in Ljungby, Vestergötland, Sweden. He received a good education in his native land, was bookkeeper in a government office in Stockholm from 1844-48, then followed the same profession in Skåne, until he emigrated to America in 1868. He came directly to Goodhue county, Minn., where he rented a farm, and farmed until he accepted his present position in 1888. He has been county commissioner for several years, and has held various local offices. Rosing was married in 1851. He has children.

Rosing, L. A., chairman of the state central committee of the Democratic party—Cannon Falls—born 29 Aug., 1861, in Malmö, Sweden. He is the son of A. G. Rosing, in Red Wing; came with his mother to this country in 1869; received a common school education in Goodhue county; worked on his father's farm until the age of twenty; then clerked in stores in Cannon Falls; and since 1888 has been conducting a shoe store of his own in that city. In the campaign of 1890 he began to take an active part in politics, and in the course of the next ten years he distinguished himself as a very able organizer, holding different positions in the Democratic organization; among which may be mentioned that of member of the congressional committee in 1892, candidate for state senator in 1894, and chairman of the state central committee since 1896. He conducted the campaigns of 1896 and 1898 with great ability, and it was largely through his masterly management that the Fusion forces succeeded in electing John Lind as governor in 1898, the first anti-Republican governor in the state of Minnesota for forty years. Gov. Lind appointed him his private secretary in 1899. Rosing was married to May B. Season, an American lady, in 1886. They have children.

Sandberg, G. P., dentist—St. Paul—born 17 Feb., 1861,

at Saltkälla, Vestergötland, Sweden.   At the age of twelve
he came to this country, directly to St. Paul, Minn., to join
his father, who had emigrated before. He received a common
school education in his native country, studied dentistry in
a private office in St, Paul, and has since 1885 successfully
practiced his profession in that city. For years he has been
the only Swedish dentist in St. Paul. In 1899 he formed a
partnership with Dr. L. R. Hoelzle. They employ several
assistant dentists. Sandberg belongs to ten different secret
societies, and has taken the highest degree in Freemasonry.
He was married in 1888 to Margarete E. Moran, an American lady. They have children.

Sandberg, J. H., botanist and physician—Minneapolis
—born 24 July, 1846, in Broby, Skåne, Sweden. He received
a college education in Lund, and studied pharmacy in his
native land; came to this country in 1868; lived in Michigan
for a while; located in Minneapolis in 1887. Sandberg
studied medicine in this country, but he is better known as
a botanist than as a physician, having for a few years been
employed by the United States as botanical collector on
the Pacific Coast. He already ranks among the leading
botanists of the country. Sandberg has discovered several
new plants, to which he, according to a universal custom
among scientists, has given his name. He is married, and
has a married daughter.

Saugstad, Christian, clergyman—Crookston—born 13
June, 1838, in Ringsaker, Kristiania stift, Norway; died
1897. In 1850 his father emigrated to the United States
and settled in Vernon county, Wis.; the following year the
mother and her two younger children crossed the Atlantic

to join her husband, leaving young Saugstad, his two brothers, and one sister in their native land to take care of themselves, but if possible to follow their parents. After having lived in Kristiania for three years, he secured an opportunity to work his way across the ocean; landed at the age of sixteen in Quebec, Canada, and followed the rest of the passengers to Milwaukee, Wis., where he, on account of being short of funds, was left alone on the pier among strangers, with only ten cents in his pocket. But after having worked for three months in Milwaukee he was able to start on his journey towards his parents, and his mother died three days after his arrival. By working on farms in the summers and in the pineries during the winters, he soon bought a farm of his own; but finally entered Augsburg Seminary, Marshall, Wis., and was ordained in 1872. Saugstad commenced his first pastoral work in Douglas and adjoining counties, Minnesota, having charge of a large field, and resided at Holmes City for eight years; then moved to Polk county, and settled in Crookston in 1886. Until the union of the different Norwegian churches he belonged to the Norwegian-Danish Conference, of which he was vice-president from 1886–90. In the early nineties he established a Norwegian colony in Bella Coola, B. C., where he died. In 1893 he published a brief history of Augsburg Seminary. He was married twice, and had eleven children.

Searle, Olaf O., emigration agent and banker—Minneapolis —born 23 June, 1859, in Fredrikshald, Norway. He came to America in 1881. In the fall of the same year he began work in the emigration department of the St. Paul, Minneapolis and Manitoba Railway, remaining there till 1883, when together with A. E. Johnson he opened business as emigration agent. This firm, known as A. E. Johnson and Company, is now doing a very extensive business in the sale of passage tickets for the various steamship companies, and also in the sale of lands. The firm has offices in New York City, Boston, St. Paul, Minneapolis, Duluth, Tacoma, and Seattle. Searle is also one of the directors of the Scandinavian American Bank in Tacoma, and vice-president of the Scandinavian American Bank in Seattle; owns considerable farm lands in central Minnesota and other real property in Western cities, notably at Little Falls, Minn. Ever since the partnership was formed, he has been the manager of the Northwestern headquarters of the firm's business, and has taken an active part in public and financial matters, especially those in which the Scandinavians have been interested. He located in Minneapolis in 1898, but in the summer lives at Lake Minnetonka, where he owns a fine house and 125 acres of land on Big Island, being one of the finest places on the lake. Searle was married in 1887 to Dagmar Johnson. They have one child.

Shaleen, John, state senator—Lindstrom—born 15 Nov., 1835, near Vexiö, Sweden. He received a common school education in his native country, and has since been an extensive reader. His parents and the whole family emigrated to the U. S. when he was twenty years of age; they settled at Chisago Lake, Minn., where both John Shaleen and his brother Peter—who died in 1898, and was one of the leading men in that part of the country—worked on the family homestead until the outbreak of the Civil War, when John Shaleen enlisted in company I of the Sixth

Minnesota Volunteer Infantry. For some time he served against the Indians on the western frontier of Minnesota; then was on duty in the South, fighting against the Confederates at Spanish Fort and at Fort Blakeley in Alabama. At the end of the war he returned to his farm; was sheriff of Chisago county from 1870–76; represented his district in the state senate during 1878–86;and has been judge of probate since 1888. He is an independent Republican and a Lutheran, and one of the first Swedish settlers in the state of Minnesota, having passed through the usual hardships incidental to pioneer life. He is considered to have been one of the most influential Scandinavian legislators in the state; public economy has been his hobby. He was married to Annie S. Stendahl in 1869; they have several children, all of whom have received a liberal education.

Sjöblom, P., clergyman—Fergus Falls—born 17 Mar., 1834, in Snöstorp, Halland, Sweden. He came to this country in 1866; was ordained the same year; had charge of a Swedish Lutheran congregation in Indiana for a couple of years; settled in Red Wing, Minn., in 1869; and moved to Fergus Falls in 1886. Since 1895 he has been located at Wakefield, Neb. Sjöblom has been vice-president and secretary of the Augustana Synod, and served on various legal and constitutional committees. He has been the parliamentarian of the synod, and one of the most influential among the Swedish-American Lutheran ministers, and has for years been associate editor of *Skaffaren*. He was married in 1855, and has children.

Skaro, J. G., physician and surgeon — Minneapolis — born 10 Jan., 1859, in St. Peter, Minn. He is the son of

Captain A. K. Skaro, who was born in Hallingdal, Norway, 4 June, 1829, came to the United States in 1846, and was killed at Nashville, Tenn., in 1865. Captain Skaro served in the United States army as a private at Fort Snelling from 1847–52, then settled at St. Peter, and enlisted in the Union army in 1862, being one of the few Scandinavians from Minnesota who rose to a higher position in the army during the Civil War. Young Skaro received a high school education in his native city, graduated from a medical college in Keokuk, Iowa, in 1880, studied medicine also in Louisville, Ky., in 1884–85, and attended the Post Graduate Medical College, New York City, in 1890. Skaro has practiced his profession in Minneapolis since 1880, having been exceptionally successful, especially in handling difficult female diseases. Indeed, in this line of practice he has few equals or superiors in the Northwest. Two of his brothers are also practicing medicine in Minneapolis. In 1890 he was married to Olive Stewart, of Nova Scotia.

Skogsbergh, Erik August, clergyman—Minneapolis— born 30 June, 1850, at Elgå, Vermland, Sweden. His father was a nail manufacturer, his mother a farmer's daughter. Young Skogsbergh attended the public schools until twelve years of age; studied three years at a college at Arvika; took charge of his father's affairs and did a large business in Norway and Sweden; became interested in a religious movement; attended for a while a missionary school in Kristinehamn, with the intention to prepare to go as a missionary to Africa; entered a missionary school in Småland; and studied privately for four years at Jönköping, with the purpose of entering the theological department in

O. O. SEARLE, MINNEAPOLIS.

A. B. DARELIUS, MINNEAPOLIS.

C. O. A. OLSON, MINNEAPOLIS.

J. A. PETERSON, MINNEAPOLIS.

G. A. PETRI, MINNEAPOLIS.

the University of Upsala; but instead accepted a call to Chicago, at the age of twenty-six. Skogsbergh traveled as a missionary throughout Vermland, Småland, and Vestergötland, preaching often in the open air to large crowds. In Sweden he was still a member of the Lutheran church, and his work was a kind of mission inside of the state church. Since, however, this movement has been separated from the Lutheran church both in this country and in Sweden. The organization of which he is a member is called the Swedish Mission Covenant of America, and its church government resembles that of the Congregationalists; but the mode of worship is more like that of the Methodists. Skogsbergh remained in Chicago for seven years, built a large church with a seating capacity of 1,500, preached in several other places, and conducted revival meetings among his countrymen throughout the Western states. Since 1884 he has resided in Minneapolis, and erected the Swedish Tabernacle, which has a seating capacity of 3,000, and is the largest church building in Minneapolis. The membership is about 400, yet the auditorium is often crowded with people. For a number of years he has also been editor of a Swedish newspaper in Minneapolis. In 1879 he was married to Tillie S. Peterson of Chicago. They have several children.

Skordalsvold, John J., journalist—Minneapolis—born 29 Oct., 1853, in Meraker, Trondhjem stift, Norway. He came with his parents to this country in 1869, directly to Goodhue county, Minn., but the family moved to Todd county the following year. Young Skordalsvold cleared his father's farm; graduated from the literary department

of Augsburg Seminary in 1881, and from the University of
Minnesota seven years later; then studied over a year at
the University of Berlin, Germany, making his own way
through school; taught some in Augsburg Seminary; was
editor of *Folkebladet* in 1883; is known as an active and
earnest temperance worker, and lost considerable money a
few years ago in connection with the Scandinavian coffee
house which he organized in Minneapolis; has served for
many years as secretary of the Minnesota Total Abstinence
Asssociation and as superintendent of the educational department of the Total Abstinence Congress; and has made
greater sacrifices for the cause of temperance than any
other Norwegian born person in the state. For some ten
years he was connected, both as principal and as teacher,
with the public evening schools of the city, and has for
several years been a contributor to many Norwegian-American and English newspapers and magazines. He is a member of the Unitarian church, and a Prohibitionist. Skordalsvold was married to Anne Romundstad in 1890. She
is one of the few women who write for the Norwegian-
American press. Skordalsvold has children.

Smith, Charles A., lumber manufacturer—Minneapolis—
born 11 Dec., 1852, in Boxholm, Ostergötland, Sweden. He
came with his father, who was a soldier in the Swedish
army for a third of a century, to the United States at the
age of fifteen, and settled in Minneapolis, Minn. He received
a common school education, both in Sweden and here, then
attended the University of Minnesota for one year, being
one of the first Swedes who attended that institution. He
received his business training in ex-Gov. J. S. Pillsbury's

hardware store in Minneapolis, where he worked for five years; then, in company with his former employer, built an elevator at Herman, Minn., remaining there until 1884, when he returned to Minneapolis. Smith has since been extensively engaged in the manufacturing of lumber; besides, he owns lumber yards in several places in North Dakota; and is one of the directors of the Swedish-American National Bank in Minneapolis. "Smith is the coming man among the Swedes," said a prominent business man during the National Republican convention at Minneapolis in 1892. But it is doubtful whether Smith has any political aspirations. He is a business man, and as such not many Scandinavian-Americans in the country are his equals. Smith is a Republican, and was one of the presidential electors of his party in 1896; but his extensive business interests prevent him from taking an active part in politics, except as counsellor, and as such he is undoubtedly one of the most influential Swedes in the state. His active co-operation in nearly every movement calculated to benefit his countrymen or the public at large has made Smith's name honored and respected far beyond the limits of his home city. But the noiseless assistance which he has bestowed upon poor people and young men endeavoring to start in life, has, perhaps, even been greater than his public generosity. Smith's great popularity and success may be due to his liberality, economy, good judgment, keen understanding of human nature, or to that unknown something often called luck. In all probability Smith does not know himself. Mankind generally calls such men well balanced. Smith deserves that distinction. He is a prominent member

of the English Lutheran church, and has been treasurer of the
English Evangelical Lutheran Synod of the Northwest for
several years. Johanna Anderson, a daughter of Olof Anderson, a *riksdagsman* from Sweden, and one of the early
settlers in Carver county, became Smith's wife in 1878.
They have several children.

Soderstrom, Alfred, newspaper manager—Minneapolis
—born 1848, in Stockholm, Sweden. After having received a
good education in his native city, he, at the age of twenty-
one, emigrated to this country; resided in Chicago for two
years; then moved to Minneapolis, Minn., where for some
time he was a teacher in Barnard Business College. Later
he associated himself with Col. Mattson as general manager of *Minnesota Stats Tidning;* but when this paper
was sold to a syndicate composed of Swedish Lutherans,
Soderstrom retired and became the chief promoter in
organizing a stock company which commenced to publish
Svenska Folkets Tidning in 1881, and of which he was
business manager up to 1899. Since he has been preparing
a Swedish history of Minneapolis, which he should be able to
make very thorough and complete, as he has resided in that
city for nearly thirty years, and has participated in all the
leading events pertaining to the Scandinavians in that
place. He was nominated for county treasurer of Hennepin county in 1892, and was the only Republican candidate
in the county that was defeated; the general opinion was
that he had been knifed by the political bosses. He is
married.

Sohlberg, Olof, physician and surgeon—St Paul—born
6 July, 1859, in Östersund, Sweden. After receiving a col-

lege training in his native country, Sohlberg emigrated to America with his parents in 1879; spent one year at Gustavus Adolphus College, and then entered Minnesota College Hospital (now the medical department of the state university) at Minneapolis; graduated from this institution after three years of study, receiving first prizes for the best examinations in pathology, medical and surgical dentistry, and clinical medicine. Sohlberg was the first foreign-born that graduated as a medical doctor in Minnesota. Since 1884 he has successfully practiced his profession in St. Paul. During the years of 1890–91 Sohlberg traveled abroad for study and observation of treatment in the European hospitals, making surgery and diseases of women his special study. He is a member of Ramsey County Medical Society and of Minnesota State and American medical associations. He is also member of the medical and surgical staff of Bethesda Hospital. He is a member of the board of directors of Gustavus Adolphus College, and takes an active part in church and public affairs. Sohlberg was married in 1886 to Helvina A. Wold. They have children.

Solem, A., journalist—Fergus Falls—born 27 April, 1850, near Trondhjem, Norway. He graduated from Kläbo seminary, near Trondhjem, in 1870. After five years spent in teaching school in the northern part of Norway, he attended the polytechnic school in Trondhjem three years. Solem came directly from Norway to Otter Tail county in 1879, and there commenced life as a carpenter. He soon learned the type-setting business and worked on both Norwegian and English papers. In 1884 he bought the *Fergus Falls Ugeblad*, of which he is still editor and proprietor.

Solem was an exponent of the principles of the People's party, but he did not endorse the methods of some of the leaders of the party. On the whole, his paper will generally be found on the side of fair play and justice whether it brings pecuniary returns or not. He is a member of the United Church. He was married to Marith Rönning in 1880.

Sorensen, Sigvart, journalist—Minneapolis—born 18 Nov., 1849, in Kristiania, Norway. Attended a Latin school at Kristiania from 1861–66, then emigrated to this country with his parents. Stayed in Chicago from 1866–68; in Madison, Wis., from 1868–70; and in La Crosse, Wis., from 1870–89, when he again removed to Chicago, where he stayed until 1891. Sorensen was elected city assessor of La Crosse for seven terms; has been connected with some newspaper or other since 1873; was for some time one of the editors of *Norsk Maanedsskrift,* published by Sorensen and Luth Jaeger; was editor of *Norden,* Chicago, from 1890–91; came to Minneapolis in 1891, becoming editor of *Budstikken,* now *Minneapolis Tidende.* Sorensen is an able and careful writer, and in 1899 wrote a history of Norway in the English language, containing about 500 pages. He was married in 1873 to Hanna Husher, a daughter of F. A. Husher. They have two children.

Stark, L. J., state legislator—Harris—born 29 July, 1826, in Lidköping, Vestergötland, Sweden. He came to this country in 1850, settling at Galesburg, Ill., where he remained about a year and a half; then moved to Chisago Lake, Minn. During the Civil War he was clerk in the quartermaster department in St. Paul. In 1864 Stark was elected to the state legislature, and re-elected ten years later, being, therefore, the first Swede who served in that capacity in Minnesota, though several Norwegians had preceded him. He had been engrossing clerk in the house of representatives before his election to this body. Stark has held many local trusts in his county, is interested in merchandising and farming, is a Lutheran in religion, and belongs to the Republican party. He has been married twice, and has grown children by both wives.

Steenerson, Halvor, lawyer and state senator —Crookston—born 30 June, 1852, in Pleasant Spring, Dane county, Wis. His parents came from Norway in 1850, moved to Houston county, Minn., in 1853, and were therefore among the very earliest Norwegian settlers in Minnesota. Young Steenerson attended the high school at Rushford, Minn., worked on his father's farm, taught school for several years, and graduated from Union College of Law in Chicago, in 1878. For two years he practiced his profession in Lanesboro, Fillmore county, moved to Crookston in 1880, and has for years been considered as one of the ablest attorneys in the state, making criminal cases his specialty. He instituted, conducted, and won, on behalf of the farmers and grain shippers, the noted Steenerson grain case, which attracted national attention and resulted in state control and regulation of railroad charges on grain shipments. He was elected county attorney of Polk county in 1880, serving two years, and represented his district in the state senate during the sessions of 1883-85. During his legislative career he took special interest in securing the establishment of railroad warehouses and the regulation of the same. He is a

Republican, was his party's delegate to the national convention in Chicago, in 1884, which nominated Blaine for the presidency, and also to the convention at which Harrison was nominated four years later. Steenerson has been city attorney, and a member of the city council and board of education; is vice-president of Scandia American Bank of Crookston, member of the I. O. O. F., and a Lutheran. In 1878 he was married to Mary Christopherson; they have two children.

Stockenstrom, Herman, journalist—St. Paul—born 13 Mar., 1853, in Stjernsund, Dalarne, Sweden. His ancestors belonged to a noble family of Sweden, and he has inherited a great deal of property. He received a college education in Falun, afterwards attended Stockholm's gymnasium and Schartau's commercial college, in Stockholm. In 1874 he went as a sailor to Philadelphia; studied for a couple of years at Augustana College, where he also taught, both in the college and privately; was editor of *Skandia* in Moline, Ill., for about one year; and came to St. Paul, Minn., in 1877. For two years Stockenstrom attended the University of Minnesota, Minneapolis, then accepted a position as editor of *Skaffaren*; but when this paper and the *Minnesota Stats Tidning* were consolidated in 1882, he became both editor and manager, a position which he exchanged in 1884 for another of the same kind as the northwestern editor of *Hemlandet*, which position he held for eleven years. He has taken a great deal of interest in politics; has been a delegate to several state and county conventions; was a strong candidate for the office of secretary of state in 1886, but retired in favor of his personal friend, Col. Matt-

C. A. SMITH, MINNEAPOLIS.

HERMAN STOCKENSTROM, ST. PAUL.

son, by whom he was twice appointed assistant secretary
of state; and was twice appointed by Brown to the same
position.   During more than a decade Stockenstrom worked
faithfully for the Republican party as a campaign speaker;
but in recent years he has not devoted much time to political
questions.   Ernst Skarstedt, in his admirable book,
Svensk-Amerikanska Poeter, says: "Stockenstrom is an
excellent orator and declaimer, and a poet of more than
ordinary talent."   As a newspaper correspondent he has
contributed many articles to several of the leading Swedish-
American papers, and is as familiar with the English language as with his native tongue.   Since 1895 he has been a
member of the editorial staff of *Svenska Amerikanska
Posten* in Minneapolis.   His poem, *Det Nya Modersmålet*,
is an excellent illustration of how the Swedish language, as
used in this country, becomes mixed with English words
supplied with Swedish endings.   Stockenstrom is a member
of the English Lutheran church, is one of the most popular
Swedes in Minnesota, and was married in 1881 to Anna
Maria Nelson, of St. Paul, Minn.

Stub, Hans Gerhard, educator—Hamline—born 23 Feb.,
1849, in Muskego, Racine county, Wis.   His parents are
Norwegians, his father being the well-known Rev. H. A.
Stub, pastor in the Norwegian Lutheran Synod.   In 1866
he graduated from Luther College, Decorah, Iowa; in 1869
he graduated with distinction from Concordia College, Fort
Wayne, Ind., and in 1872 from the Concordia Theological
Seminary at St. Louis.   He was ordained a minister the
same year and accepted a call from a Norwegian Synod congregation in Minneapolis, Minn., serving this congregation

33

till 1878, when he became professor of theology in Luther Seminary, Madison, Wis. Of this institution Stub was president from 1879–88, when he resigned from the presidency on account of ill health, but for many years retained the professorship; then was clergyman in Decorah for a few years, and returned to Luther Seminary in 1899. *The North* says: "The entire Norwegian Lutheran Synod in this country recognizes Prof. Stub as its ablest and most erudite scholar in his special branch of study. His learning is of a high order, and in addition he is a man of the highest personal attainments." He has been married twice, and his second wife is the noted musician Valborg Hovind Stub, editor of *Songs from the North*.

Sverdrup, Georg, educator—Minneapolis—born 16 Dec., 1848, in Balestrand, Bergen stift, Norway. He received a careful training at home, graduated with the highest honors from the classical department of a Latin school in Kristiania at the age of seventeen, and completed his theological course at the University of Norway in 1871. He had made a special study of the Oriental languages during his school career, and after his graduation he spent considerable time in Paris, France, for the purpose of further investigating his specialty. For years the Norwegian Lutheran church in this country had suffered from many severe storms, bitter disputes had prevailed and rent the church asunder. At last, in 1870, the Norwegian-Danish Conference was organized—an event which forms an epoch in the history of the Norwegian churches in America. The Conference, of which the well-known Rev. C. L. Clausen was the first president, began at once the erection of Augsburg Seminary in Minneapolis,

Minn. When it was completed, Sverdrup received a call to become professor of theology. He accepted, and arrived at his destination and entered upon his new duties in 1874; two years later Prof. A. Weenaas resigned from his position as theological instructor and president of the institution. Sverdrup succeeded him in the presidency, and under his able management Augsburg Seminary has in about twenty-five years become one of the foremost Scandinavian educational institutions in America. When the Conference, in 1890, was merged into the United Norwegian Lutheran Church of America, Sverdrup was again chosen president of Augsburg Seminary. When the United Church withdrew its support from Augsburg Seminary in 1893, Sverdrup remained at the head of the institution during the years of bitter struggle in which the United Church in vain tried to obtain possession of the school. When finally the matter was amicably settled in 1898 by a division of the property of the seminary between the United Church and the Augsburg Seminary corporation, this important settlement was due in part to the pronounced stand taken by Sverdrup against lawsuits in connection with the affairs of the church. Rev. J. C. Jensson in *American Lutheran Biographies* says: "He is a nephew of ex-minister Johan Sverdrup, for many years premier of Norway, and his father was a noted minister in the state church and a member of the Storthing of his native country. Born of illustrious parentage, endowed with rare mental qualities, thoroughly educated, and having inherited no small degree of the family characteristics which have made the name so prominent, Sverdrup possesses in an eminent degree the conditions for being a leader among the Norwegian Lutherans in this country." Sverdrup has been married twice: in 1874 to Katharine E. Heiberg, who died thirteen years later, and in 1890 to Elsie S. Heiberg, a younger sister of his first wife. He has had children by both wives.

Swainson, John, pioneer — St. Paul — born 1816, in Stockholm, Sweden; died 1890. He graduated from the University of Upsala; emigrated to the U. S. in 1848; settled in 1854 at Chisago Lake, Minn., where he farmed for a while, then moved to St. Paul. At the outbreak of the Civil War he was appointed quarter-master, with major's rank; and was stationed at St. Louis, Mo., remaining there until the war ended. From 1871–76 he was employed as general land agent for the Great Northern R. R., residing in St. Paul; farmed for a couple of years at Hallock, Minn.; returned to St. Paul, where he was engaged in the real estate business until he was accidentally killed by a street car. The general opinion is that Swainson left a mysterious history behind him in Sweden; yet he was the leader of several farmers who emigrated at the same time as he did. This open way of leaving his native country would hardly have been possible if he had been a criminal. But whatever might have been his career in Europe, here he became widely and most favorably known, especially among the Swedes. He was a friend to the poor people, and his wealth was often invested, with little or no security, for the benefit of needy Swedes. He quite frequently was the orator at festivals, and contributed extensively to the best Swedish and English periodicals, but many of his so-called literary productions were plagiarized.

Swärd, P. J., clergyman—St. Paul—born 1 April, 1845, in Styra, Östergötland, Sweden. At the age of twenty-three he graduated from Johannelund mission institute in Stockholm. This school has special royal privileges, and graduates from there may, after being examined, be ordained as ministers of the foreign missions and seamen's missions in foreign ports. He served one year as assistant minister in Östergötland; went to Constantinople, Turkey, in 1869, as chaplain of the Swedish-Norwegian legation and missionary for the Scandinavian seamen; remained there four years, visited Egypt and Palestine, and for some time was chaplain of the German embassy; came from Turkey to New York to take charge of the Scandinavian seamen's mission, and while there organized the first Swedish Lutheran church in Brooklyn, in 1874; went to Baltimore in 1877 to organize a Scandinavian seamen's mission; but on account of ill health accepted, the following year, a call to Vasa, Minn., where he remained for eight years, then moved to St. Paul. Swärd was president of the Minnesota Conference for two years and vice-president for six years; was theological professor in Augustana College, Rock Island, Ill., during the school year of 1888–89, but not desiring to leave his work in St. Paul unfinished, he resigned; was elected vice-president of the Augustana Synod in 1889; and served as president of the synod from 1891 to 1899. The Augustana College and Theological Seminary conferred the degree of doctor of divinity on Swärd in 1894, and the same year he was created commander of the order of the North Star, second class, by King Oscar. II. of Sweden. For several years he was one of the editors of *Skaffaren*; served a congregation in

Omaha, Neb., from 1894 to 1899; and at the latter date entered the service of the state church of his native land. Swärd ranks high as a pulpit orator. Some of his sermons, especially those delivered at gatherings of clergymen and theological students, were masterpieces. His mild, somewhat humorous, temper, his conscientious attention to the duties imposed upon him, his great knowledge of the world, his clear understanding of human nature, made him an exceptionally able president in a free church. The whole bearing of the man was democratic, and it is claimed that he returned to Sweden principally because a position there offered more time for contemplation and rest and a safer livelihood in old age than it is possible to secure here. Swärd himself said that he returned partly because he desired to leave the direction of the Swedish-American Lutheran church in younger and abler hands, which shows the modesty of the man. He was married to Selma Maria Thermaenius, of Södermanland, Sweden, in 1872. They have six children.

Swenson, John, state legislator and banker—Canby—born 1842, in Norway. He came to Minnesota in 1872, and has since been engaged in merchandising, milling, and banking. He owns several banks in the western part of the state; and is very liberal with his wealth, having in a quiet way assisted a host of needy people. He is married, and represented his district in the state legislature in 1883.

Swenson, Lars, state senator—Minneapolis—born 10 July, 1842, in Hallingdal, Norway. His great grandfather was a Scotchman. When fifteen years of age Swenson came with his parents to the United States; they settled in Nicollet county, Minn., where he worked on the farm and attended school.   He studied for some time at Luther College, and at the breaking out of the Civil War enlisted in the Second Regiment of Minnesota Volunteers.   He was wounded and taken prisoner at the battle of Chicamauga. After the war he returned to Nicollet county, where he was clerk of court for four years.   Swenson came to Minneapolis in 1879.   He was treasurer of Augsburg Seminary for thirteen years, and has ever since 1879 been manager of the Augsburg Publishing House, and treasurer of the United Church since 1890.   He was elected alderman in 1884, and served in the state senate in 1887–89.   Swenson is a Republican and a widower.

Swenson, L. S., educator and U. S. minister to Denmark —Albert Lea—born 12 June, 1865, in New Sweden, Nicollet county, Minn.   His grandfather and father were natives of Hallingdal, Norway; both emigrated to the United States and settled in Nicollet county, Minn., in 1857.   His father represented his district in the state legislature in 1887. Young Swenson entered St. Olaf College, Northfield, Minn., at the age of fourteen; graduated from Luther College, Decorah, Iowa, in 1886; then studied for some time at Johns Hopkins University, Baltimore.   When Luther Academy, in Albert Lea, was opened in 1888, Swenson accepted the call as its principal, in which capacity he served until 1897.   Ever since he located in Albert Lea, Swenson has taken an active part in politics.   In some way or another he succeeded in being regularly sent as a delegate to county, congressional, and state conventions; stumped the state in favor of Knute Nelson as governor in 1892; was appointed a member of the board of regents of the State University in

1895; and the next year was a delegate to the Republican convention at St. Louis, which nominated Wm. McKinley for president. Through the efforts of Knute Nelson more than on account of any diplomatic experience on the part of Swenson, he received the appointment as minister to Denmark in 1897. In 1887 he was married to Ingeborg Odegaard. They have two daughters.

Sunwall, G. F., grain merchant—Minneapolis—born 11 April, 1852, in Oppeby, Östergötland, Sweden. He received a college education in his native country, graduating from the *elementarlärovärk* at Eksjö in 1867. Two years later he emigrated to America, coming directly to Carver county, Minn., and clerked in stores in Carver village for three years. Then started in business for himself at Walnut Grove in 1873, which village he also founded at the same time. After having remained in the general mercantile business at that place for a couple of years, he commenced to buy grain at different points along the Omaha R. R., which occupation he followed for about five years. In 1880 he returned to Carver, where he remained until 1885, engaged in the grain business. At the latter date Sunwall settled in Minneapolis, where he organized the Central Elevator Company, a quarter million dollars' concern, of which he was manager for about ten years; then sold out his interest in said company, and started a large grain commission business in his own name in 1895. Sunwall is the only Swede in Minneapolis doing a grain commission business, and is one of the leading business men of that nationality in the Northwest. In 1877 he was married to Annie E. Kelly.

REV. P. J. SWARD, ST. PAUL.

PROF. M. WAHLSTROM, ST. PETER.

Tharaldsen, Iver, clergyman—Madison—born 10 Nov., 1847, near Stenkjär, Trondhjem stift, Norway. He received a common school education; attended an agricultural college for a couple of terms; and went to the Lofoten Islands, where two clergymen gave him private instruction for a period of two years. In 1870 he emigrated to America, and the next few years were devoted to studies as follows: at Marshall, Wis., for one year; at the University of Wisconsin for one year; at the University of Minnesota and Augsburg Seminary for two years; and he completed a theological course at the latter institution in 1874. During the next seven years he served a number of congregations in Otter Tail county, Minn., besides organizing several new churches in the northwestern part of Minnesota. While laboring in this part of the country he at one time had charge of sixteen congregations, covering a district more than one hundred and fifty miles in length, which had to be covered either driving or on horseback. In 1881 he removed to Grand Forks, N. D., where he remained three years. Also here he worked as a missionary among the new settlers on the prairies in the surrounding country in Minnesota and Dakota, and organized a number of new congregations. His health being impaired by overwork, he sought a less laborious field of action, and in 1884 located at Chippewa Falls, Wis., where he resided about fourteen years, having since resided at his present home. From 1886 to 1890 Tharaldsen was secretary of the Conference, and for some time served as secretary of the board of missions of said association. Since 1890 he and his congregations have belonged to the United Church. In the first part of 1896 he traveled extensively in the Rocky Mountain districts, Colorado and Utah, to recuperate after a long and severe siege of sickness of the preceding year. He was married in 1876 to Caroline A. Engerud, of Racine, Wis., a sister of the wife of Prof. Peter Hendrickson; they have five children, and their oldest daughter and oldest son are graduates of the Chippewa Falls high school.

Thompson, R. E., state senator and lawyer—Preston— born 7 Mar., 1857, in Fillmore county, Minn. His parents were Norwegians. He was educated in the common schools of Newburg, Minn.; in the Institute of Decorah, Decorah, Iowa; and in the State Normal School, Winona, Minn. After having taught school for some time, he commenced to study law; was admitted to the bar in 1881; served as deputy clerk of court for some time; represented his district in the state legislature during the sessions of 1883–85; and was in the state senate from 1895 to 1901, being one of the ablest and most influential members of that body. Thompson is a hard worker; very independent, and as a consequence does not always follow the party whip of the Republican bosses; and has a large legal practice. In 1884 he was married to Anna Thompson; they have two children.

Thorpe, Lars O., banker and state senator—Willmar— born 24 Dec., 1846, in Östensö, Hardanger, Norway. He came alone to the United States when not quite seventeen years old, having been a sailor a couple of years before. He worked on a farm during the summer, and attended school for a while during the winter at Jefferson Prairie, Wis.; went to Winona, Minn., in 1865, where for a couple of years he worked on farms and taught school. In 1867 he visited his native land, bringing his sister and brother with him on his return; was a railroad contractor and printer in different places for a few years, but settled permanently in Kandiyohi county, Minn., in 1871, where he assisted in publishing a paper in Kandiyohi village; and in the fall of that year moved to a farm located seven miles north of Willmar. For four years he worked on his farm, encountering many struggles and vicissitudes common to frontier life. In the fall of 1875 he was elected register of deeds, which position he filled for six years. His official duties requiring him to stay much of the time in the city, he found it necessary to move from his farm and settle in Willmar, where he has ever since resided. In 1881 he accepted his present position as cashier of Kandiyohi County Bank. Thorpe is a Republican, was a presidential elector for his party in 1884, has been a member of the school board of Willmar for several years, is president of Willmar Seminary, has been president of the city council, represented his district in the state senate in 1895-7, and has held nearly every local office. He is a member of the Norwegian Synod, and is a temperance man, being one of the most active workers in the religious, social reform, political, and financial movements of the city and county, and takes more than ordinary interest in the affairs of the state. In 1870 he was married to Martha Quale. They have several children.

Thorson, A., pioneer and county official—Norseland—born 13 Feb., 1823, in Vä, near Kristianstad, Sweden. He clerked for eleven years in Kristianstad and Sölvesborg; emigrated in 1847, in company with a couple of other young men, to this country, via France; it took them over four months to reach Charleston, S. C., where the vessel, on account of being damaged, had to anchor, instead of at New York. He happened to have a letter of introduction to a Swedish merchant who had emigrated to the U. S. in his younger days, and was now an old man; but this merchant had relatives who had settled in America in the eighteenth century, which goes to show that Swedish emigrants have in very early days crossed the Atlantic. In a short time Thorson and his companions started for New Orleans; here they ran short of money and food; but he soon secured a place as waiter in a hotel. In 1848 Thorson went to California, via Panama, working for his passage; at that time there were only a few houses in San Francisco, and not a single one in Sacramento. After having dug gold for about three years and saved about $2,000, he returned to Sweden, via Nicaragua, Jamaica, Cuba, and New York. He farmed for two years in the vicinity of his birthplace; returned to America in 1855, being the leader of thirty emigrants who accompanied him to the New World, among others his wife's parents and other relatives. Thorson and his party examined different places, but soon settled at Scandian Grove, Nicollet county, Minn., where they were the first Swedish settlers, though a few Norwegians had preceded them. Here he has farmed ever since, was register of deeds for four years, held various local offices, and has passed through many hardships incidental to pioneer life. In Sweden, in 1852, he married Anna Nelson; they have several children.

Thygeson, N. M., lawyer—St. Paul—born 11 Sept., 1862, in Martell, Pierce county, Wis. His parents came from the northern part of Norway in the early forties. He graduated from a normal school at River Falls, Wis., 1882, and from the scientific, metallurgical engineering, and modern classical courses, of the University of Wisconsin in 1885, completing his legal studies at the same institution a couple of years later. In 1888 Thygeson located in St. Paul, and is now considered to be one of the ablest Scandinavian lawyers in the Northwest. In 1891 he was married to Sylvie G. Thompson of St. Louis, Mo. They have children.

Trandberg, P. C., clergyman—Minneapolis—born 18 Aug., 1832, in Bornholm, Denmark; died 1896. In his boyhood he attended school at his birthplace and at Rönne, and during the years 1846–51 pursued a course in the Latin school at Rönne, finally graduating with the highest honors. He continued his studies in Copenhagen and was graduated from the theological department of the university in 1858. Sören Kirkegaard, the philosopher and denunciator of "official Christianity," made a deep and lasting impression upon the mind of Trandberg, and the conversion which he experienced in 1858 made him wage war against the easy-going life of the church people in his country. He was ordained for the ministry the same year, and began to serve congregations at Tjele and Vinge, Jylland; but he felt hampered by the rules and regulations of officialdom, and in 1860 he resigned his charge and returned to Bornholm, where he spent eighteen years in the most intense religious work. Indeed, the stir that he made among the people of Bornholm in the early sixties made him famous throughout the Scandinavian countries. In 1863 he formally withdrew from the state church and organized an independent congregation. This, however, was gradually torn to pieces by fierce internal contentions, and in 1878 he left his native island with a sad heart. He spent the next three years as itinerant preacher in Jylland, and emigrated to America in 1882. Though a Lutheran, but holding very liberal views, he was appointed theological professor at the Chicago Theological Seminary (Congregational) in 1885, but as he failed to bring any material additions to the Congregational church he was dismissed from that institution in 1890. An attempt made by him to establish an independent theological seminary did not prove a success, and it was abandoned in 1893. During the nineties Trandberg published *Hyrderösten*, a religious periodical, and preached occasionally until his death. He spent the last two-and-half years of his life in Minneapolis. Trandberg was married in 1863. A bust has been raised to his memory at his birthplace, and in 1899 the Danish Lutheran church people in America were raising money for another monument in his honor.

Turnblad, Magnus, journalist — Minneapolis — born 28 Jan., 1858, in Vislanda, Småland, Sweden. He came to this country with his parents in 1868 and settled in Vasa, Goodhue county, Minn., where he attended school for some time. He afterwards sought the more advanced educational institutions of Red Wing and St. Paul, always distinguishing himself as an excellent scholar. After completing his school work Turnblad established himself as a grocery merchant at Red Wing, continuing in business for ten years, when more ambitious plans induced him to move to Minneapolis. He again engaged in the grocery business in that city for some years, and also identified himself with the Swedish weekly paper, *Svenska Amerikanska Posten*, of which he became editor in 1889. This paper has, under the able management of his brother, S. J. Turnblad, met with an almost phenomenal success, having now the largest circulation of any Swedish paper in the country, although it is considerably younger than most of its colleagues, having been established in 1885. This astonishing success is largely due to the skill and ability with which Magnus Turnblad is editing the paper. For years he has taken an active part in temperance work. He has been married three times, his first wife leaving one daughter.

Turnblad, Swan J., newspaper publisher—Minneapolis— born 7 Oct., 1860, in Vislanda, Småland, Sweden. At the age of nine he came with his parents directly from his native land to Vasa, Goodhue county, Minn. Here he attended the common schools and Lindholm's high school for several years, taught school for a couple of terms, and worked on his father's farm. When nineteen years of age he moved to Minneapolis, where he worked as typesetter on *Minnesota Stats Tidning* and *Svenska Folkets Tidning* for a few years. In 1887 he became manager of *Svenska Amerikanska Posten*, which at that time had only 1,400 subscribers and was financially in a bad condition; but under Turnblad's able management it has today, 1900, a circulation of 40,000, having had, undoubtedly, taking into consideration the time, the greatest success of any Swedish paper in America, as well as being the largest in size. It is independent in politics, and advocates temperance principles. Turnblad has for years taken an active part in temperance work, having assisted in organizing several Scandinavian temperance societies in Minneapolis and throughout the state. For a couple of terms he was secretary of the grand lodge of I. O. G. T., and also organized lodges in connection with this society in different parts of Minnesota. He was the chief promoter in organizing, in about 1880, the first Scandinavian temperance society in Minneapolis, which as an open and independent organization was the means of accomplishing a great deal of good. Already in his early age Turnblad showed that he possessed singular abilities. He learned to set type by himself, and published an arithmetic, all set by himself, when he was only 14–16 years of age. In 1883 he invented a secret letter writing machine, which he patented, and which has been largely sold all over the country. In 1892 he became interested in *The North*, of which he was manager for a short time, and was also manager for *Hemmet* a couple of years. Turnblad is a member of the American Presbyterian church, and has taken the highest degrees in Freemasonry. He and his family made extensive European trips in 1895, 1897, and 1899. In the latter year Gov. John Lind appointed him a member of the board of managers of the State Reformatory at St. Cloud. At the age of twenty-two he was married to Christine Nelson, of Worthington, Minn. They have one daughter.

Ueland, A., lawyer—Minneapolis—born 21 Feb., 1853, at Heskestad, Stavanger amt, Norway. His father was Ole Gabriel Ueland, who was a member of the Norwegian Storthing from 1833 till his death in 1870, and the recognized leader of the liberal party in Norwegian politics. In 1871 young Ueland emigrated to this country, coming directly to

S. J. TURNBLAD, MINNEAPOLIS.

C. J. JOHNSON, MINNEAPOLIS.

PROF. G. JOHNSON, MINNEAPOLIS.

DR. A. LIND, MINNEAPOLIS.

J. PETERSON, ST. PETER.

Minneapolis, where for the following three years he worked hard at manual labor in the summer, and attended private school during the winter. He then began the study of law, and was admitted to the bar in 1877. In 1881 he was elected judge of the probate court, and has a very large law practice. Ueland was married to Clara Hampson in 1885. They have half a dozen children.

Valder, Hans, state legislator and pioneer—Newburg—born 18 Oct., 1813, in Stavanger amt, Norway. His father was an officer in the army. Young Valder received a good common school education in his native country, and taught for a while in the public schools. At the age of twenty-four he came to the U. S.; the journey from Stavanger to New York on a sailing vessel took three months; resided in La Salle county, Ill., for seventeen years; and for some time lived among the American Baptists at Indian Creek, Ill., accepting the religious views of his associates in 1842. He was licensed to preach, and in a couple of years about twenty Norwegians in La Salle and Kendall counties were immersed, constituting a kind of society without being regularly organized. Valder was ordained in 1844, being undoubtedly the first Norwegian Baptist preacher in the United States, and for some time received a salary of $50 a year from the American Baptists and $13 from his countrymen. He worked at manual labor part of the time, and was soon compelled to quit preaching altogether in order to support his family. He organized a small party of emigrants who settled in 1853, at Newburg, Minn.— this being one of the first Norwegian settlements in the state — where he has ever since been engaged in farming and hotel keeping.

34

Valder is not only one of the earliest settlers in the state of Minnesota, but is also one of the first Scandinavian emigrants who came to America in the nineteenth century. He has held a great many local public trusts, and represented his district in the lower branch of the state legislature in 1871. Valder is a life-long Republican; he voted for William H. Harrison as president of the U. S. in 1840 and for his grandson, Ben. Harrison, fifty-two years later. He has been married three times, namely, in 1835, 1845, and 1861; has had sixteen children; and in 1892 had over one hundred and fifty descendants, who resided in six different states of the Union. One of his sons is conducting a business college at Decorah, Iowa.

Waerner, Ninian, poet and journalist—Minneapolis—born 12 Dec., 1856, in Norrköping, Sweden. He received a college education in his native city, entered the University of Upsala in 1877, and passed his examination in philosophy three years later, but remained in the institution until 1883; then went to Berlin, Germany, to study esthetics, music, and the fine arts, remaining, however, only a short time. In 1884 Waerner emigrated to the United States; accepted a position in one of the orchestras in Chicago; afterwards became connected with newspapers, being on the editorial staff of *Kurre* and *Kuriren*; and was for one year editor-in-chief of *Svenska Amerikanaren*. He left Chicago in 1889 in order to take charge of *Svenska Korrespondenten* in Denver, Col.; was from 1891 to 1894 editor of *Friskytten*, an illustrated humorous journal published in Minneapolis, Minn.; then became connected with *Svenska Amerikanska Posten*; and settled in Motala, Sweden, in 1895.

Ernst Skarstedt says that Waerner has a large stock of ideas and a remarkable ability to express his thoughts in a poetic form; that he is one of the most praductive of all Swedish-American poets; that all his poems are original, well written, and, like his prose writings, vary from the gravest to the most comical; that he is a gifted humorist who can write long editorial articles in a serio-comic way on the most insignificant subjects. Most of the Swedish-American critics will agree with Skarstedt in placing Waerner in the front rank as a poet and humorist. He has issued three small pamphlets, but most of his numerous productions have been published in some Swedish-American newspaper. One of his poems was rewarded by the Swedish Academy in 1894, and Waerner is the only Swedish-American poet, with the exception of Magnus Elmblad, who has been recognized by that body. He is married and has children.

Wahlstrom, M., educator — St. Peter — born 28 Nov., 1851, in Gammalstorp, near Karlshamn, Sweden. When an infant of only three years of age, he came with his parents to this country; they lived in Chicago for a couple of years, and in other parts of Illinois until 1861, when they commenced to farm in Carver county, Minn. Young Wahlstrom received his elementary training at St. Ansgar's Academy— a Swedish school in Carver county, which later became Gustavus Adolphus College; graduated from the literary department of Augustana College in 1877, and from the theological department two years later. In 1886 his alma mater conferred upon him the degree of master of arts, and some years later that of doctor of philosophy. After his graduation he traveled for one year as missionary among the Indians, through Colorado, New Mexico, and Indian Territory; but his health failed, and Indian missionary work proved to be impracticable, as far as the conversion of the natives to Lutheranism or any other Christian religion was concerned. In 1880 he accepted a call as professor at Gustavus Adolphus College, St. Peter, Minn., and the following year he became the president of this institution, which under his able management has prospered beyond expectation, having an average attendance of nearly 300 students, and employing sixteen instructors. Wahlstrom is a remarkably clear and forcible speaker, and was married in 1879.

Werner, Nils O., lawyer and banker—Minneapolis—born 19 Jan., 1848, in Fjelkestad, Skåne, Sweden. Werner was graduated from a college in Kristianstad, in 1868, and, lacking the necessary means for pursuing his studies at the universities, he emigrated to America, where his parents had already gone some time previously. He came directly to Princeton, Ill., where his parents had settled. Here Werner remained for two years, studying law in private offices. In 1870 he moved to Red Wing, Minn., and was admitted to the bar the year following. Werner was elected judge of probate in 1874, remaining in office for ten years; was a member of the city council, and also member of the board of education in Red Wing. From 1886–88 he was member of the Republican state central committee. In 1888 Werner became cashier of the Swedish American Bank in Minneapolis, which had been organized shortly before by leading Swedes in the state, and was elected its president in 1894. The great success with which this important financial undertaking has met is due in no small degree to Werner's able service. Werner is a Republican, and a member of the English Lutheran Church. He was married in 1872 to Eva Charlotte Anderson. They have children, and one of their sons is practicing law in Minneapolis.

Widstrand, Frans Herman, socialist—Litchfield—born 1824, in Stockholm, Sweden; died 1891. He received a careful education at the University of Upsala; was employed in the governmental department in Stockholm for a while; but his radical ideas soon made it impossible for him to retain such a position, especially as he began to publish an anarchical paper. In 1855 he emigrated to this country; resided for quite a long time in Minneapolis, Minn., and vicinity, then started a social community in Wright county. In this settlement all property was common, all should work alike; no liquor, tobacco, meat, or women were allowed in the community, which was intended to be a heaven on earth, and in a certain sense it became a paradise, for no one worked. Such a gathering of idealists and idlers—not to say idiots—had soon to disband. A Yankee succeeded in securing the deed for all the property; Widstrand lost everything, and moved to Litchfield in 1880. Here he endeavored to avenge himself upon mankind by publishing *Rothuggaren*—a paper which made war upon religion, government, and the human race. He was one of the most eccentric Swedes in America, and possessed many noble qualities, but was so unpractical that he seemed insane.

Ylvisaker, John, educator—Robbinsdale—born 24 April, 1845, in Sogndal, Bergen stift, Norway. After being confirmed Ylvisaker entered a teachers' seminary, and after

graduating served as teacher in the public schools of Norway for a period of three years, studying during that time
Old Norse, German, and English, with private tutors. In
1871 he emigrated to America, entering Luther College,
from which institution he graduated three years later. In
1874 Ylvisaker began the study of theology at Concordia
Seminary, and three years later became pastor of the Norwegian Synod congregation at Zumbrota, Minn., where
he remained till 1879. He was now called as professor of
theology of Luther Seminary, and for the sake of further
preparing himself for his duties as professor Ylvisaker, in
1881, made a trip to Europe, studying theology at the
University of Norway, the University of Denmark, and the
University of Leipzig, Germany, having received a stipend
from the Norwegian Synod, to which he belongs. He has
been secretary of the faculty since 1882, and vice-president
of the institution since 1896. Ylvisaker is considered to be
one of the ablest Norwegian-American theologians. He was
married in 1877.

　　Ytterboe, Halvor T., educator — Northfield — born 25
Nov., 1857, near Calmar, Iowa. His parents came from
Telemarken, Norway, in 1852. He worked on his father's
farm until seventeen years of age; graduated from Luther
College in 1881; studied for one year at the University of
Iowa; became teacher in St. Olaf College in 1882, and for a
number of years devoted his whole time as its financial secretary; and it is claimed that the institution would have
been financially crippled but for his success in securing voluntary subscriptions. He was married to Elise Amalia
Kittilsby, of Calmar, Ia., in 1886. They have children.